Bernhard Felderer Stefan Homburg

Macroeconomics and New Macroeconomics

With 97 Figures

Springer-Verlag
Berlin Heidelberg New York
London Paris Tokyo

Prof. Dr. Bernhard Felderer
Dipl.-Vw. Stefan Homburg
Universität zu Köln
Albertus-Magnus-Platz
5000 Köln 41
FRG

Title of the German edition: "Heidelberger Taschenbücher, Bd. 239, Felderer/Homburg, Makroökonomik und neue Makroökonomik", 2nd corrected edition
ISBN 3-540-15795-6 Springer-Verlag Berlin Heidelberg New York Tokyo
ISBN 0-387-15795-6 Springer-Verlag New York Heidelberg Berlin Tokyo

ISBN 3-540-16961-X Springer-Verlag Berlin Heidelberg New York
ISBN 0-387-16961-X Springer-Verlag New York Berlin Heidelberg

Library of Congress Cataloging-in-Publication Data
Felderer, B. (Bernhard)
Macroeconomics and new macroeconomics.
Translation of: Makroökonomik und neue Makroökonomik. 2nd corr. ed. 1985.
Bibliography: p.
Includes indexes.
1. Macroeconomics. I. Homburg, Stefan, 1961–. II. Title.
HB172.5.F4513 1987 339 86-21896
ISBN 0-387-16961-X (U.S.)

This work is subject to copyright. All rights are reserved, whether the whole or part of the material is concerned, specifically those of translation, reprinting, re-use of illustrations, broadcasting, reproduction by photocopying machine or similar means, and storage in data banks. Under § 54 of the German Copyright Law where copies are made for other than private use, a fee is payable to "Verwertungsgesellschaft Wort", Munich.

© Springer-Verlag Berlin Heidelberg 1987
Printed in Germany

Media conversion: Daten- und Lichtsatz-Service, Würzburg
Printing and bookbinding: Konrad Triltsch, Würzburg
2142/3140-543210

"The present treatise is an attempt to present a modern version of old doctrines with the aid of new work, and with reference to the new problems, of our own age."

ALFRED MARSHALL

Preface

This macroeconomic textbook is a revised translation of the second edition of our "Makroökonomik und Neue Makroökonomik", originally published in 1984. When looking at the vast number of macroeconomic textbooks the reader may wonder why he should read this one; thus a few remarks seem appropriate.

The characteristic feature of the present book is that we do not discuss topic by topic but orthodoxy by orthodoxy. This procedure was suggested by the fact that, today, we have no unique economic doctrine but a variety of approaches which are all relevant to economic and especially policy decisionmaking. We think any student of economics should be thoroughly acquainted with the *meaning* of such terms as "Keynesianism" or "Monetarism" because these, along with the other, orthodoxies form the basis of all current opinions and issues in macroeconomic theory and policy. The aims of the book are to discuss the most important orthodoxies in a historical order; to substantiate and criticize each of them; and to bring out the main differences. We do not intend to present a "Keynesian" or "Monetarist" view or to play the referee.

Since "there is no such thing as a free lunch" we must point out the price we have had to pay for our approach. Some close relatives of macroeconomic theory, such as the theories of foreign trade or economic growth, have been excluded – not only in accordance with SMITH's principle of the division of labor, but also because we aimed at providing a text that is not too voluminous. Moreover, we have resisted the temptation to pretend "realism" or "empirical relevance" by presenting some figures and estimates. Our subject has been confined to pure theory.

Parts One and Two are designed for one-semester undergraduate courses. They make the reader familiar with the two outstanding orthodoxies, namely, Classical and Keynesian macroeconomics. Some teachers will find it useful to include Chapter VII on the real-balance effect too. Part Three, dealing with the more recent developments in macroeconomic theory, is written for advanced undergraduates. In these chapters, we discuss the theory of portfolio selection, Monetarism, Rational expectations theory, and Neokeynesian "disequilibrium" theory. It is important to our arrangement that many shortcomings of the simple forms of Classical and Keynesian theory are not discussed in Part Two but postponed till Part Three.

In order to make the text easy to grasp we have dispensed with mathematics as far as possible. But since mathematical methods are used in almost all macroeconomic papers and studies we have added a *Mathematical Appendix,* designed for advanced (graduate) students. This appendix deals with some tricky problems which were not resolved in the text itself, and contains mathematical reviews written especially for macroeconomics.

Thanks go to Prof. Dr. Manfred Feldsieper, Prof. Dr. Manfred Neumann, Prof. Dr. Werner Rothengatter, Prof. Dr. Hans-Karl Schneider, Prof. Dr. Christian Watrin, Dr. Ingo Barens, Dipl.-Phys. Dirk Müller and Dipl.-Vw. Bernd Prüfer who made many useful comments on the German editions. Moreover, we are especially grateful to Mrs. Irene Cameron who had the tough task of improving our English.

Despite Mrs. Cameron's excellent work, it is to be feared that the final remark of our German preface will prove true once more: The second principle of thermodynamics is easily transferred to the operation of making a textbook: sense turns into nonsense *by itself*, and *energy* is required to reverse that process. Hence, we are indebted to any reader who will devote some part of *his* energy to eliminating the remaining nonsense.

Cologne, October 1986   Bernhard Felderer
                                                        Stefan Homburg

Contents

Definitions of Variables 1

Part One. Fundamentals

Chapter I. Some Methodological Considerations 5

§ 1   Economic Theories 5
§ 2   Economic Models 6
§ 3   Methods 7
§ 4   Equilibrium and Disequilibrium. Stability 7
§ 5   Statics, Comparative Statics, and Dynamics 9
§ 6   Ex Post versus Ex Ante Analysis 10
§ 7   Partial versus Total Analysis. The Ceteris Paribus Clause 10
§ 8   Microeconomics versus Macroeconomics 11

Chapter II. A Historical Survey 13

§ 9   The Predecessors 13
§ 10 The Classical Economists 14
§ 11 The Neoclassical Economists 15
§ 12 From KEYNES to the Present 17
Further Reading 18

Chapter III. National Income Accounting 19

§ 13 The Economy as a Circular Flow 19
§ 14 The Circular Flow-Model of FRANÇOIS QUESNAY 20
§ 15 The System of Income Accounts 21
§ 16 Notions of Income in the System of Income Accounts 24

Part Two. Macroeconomics

§ 17 Introduction to Part Two 31

Chapter IV. The Classical Theory 33

§ 18 The Classical Vision. Plan of the Chapter 33
§ 19 Production Functions 35

§20 The Firms   38
§21 The Households   45
§22 The Labor Market   48
§23 The Capital Market   50
§24 The Commodity Market   51
§25 The Quantity Theory of Money   53
§26 Say's Law   58
§27 The Classical Model   59
§28 Digression: Walras' Model   62
§29 Conclusion   66
Further Reading   67

Chapter V. The Keynesian Theory   69

§30 The Crisis   69
§31 The "General Theory" and Its Interpreters   70
§32 The Effective Demand   72
§33 Consumption Demand   73
§34 Investment Demand   78
§35 The Income-Expenditure Model   80
§36 The Simple Multiplier   83
§37 The Markets for Money and Bonds. The LM Curve   85
§38 The Capital Market. The IS Curve   92
§39 The IS/LM Model   94
§40 The Complete Keynesian Model   97
§41 First Scenario: The Investment Trap   101
§42 Second Scenario: The Liquidity Trap   105
§43 An Under-employment Equilibrium with a Flexible Real Wage? . .   108
§44 Third Scenario: Sticky Wages   109
§45 Conclusion   112
Further Reading   113

Chapter VI. Political Implications: A Comparison   115

§46 The Role of Government. Goals and Means of Economic Policy . .   115
§47 Fiscal Policy   117
§48 Fiscal Policy in the Classical Case   118
§49 Fiscal Policy in the Complete Keynesian Case   121
§50 Fiscal Policy with an Investment or Liquidity Trap   126
§51 Fiscal Policy with Sticky Wages   129
§52 The Concept of Counter-cyclical Fiscal Policy   130
§53 Monetary Policy   133
§54 Monetary Policy in the Classical Case   134
§55 Monetary Policy in the Complete Keynesian Case   134
§56 Monetary Policy with an Investment or Liquidity Trap   135
§57 Monetary Policy with Sticky Wages   137
§58 Conclusion   138
Further Reading   138

Part Three. New Macroeconomics

§ 59 Introduction to Part Three   141

Chapter VII. The Real-Balance Effect   143

§ 60 A Criticism of Classical Monetary Theory   143
§ 61 A Criticism of Keynesian Monetary Thoery   148
§ 62 Conclusion   151
Further Reading   152

Chapter VIII. The Theory of Portfolio Selection   153

§ 63 Microeconomic Foundations   153
§ 64 Macroeconomic Applications   161
§ 65 Conclusion   168
Further Reading   170

Chapter IX. Monetarism   171

§ 66 The Theoretical Foundations, or: Monetarism versus Keynesianism .   172
§ 67 The Empirical Investigations, or: Monetarism versus Fiscalism . . .   180
§ 68 The Political Inferences, or: Monetarism versus Activism   183
§ 69 Conclusion   184
Further Reading   185

Chapter X. New Classical Economics   187

§ 70 Expectations and Rational Expectations   188
§ 71 The Phillips-Curve. Stagflation   191
§ 72 The New Classical Vision   196
§ 73 The New Classical Model   197
§ 74 Political Inferences   200
§ 75 Conclusion   205
Further Reading   208

Chapter XI. Neokeynesian Theory   209

§ 76 The Evolution of Neokeynesian Economics   209
§ 77 The Dual Decision Hypothesis   212
§ 78 The Logic of the Fix Price-Method   218
§ 79 A Reconsideration of the Consumption Function   225
§ 80 The Neokeynesian Model   229
§ 81 Political Inferences   240
§ 82 Walras' Law with Quantity Constraints   245
§ 83 Conclusion   247
Further Reading   249

Mathematical Appendix

Introduction 253

1. Calculus of Functions of a Single Variable 255
   1.1 Functions of a Single Variable 255
   1.2 Derivatives 255
   1.3 Taylor's Theorem 258
   1.4 Differentials 260
   1.5 Concavity and Convexity 161
   1.6 Maxima and Minima 263
 * 1.7 Profit Maximization 265

2. Linear Algebra 267
   2.1 Vectors 267
   2.2 Matrices and Determinants 268
   2.3 Simultaneous Linear Equations 271
   2.4 Characteristic Value Problems 273
   2.5 Quadratic Forms 274

3. Calculus of Functions of Several Variables 277
   3.1 Functions of Several Variables 277
   3.2 Partial Derivatives. Gradients 277
   3.3 Chain Rule 279
   3.4 Taylor's Theorem 281
   3.5 Partial and Total Differentials 282
   3.6 Concavity and Convexity 283
   3.7 Maxima and Minima 284
   3.8 Maxima and Minima under Constraints 286
 * 3.9 Profit Maximization 288

4. Implicit Functions 291
   4.1 Explicit and Implicit Functions 291
   4.2 Implicit Differentiation with Two Variables 292
   4.3 Implicit Function Theorem 293
 * 4.4 The Slope of Equilibrium Loci 294
 * 4.5 Properties of Demand Functions 298
 * 4.6 Fiscal Policy in the Keynesian Model 300

5. Ordinary Differential Equations 303
   5.1 Function Equations and Functional Equations 303
   5.2 Solution of a Linear Differential Equation 304
 * 5.3 Stability of a Market 305
   5.4 Solution of Simultaneous Differential Equations 307

* 5.5 Stability of the IS/LM Model   312
* 5.6 Stability of the Neokeynesian Model   313
   Further Reading   315

Bibliography   317

Author Index   323

Subject Index   325

Definitions of Variables

Here all symbols are defined – in so far as they are not merely functions or coefficients – so that the reader can look them up quickly. Their dimensions indicate among other things, whether they are stock or flow variables.

A – autonomous demand measured in commodity units per period

α – vector of exogeneous variables; $\alpha := (P, w, \pi_0, M_0, T)$ or $\alpha := (P, w, \pi)$

B – nominal stock of bonds measured in money units

C – real consumption measured in commodity units per period

c – propensity to consume, absolute measure

c′ – marginal propensity to consume, absolute measure

D – a) real budget deficit of the government measured in commodity units per period
   b) market demand measured in commodity units per period

E – a) expenditures measured in money units per period
   b) excess demand on a market measured in money units per period
   c) expected value of a variable

G – government expenditure measured in commodity units per period

I – real investment demand measured in commodity units per period

i – nominal interest rate measured in 1/period

K – real stock of capital measured in commodity units

k – a) cash balance coefficient (i.e. $1/v$)
   b) arbitrary coefficient

L – real liquidity demand measured in commodity units per period

M – nominal money supply measured in money units

m – a) multiplier, absolute measure
   b) natural logarithm of M

N – number of working hours per period (employment)

n′ – marginal propensity to work, absolute measure

π – nominal profits measured in money units per period

P – price level measured in money units per commodity unit

p – natural logarithm of P

Q – net receipts measured in money units per period

q – relative market rate of real capital, absolute measure

R – a) receipts measured in money units per period
   b) marginal efficiency of capital measured in per cent per period

r – rate of return

r_B – nominal rate of return on bonds

r_E – nominal rate of return on equities

r_K – market rate of real capital

S – a) real savings measured in commodity units per period
  b) market supply measured in commodity units per period
  c) standard deviation of a variable

T – real tax revenue measured in commodity units per period

U – rate of unemployment, absolute measure

u_t – stochastic variable

v – circular velocity of money

v_t – stochastic variable

W – real wealth measured in commodity units

w – a) nominal wage rate measured in money units per working hour
  b) rate of non-human capital in proportion to human capital, absolute measure

x – real quantity of a good measured in commodity units per period

Y – real yield or real income or real production of an entire economy measured in commodity units per period

Part One   Fundamentals

Chapter I. Some Methodological Considerations

This is a book about macroeconomics. But since we consider some basic methodological background essential to the study of macroeconomics, that must be our concern in this opening chapter. Our aim, however, is to be as concise and relevant as possible, and hence the reader will become familiar only with some elementary issues that are important, if not to real life, then at least to the following text.

§1 Economic Theories

Economics as a science deals with the activities of the individual, the community, and the government in so far as they participate in the production and consumption of scarce commodities. Scarce commodities are those which are both desired and not freely available. From the earliest times man has been inspired for three basic reasons to discuss these themes: First he tried to understand and *explain* economic events; second he sought to *forecast* economic events of the future; and third he was interested in understanding the economic order and specific policies that might best serve the needs of the community, i.e. economics was used to *organize* the economy's affairs. Explanation, forecasting, and organization are the three goals of economics.

The means of pursuing these goals are evidence and theory. By *theory* we mean a system of definitions, premises, and hypotheses. There are several kinds of theories. Some of them merely give a *classification*: they put some important aspects of reality into a system of definitions. Such a theory serves as an "apparatus of the mind" and can be used to describe reality in a precise way. The System of National Accounts is an example of this type of theory.

Other theories, sometimes called *nomological*, try to uncover the laws that govern economic events. They might state, for instance, the connection between the quantity of money and the price level.

In order to make recommendations, theories can be based on value judgements; they are then called *normative* in contrast to *positive* theories which do not imply certain value judgements. Conceptually these two types of theory can easily be distinguished – but in practice this may be difficult. You will soon see that most economic theories contain both normative and positive elements.

To attain the objectives mentioned above, it is necessary that theories correspond to reality. For example the proposition in physics

"All heavy bodies fall to the ground."

seems to match the empirical facts exactly. Laws such as this can be discovered by *induction*: many isolated observations lead to a proposition that is likely to be universally valid. But the trouble with this is that such propositions, even under ideal conditions, can be confirmed in nothing but a finite number of cases. This is the famous *induction problem*: Because we are unable to confirm empirical propositions in *all* cases where they could apply, the former cannot be proved universally valid. Induction therefore, though very important for most sciences, leads to conclusions that are not valid in the strict logical sense.

This being so it is impossible to *verify* an empirical law, i.e. to show its universal validity; but such a law can be *falsified* by means of an example showing a contradiction. If you happened to meet a heavy body that did *not* fall to the ground you would have disproved the above-mentioned law.

In addition to induction, theorists also employ *deduction*: from the validity of a general proposition they derive the validity of a more special one. Suppose for instance that in fact all heavy bodies fall to the ground. Then you can obviously deduce from this:

"This particular heavy body will fall to the ground."

Starting from the induction problem, the development of science has been imagined in the following way[1]: Theories are employed until they happen to become falsified by at least one example demonstrating a contradiction; they are then substituted by new theories which do fit the facts and in this sense are more general than the "old" ones. This is the position of *critical rationalism*. Hence critical rationalism, developed by KARL R. POPPER some fifty years ago, considers empirical falsification as the main "engine of progress" in science. Though this view has some merits, a few critical remarks with respect to economics are in order.

In the first place the opportunities for carrying out controlled experiments in economics are very rare; it is therefore extremely difficult to reject a theory on empirical grounds and this holds all the more since economic propositions are often looked at as probabilistic laws and not as laws that can be applied strictly. Hence empirical observations, which are themselves subject to error, rarely lead to the rejection of well established theories; on the contrary the latter display considerable inertia and are dismissed only if new, superior theories are available[2]. There is never a "theory-vacuum".

§2 Economic Models

At first glance economic events as a whole look almost chaotic and impenetrable – and this may be the first insight of every economist. He therefore develops for the time being a very simplified image of reality, i.e. a *model*, before he starts analysing a certain subject.

A model should depict those parts of reality that are considered relevant to a certain problem. The model is not merely allowed to abstract from reality – on the

---

1 Cf. POPPER, K.R. (1936) The Logic of Scientific Enquiry. Reprint New York 1961: Basic Books
2 Cf. KUHN, Th.S. (1970) The Structure of Scientific Revolutions. Chicago: Chicago University Press

contrary it is obliged to! Abstraction and simplification are the inherant functions of a model. A "good" model yields economic insight, and it is less important how well the premises fit reality.

Readers who find this attitude somewhat awkward should consider the following example: When describing the movement of the moon around the earth, astronomers treat both moon and earth as balls in the mathematical sense. Isn't this an unwarranted simplification – look at the hills and valleys! But, as everybody knows, it is not unwarranted and this model leads to extremely accurate conclusions. Nevertheless, astronomers can subsequently refine the model to yield even better results, this being the second step after they have learned from the first. It is the same in economics.

Typically an economic model includes the following elements. First there are *definitions* of the economic institutions and the exogenous and endogenous variables. *Exogenous* variables are those which are treated as given in the model while the *endogenous* variables are to be explored. Second there are *premises* (or *axioms*), i.e. unexplained and unproved propositions that are assumed true in the model. Finally there are *empirical laws* gathered perhaps from some systematic observations.

The results are then deduced. They are called *theorems*, *implications*, or *conclusions*. The reader should note the similarity between models and theories. Models are means of developing theories and these two cannot be strictly separated.

§3 Methods

By a *method* we mean a special procedure for obtaining scientific results. Hence a method is a technique of analysis or a way of looking at things. For example, both induction and deduction are methods; but there are also more specialized ones designed specifically for economic theory-building. These are to be explained in the following paragraphs.

§4 Equilibrium and Disequilibrium. Stability

"How many times has the reader seen an egg standing upon its end?"

(P. A. SAMUELSON)

Since the birth of economics, the notion of equilibrium has been essential to economic thought. This being the case it is a pity that the term is not used in a unique, or at least predominant, sense, and therefore frequently gives rise to confusion. Still, three primary meanings of equilibrium can be distinguished.

The idea of *equilibrium in the methodical sense* comes from the natural sciences. Equilibrium is conceived as a state of rest. An economic system with given parameters is said to be in equilibrium if the endogeneous variables do not change over time. To economics, the idea of equilibrium in the methodical sense is well-suited since it is rather general and does not refer to special occurences such as fulfilled plans. Therefore it can be applied almost universally: for example to a single market, the balance of payments, or economic growth.[1]

Equilibrium in the theoretical sense is known to the reader from his microeconomic courses. It refers to one or more markets which are said to be in equilibrium if and only if supply equals demand. This is a much narrower meaning of the term since a market can be at rest also if supply and demand do *not* coincide. This will be shown later on. Therefore, we prefer to speak of *market clearance* if supply equals demand and we call this an "equilibrium" only to the extent that it is an equilibrium in the methodical sense.

Finally, the concept of *equilibrium in the normative sense* has been as important as the two previous interpretations. A state is often called an equilibrium if it is considered optimal in some sense; and the reader will certainly know from experience that this is the predominant use of "equilibrium" in politics. But what about an under-employment-equilibrium that is by no means regarded as optimal? Obviously using the different meanings of "equilibrium" simultaneously causes confusion; and hence we will never use "equilibrium" in the normative sense.

Equilibria may be either stable, unstable, or what one might call "indifferent". With a *stable* equilibrium, a displacement from equilibrium is followed by a return to equilibrium, the return being caused by internal forces of the system. With an *indifferent* equilibrium, such forces are missing and the original equilibrium is not re-attained. And with an *unstable* equilibrium, the internal forces cause a progressive deviation from the equilibrium position:

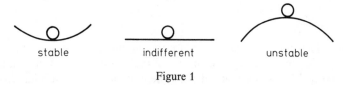

stable   indifferent   unstable

Figure 1

Thus we may conclude that an equilibrium must be *stable* if it is to be economically meaningful. The realization of any unstable equilibrium is as improbable as the realization of a disequilibrium (remember SAMUELSON's "egg"). Only a stable equilibrium constitutes a state which will be approached or maintained by the economic system permanently.

In order to grasp the significance of stable equilibria to economic analysis, the reader should observe: If we were unable to find a stable equilibrium as the economy's "center of gravity", we could state literally nothing about economic laws or future evolutions. This is the proper justification of "equilibrium analysis", interpreted in a non-normative sense.

---

1 Growth equilibrium is a *dynamic* equilibrium because the magnitudes are subject to permanent change. Yet, this is a "state of rest" since the *rate* of change remains constant.

§ 5 Statics, Comparative Statics, and Dynamics

We now turn to three techniques of analysis that are very important to economic theory. A theory can be called static, comparative static, or dynamic according to its treatment of *time*.

In *statics*, all variables relate to the same time period. An example of this is shown in the original curves of the following figure. Their point of intersection determines both price and quantity sold; and, obviously, it is unnecessary to date the variables because only a single instant is considered.

Comparative statics deals with "shifting of curves" or, more precisely, with variables that refer to different time periods. In the figure above, the demand curve was shifted outward while the supply curve remained constant. Now the changes of price and quantity can be analysed. Obviously, they both increase.

Certainly this kind of analysis does not raise the issue whether an adjustment process takes place and how it could be conceived to work. On the contrary, we *postulate* that before and after the curve-shift there is an equilibrium. So comparative statics, though of great value to the theorist, is incomplete in this respect and needs to be supported by an explanation of the adjustment process.

This is the proper task of *dynamics*. Price p and quantity x are here regarded as functions of time, i.e. $p(t)$ and $x(t)$; they are not dated to a certain time period. Now a simple hypothesis can be made, e.g. that the price rises when there is excess demand and falls when there is excess supply. Such hypotheses, formulated either verbally or mathematically, yield a description of the adjustment process; they can also be used to analyze the stability characteristics of the system. Moreover, there are often intimate relationships between comparative static and dynamic characteristics of a system; this was called the *correspondence principle* by SAMUELSON[1].

It may be that some readers now consider dynamics superior to comparative statics and the latter superior to statics. This is not quite correct. On the contrary,

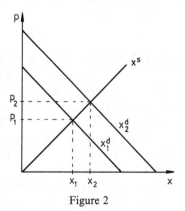

Figure 2

---

1 SAMUELSON, P.A. (1947) Foundations of Economic Analysis. Second edition 1983 Cambridge etc.: Harvard University Press

statics and comparative statics have the advantage of being simpler methods and, given the bounded mind of man, frequently yield more fruitful results. So each of the three methods has its own place[2].

§6 Ex Post versus Ex Ante Analysis

In economics, and especially in macroeconomics, two methods are employed which must be carefully distinguished. We want to demonstrate them by means of the well-known equation

$$x^s = x^d.$$ (1)

At one level, this "supply equals demand" can be regarded as an *ex post* equation where "ex post" simply means "afterwards". It then states that, in the past, *purchases* and *sales* were the same – a fact that is clearly inevitable. If, for instance, one thousand pounds of steel were sold in the steel-market within a certain period, then these thousand pounds of steel were necessarily also bought.

Ex ante analysis, on the contrary, regards the quantities in (1) as *planned* purchases and sales, i.e. as *demand* and *supply*; it follows that these two do not of necessity coincide and the equation above must be regarded as an *equilibrium condition*.

Thus we sharply distinguish between purchases and sales on the one hand and demand and supply on the other hand. The former are equal by definition while the latter are not: they require the theorist to work out the conditions for an equilibrium.

In more general terms, ex post analysis can be said to deal with *observed* economic magnitudes without explaining how they were generated, whereas ex ante analysis concerns itself with the *planned* magnitudes which produce the economic forces that ultimately generate the observed phenomena. Yet both methods are necessary for macroeconomics, and the reader should attempt to keep them strictly separate. This is not too easy because, as equation (1) suggests, mathematical formulations do not indicate whether they are meant ex post or ex ante – thus they have to be interpreted from the context.

§7 Partial versus Total Analysis. The Ceteris Paribus Clause

Economic analysis of a market economy can either cover all markets or just some of them, and accordingly we distinguish between *partial* or *total analyses*. It should be stressed that this distinction does *not* refer to whether "all relevant factors" or just some of them are included in the analysis. In the latter sense, all theory must be regarded as "partial" since human understanding is unable to take account of all factors simultaneously – and thus the distinction would be superfluous.

An instrument used both in partial and total analysis is the so-called *ceteris paribus-clause*, often stated using the notorious phrase "other things being equal". It

---

2 This was pointed out by BOULDING, K.E. (1955) In Defence of Statics. Quarterly Journal of Economics **69**, pp. 485–502

enables the theorist to hold constant a certain set of factors while others are varied so as to analyse their specific effects.

In the theory of consumer behaviour, for instance, preferences and prices may be kept constant in order to discover the reaction of demand to a pure variation in income. This is not at all "restrictive" – because, afterwards, prices may be varied in order to analyse their effect. And, after all, these different causes can even be combined to give the result of a simultaneous change in income and prices.

Considered in this way, the ceteris paribus-clause is not a specific "trick" of economists but rather quite natural to scientific discovery. However, we do not want to suggest that it is always legitimate to keep things constant – often it is not! There is an incorrect use of the ceteris paribus clause which sometimes causes errors. It consists of keeping a factor A constant while simultaneously varying a factor B, where in fact they are not independent of each other. (For example, you increase the speed of a car "other things being equal", i.e. the revolutions of the motor and its momentum.) Thus the use of the ceteris paribus clause is legitimate only if the factors involved can be treated as independent[1].

§ 8 Microeconomics versus Macroeconomics

In accordance with prevailing (!) opinion, microeconomics and macroeconomics can be distinguished in the following manner.

Microeconomics proceeds from the individual economic agent. Every such individual has to make various economic decisions: a household has to decide on its consumption, for example, an entrepreneur on his investments. Microeconomic theory seeks to relate economic events back to these individual decisions. On this basis the conditions for an equilibrium in a single market (partial analysis) and in the whole economy (total analysis) are considered. Thus the characteristic feature of microeconomics is decidedly not that it is restricted to a single market but rather that economic events are explained by means of individual decisions.

Macroeconomics differs from this approach in that it starts from the *aggregate* of several (or all) households or entrepreneurs. Correspondingly, macroeconomics does not worry about supply and demand of certain goods – indeed, it does not worry about the existence of single goods at all. Rather, all goods are taken together and only the resulting *bundle* is considered. Thus the distinguishing feature of macroeconomics is that it collects both individuals and goods together to aggregates and bundles, respectively. Like microeconomics, macroeconomics is concerned with partial and total analysis alike, though it is true to say that the stress is more on total analysis.

The choice between micro- and macroeconomics has important consequences for theory: A macroeconomic theory is often more clear and easier to understand than a microeconomic one; due to its simplicity it is more likely to yield unique results; and what is more, macroeconomics allows a rather easier approach to empirical investiga-

---

1 In mathematics, we encounter the ceteris paribus clause when computing partial derivatives. The possible abuse is here obvious: The partial derivative $\partial z(x,y)/\partial x$ gives the change in z caused by changes in x only on the condition that x and y are independent of each other.

tions. But these three advantages have to be paid for by a *loss of information* due to the aggregation. Thus, in macroeconomics, it is always to be hoped that no information has been lost that is important to the problem at hand.

By now, it should have become clear to the reader that the terms microeconomics and macroeconomics do not refer to certain theories but to *methods*. (In fact, there is a variety of different theories both in microeconomics and in macroeconomics.) The two do not compete but complement one another, and each of them has its own domain.

Microeconomics is primarily concerned with the problem of *allocation*: the question of how scarce resources are utilized, which goods are produced in what quantities, and how the output is distributed. Allocation and distribution are by nature microeconomic problems.

Macroeconomics, on the other hand, deals chiefly with the problems of economic activity, employment, inflation, and growth. Obviously, these questions all refer to aggregate magnitudes, e.g. to the rates of unemployment and inflation. Thus it is evident that the choice of the method is governed by the problem to be explained.

Since the use of terms in the literature, to put it mildly, is not unique, we cannot conclude this section without indicating what the distinction "microeconomics-macroeconomics" does *not* mean: Firstly, these terms are not equivalent to "partial analysis – total analysis". Furthermore, they do not coincide with "equilibrium theory – disequilibrium theory" or even "Classical theory – Keynesian theory". And, finally, it is neither true that microeconomic theories are always based on maximization behaviour nor that macroeconomic theories never are. In the following it will become clear that these distinctions all overlap.

Chapter II. A Historical Survey

According to SCHUMPETER, the three benefits from studying the history of economics thought are pedagogical advantages, new ideas, and insights into the ways of the human mind – but, in a book on macroeconomics, matters stand quite differently. In this chapter, we merely want to discuss some subjects that are important to macro-economic theory.

§9 The Predecessors

Reflections on economic problems can be traced back to antiquity. In PLATO's "Politeia", for example, we already find remarks about the advantages of the division of labor; and ARISTOTLE discussed problems of value, money, and interest in detail. These two certainly summed up thoughts that were even more ancient.

However, it is typical of Romans and Greeks, of scholastics and the philosophers of natural law that they never pursued economics in its own right but always in connection with another, a 'proper', science – be it ethics, law, or political philosophy. Hence, at this time, there was no genuine economic science; but it would be wrong to underestimate the contributions of these authors *to* economics because their work is one of the two sources of systematic economic inquiry.

The other source is composed of the work of innumerable authors who were occupied with more practical or political problems. This illustrious group consisted mainly of teachers of administration, bureaucrats, politicians, and business men. As practical men, they were naturally less concerned with an analytic and systematic treatment of their ideas; but they enriched their writings with a considerable amount of factual information. In the sixteenth and seventeenth centuries, the number of such publications increased so rapidly that, later on, the development of thought in this era was called *mercantilism*. The mercantilists focused on promoting national exports and trading power as well as on fiscal targets, i.e. providing receipts for the sovereign's treasury (*camera*). From this the name *cameralism* was derived for German mercantilism which is a forerunner of modern public finance.

Sir Willam PETTY (1623–1687) is one of the forerunners in the development of economic *analysis* which, according to SCHUMPETER, must be distinguished from the development of economic *reasoning*. PETTY established the concept of national *surplus* that was to become a characteristic feature of Classical economics. Let us briefly describe this approach.

Imagine an economy that only produces "corn" by means of labor and "corn", i.e. capital. In order to produce 100 units of corn, 10 hours of labor and 20 units of "corn" are assumed to be necessary. The latter are a flow; they represent the use of "corn" in production or, to use contemporary jargon, capital amortization. The workers receive a *subsistence wage*, which just enables them to maintain their and their families' capacity to work. This subsistence wage, which possibly satisfies cultural needs as well, may amount to 6 units of "corn" per manhour.

Hence, for producing 100 units of "corn" 10 · 6 + 20 = 80 units of "corn" are required; after deducing the cost of production there remains a *surplus* of 20 units. Now this surplus can either be used for consuming non-essential goods ("luxury consumption") or for capital accumulation. The latter would increase production later on and hereby increase the general wealth.

Around the mid eighteenth century in France a school of men came into being who called themselves "les économistes"; today they are called the *physiocrats*. Founder and head of the school was the medical practitioner FRANÇOIS QUESNAY who was the first to give a comprehensive analysis of the economic process. It was an achievement of the first magnitude. The physiocrats were influenced by RICHARD CANTILLON (1680?–1734) who was the first to consider the problem of resource allocation and also showed for the first time how demand controls the pattern of production via changes in relative prices. ANNE ROBERT JACQUES TURGOT (1727–1781), who was associated with the physiocrats, also developed an elaborated economic theory at this time and he made fruitful contributions that put him among the most important of the predecessors.

§ 10 The Classical Economists

The Classical period of economics can be said to begin in 1770. This decade covers TURGOT's major work and, above all, saw the appearance of the most celebrated economic book of all times, namely, "An Inquiry into the Nature and Causes of the Wealth of Nations". Its author ADAM SMITH (1723–1790) was Professor of Moral Sciences at the University of Glasgow. The significance of his work is partly due to his own analytic contribution but mainly to his arrangement of existing thought, which he forcefully unified. Through the work of SMITH, economics was established as an autonomous field of knowledge for the first time; and, in agreement with SCHUMPETER's dictum that the first discovery of a science is the discovery of itself, she became a proper science.

The Classical age is to be understood in conjunction with its predecessors since, of course, no definite break did take place as suggested at the date 1770. Proceeding from SMITH's work, the Classical economists dealt with nearly all the problems which form the body of present economics; but their doctrine can hardly be summed up in a few words. It has been said that, in the classical writings, a single sentence is more convincing than the whole chapter and the latter, in turn, is more convincing than the entire doctrine. The reader should study at least one Classical book to become conscious of the rather casuistic line of reasoning that makes it so difficult to appreciate the Classics from a modern standpoint.

However, some crucial points of Classical economics can be established. One of them is SMITH's "invisible hand" which symbolizes the working of a market economy (and the Classics were convinced that a market economy would work). This "invisible hand", i.e. the pricing mechanism, coordinates the plans of individuals in spite of –

or due to – their selfish behaviour. Underlying this is the notion of a *natural order* to which the given order should come as close as possible so as to achieve the "optimum optimorum". Consistently, the Classics required that the *state* refrains from intervening in the economic process; later on, this notion was ridiculed as the "nightwatchman state" by F. LASALLE.

The idea, or ideology, of "laissez faire" was not only an attack on the mercantilists, who considered import restrictions and other regulations suitable tools of economic policy, but rather a rejection of interventionism and activism in general. Only two functions were assigned to the government, namely, to take responsibility for security and to establish a legal system that maintains freedom of trade and private property.

What was the main concern of the Classical economists? It was not the allocation problem or the theory of the pricing mechanism though these two were very important also. Rather, the Classics focused on problems that were all connected with the above mentioned *surplus* of the economy; and their main questions referred to the *formation* of that surplus, its *distribution* among the different classes of society, and its *utilization* as "luxury consumption" or "investment". This latter problem – we would now call it a problem of economic growth – was exceptionally important to Classical theory. The Classics uniquivocally favoured the second alternative (investment) because, in the long run, it increases the capital stock and thus the "wealth of nation".

Outstanding economists of the Classical age besides SMITH are: THOMAS MALTHUS (1766–1834) who was both the first economist of population and stagnation; JEAN BAPTISTE SAY (1767–1832), a french adherant to SMITH's doctrines who systematized and popularized them; DAVID RICARDO (1772–1832) who first developed the labor theory of value and was especially interested in problems of distribution; and JOHN STUART MILL (1806–1873), the great philosopher, who elaborated the Classical doctrine in its perfection.

The suggestion of a "Classical" period is due to KARL MARX (1818–1883) who himself is at least as influential and prominent as the Classics and who considered JOHN STUART MILL the last of them. Here we follow his classification, although for other reasons, and date the end of the Classical age to the year 1870 which we regard as the beginning of the Neoclassical period.

But before we pass to the latter, a terminological remark must be made. Nowadays the term "Classics" is used in two entirely different senses. This is because in 1936 Lord KEYNES – immodest as he was – embraced all economists before *his* time under this heading, thus he combined the Classical and Neoclassical economists. We do not want to adopt KEYNES' terminology throughout since there are important differences between Classical and Neoclassical economics; though we will frequently use the short-hand "Classical theory" instead of "Classical-Neoclassical theory". But the reader should beware of the very confusing use of words that takes place today.

§11 The Neoclassical Economists

Usually, Classical and Neoclassical economics are delimited by the so-called "marginal revolution" though this term, like some other "revolutions", may overvalue somewhat the real development. Nevertheless, important changes in analysis took place at this time; and they suggest the separation of two periods.

Marginalism as the central innovation of Neoclassical economics is the generic term for all those "marginal" considerations that are embodied in expressions such as "marginal utility" or "marginal cost". Later on we will use this approach in such great detail that it is unnecessary to explain it now. Using the marginalistic approach, it became possible to trace economic behaviour back to the solution of individual optimization problems. This method differs from that of the Classical economists who rather tended to argue macroeconomically. The Classics were more concerned with the behaviour of certain "classes" of society whereas the Neoclassics focused on the individual. From this point, the economic process was chiefly analysed proceeding from individual behaviour.

Neoclassical marginalism was firstly used in *value theory*, and here it gave rise to an incisive change: The Classics unequivocally conceived of the value of a certain good as determined by its cost of production. This is the *production theory of value* which was developed into the *labor theory of value* by RICARDO and MARX. In contrast, the early Neoclassics thought that it was the marginal utility of a good which would control the price offered by the customers and hence its value. This is a *subjective* theory of value in contrast to the *objective* one of the Classics; but we point out that it was only employed by the early Neoclassics.

These seemingly far-reaching changes in analysis can only be understood in full when considered alongside the change in the subjects that were to be explained: The Classics aimed at exploring the formation, distribution, and utilization of the national surplus whereas the Neoclassics were chiefly concerned with the problem of allocation. The latter sought to explain what determines the allocation of scarce resources among different uses. They finally stated that the pattern of production adapts to the pattern of demand by changes in relative prices; and, above all, that the economy thereby reaches a state that is in a certain sense optimal.

To conclude, the most important difference between Classical and Neoclassical economics can be put as follows: The Classics examined the economic events that would take place over time, whereas the Neoclassics selected a single instant and then analysed the economy in an essential static manner. Hence the interest had shifted from the theory of growth to the theory of value.

At the beginning of the Neoclassical period, there are three authors who independently and almost simultaneously initiated the "marginal revolution"; they are WILLIAM STANLEY JEVONS (1835–1882), CARL MENGER (1840–1921), and LÉON WALRAS (1834–1910). The central point of their writings is the notion of *marginal utility*, i.e. the utility of the last "small" unit of a commodity. The introduction of marginal utility theory brought about still another change, namely, the utilization of mathematical methods which are now so commonplace and yet had scarcely been employed before.

While JEVONS had only worked out a purely subjective theory of value, two authors independently succeeded in combining the subjective and the objective approach and, again, WALRAS was one of them. The other was ALFRED MARSHALL (1842–1924) who held the Chair of Political Economy at Cambridge/Britain and who was, if measured by his influence, the outstanding author of that period. Today, MARSHALL's brilliant synthesis of the objective and subjective components of value (cost and utility, respectively) is illustrated by the well-known schedules of supply and demand which he also developed. Here, the supply curve represents the objective, the demand curve the subjective component of value; and their point of intersection determines both market price (in the short run) and natural price (in the long run).

Other distinguished representatives of Neoclassicism are Irving Fisher (1867–1947), Vilfredo Pareto (1848–1923), Knut Wicksell (1851–1926), and Marshall's successor Arthur Cecil Pigou (1877–1959) to name merely a few that are important to the following.

Defined *historically*, the Neoclassical period can be said to end in 1914 when World War I began, or at the latest in 1930. But viewed *analytically*, an end cannot be discovered: the technique of analysis that was introduced by the Neoclassics predominates up to this day, though several advances have taken place in our century. Hence it should be clear that, for present purposes in referring to the Neoclassics, we will use the historical definition only.

§ 12 From Keynes to the Present

At the beginning of our century, an economist entered the scene whose theoretical work culminated, in 1936, in the "General Theory of Employment, Interest and Money" and who was to become fairly important to the future development of economics: John Maynard Keynes (1883–1946), a versatile and politically engaged Englishman.

Due to Keynes, the macroeconomic theory of today came into being, whereas microeconomics was somewhat restrained. Once again, this was caused by a shift in the subjects that were to be explained: Neoclassical theory, as we saw above, focused chiefly on the problem of resource allocation while the work of Keynes and his supporters is more concerned with the problem of *employment*.

Henceforth, the main question was not "How are scarce – and therefore fully employed – resources allocated to different uses?" but "Why are scarce resources, especially labor, sometimes not fully employed?" This change of question, in turn, partly was due to a historical event, i.e. the Great Depression, and partly to the interest in short-run problems that is so characteristic of our century.

An important outcome of Keynes' work was the creation of a split or schism in economic theory. Our previous assertion that Neoclassical analysis has survived up to the present is only half the truth – the fact is that, under the influence of Keynes, a second orthodoxy came into being. The second part of our book is organized according to this schism.

It would, of course, be an over-simplification to state that Neoclassical and Keynesian theories exhaust the content of contemporary economics; the real development has gone beyond them and it would only be fair to describe it here. The experience of the historians, however, teaches us that historiography becomes harder as we approach the present; and in economics there is the additional thorny problem of an utterly diffuse terminology.

Therefore, in conclusion, we propose a graphical schema that incorporates the various schools of thought in so far as they relate to our subject: macroeconomics. The labels used are far from being uniquely definitive – but we have tried hard to represent the prevailing opinion. A second danger is that the schema has become somewhat "schematic"; nevertheless it may serve as a useful preliminary orientation for the reader. Our principal task in the following chapters is to explore the content of the various "boxes".

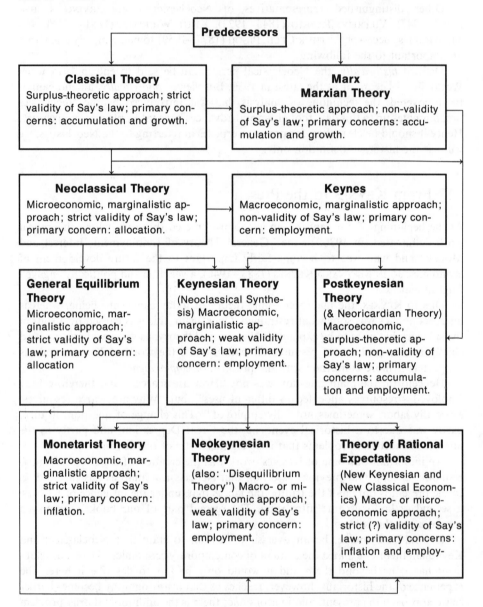

Further Reading

BLAUG, M. (1968) Economic Theory in Retrospect. London: Heinemann
ROBINSON, J. (1962) Economiy Philosophy. London: Watts
SCHUMPETER, J.A. (1954) History of Economic Analysis. London: Allen and Unwin

Chapter III. National Income Accounting

§13 The Economy as a Circular Flow

As stated above, the economic process is a subject quite hard to comprehend. Taking a bird's-eye view of the economy, however, *exchange* appears to be a central phenomenon. Considering first a pure barter economy with only two persons, the exchanges between them can be depicted in the following manner:

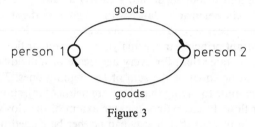

Figure 3

This diagram represents the exchange of goods without use of money; and we assume that only value equivalents are exchanged. Hence, the goods going from person 1 to person 2 are worth as much as those which are going the opposite direction. When money is introduced as a generally accepted medium of exchange, the scheme would look like this:

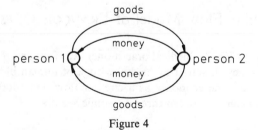

Figure 4

Obviously, the circular flow of commodities is complemented by a circular flow of money. The directions of these two circular flows are opposed – but, in other respects, they are equivalent: If you buy a car worth $10,000, the car of this value accrues to you and money of the same value accrues to the dealer, and these two flows are essentially identical. Hence, when looking at the economy as a whole, one of the two flows can be *eliminated*.

It is appropriate to eliminate the commodity flow for two reasons. First, it is often necessary to calculate sums of different commodities; and this is possible only if they are expressed in money terms. You cannot, for instance, add two pounds of apple and five tons of steel; but if both are valued at market prices, the sum of their values, expressed in money terms, can easily be calculated. The second reason for taking the money flow is that many transactions take place in monetary form only, e.g. tax-payments.

The above model of the circular flow can be made more realistic if, in addition to commodities (goods and services), we introduce claims and productive services.

The exchanges in a complex economy with millions of individuals and goods can also be described in this manner, at least in principle. But the results, due to the complexity, would hardly tell us much; it would be as informative as a TV-picture which is approached so closely that the single points of which it consists can be perceived – but not the picture itself.

Hence, in practice, the innumerable individuals are combined to *aggregates*, as are the various commodities. Subsequently, it becomes possible to assign empirical values to these aggregates and to put them into a clearly arranged scheme. The degree of aggregation must be chosen in accordance with the goals of the study because a higher degree makes things easier to understand but also causes a loss of information.

The most important principle in the analyis of the circular flow is called the *axiom of the closed flow*. It states that, for every aggregate of individuals, the sum of the outgoing flows must be equal to the sum of the ingoing ones. The economic interpretation of this amounts to saying that there are neither "injections" nor "leakages" within the circular flow. In a certain sense, the axiom of the closed flow is a parallel to the proposition in physics that energy can neither be gained nor lost.

It should be clear by now that the analysis of the circular flow can be characterized in two ways. First, it is a *theory* which yields classifications; for it combines the various elements of the economy into certain aggregates. Second, this analysis embodies *empirical investigations* of the economy as a whole.

§14 The Circular Flow-Model of FRANÇOIS QUESNAY

FRANÇOIS QUESNAY, a French medical practitioner, was founder of the first economic school, the physiocracy. Inspired by his knowledge of human blood circulation, he was the first to model the economy as a circular flow. His model, called *Tableau économique*, distinguished between three economic sectors:

- The *productive class* (classe producitive) which consists of peasants and tenant farmers. Only these were said to increase social wealth because, according to the physiocratic view, only nature was able to produce values.
- The *class of the land owners* (classe propiétaire) that consisted of the nobility and clergy.
- The *sterile class* (classe stérile), covering all other occupations, especially commerce and handicraft. According to the physiocratic view, this class was unable to produce value; it merely recasted those values produced by the productive class.

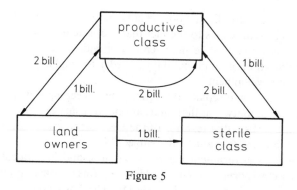

Figure 5

QUESNAY's Tableau shows the relations of supply and demand that take place between these three sectors, depicting the monetary flows only:

Within a given year, the productive class produces food and raw materials to the value of 5 billion livres, using 2 billion livres worth of them as seed, foodstuff, and means of subsistance. Furthermore, it uses one billion to pay for goods manufactured by the sterile class and, finally, has to pass on the sum of 2 billion livres to the land owners as rent.

The land owners in turn buy food from the productive class as well as manufactured goods from the sterile class valued at 1 billion livres each.

Finally, the sterile class acquires agricultural goods to the value of 2 billion livres from the productive class, uses some part of them for its own needs, and sells the reminder in "refined" form to the other classes. It is very important to QUESNAY's model that the value produced by the sterile class merely compensates for its own consumption: hence this class does not contribute to the *net* social wealth.

It is true that the physiocratic model of a feudal economy has largely become obsolete – except for the central idea: the notion of a *circular flow*. In the Classical age, only one economist, MARX, made the idea of the circular flow the focus of his approach. It was only in the 1930s that this concept attained its present importance to economic theory.

§15 The System of Income Accounts

The contemporary *system of product and income accounts* as used in the United States and, in similar form, in all other countries emerged as the synthesis of two distinct lines of research: First, the analysis of circular flows and, second, national income accounting. While the former approach aims at representing the full extend of economic interdependence, referred to as the "circular flow", the latter seeks to determine the value of annual national income. Making allowance for this two-fold goal, the present section is devoted to circular flow aspects of the US system; and the next one to notions of total income and techniques of measuring it.

In the United States, unlike other countries, such as France or Western Germany, there is no central institution reporting national income accounts. Regular data are issued by the Bureau of Economic Analysis (Department of Commerce), and the Federal Reserve Board. The US system presents the circular flow of income ex post in a macroeconomic, periodical, bookkeeping, numerical form. The bookkeeping nature of the US system relates to the fact that the system registers the circular flow by means of double-entry bookkeeping. Thus it provides a suitable scheme for classification and publication of empirical data in order to yield a comprehensive survey of past economic development.

In what follows we will replace the original bookkeeping-type presentation by a graphical one, and simplify it in that international transactions are ignored. Our aim is only to explain the essential features of the US system; more detailed information is given in the literature relevant to the subject.

Abstracting from government activities, savings, and investment, the economy consists of two sectors, *firms* and *households*. The firms produce commodities (goods and services) and sell them to the households. The households, in turn, consume commodities and sell factor services (especially labor) to the firms. Hence, when depicting the monetary flows only, we arrive at the following figure:

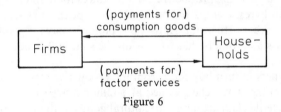

Figure 6

Such a formulation using two sectors appears trivial – but a couple of significant differences from the physiocratic model show, that it is not. First, the economy is partitioned *functionally* and not *personally*. A person does not belong to one of the two sectors pure and simple; but he belongs to the firms when producing, and to the households when consuming. In the second place – and even more important – the US system proceeds from the assumption that *any* commercial activity results in added value, not only the agricultural one.

In the basic model above, the firms produce solely consumption commodities, and the households spend all of their income on consumption. Owing to the axiom of the closed flow, the sum of factor incomes equals total consumption expenditure:

$$\text{total factor income} = \text{total consumption expenditure} \qquad (2)$$

As a result, the productive equipment of the economy remains unchanged since there is no investment. This is a *stationary economy*. In an *evolutory economy*, total productive equipment is changed by means of *net investment*:

$$\text{net investment} := \text{gross investment} - \text{reinvestment} \qquad (3)$$

The symbol ":=" indicates that this is a *definition*. We refer to gross investment as the value of all produced commodities which have not been sold for consumption. Thus, gross investment may consist of produced means of production, and of voluntary or unvoluntary stockkeeping. *Reinvestment*, or *depreciation*, refers to the replacement of old and worn out machines, plant, and buildings with new ones. Now, net investment is the difference between gross investment and reinvestment. Hence net investment indicates the *increase* in productive equipment and stockkeeping.

Denoting the value of total production as Y (yield), the value of consumption as C, and the value of gross investment as I^g, we obtain the fundamental equation

$$Y := C + I^g \qquad (4)$$

It describes the distribution of the total product between consumption and investment.

Refining our simple model once more, we will assume that households and firms do not spend their entire income, but form savings, too. Households save when their consumption falls short of their factor income; while, in the firms sector, corporate firms can retain some share of total profits. Savings, denoted by S, are defined as the sum of depreciation, firms' savings, and households' savings. Since any savings, whether made by firms or households, amount to a reduction of consumption, we arrive at our second fundamental equation

$$Y := C + S \qquad (5)$$

Equations (4) and (5) indicate the *double meaning of Y*: First, Y is the total value of commodities produced; second, it is the sum of all factor incomes. Together these two equations immediately yield:

$$I^g = S \qquad (6)$$

Hence, gross investment and savings are identical *ex post*; indeed, investment is feasible only by reducing consumption by an equivalent amount. The ex post identity of investment and savings is very important to macroeconomic theory; yet it has to be stressed that this tells us nothing about the coincidence of the *plans* to save and to invest. Such questions are the subject of our macroeconomic ex ante analysis.

Now, introducing investment and savings raises a problem: The axiom of the closed flow is *violated* because households' factor incomes exceed consumption expenditures. In order to maintain the closed flow, we have to add an imaginary sector, called *capital formation*. It absorbs savings, and serves to finance investment. The sector "capital formation" is imaginary in that it is merely a theoretical creation with the purpose of closing the flow and indicating changes in asset holdings. The circular flow depicted below again satifies the axiom of the closed flow:

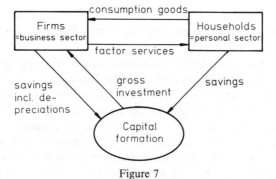

Figure 7

A final extension may cover receipts and expenses of the *government sector*. Households pay direct taxes and fiscal charges to the government; and receive factor incomes as well as transfer incomes from it. Firms pay taxes as well as non-tax payments, such as fees and contributions; they receive subsidies and payments for delivered goods and intermediate inputs from the government. Government makes positive or negative savings, carries out investment, and sells commodities to the firms and households:

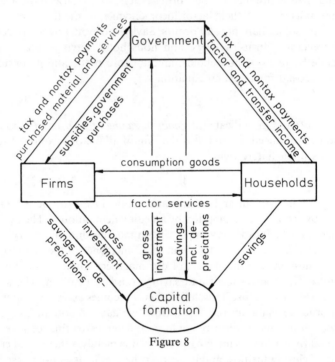

Figure 8

The actual US system of product and income accounts includes various extensions; most important, a sector for the "rest of the world" is added, and all of the above sectors are subdivided. Our brief introduction, however, should have sufficed to bring out the basic idea.

§ 16 Notions of Income in the System of Income Accounts

In contemporary discussion, both theoretical and political, "aggregate income" is of outstanding significance: it serves as a "business barometer"; it is the strategic variable of growth policy; and it is even employed as a "welfare indicator". This overwhelming importance of "aggregate income" necessitates that it be determined *empirically*; and this constitutes a further duty of income accounting.

While aggregate income is often referred to as "national product" in economic life, the US system of product and income accounts distinguishes several meanings of this seemingly simple term. Four distictions are to be considered here.

Net and gross product. The distinction between net and gross product is analogous to that between net and gross investment: we calculate net product by deducting depreciation (or reinvestment) from gross product. Hence, gross product measures total income, whereas net product comprises only that fraction of it which is available for consumption or net investment.

Domestic and national product. This distinction makes allowance for the economy's foreign relationships. Domestic product measures total income created within the boundaries of the country, including that fraction which belongs to foreign residents. National product, on the other hand, measures all income accruing to nationals – be it created in the country, or abroad. Thus, the profits of a US firm's foreign branch in Germany belong to the US national product, but not to the US domestic product. Conversely, they belong to Germany's domestic product, but not to her national product. – The difference between domestic and national products is called "net factor income accruing to residents from abroad". It may be positve or negative.

Products at market prices and at factor cost. These two differ by the amount of indirect taxes and subsidies. The product at factor cost represents the value of output as measured by the total costs incurred in its production. Adding indirect taxes and deducing subsidies from this yields the product at market prices.

Nominal and real product. The basic idea of this last distinction is that any value increment is capable of being split up into an increment in output, and an increment in prices. If the measured value of a given product has increased by 5 per cent annually, this can mean that purchased quantities have risen by 5 per cent, or that prices haven risen by 5 per cent, or that some combination of these two events has taken place. With respect to "social wealth", it is only the change in output that matters. Therefore, the nominal products are divided by an appropriate price index in order to obtain the real product. The growth rate of the real product is meant to represent the annual increase in output.

On the basis of these four distinctions, we could form $2^4 = 16$ definitions of income; but only some of these are actually employed. To give an impression of the magnitude of the most important measures, we present here some figures for the United States (1984)[1]:

Gross domestic product at market prices:	$ 3,619 bill.
Gross national product at market prices:	$ 3,663 bill.
Net national product at market prices:	$ 3,259 bill.
Net national product at factor cost:	$ 2,960 bill.

The net national product at factor cost is often referred to as *national income* because

– it does not include depreciation;
– it refers to the income of nationals; and
– it does not include indirect taxes (minus subsidies).

Therefore, national income is a suitable measure of the material living standards of nationals. Yet, the habitual indicator of a country's economic strength is the gross

---

1 Source: Department of Commerce (Bureau of Economic Analysis and Bureau of the Census).

national product at market prices (GNP_M). The following figure depicts the real growth of GNP in the United States[1]:

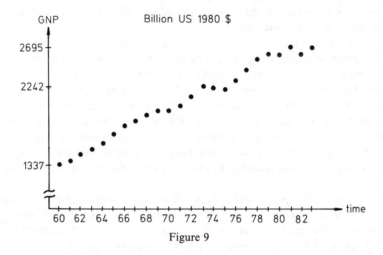

Figure 9

There are three different ways to calculate aggregate products. First, one can add the *values of all commodities* produced; second, one can compute the *sum of all expenditures*; and, finally, one can total *all factor incomes*. These three ways of determining aggregate income are called the *commodity-service method*, the *consumption-plus-investment method*, and the *incomes received method*, respectively. It is of the utmost importance to understand that they are bound to yield the same results. This is because the value of all commodities produced constitutes aggregate factor income, and this factor income is spent totally in one way or another. Therefore, the commodity-service method, the consumption-plus-investment method, and the incomes received method are just three ways of considering the same phenomena.

The procedure using the *commodity-service method* is very simple indeed. For every producing unit in the economy, one calculates *net output* by deducting purchases of goods and services from its annual sales. Gross domestic product at market prices is the simple addition of all net outputs:

$$GDP_M = \sum \text{Net outputs} \qquad (7)$$

According to the *consumption-plus-investment method*, four types of expenditure are to be distinguished, namely, *consumption*, *investment*, *government purchases*, and *net export*. Net exports represent the difference between exports and imports. Thus, we can split up gross national product at market prices into four components:

$$GNP_M = C + I^g + G + (Ex - Im) \qquad (8)$$

Here, G denotes government purchases, Ex denotes exports, and Im denotes imports. The relative significance of the four components of GNP is illustrated in the following table[2]:

---

1 Source: same as above.
2 Source: same as above.

GNP	C	I	G	Ex	Im
$3663	$2342	$638	$747	$364	$429
100%	64%	17%	20%	-2%	

The *income-received method* describes how national income is distributed among empoyees, and entrepreneurs and property-owners. In the US system, the components of national income consist of *income from employment* on the one hand and *income from property and entrepreneurship* on the other:

$$NNP_F = Y \text{ employees} + Y \text{ property and entrepreneurship} \qquad (9)$$

The quotient Y employees/NNP_F is called *labor's share*. When judging on the significance of this magnitude, one must take into account that top managers belong to the group of wage-earners whereas small retail traders are entrepreneurs. Hence, labor's share cannot serve as a measure of the justice of distribution or the like. The corresponding figures for the United States (1984) are[1]:

NNP	Y employees	Y property and entrepreneurship
$2960	$2173	$787
100%	73%	27%

In order to illustrate the basic structure of the US system as a whole, we want to combine the three ways of measuring aggregate income in a synoptic diagram:

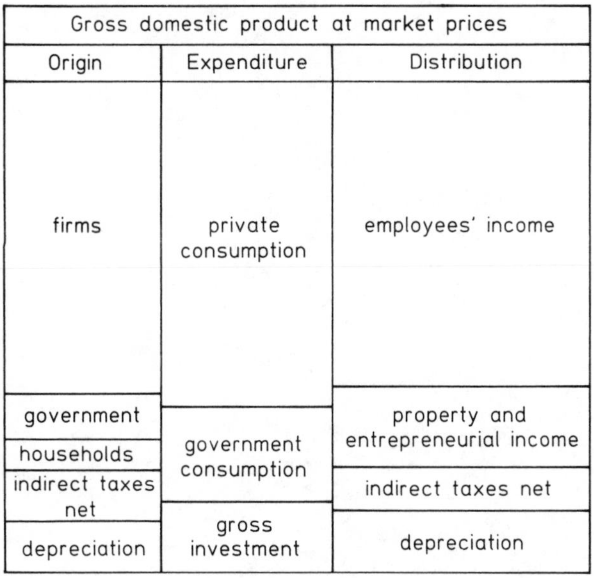

Gross domestic product at market prices		
Origin	Expenditure	Distribution
firms	private consumption	employees' income
government	government consumption	property and entrepreneurial income
households		
indirect taxes net		indirect taxes net
depreciation	gross investment	depreciation

Figure 10

---

1 Source: same as above.

The areas of the diagram above are proportional to the corresponding magnitudes so that the figure yields a good impression of relative shares[2]:

We do not want to conclude the present chapter without emphasizing that the informative power of the US income account is limited by innumerable problems. Problems of definition veil the border line between investment and consumption (is a professor's salary investment in human capital, or government consumption?) as well as blurring the somewhat misleading distinction between income from employment and income from property and entrepreneurship. The problems of empirical measurement are by no means less serious, and the advanced reader will soon recognize that aggregate product cannot be measured like velocity or temperature.

---

2 Source: United Nations (1985) National Accounts Statistics. The numbers refer to United States 1982. Minor items have been neglected.

Part Two   Macroeconomics

The essence of an orthodoxy of any kind is to reduce the subtle and sophisticated thoughts of great men to a set of simple principles and straightforward slogans that more mediocre brains can think they understand well enough to live by.

(HARRY G. JOHNSON)

§17 Introduction to Part Two

For some fifty years macroeconomic discussion has been dominated by two competing orthodoxies, called Classical-Neoclassical and Keynesian Theory respectively. While these two approaches have been considerably elaborated since, their "cores" have remained unchanged, and hence it is worth examining them more closely. Thereafter we will be able to debate their implications for economic policy, and then pass on to more recent developments in macroeconomics. But initially, we should specify the general assumptions of our approach.

First, we will represent both Classical-Neoclassical and Keynesian theory in highly condensed form. The interconnected strands of thought, characteristic of the historical development of ideas, cannot be followed here because theory, not history, is at the center of our interst. Hence we combine Classical and Neoclassical theory in spite of the analytical differences between them since there are also important similarities. For short, we will speak of the *Classical theory* from now on. As a result of this very condensed exposition, every judgement of "Classicism" or "Keynesianism" is a judgement of the central arguments only and cannot do justice to single authors.

Secondly, the theories are put in contemporary terms. For example, we will speak of a "production function" in connection with Classical theory – although this mathematical notion was perfectly unknown to the Classics. This procedure suits our purpose because it helps in comparing the different theories; and it is legitimate because only the form and not the essence of the original ideas is changed.

Thirdly, we limit our subject in several respects. We consider only

- a market economy with private property,
- where all markets are perfectly competitive,
- no external economic relations exist,
- and where, initially, there is no government.

These premises are, no doubt, very restrictive and we hope that they do not prevent the reader from reading further. In most cases it is suitable to start with the simplest model; but the simplest is also the most abstract model and hence rather remote from reality. But, with increasing knowledge and proficiency, the model can subsequently be made more realistic; and this will happen in Chapter 5, for example, where government is introduced in order to analyze the impacts of fiscal and monetary policy.

Nonetheless, the models are perfectly adequate to bring out the central ideas of Classical-Neoclassical and Keynesian theory. What is more, they are quite difficult enough.

Chapter IV. The Classical Theory

§18 The Classical Vision. Plan of the Chapter

The early economists were confronted by the theoretical problem that, in a market economy, the individuals formulate their economic plans rather independently from one another, and yet these plans are normally fulfilled. How could this be possible? The answer was: The *pricing mechanism* brings about a coordination of those individual economic plans. Due to this mechanism, the pattern of production tends to adjusts to the pattern of demand.

If there is excess demand in a certain market, for example, the customers will overbid one another to get the desired good, or the suppliers will be able to charge them higher prices. Thus the production of the good becomes more profitable, which induces some suppliers to produce more of it. At the same time some customers will be inclined to buy other goods because this one now seems too expensive to them. Hence, the price change is likely to result in a market clearance. But if this is true for any market – so the early economists thought – it would be true for all markets, too.

With regard to the above mechanism, Classical and Neoclassical economists also considered *adjustment problems*; indeed, they are the last to be accused of unrealistic lines of reasoning. Nevertheless, the tenor of their analysis reads as follows: *Ultimately*, a market economy tends towards a state of general equilibrium, i.e. clearance of all markets; and in this sense, general equilibrium is the center of gravity of a market economy.

Classical and Neoclassical economists did *not* want to deny the possiblity of temporary crises: they only maintained that a convergence towards general equilibrium would occur *in the long run*, even if this "long run" would take some five or even thirty years. Furthermore, they considered general equilibrium an *optimal state for society*. They asked: What could be better than an economic order which allows individuals to plan freely and independently and yet typically fulfills their plans? So the early economists recommended an economic order that guarantees economic freedom to the citizen: they advocated the market directed economy.

Beside the analysis of the pricing mechanism that we call price or value theory, a second achievement of the Classics consisted in discovering the *veil of money*. Viewed naively, money seems to play the outstanding role in the economic process: Those who possess plenty of it are considered rich; and nearly everyone tries to earn lots of money and to spend as little as possible on any given quantity of goods. The Classics opposed this common opinion by declaring: *Money and wealth are entirely different*. The social wealth consists of the annual production or the existing stock of goods whereas money is a mere medium of exchange. No one wants money for its own sake but only because of the goods he can buy with it. Hence, money is a "veil" over the real events.

The exaggeration of this view led to the *macroeconomic dichotomy* (bipartition), as it is called today. This is the proposition that in a market economy the monetary and the real magnitudes are entirely independent of one another. An increase in the quantity of money, for instance, does not bring about any change in real wealth, but only a proportionate increase in prices. Accordingly, analysis was divided into *value theory* and *monetary theory*. Value theory deals with real magnitudes as well as with relative prices whereas monetary theory deals with pure money prices. We mention this "dichotomy" because it is decisive for what is to follow: To maintain the "Classical spirit", we will first discuss the determination of real magnitudes only; afterwards we will supplement this pure value theory with the quantity theory of money.

Two macroeconomic simplifications are basic to the following procedure. First, in the economy considered there are only two kinds of individuals, called *firms* and *households* respectively, and these are combined into two sectors. The sectors each pursue three economic activities:

The firms   – produce commodities,
          – demand labor power, and
          – undertake investments.
The households – consume commodities,
          – supply their capacity to work, and
          – make savings.

Our second assumption implies that only a *single homogeneous* commodity is considered whose quantity is designated as Y. Looked at ex post, Y is the *real income* of the whole economy and, as only one commodity is supposed to exist, "real income" means the same as "the number of annually produced units of that commodity"; hence real income is measured in commodity units.

But in ex ante-analysis, three meanings of "Y" must be carefully distinguished. Y can be interpreted as

– the total quantity of *planned* production (Y^s);
– the total quantity of *planned* demand for goods (Y^d); or
– the sum of labor incomes, interest incomes, and profit incomes.

Our model covers four markets in total, namely

– the *commodity market* where the supply of commodity Y^s meets consumption demand C and investment demand I;
– the *labor market* where labor supply N^s and labor demand N^d meet;
– the *capital market* where capital supply S (savings) and capital demand $I \equiv \Delta B^s/P$ meet (in fact, as explained later, I denotes both investment demand and capital demand);
– and the *money market* which is described by the quantity theory of money.

Since the first three markets are assumed to be perfectly competitive, in each of them a single price is established, i.e.

– the *price level* P which denotes the money price of the homogeneous commodity;
– the *nominal wage* w as the money price of labor; and
– the *rate of interest* i as the price of capital.

In so far as we are abstracting from money, it is not the money price level P and the nominal wage w that are crucial, but only their quotient, i.e. the *real wage* w/P. The real wage denotes the number of commodity units paid for one working hour.

In the following, we will first analyze the behaviour of firms and households; subsequently we let them trade in the various markets; then we introduce money; and finally we sum up these isolated results by means of the Classical model.

§19 Production Functions

In the firms sector, commodities are produced by means of *factors of production*. Clearly the technology of production exerts a strong influence on the behaviour of firms; so we first turn our attention to this. Classical theory distinguishes between three factors of production, namely, labor, capital, and land.

The term *labor* here covers all work done by blue-collar and white-collar workers; the work of the enterpreneur himself, however, was either neglected or conceived of as a special factor.

Capital in general means either the entirety of producible means of production, or the financial funds to pay for them; here we use the term in its first sense. In the theoretical analysis of production, inventories do not constitute capital because they cannot be used as a means of production.

Land, finally, covers all natural resources or, in other words, all non-producible means of production. Land in the narrow sense belongs to this category, but so do ore deposits, oil springs, and the like.

The relationship between input of factors of production and output can be described by a *production function*:

$$Y = F(N, K). \tag{10}$$

Here Y denotes the quantity of goods produced, N the number of working hours, and K the size of the capital stock. In our macroeconomic model, capital consists of a homogeneous commodity that is identical to the produced commodity. Thus the output can be used either for consumption or investment; in the latter case, the stock of capital increases.

Equation (10) assumes nothing but the existence of a *maximum output* corresponding to any combination of labor and capital. The functional relationship between them depends on

– the given quantity and quality of land; and
– the given level of technical and organizational knowledge.

By equation (10) it is not meant that land and knowlegde exert no influence on output, but only that these two are given and *constant* within the considered period. In the short run, the enterpreneurs can vary output by variations in labor and capital input only.

To obtain analytical results, the foregoing premises do not suffice; certain assumptions with respect to the kind of functional relationship must be made. We will assume a *Neoclassical production function*:

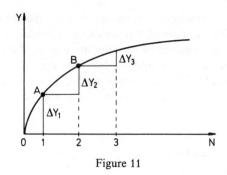

Figure 11

This figure shows the relationship between the number of working hours and output where the quantity of capital is taken as given. This Neoclassical production function clearly exhibits the following features:

- The graph runs through the origin,
- its slope is always positive,
- but decreases over the whole range.

What does this mean in economic terms? First, nothing can be produced without any effort; therefore, the graph runs through the origin. Second, more work yields more output; therefore, the slope is always positive.

We now have to ask why the slope decreases over the whole range. Imagine a firm with a certain amount of equipment where no work is done at all. This is point O in the figure above. An increase in labor input up to one hour will bring about an extra yield of ΔY_1, and point A is reached. A second hour of work will also increase output but by *less* than the first because the first hour is likely to have been used for the most urgent activity.

At this level of abstraction – only two variable factors of production which are both perfectly homogeneous – it is quite reasonable to suppose that both factors exhibit decreasing returns: For if the quantity of some factor is increased gradually, the quantity of the other being held constant, the former is rather "scarce" at first; and then gradually becomes more and more "abundant" in relation to the other. Thus the increase in output caused by a given increase in the variable factor is likely to diminish. This is the essence of the Neoclassical production function.

The additional yield of the last unit of labor is called the *marginal product of labor*. Thus we can say that the Neoclassical production function implies diminishing marginal product of labor as the quantity of labor is increased.

This line of thought can also be directly applied to the other factor, i.e. capital, since it is appropriate to assume that the law of diminishing marginal product applies to this factor, too: Starting with a positive number of working hours and without any capital in the sense of equipment, the first unit of capital will be put to the most urgent utilization, the second unit to the next most urgent utilization, and so on; hence capital will also show a diminishing marginal product.

It is to be noted that the foregoing reasoning applies only to *partial factor variations*, i.e. to variations of a single input (or some inputs) keeping at least one other constant. In the case of a *total factor variation*, i.e. a proportionate increase of *all* inputs, the law of diminishing returns is unlikely to hold because the relative scarcity of the factors remains unchanged. On the contrary, it would be supposed that a doubling of *every* input results in a doubling of output.

In three-dimensional space, the Neoclassical production function has the following shape:

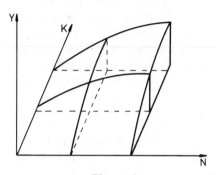

Figure 12

Obviously, the slopes of the surface of this graph with respect to the N- and K-axes are both positive and decreasing. They are called *marginal productivities*. For example, the marginal productivity of labor is equal to the marginal product of the last "small" unit of labor divided by exactly that "small" unit. In the limit of infinitesimal variations, the marginal productivities are identical to the partial derivatives of the production function with respect to N and K.

The difference between marginal products and marginal productivities is that the former represent certain quantities of output while the latter are *ratios*. In contrast to marginal products, marginal productivities do not increase if the additional output produced increases but only if additional output *per unit of input* increases.

The Neoclassical production function has first partial derivatives[1] that are strictly positive: any extra input yields some extra output; furthermore, it has second partial derivatives that are strictly negative: the additional output per unit of additional input decreases; and, finally, we suppose for simplicity that its cross derivatives vanish: the marginal productivity of labor is independent of the quantity of capital, and conversely.

To sum up:

$$\frac{\partial F}{\partial N} > 0 \quad \text{and} \quad \frac{\partial F}{\partial K} > 0. \tag{11}$$

$$\frac{\partial^2 F}{\partial N^2} < 0 \quad \text{and} \quad \frac{\partial^2 F}{\partial K^2} < 0. \tag{12}$$

$$\frac{\partial^2 F}{\partial N \, \partial K} = \frac{\partial^2 F}{\partial K \, \partial N} = 0. \tag{13}$$

---

[1] Partial derivatives are introduced in the mathematical appendix. Assumption (13) is also explained there, in subsection *4.5.

Some qualifications concerning the empirical validity of the Neoclassical production function must be made. First, this function implies perfect *substitutability* of the two factors of production: they can be combined in any arbitrary ratio. This is rather unrealistic if a specific capital equipment is given and a certain number of workers is required to operate it. Here we speak of a *limitational* production function. However, the Neoclassical production function does not relate to such a situation but rather to the *planning stage* in which it is perfectly reasonable to assume that the entrepreneur can make a choice between different methods of producing a given output. We thus recognize that the Neoclassical production function deals with a not too short time horizon which enables the enterpreneur to decide on the method of production; and it neclects the time scale in which equipment is already installed and no choice of this kind can be made.

Second, the Neoclassical production function contradicts the original *law of diminishing returns* as put forward by TURGOT. TURGOT proceeded from an observation in agriculture: If land is cultivated, the second hour of work potentially brings in a *higher* yield than the first because the first hour does not allow an intense enough cultivation. Thus, TURGOT proposed returns to labor which *increase* at first; but he also thought marginal productivity of labor would decrease after a certain optimal point was passed. To conclude, TURGOT's production function showed a marginal productivity of labor which, starting from the origin, first rose up to a certain point, and then declined in the familiar manner. Generally, the assumption of a Neoclassical production function is likely to be violated if there are special technical relationships. In many cases, especially that of TURGOT, it is not an unwarranted simplification however because it can be shown that, in perfect competition, firms always produce in the range of diminishing marginal productivity[1]. Hence, the range of increasing marginal productivity is economically irrelevant and can be neglected accordingly without loss of generality.

For the purpose of empirical investigation, special production functions have been constructed, such as the famous *Cobb-Douglas production function*. Such formulations need not detain us here since our primary concern is theoretical rather than practical.

§ 20 The Firms

Having considered the production function, we are now ready to turn to the behaviour of firms. In a market economy, the behaviour of the productive sector depends crucially on the decisions of the various single enterpreneurs, and this obvious fact has to be our point of departure. Hence, we take up MARSHALL's famous notion of the representative firm.

The *representative firm* is an imaginary single firm which behaves, except in scale, exactly as the average of all firms, i.e. it works under normal conditions. If there are 100 firms, for example, which produce in total 1000 units of a certain commodity, the representative firm will produce precisely 10 units of it. Because we are searching for qualitative results only, the difference of scale can be neglected, and we can speak of "the representative firm" and "the sector of firms", as well.

---

1 This is shown in the Mathematical Appendix, Subsection *3.9.

The representative firm is supposed to aim at maximizing its profit. This assumption does not suit reality perfectly; but it seems more reasonable than any simple alternative (e.g. revenue maximization). *Planned nominal profits* are expressed as money units per period and they consist of revenues minus labor and capital costs:

$$\pi = P \cdot Y^s - w \cdot N^d - i \cdot B^s$$

profits = revenues − labor costs − capital costs

(14)

In this formula, π represents annual nominal profits, P the commodity price, w the nominal stage rate, N^d planned demand for labor, and i the rate of interest. B^s is the planned debt of the firm, that is the stock of bonds that are to be issued up to the end of the period. Hence $i \cdot B^s$ represent the future interest payments.

Trying to maximize profits, the representative firm has to take into account its production possibilities which are given by a Neoclassical production function:

$$Y = F(N, K).$$

(15)

Changes in the physical stock of capital within a single period are called *investment*. If K denotes the optimal equipment and K_0 that equipment given at the beginning of the period, investment amounts to

$$I := K - K_0.$$

(16)

where we assume absence of bottlenecks, so that the optimal stock of capital can be realized by means of a single investment decision. The representative firm *finances* its investment by issuing bonds[1]:

$$P \cdot I = \Delta B^s.$$

(17)

This equation amounts to the assertion that the *value* of the investment, calculated as commodity price times the number of capital goods required, is wholly financed by borrowing; hence ΔB is the nominal change in the debt within the period. Of course, it is also conceivable that investment is financed out of current profits; but we can interpret this as if the profits were first distributed and then given to the firm as outside debt immediately afterwards. Here, we implicitly acknowledge the fact that self-financing gives rise to (opportunity-) costs since the owners have to forego other way of using their funds. This difficulty is avoided here since capital consists of outside debt only.

By rearranging terms in equation (17)

$$I = \frac{\Delta B^s}{P}$$

(18)

it becomes clear that the demand for physical capital (equipment), I, is identical to the real demand for financial capital (funds), $\Delta B^s/P$.

We now substitute the production function (15) and equations (16) and (17) into the profit function (14) to get:

$$\pi = P \cdot F(N, K) - w \cdot N^d - i(B_0 + P(K - K_0)).$$

(19)

---

1 Note that every *supply* of bonds is equivalent to a *demand* for capital. Therefore we use the subscript "s" referring to bonds rather than capital.

Since we deal with perfect competition only, the representative firm acts as price taker: It considers the price, the wage rate, and the rate of interst given and adjusts output, labor and capital input so as to maximize its profits. As equation (19) suggests, profit is indeed merely a function of two variables, i.e. labor and capital, because the latter determine output uniquely. Thus, the conditions for maximum profit[1] consist in setting the partial derivatives of the profit function to zero:

$$\frac{\partial \pi}{\partial N} = P \cdot \frac{\partial F}{\partial N} - w \overset{!}{=} 0, \tag{20}$$

$$\frac{\partial \pi}{\partial K} = P \cdot \frac{\partial F}{\partial K} - i \cdot P \overset{!}{=} 0. \tag{21}$$

Solution immediately yields:

Condition for
optimal labor demand:
$$P \cdot \frac{\partial F}{\partial N} = w, \tag{22}$$

Condition for
optimal capital demand:
$$\frac{\partial F}{\partial K} = i. \tag{23}$$

$P \cdot \partial F / \partial N$ is called the *marginal value productivity* of labor as opposed to $\partial F / \partial N$, the marginal physical productivity. It is the increase in monetary revenue caused by a "small" increase in labor – as opposed to the increase in physical output. According to equations (22) and (23), marginal value productivity of labor must equal the nominal wage in equilibrium; and marginal value productivity of capital must equal the rate of interest.

What is the economic interpretation of these formulae? Let us turn to labor first. The effect of the employment of a small additional quantity of labor is two-fold:

– revenue rises approximately by $P \cdot \partial F / \partial N \cdot dN^d$ (*marginal revenue*);
– and costs increase by $w \cdot dN^d$ (*marginal cost*)[2].

From the standpoint of profit maximization, the employment of an additional labor unit is sensible only if marginal revenue exceeds marginal cost:

$$P \cdot \frac{\partial F}{\partial N} \cdot dN^d > w \cdot dN^d \tag{24}$$

marginal revenue > marginal cost

As long as this condition holds, the representative firm will find it advantageous to *increase* its labor demand, since revenue increases more than cost. Now the central idea is that marginal productivity will *decline* due to the assumption of a Neoclassical production function. The reader will recognize this immediately from Figure 11. Hence, if labor demand goes up, and marginal productivity of labor declines accord-

---

1 Owing to our assumptions regarding the production function, these conditions are both necessary and sufficient when we abstract from corner solutions.

2 The terms "marginal revenue" and "marginal costs" refer to one *factor unit* here. Instead, we could also use them referring to one *output unit*, writing $P \cdot dy$ for marginal revenue and $w \cdot \partial N / \partial Y \cdot dY$ for marginal costs.

ingly, a point will finally be reached where

$$P \cdot \frac{\partial F}{\partial N} \cdot dN^d = w \cdot dN^d, \tag{25}$$

and this is the point of maximum profit with respect to labor! If the firm were to increase its labor demand further, profits would decline because marginal cost is *constant* and marginal revenue *diminishes* (due to diminishing marginal productivity). On the other hand, it would also be unwise to demand less labor than indicated by equation (25) since, before reaching this equality, (24) applies and profits can be increased by employing more labor. Therefore, the point where marginal cost equals marginal revenue is optimal. Dividing (25) by dN^d immediately yields equation (22) which basically makes the same statement but with respect to infinitesimally small changes.

The condition for the profit maximizing stock of capital can be explored similarly. Any increase in the capital stock causes both

– an increase in revenues of approximately $P \cdot \partial F/\partial K \cdot dK^d$;
– and an increase in cost by $i \cdot P \cdot dK^d$.

dK^d represents the change in the capital stock, i.e. investment. The increase in costs is due to the fact that investment is financed by debt for which interst must be paid. Starting from zero and increasing capital gradually, marginal revenue will at first exceed marginal cost; but whereas the latter is constant due to given prices, marginal revenue declines. It declines until

$$P \cdot \frac{\partial F}{\partial K} \cdot dK^d = i \cdot P \cdot dK^d. \tag{26}$$

marginal revenue = marginal cost

This is the optimum condition for the stock of capital. Dividing both sides by dK^d yields equation (23) which states the equivalent with respect to infinitesimal changes.

Using those maximum conditions we are ready to turn to the ultimate goal of our model: to explore how the representative firm reacts to *price changes*. Again, we start by considering labor, and divide equation (22) by the commodity price or price level:

$$\frac{\partial F}{\partial N} = \frac{w}{P}. \tag{27}$$

Equation (27) states that the marginal physical product of labor must equal the *real wage rate*. How can we expect the firm to react when the real wage rate rises? The firm will again choose labor input so as to equalize marginal productivity and the given real wage rate; because, as we saw before, only in this case profits will be maximized. If the real wage *rises*, marginal productivity of labor must also *rise*, and this means that labor demand *diminishes* (see Fig. 13).

Therefore, as a rule, labor demand declines as the real wage rate goes up. The same result is obtained mathematically if we differentiate (27) by means of the chain rule[1]

---

1 Cf. the mathematical appendix, passim. We have to point out that in the simple case we need not solve two *simultaneous* equations (20) and (21) because the cross derivatives of the production function were assumed to vanish. In Subsection *4.5 of the Mathematical Appendix we deal with the more tricky case of non-vanishing cross derivatives.

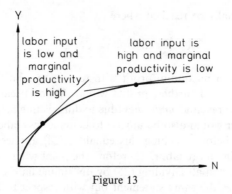

Figure 13

with respect to w/P (i.e., $\partial F/\partial N$ must be differentiated with respect to N first, and then N with respect to w/P):

$$\frac{\partial^2 F}{\partial N^2} \cdot \frac{dN}{d(w/P)} = 1 , \tag{28}$$

$$\Leftrightarrow \frac{dN}{d(w/P)} = \frac{1}{\dfrac{\partial^2 F}{\partial N^2}} < 0 . \tag{29}$$

The negative impact of a rise in the real wage rate on labor demand follows directly from assumptions (12) and (13). The impact of changes in the interest rate on capital demand is derived similarly:

$$\frac{\partial^2 F}{\partial K^2} \cdot \frac{dK}{dI} \cdot \frac{dI}{di} = 1 \quad \left(\frac{dK}{dI} = 1; \text{ cf. (16)} \right) \tag{30}$$

$$\Leftrightarrow \frac{dI}{di} = \frac{1}{\dfrac{\partial^2 F}{\partial K^2}} < 0 . \tag{31}$$

We can summarize the results of this section by the *labor demand function* and the *capital demand function* of the representative firm:

$$N^d = N^d \underset{(-)}{\left(\frac{w}{P} \right)} \tag{32}$$

$$I = I(\underset{(-)}{i}) . \tag{33}$$

The following two figures illustrate that any rise in the real wage diminishes the demand for labor; and any rise in the interst rate diminishes the demand for capital.

In addition to these two functions, there exists a *demand for financial capital* or, equivalently, a *supply of bonds*. (Recall that, if someone offers a bond he demands financial capital, i.e. money; thus demand for capital and supply of bonds are equivalent.) This demand for financial capital is here identical to real investment since we supposed the latter to be entirely financed by outside debt. Thus, "investment" has a two-fold meaning.

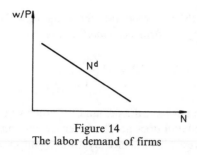

Figure 14
The labor demand of firms

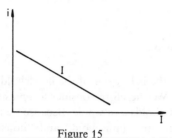

Figure 15
The investment demand of firms

Our description of the representative firm's decisions is now complete. We recognized that the firm – when price, wage, and interest are given – chooses its demand for labor and capital so as to maximize its profits.

In the following we will employ the very important assumption that the stock of capital *does not change within the current period*, or, to put it differently, that one period is required for the installation of new capital goods. Under these circumstances, the current production depends only on the initial capital stock and on the level of employment, whereas the new capital goods have no impact before the next period. The resulting model is not exactly the same as that we discussed above – because there we supposed new capital goods to increase production instantaneously – but it simplifies analysis considerably, and it is for this reason alone that we employ it from now on. Changes in the stock of capital are rather difficult to handle, and that is why they are chiefly dealt with in growth theory[1].

Due to our new assumption, we can rewrite the production function as

$$Y = f(N). \tag{34}$$

because the only *variable* factor that influences current production is labor. Investment, on the other hand, shows a *demand effect* within the current period, but not a *capacity effect*; capacity to produce cannot be enlarged before the following period. According to (34), current production depends exclusively on labor; but the latter, in

---

1 Since there is no capacity effect in the first period, the profit function (14) must be interpreted as to refer to two-period profit maximization. Strictly speaking, we should allow for expectations. But that would make the analysis harder without changing the qualitative results.

turn, is conditional on the real wage rate (cf. equation (32)). Combining these two functions, we can specify the firm's *commodity supply function*:

$$Y^s = Y^s \left(\frac{w}{P} \right) \atop (-) \tag{35}$$

If the real wage rate goes up, the demand for labor will decrease and so will the commodity supply. The latter does not, however, depend on the rate of interest. It is true that the rate of interest will influence investment; but since we neglect the capacity effect of investment it will not have any impact on current production.

§21 The Households

As in the sector of firms, the behaviour of the household sector also depends on the decisions of single units. We therefore consider a *representative household* that acts, save in scale, like the households as a whole. Because we look for qualititative results only, the terms "representative household" and "household sector" can be used synonymously.

Within any period, the representative household receives *labor income, interest income*, and *profit income*:

$$P \cdot Y = w \cdot N^s + i \cdot B^d + \pi. \tag{36}$$

As we know from national income accounting, $P \cdot Y$, i.e. the price-level times the physical output of a period, is identical to total nominal income if depreciation is neglected. Or, to put it another way, profits are simply defined as the value of production minus labor and interest income by equation (14). Hence, the sum of labor, interest, and profit income must be equal to the value of production *ex post*. But what holds ex post trivially, holds ex ante only if the individual *plans* are compatible. Therefore, in ex ante analysis, we have to distinguish between planned supply (Y^s), planned demand (Y^d), and income (Y).

In that we are abstracting from money for the time being, the representative household divides its real income between consumption and savings:

$$Y = C + S; \quad S := \frac{\Delta B^d}{P}. \tag{37}$$

In this equation, C represents real consumption, and S real savings, i.e. real demand for bonds. (37) is called a *budget constraint* because it forces the household to balance income and expenditure. The concept of a budget constraint is important and should not be misunderstood: it does not state that some income is given to the household and the latter has only to decide how to spend it. On the contrary, incomes and expenditures are planned simultaneously; by manipulating its labor and capital supply, the household can decide on its labor and interest income. This point is very important to Classical theory.

In order to choose a certain *labor supply*, the household weighs the advantages of income against the disadvantages of giving up leisure. The Classics described this by means of *cardinal utility theory*. Cardinal utility theory conceives of utility as a quantity that is measureable, at least in principle, and *marginal utility* is simply that utility received from the consumption of the last "small" unit of some good.

The representatives of marginal utility theory proceeded from the empirical observation that the intensity of a stimulus declines when the cause of that stimulus (e.g. the consumption of a certain good) is repeated. Or alternatively: marginal utility decreases as consumption increases. This principle is known today as *Gossen's first law*. According to it, the relationship between income (or consumption) and utility exhibits the following shape:

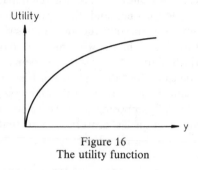

Figure 16
The utility function

The graph of this utility function shows that marginal utility of consumption – though always positive – diminishes over the whole range. In contrast, labor was assumed to yield dissatifaction because it involves giving up some leisure. Since leisure is treated like any other good, and therefore also shows diminishing marginal utility, marginal disutility of labor must increase as labor supplied itself increases.

The household receives additional real labor income

$$dY = \frac{w}{P} \cdot dN^s. \tag{38}$$

if it supplies dN^s additional units of labor at the given real wage rate w/P. When total labor supply and labor income are small, marginal utility of income will be high but marginal disutility of labor will be low. Accordingly, the household will increase its labor supply gradually until the marginal disutility of labor and marginal utility of income are just in balance. This point is optimal to the household.

If the given real wage increases, marginal utility of labor income will rise too, because now a greater quantity of goods is paid for every working hour, and labor supply will be increased until the new optimum is reached. Hence, marginal utility theory yields the result that high wages correspond to a high labor supply, and from this the *Classical labor supply function* can be derived:

$$N^s = N^s \underset{(+)}{\left(\frac{w}{P}\right)}. \tag{39}$$

This theory should be qualified a little in view of contemporary theory. From modern "indifference curve analysis", such a monotonic relationship between real

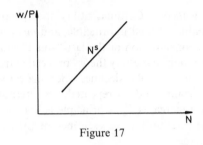

Figure 17

wages and labor supply can *not* be inferred because the impact of an increase in the real wage rate is two-fold. On the one hand, there is certainly a *substitution effect*: When the wage rate goes up, leisure becomes dearer and this will induce the household to demand less of it, i.e. it will induce him to work more. But, on the other hand, there is an *income effect*, too, which enables the household to demand both more goods and leisure. Thus, the household can afford the now dearer leisure, and it is even possible that more of it will be consumed than before, i.e. that labor supply will diminish. The *net effect* of these two potentially opposing impacts cannot be determined theoretically; but empirical evidence over the last century suggests that, on the average, labor supply *diminishes* due to rising real wages. Nevertheless, we will employ function (39) in the following analysis.

If we now turn to the household's choice between consumption and savings, it has to be stressed from the outset that this decision is not independent of the one above. The household does not decide on its income first, and on the utilization of income afterwards: but he makes these decisions *simultaneously*. It is only for pedagogical purposes that we discuss these problems independently.

When the Classics spoke of "savings", they thought primarily of the investing entrepreneur, and "savings" and "investment" appeared almost identical to them. This view was quite appropriate in those days. But the Neoclassics – and we will follow them in this respect – were well aware of the fact that the decisions to save and to invest are entirely different. Firms undertake investments in order to make profits in the future; but it is primarily households that decide how much to save, and they do this in order to distribute their income over time, to receive an interest, or to leave a bequest.

The *abstinence theory of interest*, put forward by WILLIAM NASSAU SENIOR, was one of the Classical explanations of savings and interest, and it was perhaps the most important. According to this theory, the household generally prefers present to future consumption (where future consumption is the same as savings) on purely subjective grounds, as well as because of *risk-aversion*. It was argued that the household saved only if interest high enough to counteract the sacrifice and the risk of waiting was offered to him.

Considered with the aid of marginal utility theory, the household will increase its savings up to the point where the marginal utility of the interest payment and the marginal disutility of waiting just balance. A rise in the given rate of interest increases the marginal utility of a certain level of savings and, hence, induces the household to save more.

Furthermore, we will assume for simplicity's sake that the decision to save is not influenced by the real wage rate and that the decision to work is not influenced by the

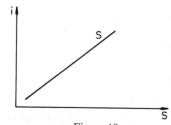

Figure 18
The savings (or capital supply) of households

rate of interest. This yields the *Classical capital supply function* which states that savings depend on the rate of interest only, and increase in line with rising interest:

$$S = S(\underset{(+)}{i}).\tag{40}$$

The Classical abstinence theory of interest is not to be taken too seriously. In order to explore the positive interest rates that occur in reality, we do not need the assumption that savings mean a "sacrifice" to the household generally. Rather, it is perfectly adequate to assume that the households' capital supply is *scarce* in comparison with the firms' demand for it. If, at an interest rate equal to zero, the households would wish to save an amount of $ 100.000, but the firms would like to get $ 2.000.000, the latter will overbid one another until an equilibrium interest rate of, say, 10 per cent is established. It is even conceivable that capital supply would remain at $ 100.000, i.e. that not a single household would be induced to save more, because substitution and income effects cancelled each other out. In this case, the economic function of the interest rate would merely consist in directing capital into its most efficient uses.

In so far as interest receipts constitute a negligible part of total income, (40) and (37) suggest that the household will consume *less* when the rate of interest goes up. This is because total income remains almost the same; and because the household's aim to save more it must reduce consumption accordingly. Therefore, the *Classical consumption function* reads

$$C = C(\underset{(-)}{i}).\tag{41}$$

Our description of the household's behaviour is now complete, and we want to summarize the results. According to Classical theory, the representative household receives labor, interest, and profit income. It decides on labor and interest income by itself; only profits are given because they depend on the prevailing profitability of the firms. (In the long run, however, the household can change its equity interests; and then, all components of total income are endogenous.)

For simplicity only we assumed that the choice between labor and leisure is independent of the rate of interest, and that the choice between present and future consumption is independent of the real wage rate [1]. Owing to the special assumptions

1 We admit freely that this is an inconsistent assumption: If the household increases its labor supply subsequent to a rise in the real wage rate, it must necessarily either spend or save more, which contradicts the premise that both consumption and savings are independent of the real wage rate. Allowing for the dependency, however, would involve no different results but prevent any graphical demonstration of the model.

of marginal utility theory, labor supply and savings proved to be positively correlated to the real wage and the interest rate, respectively, while consumption was seen to decline as the rate of interest rises.

The representative household formulated its plans subject to the budget constraint (37) which may be rewritten as

$$P \cdot C + P \cdot S = w \cdot N^s + i(B_0 + P \cdot S) + \pi. \tag{42}$$

On the left hand side of this equation, consumption and savings are the two possible utilizations of income, whereas, on the right, there are the three sources of income. $B_0 + P \cdot S$ is identical to B^d: the initial stock of bonds, plus current savings, is identical to the planned stock at the end of the period, and interest income stems from the latter stock.

§ 22 The Labor Market

We have already derived the labor demand of the firms and the labor supply of the households. In this section, we combine these two constituents of the *labor market* in order to establish the equilibrium levels of employment and the real wage rate. From the Classical point of view, *full employment* and the *equilibrium real wage rate* result from equating labor demand and supply:

$$N^d\left(\left(\frac{w}{P}\right)^*\right) = N^* = N^s\left(\left(\frac{w}{P}\right)^*\right). \tag{43}$$

Looked at mathematically, these are two simultaneous equations with two unknowns: N and w/P. Provided that a solution exists at all, it is unique given our assumptions. In a graphical representation, the solution is determined at the point of intersection of the demand and supply schedules:

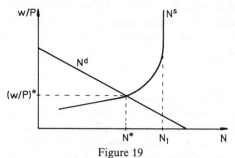

Figure 19
Equilibrium in the labor market

The plans of firms and households are compatible only when the equilibrium real wage rate (w/P)* prevails: in this case, every demand for labor is fulfilled, and every household can sell its labor supply.

We now have to ask what happens when the real wage rate *differs* from its equilibrium level; for our equilibrium analysis makes sense only if there is a tendency of the real wage rate to move towards the equilibrium rate. Let us, therefore, consider a situation where the real wage is too high:

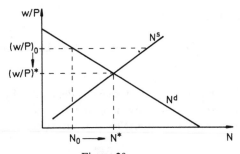

Figure 20
Disequilibrium in the labor market

In the Classical model – as in reality –, the price level P is *exogenous* to the labor market so that only the nominal wage rate can change. Hence the excessive real wage rate $(w/P)_0$ is due to an excessive nominal wage rate. As seen from the figure above, this causes an excess supply of labor, i.e. *unemployment*. The Classics presumed that in such a case, the unemployed would be willing to work at a lower nominal wage rate, and that they would underbid the employed. It was also considered possible that the employers could now enforce a reduction in wages.

Both possibilities entail a reduction in *real wage rates*, and – according to the Classics – this reduction would continue until the equilibrium real wage rate $(w/P)^*$ and full employment were regained.

With regard to the converse case of a real wage below the equilibrium rate we can argue analogously: The firms will want to get more labor than they can at the prevailing wage rate; accordingly, some of them will offer higher wages to entice workers away from other firms; and this will last until the equilibrium is re-established. Obviously, the Classical adjustment process can only be expected to work smoothly if there are no arrangements or cartels, like employers' federations and unions.

The reader should notice that the theoretical notion of "full employment" is not necessarily identical to that of labor market statistics. Full employment N^* is consistent with the fact that some members of the working population do *not* work; in Figure 19, these are $N_1 - N^*$ persons. But, and this is the central point, they *voluntarily* do not take up employment because the prevailing wage appears insufficient to them.

Therefore, we will reserve the term *unemployment* for involuntary unemployment only, and N^* is called full employment equilibrium since no one is involuntarily unemployed. This terminology is suggested by a *normative* consideration: At N^*, all workers are acting in accordance to their preferences, and in this special sense the result can be called "optimal". On the other hand, a state can hardly be regarded as optimal in which the working population is *forced* to work as much as possible.

The results of Classical labor market theory can be summarized as follows. Long-lasting involuntary unemployment is impossible since the wage rate can always adjust as to bring about an equilibrium; in equilibrium, the plans of both firms and households are fulfilled; and these hypotheses are *only* subject to the premise that there are no institutional constraints that hinder a wage adjustment.

§23 The Capital Market

"Interest is commonly reckoned for Money ... but this is a mistake."

(NICHOLAS BARBON)

In the *capital market*, bonds are traded; they are demanded by the firms and supplied by the households. We have already derived the firms' *real demand for financial capital*, in §20, which proved identical to their investment:

$$I(i) \equiv \frac{\Delta B^s}{P}. \tag{44}$$

The firms' capital demand was seen to be a declining function of the interest rate because any increase in the interest rate increases capital costs. Similarly, in §21, we derived the households' saving function, i.e. their *real supply of financial capital*, which turned out to be an increasing function of the interest rate:

$$S(i) := \frac{\Delta B^d}{P}. \tag{45}$$

The Classics, as already indicated, conceived of investment and saving as almost identical processes carried out by the same persons. To them, "saving" meant not only a sacrifice of consumption but also a demand for real capital goods; and hence it is hardly astonishing that the equality of savings and investment did not seem a severe problem to them.

The Neoclassics came closer to the present view as they clearly perceived the difference between decisions to save (i.e. to postpone consumption) and decisions to invest (i.e. to undertake an enterprise). If these decisions are reached independently, there must be an adjustment mechanism that reconciles them. This adjustment mechanism is the *rate of interest*. Equating investment and saving yields the equilibrium condition

$$I(i^*) = S(i^*) \tag{46}$$

which determines the *natural rate of interest* i*. The natural (or equilibrium) rate of interest entails the equality of savings and investment. It is equal to the equilibrium marginal productivity of capital because equation (23)

$$i = \frac{\partial F}{\partial K}. \tag{47}$$

shows that the firms always adjust the capital stock in order to equate the marginal productivity of capital to the rate of interest. The natural rate of interest is also equal to the marginal disutility of waiting since the households increase savings up to this point. Hence, the rate of interest can be said to equalize the marginal productivity of capital and the marginal disadvantage of waiting (see Fig. 21).

The *actual* rate of interest may, of course, depart from the equilibrium rate for some time – but not for too long. For if it is above i*, for instance, investment will decrease whereas savings may increase; thus capital supply will be abundant and some households will not succeed in selling the capital they wish to supply. They are then

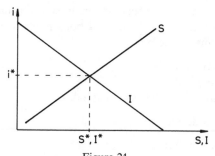

Figure 21
Equilibrium in the capital market

likely to accept a lower return because it is better to receive this than none at all. Therefore, the rate of interest will decline until equilibrium is regained where every firm and every household can realize its plans and where, accordingly, there is no reason for the interest rate to change. Since the capital market comes rather close to a perfect market in the theoretical sense, we can expect a fairly quick adjustment.

We have to stress that it is *claims* that are traded in the capital market – not commodities and not money either. Commodities are supplied and demanded only in the commodity market (which we will be considering next), and money is not regarded as capital (which does not deny that it serves as a medium of exchange in the capital market).

This point is all the more important to Classical economics to the extent that it conflicts with common opinion. NICHOLAS BARBON, in 1690, was the first to suggest this model of the capital market. He maintained that borrowers, if they take a loan, do not want the money for itself but the *goods* it can procure and that the capital market can be conceptualized as the exchange of goods for claims (bonds). Therefore, money does not enter into the determination of the interest rate: the latter is influenced only by real forces, i.e. marginal productivity of capital and marginal disutility of waiting.

Thus, any abstention from consumption on the part of households results in an increase in the social stock of capital because this abstention is equivalent to saving, and savings become equal to investment by means of the interest rate. The results of this analysis are that, in the Classical model, claims (bonds) are supplied and demanded in the capital market, and the interest rate is expected to bring about a quick market clearance.

§24 The Commodity Market

To conclude our non-monetary analysis, we discuss the *commodity market* in which commodity supply and investment and consumption demand meet. Equilibrium in the Classical sense means equality of commodity supply and demand:

$$Y^s\left(\frac{w}{P}\right) = C(i) + I(i). \tag{48}$$

We now want to explain why a seperate analysis of this market is not necessary: The two sectors of the economy, firms and households, make decisions on three activities each. The firms decide on

- the supply of commodities,
- the demand for labor, and
- the demand for financial and physical capital,

whereas the households decide on

- the demand for consumption goods,
- the supply of labor, and
- the supply of capital, i.e. savings.

It can easily be seen that both sectors have *two degrees of freedom*. If the firms choose some investment and labor demand, they have also committed themselves to a certain supply of commodities; and the households have implicitly decided on their consumption once they have chosen certain amounts of labor supply and savings.

If the firms' demand for labor matches the households' supply of it, and if capital demand and supply also coincide, then commodity supply must equal commodity demand, too. Or, to put it differently, simultaneous equilibrium in the labor and capital markets *implies* equilibrium in the commodity market. This can be proved mathematically in the following manner.

Using the definition of profits (19) and replacing $F(N, K)$ and $K - K_0$ with their respective equivalents Y and I yields:

$$\pi = P \cdot Y^s - w \cdot N^d - i(B_0 + PI). \tag{49}$$

The firms' financial constraint (17) stated that any investment must be financed by an equivalent supply of bonds:

$$I \equiv \frac{\Delta B^s}{P}. \tag{50}$$

Furthermore, we retain the households' budget constraint (42):

$$P \cdot C + P \cdot S = w \cdot N^s + i(B_0 + PS) + \pi. \tag{51}$$

Putting all terms of these equations on the left hand side and rewriting (50) as $P \cdot I - P \cdot I = 0$ yields

$$\pi - P \cdot Y^s + w \cdot N^d + i(B_0 + PI) = 0 \tag{52}$$

$$P \cdot I - P \cdot I = 0 \tag{53}$$

$$P \cdot C + P \cdot S - w \cdot N^s - i(B_0 + PS) - \pi = 0. \tag{54}$$

Finally, adding (52) to (54) and rearranging terms amounts to

$$\underset{\text{commodity market}}{P(C + I - Y^s)} + \underset{\text{capital market}}{(1 - i)P(S - I)} + \underset{\text{labor market}}{w(N^d - N^s)} = 0 \tag{55}$$

According to (55), the excess demands in the three markets, each of them multiplied by the respective market price, sum to zero. This is called *Walras' law*. Walras's law does not hold only in equilibrium but under any circumstances: If an excess demand occurs in one market, there must be at least one other market where excess supply exists because, otherwise, the sum of the excess demands would not vanish.

We can conclude from this that there must be an equilibrium in the commodity market if the labor and capital markets are both cleared. Hence, the commodity market can be neglected in our non-monetary analysis.

Note: When studying the literature, one frequently encounters the opinion that equality of savings and investment is in itself sufficient to ensure equilibrium in the commodity market. The usual motivation of this runs as follows:

$$Y = C + I \quad \text{and} \quad Y = C + S. \tag{56}$$

From this it follows that $S = I$ implies $Y = Y$ (57)

This, though a truism, holds perfectly only in ex post analysis. In ex ante analysis, however, the two "Y" do not mean the same, since the Y on the left hand side represents planned commodity demand, and that on the right, planned income of households. Equalization of S and I amounts to deducing that commodity demand equals income – and this has hardly anything to do with equilibrium in the commodity market. An equilibrium in the commodity market requires that commodity supply and demand match, and planned commodity supply, in turn, is entirely different from households' planned income because it is planned by the firm sector.

By means of Walras's law we can infer that $S = I$ implies an equilibrium in the commodity market *on the condition that* an equilibrium in the labor market prevails simultaneously[1]. It is hence a fallacy that $S = I$ implies an equilibrium in the commodity market; and it is downright absurd to refer to the capital market as a commodity market.

To conclude, let us discuss the possibilty of a *demand gap* in the commodity market, i.e. unsufficient demand for commodities. At first sight, it would seem that this situation is likely to arise because the households do not spend all their income – which, in equilibrium, is equal to commodity supply – but save a certain amount. But, in equilibrium, these savings are equal to investment demand so that investment fills the gap exactly. Hence, in the Classical model, a demand gap is utterly inconceivable.

§ 25 The Quantity Theory of Money

"Money is a veil." (ARTHUR CECIL PIGOU)

The Classical non-monetary analysis which we have been discussing up to now was complemented by the so-called *quantity theory of money*. *Money*, looked at from the Classics' point of view, is chiefly commodity money: it consists of gold, silver, and coins of precious metal. Bills of exchange and banknotes were not included in the quantity of money for reasons that we will explain later. Money was supposed to serve as

– a generally accepted means of payment and
– a general measure of value.

---

1 This will become only too obvious in Keynesian theory.

As a *generally accepted means of payment*, money permits an indirect exchange of commodities. This is an enormous advantage as should become evident by the following example: Imagine a peasant who wishes to sell grain in exchange for tools, and an artisan who wants to sell tools in order to get some meat. No exchange at all can take place between these two, because the peasant's offer does not match the artisan's need. It will probably take a great deal of searching until they find someone whose wishes correspond to their own.

In a monetary economy things are much easier: The peasant can sell his grain to another person first and then exchange the revenue for the tools. Finally, the artisan can use this money to buy his meat. Thus the advantages of indirect exchange originate from the fact that there need not be a *double* coincidence of wants (i.e. one person demands what is supplied by the other, and vice versa) but only a *single* coincidence – and, of course, an agreement on the price. This constitutes the *transactions motive for using money*.

Due to its function as *general measure of value*, money serves for reckoning the values of all other commodities: these values are expressed in money terms. This yields remarkable efficiency gains, too. In an economy where there are 1.000.000 different goods – and that is not very many –, about 500 billion *relative prices* do exist which specify the pairwise exchange ratios of the goods. Thus, using a general measure of value reduces the number of prices to a 500.000th of the original number (i.e. to 1.000.000), and this considerably facilitates comparisons. A general measure of value need not physically exist: MONTESQUIEU, for instance, gave an account of African tribes who used a purely imagininary measure of value, so-called "makuten", for expressing the value of different goods. Contemporary examples of imaginary measures of value are the British guinea and the Special Drawing Rights of the International Monetary Fund. In the following, we will speak of *abstract prices* if the measure of value is not identical to the means of payments; otherwise, we will speak of *money prices*.

Money's function as a *store of value* was assigned to it by the Classical authors in a restricted sense only: In order to serve as a means of exchange, money must also be a temporary store of value; and this is the reason why it is always durable goods that are selected to serve as money. On the other hand, the Classics denied that money acts as a *store of value proper* because, in contrast to other stores of value, it yields no *interest*. Hence, as they argued, it would be unwise to hold more cash than was required for transaction purposes thus incurring a loss of interest on the assets that could otherwise have been held. Consequently, the Classics considered *hoarding* an irrational exception.

Now we are able to turn to the core of Classical monetary theory, i.e. the principle of the *neutrality of money*. According to this, money is a mere "veil" over real events; it sometimes obscures them; but, apart from the efficiency gains described above, it does not influence the real events at all. The last great Classic, JOHN STUART MILL, for instance, opens the second volume of his "Principles", after he has completed more than 700 pages of real analysis, with the following words:

"Having proceeded thus far in ascertaining the general laws of Value, without the idea of Money (except occasionally for illustration) it is time that we should now superadd this idea. ... It must be evident however, that the mere introduction of a particular mode of exchanging things for one another, by first exchanging a thing for money and the exchanging the money for something else, makes no difference in the essential character of transactions. It is not with money that things are really purchased. ... There cannot, in short, be intrinsically a more insignificant thing, in the economy of society, than money." [1]

The interpretation of this passage must not be pushed too far, however, since MILL conceded a short-run impact of money on real variables. Nevertheless, the central idea is maintained: Money is, so to speak, the lubricant of the economic process; without its aid exchange would be much more troublesome; but a single "drop" of it is sufficient – the quantity makes no difference to the real variables. These thoughts gave rise to the notion of a "dichotomy" between the real and the monetary sectors of the economy whereby the two have no influence on each other.

Hence, with respect to the monetary sector, only the *price level* is to be explained and this is achieved by the quantity theory of money. The Classics chose the following point of departure: The price level, being the average price of all commodities, is the ratio at which money exchanges for the other commodities and can be determined by equating demand and supply in a fictitious money market. Fictitious, because money is not actually traded in a specific market, but is exchanged for commodities in *every* market. Yet this does not preclude us from mentally distinguishing a money market. The "money market" in this sense must not be confused with those markets for short-term loans which are called money markets in business language.

In the following we suppose that money is not produced and supplied as other goods but that its quantity is given by the available quantity of precious metals or by the policy of the central bank. In doing so we neglect the possibility of gold production or creation of money by modern banks. This amounts to assuming an *exogenous money supply*.

If the money supply is a given *stock*, the demand for money must also be a stock. According to the quantity theory of money, the demand for a cash stock arises from the time-lag between receipts and expenditures. When people receive their money income, they do not spend it instantaneously but need some time to decide on their consumption and savings. This time-lag causes a permanent average stock of cash to be held by the individuals. Let us calculate this by means of a representative individual who holds every dollar for three months. Thus the *average duration of holding cash balances*, k, amounts to

$$k = \text{three months} = 1/4 \text{ year}. \tag{58}$$

Henceforth we will call this variable the *Cambridge k*, for short, since it was first introduced by the economists MARSHALL and PIGOU from Cambridge. Let us further assume nominal national income of $ 100 annually:

$$P \cdot Y = \$ 100. \tag{59}$$

Now, what quantity of money will be called for? If each dollar were to be kept for the whole year (on average) then $ 100 would be necessary to match the demand for money because the nominal income is exactly $ 100. But if, on the other hand, each

---

1 MILL, J.St. (1848) Principles of Political Economy. London: Parker. Reprint Toronto 1965: University Press. pp. 2 ff.

dollar is kept for a quarter of a year, only $\$25$ are required. These $\$25$ circulate four times a year and hence support an annual sales volume of $\$100$.

In general terms, we can calculate the nominal demand for money (L^n) as the product of nominal income and the Cambridge k:

$$L^n = k \cdot P \cdot Y. \tag{60}$$

The demand for money must equal the exogeneous money supply in equilibrium:

$$M = k \cdot P \cdot Y. \tag{61}$$

This is called the *Cambridge equation*; it is one way of expressing the quantity theory of money. Another way was chosen by the American economist IRVING FISHER who considered the *velocity of circulation* instead of the Cambridge k. In the above example, the Cambrige k came to a quarter of a year and this, as we saw, meant that money circulated four times a year, i.e. the velocity of circulation amounted to four. Thus the velocity of circulation is merely the reciprocal of the Cambridge k:

$$v = \frac{1}{k}. \tag{62}$$

Substituting v for k in the Cambridge equation and rearranging terms yields the *quantity equation*:

$$M \cdot v = P \cdot Y. \tag{63}$$

The Cambridge equation and the quantity equation are basically equivalent as v proved to be the reciprocal of k. But the former clearly indicates the individual decisions to hold money whereas the latter refers to the somewhat mechanistical notion of a "given" velocity of circulation. Therefore, we will use the Cambridge equation from now on; but we stress that the quantity equation could be employed equally well.

Let us now have a closer look at the four variables of the Cambridge equation. The money supply (M), as stated above, is a given stock. The Cambridge k depends on how much cash the individuals want to hold. We assume – and this assumption is crucial – that it is constant in the short run. Finally, real income (Y), as we recognized above, is determined by the preferences of the households and the production technology.

$$M = k \cdot P \cdot Y. \tag{64}$$

Therefore, the *price level* is the only variable not given from elsewhere and this immediately yields the conclusion of the quantity theorists: The quantity of money, k and Y being given, determines the price level *uniquely and causally*; and k and Y themselves are independent of the quantity of money. For example, any doubling of the quantity of money must entail a doubling of prices. This is the quintessence of the quantity theory of money.

A doubling of the quantity of money must entail a doubling of the price level – O.K. But, as economomists, we should not trust in such "musts", but ought to ask what is the *adjustment process* which brings about this doubling. On this score, let us listen to JOHN STUART MILL:

"Let us suppose, therefore, that to every pound, or shilling, or penny in possession of any one, another pound, or shilling, or penny were suddenly added. There would be an increased money demand, and consequently an increased money value, or price, for things of all sorts. This increased value would do no good to any one; would make no difference, except that of having to reckon pounds, shillings, and pence in higher numbers... If the whole money in circulation was doubled, prices would be doubled." [1]

MILL's Neoclassical succesors specified the crucial point more exactly: They assumed, as MILL did, that the cash balance of every individual is doubled instantaneously. Starting from an original equilibrium, this means that real cash balances are now considered *too high* because prior to the increase they were considered just appropriate. To reduce their excess cash balances, individuals will increase their demand for commodities. This increased commodity demand, however, will not be accompanied by a higher commodity supply since the latter depends on real variables that have not changed. Our first result, therefore, is that there will be an *excess demand* in the commodity market which, over time, will bid up prices.

When can we expect this increase in prices to stop? It would be a fallacy to suppose that this would occur when all individuals have spent their surplus cash balances. Though a *single* individual unquestionably can reduce his cash balance, this is not possible for the economy as a whole since one individual's expenditures are the receipts of another. The price pressure hence is not eliminated by reducing nominal cash balances. We unravel this problem as soon as we realize that the individuals do not want to maintain a certain *nominal* but a certain *real* cash balance, i.e. command over a certain quantity of goods. Therefore, prices will rise until real cash balances, M/P, have resumed their original level. When this happens, the purchasing power of cash balances is just the same as before, and hence the latter match the individuals' preferences. In order to keep the original level of M/P, prices must clearly rise in proportion to the quantity of money.

We refer to the dependence of commodity expenditures on real cash balances as the *Cambridge-effect*. The Cambridge effect is the link between changes in the quantity of money and changes in the price level; and it ensures that prices move in proportion to the quantity of money.

The Neoclassical economist KNUT WICKSELL, one of the most outstanding monetary theorists, confessed in his critique of the quantity theory of money [2] that the latter gives a logically valid explanation but can be attacked on empirical grounds. While the space at our disposal does not permit a full account of WICKSELL's own contribution (which, in fact, is similar to that of KEYNES) we would, at least, want to take note of his central criticisms:

First, WICKSELL doubts the constancy of the velocity of circulation (or the Cambridge k) which he believes to be one of "the most airy and less seizable variables of the economy". But if the velocity of circulation is not constant at least in the short run, then the impact of a change in the quantity of money on the price level cannot be forecasted.

Second, WICKSELL criticizes the quantity theorists' narrow definition of money, pointing out that precious metals and coins can be substituted by notes, bills of

1 MILL, op.cit. p. 15
2 WICKSELL, K. (1898) Geldzins und Güterpreise. Jena: Fischer. English translation (1965) Interest and Prices. New York: Kelly

exchange, or cheques. If a wider definition of the quantity of money is considered appropriate, the latter can hardly be treated as *exogenous* since, for example, the individuals can decide freely on how many bills of exchange they want to draw. It may also happen that an increase in the quantity of precious metals entails a decrease in the quantity of bills of exchange such that the total quantity of money remains constant.

Third, WICKSELL doubted the crucial link between the quantity of money and the price level, namely, the strength of the Cambridge-effect. Later on we will encounter a similar critique that suggests substituting the Cambridge-effect by another one (the Keynes-effect).

To conclude. The prevailing monetary doctrine of the Classical age is the quantity theory of money. It implies a dichotomy between the real and the monetary sector of an economy and states, essentially, that changes in the quantity of money cause proportional changes in the price level *only*, whereas all real variables remain constant.

For clarity of exposition, we have considered only the "pure core" of this theory; and hence we want to add that the quantity theorists were indeed far from denying every real impact of monetary changes – though they were also far from stressing this point[1]. As ALFRED MARSHALL once put it:

"This so-called 'quantity theory of the value of money' is true in just the same way as it is true that the day's temperature varies with the length of the day, other things being equal; but other things are seldom equal."[2]

§26 Say's Law

"The fundamental things apply, as time goes by." (From "Casablanca")

The law named after JEAN BAPTISTE SAY is one of the most famous propositions of Classical doctrine. One familiar definition of it reads:

Any supply creates its own demand. This is because every expansion of production entails additional factor incomes that are used by their recipients for demanding commodities.

However innocent a statement this may seem, vehement discussions have attended to it up to the present. Let us try to gain a closer insight into this. In the first instance, Say's law does not refer to the identity *ex post* of sales and purchases but to *planned* magnitudes; it is not a mere truism. Second, Say's law is not an *axiom* but a *theorem*, i.e., a proposition which is not supposed true but can be derived from others. The following passage from MILL brings this home:

"... is it ... possible that there should be a deficiency of demand for all commodities, for want of the means of payment? Those who think so cannot have considered what it is which constitutes the means of payment for commodities. It is simply, commodities. Each person's means of paying for the productions of other people consists of those which he himself possesses. All sellers are inevitable and ex vi termini

---

1 Cf. ESHAG, E.(1963) From Marshall to Keynes. Oxford. Basil Blackwell
2 MARSHALL, A. (1926) Official Papers by Alfred Marshall. London: Macmillan. p.267

buyers. A general over-supply, or excess of all commodities over demand, so far as demand consists in means of payments, is thus *shown to be* an impossibility".[1]

Anyone who accepts all the arguments of Classical theory up to this point must also accept Say's law. For what could be the cause of a general "glut" or a general "demand gap"?

- Sudden *hoarding* of money is eliminated as a possible cause of inadequate commodity demand because hoarding was considered irrational by the Classics. Yet even if we *do* admit this possiblity, it only implies a change in the circulating quantity of money that will soon be offset by a corresponding change in prices.
- *Real savings* are still less suited for explaining a general glut since they are matched by an equivalent investment demand almost instantaneously.

Yet these two arguments are superficial. The deeper case for Say's law lies in the obvious fact that nobody *plans* to produce something without simultaneously *planning* to demand something else. Because decisions to supply and demand take place at the same instant, it is impossible that demand and supply differ *in total*. This does not mean, of course, that they match *in each market* (this is the very meaning of Say's law that the newspapers usually assign to it; but it is completely absurd). On the contrary, it was SAY himself who analyzed the disturbances which can take place in a single market. And RICARDO states:

"Too much of a particular commodity may be produced, of which there may be such a glut in the market; but this cannot be the case with respect to all commodities."[2]

What is more, Say's law was not meant to deny the possibility of *temporary* crises which could arise, for instance, from slow price adjustments. Rather, the Classics wanted to contest the possiblity of a *general* and *lasting* glut – a thesis proposed so frequently in the popular (and even scientific) literature. They argued: Everybody supplies goods and services only in order to buy some other commodities; in the course of capital accumulation and rationalization, therefore, production will increase only; but a general market saturation is downright inconceivable since no one already saturated would supply anything more. And some of them added that the saturation of all individuals with respect to all their wants would not be an economic problem, but the solution of all economic problems.

§27 The Classical Model

In the preceding section we discussed the various individual markets of Classical economics covering in the process all essential issues. In order to get a comprehensive impression of this doctrine, we are now ready to integrate these isolated elements into an algebraic and geometric Classical model.

The algebraic Classical model summarizes the labor demand and supply functions, (32) and (39), the production function, (34), the savings and investment func-

---

1 MILL, op.cit. vol. 2, p.91. Italics added.
2 RICARDO, D. (1817) Principles of Political Economy and Taxation. Reprint of the 3rd edition London 1924: Bell and Sons. p. 275.

tions, (40) and (33), and the Cambridge equation, (61). Supplementing this with the identity w = (w/P) P yields the simultanous equations C, for **Classics**:

$$N^d\left(\frac{w}{P}\right) = N^* = N^s\left(\frac{w}{P}\right) \quad \rightarrow N^*, \left(\frac{w}{P}\right)^* \tag{C.1}$$

$$Y = f(N) \quad \rightarrow Y^* \tag{C.2}$$

$$S(i) = I(i) \quad \rightarrow i^* \tag{C.3}$$

$$M = k \cdot P \cdot Y \quad \rightarrow P^* \tag{C.4}$$

$$w = \left(\frac{w}{P}\right) \cdot P \quad \rightarrow w^*. \tag{C.5}$$

These are *six* simultaneous equations – since (C.1) contains two – which, due to our previous assumptions, determine the *six* indicated variables uniquely.

(C.1) represents the equilibrium condition of the labor market which yields full employment, N^*, as well as the equilibrium real wage rate, $(w/P)^*$.

(C.2) is the production function. Given that we ruled out changes in the capital stock, production depends solely on the variable employment. The commodity supply function could have been written down as well; but this formula indicates more clearly that commodity supply directly follows from the employment level, N^*.

(C.3), the market clearance condition of the capital market, determines the natural interest rate, i^*. Of course, the latter implies a certain amount of savings and investment.

(C.4) is the Cambridge equation. Since the quantity of money and its velocity of circulation are assumed given, the equilibrium price level, P^*, is implied by real output, Y^*.

(C.5), finally, is a purely formal identity. It states that a certain nominal wage rate, w^*, is implied by the equilibrium real wage rate, $(w/P)^*$, and the equilibrium price level, P^*. The working of the model requires that this nominal wage rate is not given from outside.

The algebraic model, among other things, elucidates the Classical *dichotomy*: The real sector of the economy is covered by the equations (C.1) to (C.3) where all real magnitudes are determined. From (C.4) and (C.5), the price level and the nominal wage rate are derived as purely monetary variables which do not influence the real sector.

Such an algebraic model serves very well to demonstrate the core of a doctrine. Recollecting the various equations facilitates recollecting the whole theory – but the danger exists that one develops too mechanistic an understanding of the doctrine. We want to stress, therefore, that the equations are not put as natural laws but merely give a brief account of a few seemingly important relationships.

Next we turn our attention to the geometric exposition. This usually has the advantage of depicting events simultaneously which, in reality, also take place simultaneously; in this respect they are similar to algebraic models but superior to verbal description. Assembling Figures 11, 19, 21, and supplementing them by two new graphs results in the total model (see Fig. 22).

Any quadrant of Figure 22 corresponds to the accordingly numbered equation of the algebraic model. It should be read in numerical order:

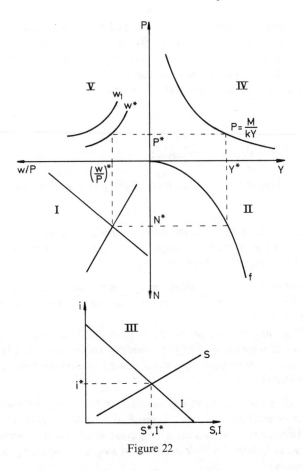

Figure 22

Quadrant I reproduces Figure 19 of the labor market which has simply been inverted. The axes always represent positive values.

Quadrant II reproduces Figure 11 of the production function which has also been inverted.

Quadrant III depicts the capital market.

Quadrant IV must be explained in greater detail. The hyperbola there represents the Cambridge equation. This becomes clear if you recognize that the Cambridge equation can be converted to

$$P = \frac{M}{k \cdot Y}. \qquad (65)$$

where P is the dependent and Y the independent variable. The given magnitudes, M and k, determine the position of this hyperbola and any real income (Y) yields a specific equilibrium price level (P).

Quadrant V, finally, is the equivalent of equation (C.5). Since w/P and P are the two variables involved, we encounter a family of curves

$$P = \frac{w}{w/P} \qquad (66)$$

here with parameter w. In this quadrant, w/P and P are given from the labor market and the Cambridge equation, respectively. By means of these magnitudes, a particular hyperbola is "singled out", such that it covers the point ((w/P)*,P*).

The Classical model is now described completely. In Chapter VI we will use both the algebraic and geometric representations in order to analyze macroeconomic policies.

§28 Digression: Walras' Model

"The Walrasian Auctioneer is a great myth; I emphasize both words."

(JAMES TOBIN)

Finally we want to cast a glance at the *microeconomic model of general equilibrium* as first proposed by LÉON WALRAS. Though our concern is with macroeconomics, this digression is almost inevitable because

- in the first instance, (Neo-) Classical theory was primarily microeconomic in spirit; thus taking note of its microeconomic formulation will deepen our understanding of this doctrine.
- Second, *Walras' model* is the prototype of *general equilibrium theory* which offers a microeconomic total analysis of the economy. In this respect, it is both point of departure and reference point for various further developments that are to be discussed in Part Three.

The Frenchman LÉON WALRAS was the first, in 1874, to put forward a theory of microeconomic general equilibrium[1]. Having at first been refuted or ignored, his model was to become the "magna carta" of economics, as SCHUMPETER put it. In the following, we want to describe Walras' model in a rather simplifying manner so as to bring out its essence.

An economy may consist of households and firms, H and F in number. They are indicated by h and f, respectively. Furthermore, G different goods exist, indicated by g, which are traded in the same number of markets. The term "good" is used in its broad sense and also covers services and claims. The model refers to an economy without money.

Prices $p_1, p_2, \ldots, p_G$ of the G goods are expressed by an imaginary measure of value: they are abstract prices. Thus, the relative price of goods i and j is reckoned as p_i/p_j.

The quantity of a certain good, g, that is supplied or demanded by household h is labeled as x_{hg}. We denote it by a *negative* sign if it is demanded and by a *positive* sign if it is supplied by the household. Take an example: If household no. 9 supplies 20 hours of a certain quality of labor which is good no. 6, we write $x_{9,6} = 20$. But if it demands apples of some sort, referred to as good no. 4, we have $x_{9,4} = -3$.

---

1 WALRAS, L. (1884) Eléments d'économie politique pure ou théorie de la richesse sociale. Lausanne. English translation (1954) Elements of pure Economics. London: Allen and Unwin

The subjective preferences of a household are described by a preference function

$$U_h(x_{h1}, \ldots, x_{hG}); \quad h = 1 \ldots H \tag{67}$$

which it seeks to maximize. This means, the household chooses all its demands and supplies of goods such that its utility attains a maximum. But it has to take notice of its *budget constraint* by which it is forced to keep expenditures and receipts in balance:

$$\sum_{g=1}^{G} p_g x_{hg} + \sum_{f=1}^{F} \pi_{hf} = 0 \tag{68}$$

The budget constraint requires the (positive) receipts to match the (negative) expenditures: i.e., the sum of both must vanish. π_{hf} denotes the profit income household h receives from firm f. We take the profit shares as givens and define

$$\pi_f := \sum_{h=1}^{H} \pi_{hf}.$$

Under certain conditions which cannot be adduced here, the optimization process yields the *supply and demand functions* of the H households:

$$x_{hg} = x_{hg}(p_1, \ldots, p_G); \quad h = 1 \ldots H; \ g = 1 \ldots G. \tag{69}$$

Any of these H times G functions depends on

- individual preferences,
- original stocks of durable goods, and
- prices.

Since preferences and original stocks are exogenous, only prices are explicitly noted in (69).

Let us turn to the firms, F in number. Here, again, we denote demands by *negative* and supplies by *positive* signs. Every firm seeks to maximize its profits which can be written in the familiar form "revenues minus costs" as

$$\pi_f = \sum_{g=1}^{G} p_g \cdot x_{fg}; \quad f = 1 \ldots F. \tag{70}$$

Trying to maximize profits, the firms are constrained by their production functions:

$$x_{fg} = x_{fg}(x_{f1}, \ldots, x_{fG}); \quad f = 1 \ldots F; \ g = 1 \ldots G. \tag{71}$$

The production functions are indexed by g, because for any firm there are precisely as many production functions as there are goods; and they are indexed by f, because each firm's productivity will tend to be different from the others'. Equations (70) and (71) yield, under certain conditions, the *demand and supply functions* of the firms:

$$x_{fg} = x_{fg}(p_1, \ldots, p_G); \quad f = 1 \ldots F; \ g = 1 \ldots G. \tag{72}$$

Our description of individual behaviour is now complete, and we merely have to go a small step further to obtain the results of Walras' model. A general equilibrium requires that demand and supply be equated in each market:

$$\sum_{h=1}^{H} p_g \cdot x_{hg} + \sum_{f=1}^{F} p_g \cdot x_{fg} = 0; \quad g = 1 \ldots G. \tag{73}$$

This equation says that the sum of all individuals' (negative) demands for a certain good (g) must be equal to total (positive) supply of this good. Let us, for instance, consider the market of good no. 5 ("potatoes"):

$$\sum_{h=1}^{H} p_5 \cdot x_{h5} + \sum_{f=1}^{F} p_5 \cdot x_{f5} = 0. \tag{74}$$

The sum of demands for potatoes must equal the sum of supplies in order to establish an equilibrium in the potatoes market. In (73), this condition is applied to all markets.

Equations (69), (72), and (73) can be combined to yield **Walras'** model:

$$x_{hg} = x_{hg}(p_1, \ldots, p_G) \tag{W.1}$$

$$x_{hf} = x_{hf}(p_1, \ldots, p_G) \tag{W.2}$$

$$\sum_{h=1}^{H} p_g \cdot x_{hg} + \sum_{f=1}^{F} p_g \cdot x_{fg} = 0. \tag{W.3}$$

Hence, Walras' model consists of

– H times G demand functions of the households,
– F times G demand functions of the firms, and
– G equilibrium conditions,

where "demand" is used as a generic term to refer to demand (denoted negatively) and supply (denoted positively). The model determines

– H times G demands of the households,
– F times G supplies of the firms, and
– G equilibrium prices.

Thus, the model consists of just as many equations as unknowns which is, of course, neither necessary nor sufficient for a unique solution but can be regarded as a "hint". However, adding all budget restrictions, (68), and all profit definitions, (70), yields

$$\sum_{h=1}^{H} \left(\sum_{g=1}^{G} p_g x_{hg} + \sum_{f=1}^{F} \pi_{hf} \right) + \sum_{f=1}^{F} \left(\sum_{g=1}^{G} p_g x_{fg} - \pi_f \right) = 0 \tag{75}$$

and, after cancelling out the π_{hg} (all profits are distributed) and rearranging terms, this becomes

$$\sum_{g=1}^{G} \left(\sum_{h=1}^{H} p_g \cdot x_{hg} + \sum_{f=1}^{F} p_g \cdot x_{fg} \right) = 0. \tag{76}$$

This very important equation follows directly from the households' budget constraints and the firms' profit definitions. Thus, its validity is independent of equilibrium conditions, and the equation holds in equilibrium as well as in disequilibrium. It is called *Walras' law*. Comparing (76) with (W.3) shows that (76) is just the *sum of the equilibrium conditions*. This sum must vanish. Therefore, an equilibrium in $G - 1$ markets *implies* an equilibrium in all markets: if $G - 1$ terms in (76) are zero, and the sum of all terms is zero, then the Gth term must vanish also.

Walras' Law: The sum of the excess demands in all (G) markets is equal to zero. Therefore, an equilibrium in G − 1 markets implies that there is also an equilibrium in the Gth market.

Walras' law gives rise to the following problem: Since the sum of the excess demands is given (i.e. zero), we are left with G − 1 *independent* equilibrium conditions and, therefore, the number of independent equations (G − 1) is less than the number of unknowns (G).

Walras himself arrived at the result that only G − 1 *relative* prices are determined by the equilibrium conditions, but not the G *abstract* prices. He chose an arbitrary good as *numéraire*, i.e. as measure of value, and argued that the G − 1 independent equations are just sufficient to determine the G − 1 relative prices with respect to the numéraire. Thus, all G − 1 relative prices, in the sense of exchange ratios, are determined.

It is easily seen why the G abstract prices, sometimes called "money prices", are not determined within the model. A doubling of all abstract prices has no impact on utility functions or the budget constraints; and all relative prices, demands, and supplies remain the same as before:

$$x_{hg}(p_1,\ldots,p_G) = x_{hg}(2p_1,\ldots,2p_G) \qquad (77)$$

$$x_{fg}(p_1,\ldots,p_G) = x_{fg}(2p_1,\ldots,2p_G). \qquad (78)$$

Demands and supplies are said to be *homogeneous of degree zero* in abstract prices. Considered in economic terms, this is obvious because an alternative way of expressing values in no way alters real events in an economy without money. Indeed, this doubling of abstract prices is equivalent to the situation in which, from a certain day on, prices are not reckoned in dollars but in half-dollars. It is hardly conceivable that – for this reason alone – demands or supplies should change.

Finally, we want to reproduce the *adjustment process of prices* as put forward by WALRAS. For this purpose, Walras developed the famous (or notorious) notion of the *auctioneer*: At the beginning of any period, the auctioneer cries out a certain trial price vector. After doing so, he collects the demand and supply plans of households and firms, these plans being determined with respect to the announced price vector. The auctioneer compares demands and supplies in every market; he increases prices where there is an excess demand; and lowers them where there is excess supply. Afterwards, the new price vector is announced. Now, the individuals formulate their plans again; and this interplay lasts until a price vector is found which establishes a general

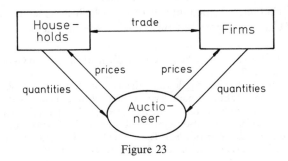

Figure 23

equilibrium. *Not before then are the transactions carried out.* This "cybernetic" process is illustrated in Figure 23.

WALRAS believed that this process of trial and error, he spoke of a *tatônnement* (groping), would finally arrive at the general equilibrium. In short, he was the first to give a mathematical account of SMITH's invisible hand.

More recent research work in the field of general equilibrium theory, starting with a paper by ABRAHAM WALD[1], thoroughly investigated the problems of *existence*, *uniqueness* and *stability* of the general equilibrium because, as we already mentioned, these issues can not be solved by counting equations and unknowns. However, it is impossible to give even a brief account of this work here[2].

§ 29 Conclusion

Our discussion of Classical theory is now complete, and we have obtained some first insight into the "vision" of the Classical economists. From the partial analyses of the labor, capital, and commodity markets, the quantity theory of money, Say's law, and the complete model, it has emerged that the Classical doctrine has no place for involuntary unemployment, overinvestment, underconsumption, and general crises. On the contrary, the "invisible hand", i.e. the princing mechanism, always results in a general market clearance.

In view of the *real depressions* which arise so frequently, the reader may wonder whether the Classical theory is really to be taken as a serious doctrine. With respect to this, two remarks are in order.

First and foremost, it must be emphasized that the Classical and Neoclassical authors were primarily concerned with the analysis of long periods. They only maintained that there is a strong *tendency* of market economies to converge towards the general equilibrium; and that this equilibrium would *finally* be attained – even if the adjustment process might last for many years. On the other hand, the Classics *denied* a long-run tendency towards ever aggravating crises as MARX and others had expected.

In the second place, the Classics were in fact well aware of real enonomic problems – but they traced them back to specific disturbances of the market process: to monopolies, cartels, unions, and state intervention. Hence, it is altogether wrong to think, for instance, that the Classical doctrine is refuted by the unemployment which actually exists: The statement "Perfectly flexible wages entail steady full employment." Is not disproved by the fact that unemployment arises frequently – wages *not* being perfectly flexible. We will return to this later.

In our next chapter, we encounter a theory which not merely criticizes several assumptions of Classical theory but turns some issues upside-down.

1 WALD, A. (1936) Über einige Gleichungssysteme der mathematischen Ökonomie. Zeitschrift für Nationalökonomie **7**, pp. 637–670
2 Good introductions to general equilibrium theory are QUIRK, J. and R. SAPOSNIK (1968) Introduction to General Equilibrium Theory and Welfare Economics. New York etc.: McGraw-Hill as well as ARROW, K.J. and F.H. HAHN (1971) General Competitive Analysis. San Francisco: Holden-Day. We also recommend the article of WEINTRAUB that sets aside the more technical difficulties: WEINTRAUB, E.R. (1983) On the Existence of a Competitive Equilibrium: 1930–1954. Journal of Economic Literature **21**, pp. 1–39

Further Reading

ACKLEY, G. (1978) Macroeconomics: Theory and Policy. New York etc.: Macmillan

MARSHALL, A. (1990) Principles of Economics. Reprint of the 8th edition London 1952: Macmillan

MILL, J.St. (1848) Principles of Political Economy. London: Parker. Reprint Toronto 1965: University Press

RICARDO, D. (1817) Principles of Political Economy and Taxation. Reprint of the 3rd edition London 1924: Bell and Sons

SMITH, A. (1776) An Inquiry into the Nature and Causes of the Wealth of Nations. Reprint Oxford 1976: Clarendon

WALSH, V.Ch. and H. GRAM (1980) Classical and New Classical Theories of General Equilibrium. New York etc.: Oxford University Press

Chapter V. The Keynesian Theory

§ 30 The Crisis

"In the long run, we are all dead." (JOHN MAYNARD KEYNES)

Starting with the collapse of the New York stock exchange in 1929, an economic crisis broke out in the United States of America which soon spread over Europe and throughout most other countries and was to become the worst economic crisis of the twentieth century so far. Nowadays, we call it the *Great Depression*. It entailed a considerable fall in production, much social misery, and – above all – mass unemployment on a hitherto unknown scale.

It is hardly surprising that Classical theory lost credibility in those days, and that trust into the self-regulating forces of the market gave way to increasing scepticism. Thus, the crisis in the real economy became a crisis in Classical theory.

Sometimes it was – and still is – argued that the orthodoxy was defeated by the facts, but this is a hasty conclusion for at least two reasons. First, the Classical theory, like any theory, was specified as a set of conditional clauses like *"If* all prices, wage rates, and interest rates are perfectly flexible *then* every market will tend towards an equilibrium." Thus, hinting at the various market imperfections in reality, the orthodoxy could defend itself. On the other hand, Classical theory had never denied the possibility of temporary crises (indeed, it had always been unwise to do so because of their reality) but only maintained that a market economy would finally attain the general equilibrium.

Hence, the uneasiness with the Classical doctrine must be formulated more carefully, and here, two thrusts can be traced out:

- The *political criticism*: What help is a theory proclaiming full employment in the long run if this time scale is politically unacceptable?
- The *theoretical criticism*: What are the merits of a doctrine which proceeds from utterly unrealistic assumptions and thus cannot be attacked on empirical grounds? Who could guarantee that the *theoretical foundations* of this theory are correct?

The political criticism led to calls for public remedies which later, and relatively independent of theoretical foundations, were actually employed. With respect to practical policy, this meant the bankruptcy of the prevailing doctrine.

The theoretical criticism, in contrast to popular opinion, was elaborated by various economists and in various ways[1]. But it found its most eminent expression in

1 GARVY, G. (1975) Keynes and the Economic Activities of Pre-Hitler Germany. Journal of Political Economy **83**, pp. 391–405.

"The General Theory of Employment, Interest and Money"[2] by JOHN MAYNARD KEYNES. This book, which influenced practical policy more than almost any other, is the subject of our next section.

§ 31 The "General Theory" and Its Interpreters

"All economists claim to have read it. Only a few have.
The rest feel a secret guilt that they never will."   (JOHN K. GALBRAITH)

Probably, the "General Theory" is the most often cited economic book of our century. This outstanding influence can be explained partly by the fact that the author was one of the most prominent and influential economists even before its publication; therefore, an eager audience was already awaiting its appearance.

According to the title, KEYNES sought to offer a general explanation of employment, interest, and money. The term "general" is decisive and indicates that KEYNES ascribed validity to the Classical theory for the *special* case of full employment only, while considering his own doctrine to apply to situations of underemployment, too.

Ten years after its publication, PAUL A. SAMUELSON remarked on the "General Theory":

"It is a badly written book, poorly organized; any layman who, beguiled by the authors's previous reputation, bought the book was cheated of his 5 shillings. It is not well suited for classroom use. It is arrogant, bad-tempered, polemical, and not overly-generous in its acknowledgements... In it the Keynesian system stands out indistinctly, as if the author were hardly aware of its existence or cognizant of its properties; and certainly he is at his worst when expounding its relations to its predecessors. Flashes of insight and intuition intersperse tedious algebra. An awkward definition gives way to an unforgettable cadenza. When it finally is mastered, we find its analysis to be obvious and at the same time new. In short, it is a work of genius."[3]

Of course, this review is rather pointed, but nevertheless explains why there exists no consensus opinion on the issue "what KEYNES had really said and meant". On the contrary, several interpretations have come into being thus far; and it has been the latter which have popularized KEYNES' thoughts and made them politically efficacious:

"As a result, Keynes has become 'the greatest economist of our time' (an obituary remark indicating that his contribution was so indisputable as to require no explanation) and the *General Theory* has been shelved as a 'classic' (meaning an acknowledged book that no one reads, for fear of discovering that the author was himself not clear about the message his disciples derived from his work)."[4]

---

2 KEYNES, J.M. (1936) The General Theory of Employment, Interest and Money. London. Reprinted 1964 New York etc.: Harcourt and Brace. Subsequently, we refer to it as the "General Theory".
3 SAMUELSON, P.A. (1946) Lord Keynes and the General Theory. Econometrica **14**, p. 190.
4 JOHNSON, H.G. (1970) Recent Developments in Monetary Theory – A Comment. In: CROOME, D. and H.G. JOHNSON Ed. Money in Britain, 1959–1969. London: Oxford University Press.

Although the designations of the various interpretations are by no means used uniquely, three of them seem to be the most important[5]:

a) *The Keynesian theory*, which must not be confused with KEYNES' own theory, has become the most momentous one. It has one foot firmly on the ground of Classical theory, and the other on what it considers to be the "new" and "progressive" ground of the "General Theory". For this reason, we call it the *Neoclassical Synthesis*. The best known adherants of Keynesian theory are ALVIN H. HANSEN, JOHN R. HICKS, LAWRENCE R. KLEIN, FRANCO MODIGLIANI, DON PATINKIN, PAUL A. SAMUELSON, and JAMES TOBIN. The Keynesian theory, or Neoclassical Synthesis, is the theme of the present chapter.

b) *Postkeynesian theory*, unlike Keynesian theory, opposes the Classical doctrine fundamentally. Its advocates, especially PAUL DAVIDSON, ROY F. HARROD, RICHARD F. KAHN, NICHOLAS KALDOR, MICHAL KALECKI, JAN A. KREGEL, HYMAN P. MINSKY, JOAN ROBINSON, and GEORGE L.S. SHACKLE, object to pocketing KEYNES into a Neoclassical Synthesis. According to the Postkeynesians, KEYNES' contribution is altogether irreconcilable with theories of the (Neo-) Classical type; and hence it is hardly astonishing that they label the Neoclassical Synthesis as "bastard Keynesianism" (JOAN ROBINSON).

The Postkeynesian authors are far from forming a homogeneous crew; yet, two lines of thought can be distiguished. Both, purportedly, originate in KEYNES' work, and they differ in stressing *real* and *monetary* forces, respectively:

Those Postkeynesians who are primarily concerned with real analysis[6] reject Neoclassical marginalism and employ the Classical surplus-theoretic approach instead. There are three characteric features of their theory:

- Price effects play merely a subordinate role within the analysis whereas *income effects* dominate. Employment, for instance, is primarily determined by aggregate commodity demand – not by the real wage rate.
- The economic process is not explored in a static model of allocation (WALRAS), in a model of economic growth with presupposed full employment (SOLOW-type theory of economic growth) but within the framework of a dynamic process. In this respect, Postkeynesianism comes close to the Classical theory of accumulation and economic growth.
- Third, income distribution is intimately connected with economic growth. "Strategic" variables of analysis are the profit share and the investment activity.

The second Postkeynesian line of thought can be embraced under the heading "money and uncertainty"[7]. These authors assign such a great significance to monetary disturbances and uncertainty that they regard Neoclassical equilibrium analysis

---

5 New Keynesian Economics dealt with in chapter X do not claim to be another KEYNES-interpretation.
6 Cf. KREGEL, J.A. (1975) The Reconstruction of Political Economy. An Introduction to Post-Keynesian Economics. London: Macmillan. ROBINSON, J. (1965) The Accumulation of Capital. London: Macmillan.
7 Cf. DAVIDSON, P. (1978) Money and the Real World. Basingstoke etc.: Macmillan. MINSKY, H.P. (1975) John Maynard Keynes. Columbia: Columbia University Press. SHACKLE, G.L.S. (1955) Uncertainty in Economics. Cambridge: Cambridge University Press.

as utterly irrelevant. Furthermore, they consider KEYNES' stress on *uncertainty* as his genuine contribution.

Because Postkeynesianism is somewhat removed from the prevailing orthodoxies and does not offer a coherant theory, we cannot describe it in more detail[8].

c) *Neokeynesian theory*, finally, springs from a re-interpretation of KEYNES by ROBERT W. CLOWER and AXEL LEIJONHUFVUD. Our Chapter 11 will deal with Neokeynesian theory in some detail, but it is to be noted here that the initial enthusiam from this "re-interpretation" soon dwindled, and LEIJONHUFVUD had to retract his claim. This does not lessen, however, the theoretical significance of Neokeynesian theory.

Considered in all, Keynesians and Neokeynesians on the one hand and Postkeynesians on the other hand form two groups who can be referred to as *imperfectionists* and *fundamentalists*, respectively. Imperfectionists (Keynesians and Neokeynesians) share the Classic's opinion that, in general, forces do exist which direct the economy towards full employment equilibrium. But – owing to certain "imperfections" in the market mechanism – they believe it does not work very smoothly and therefore propose government interventions instead of a "laissez-faire" policy.

Fundamentalists (Postkeynesians), on the other hand, deny the existence of such market forces. They claim that, in a free market economy, there is *no* automatic tendency towards full employment. This view does not necessarily lead Postkeynesians to a rejection of the free market system; but they recommend at least some institutional changes.

§ 32 The Effective Demand

Now we pass on to the essence of the "General Theory", as it is interpreted by the Keynesians. Of central importance is the attention KEYNES gives to *effective demand:* the actual aggregate demand for commodities in a closed economy. He denies the validity of Say's law, according to which supply creates its own demand, and argues that, quite on the contrary, effective demand determines the level of production.

Let us briefly recollect the Classical analysis of income and production. Following this theory, production as a whole is limited only by

– the households' preferences (giving rise to the labor supply function) and
– the accumulated stock of capital together with the technical determinants of production (which yield the production function and the labor demand function).

Expressed in short, the labor market is the *strategic market* of the model since in this market, employment is determined which itself determines the level of production. Unsufficient commodity demand is impossible.

Looked at in the Classical way, it is hard to understand a situation where, on the one hand, many persons want to work while, on the other hand, there is an universal desire to consume more. This is because an increase in employment and production

---

8 Introductions are ROBINSON, J. and J. EATWELL (1974) An Introduction to Modern Economics. London: McGraw-Hill. EATWELL, J. and M. MILGATE (1983) Keynes' Economics and the Theory of Value and Distribution. London: Gerald Duckworth.

would meet both wishes. KEYNES tried to solve this *paradox of unemployment* by distinguishing the pure wants from the *effective* demands as they actually occur in the markets. An inadequate effective demand restricts the level of production; this causes factor incomes to decrease; and thus, effective demand drops even more until an underemployment equilibrium may eventually be reached. This line of thought is the core of the "General Theory". It can be summarized by the statement:

The level of production is determined by effective demand. Demand creates its own supply – not the reverse.

Say's law is virtually turned upside-down – yet we remember that it was not proclaimed as a dogma by the Classics but derived from more general principles. Hence, if KEYNES wanted to attack Say's law he had to attack the premises of Classical economics, too. According to the Keynesians' opinion, four important departures from orthodoxy can be found in the "General Theory":

1) The *consumption function*, which establishes a stable connection between current real income and real consumption expenditure.
2) A modified theory of investment, based on the *marginal efficiency of capital*.
3) The *liquidity preference theory*, as an alternative to the quantity theory of money.
4) Possible *rigidities* of prices and wages.

The respective importance of these four matters is subject to controversy; repeatedly, one of them is given precedence as the "truly revolutionary contribution" of the "General Theory". Sometimes, a so-called money illusion (of the labor suppliers) is added to these four points; but this seems to be neither theoretically nor empirically significant, and is not referred to by KEYNES in his "General Theory".

In the following, we want to analyze effective demand in greater detail since it has proven to be at the heart of Keynesian theory. For this purpose, we first examine the determinants of consumption and then those of investment.

§ 33 Consumption Demand

The first hypothesis essential to Keynesian economic states that real consumption is influenced primarily by current real income. This functional relationship is called the Keynesian *consumption function*:

$$C = C(Y). \tag{79}$$

Consumption (C) and income (Y) are measured in commodity units. The function (79) seems to be generally acceptable – for what could be more plausible than the dependence of consumption on income? We now have to examine the implied premises.

First of all, (79) presupposes a *stable* relationship between current real consumption and current real income; and the formula suggests that consumption is the dependent, and income the independent, variable. This is altogether *inconceivable* from the Classical point of view because, in Classical analysis, consumption, labor and capital supply, and thus income are planned *simultaneously*, in accordance with individual preferences and prices. Though consumption and income are connected by means of the budget constraint, there is nothing like a causality running from Y to C. Hence, the Keynesian consumption function contradicts (Neo-) Classical theory[9].

Second, the formula suggests that real income is the *only* determinant of real consumption, but this is not exactly what is meant: Rather, the consumption function expresses that real income – among the various determinants of consumption – is the only important one which is *variable* in the short run. Implicitly, the consumption function contains many more variables: KEYNES himself considered 24 of them in chapters 8 and 10 of his "General Theory". One of these additional factors is the *rate of interest*, which plays such an important role in Classical theory (you remember: the decision as to consumption versus savings). With respect to this, KEYNES remarked:

"There are not many people who will alter their way of living because the rate of interest has fallen from 5 to 4 per cent, if their aggregate income is the same as before."[10]

Thus, KEYNES doubted the interest elasticity of consumption and savings: experience showed that the rate of interest has no strong impact on the decisions to consume or save. He intensified his argument by pointing out that the substitution and income effects of a change in the rate of interest probably cancel out – a fact that had already been granted by most Neoclassical authors.

Third, we have to note that, according to (79), consumption depends on *current* real income, not on past or expected future incomes. This hypothesis has been disputed since; we call it the *absolute income hypothesis*.

Following these general remarks, we can turn to the special properties of the consumption function, that is, to KEYNES' *fundamental-psychological law* as he called it. It states that

– due to a rise in income, consumption always increases;
– but the additional consumption falls short of the additional income[11].

We can state this exactly by means of the marginal propensity to consume. The *marginal propensity to consume* gives the approximate increase in consumption that is brought about by a small increase of income. It is defined as the differential quotient

$$C' := \frac{dC}{dY}. \tag{80}$$

According to the fundamental-psychological law, the marginal propensity to consume must be greater than zero but less than one:

$$0 < \frac{dC}{dY} < 1. \tag{81}$$

Let us suppose, for instance, that the marginal propensity to consume is constant and equals 0.8. In this case, an increase in income of 1 will cause an increase in

---

9 Until very recently, this fact has not gained enough attention in the literature. We will return to the issue in Chapter XI.
10 "General Theory", op.cit., p. 94
11 "General Theory", op.cit., p. 96. It is not true that the fundamental psychological law implies also a *decreasing* marginal propensity to consume.

consumption of 0.8. The fundamental-psychogical law is satisfied since the change in consumption is positive but less than the change in income.

Next, we consider the households' budget constraint

$$Y = C + S. \tag{82}$$

If 0.8 units of an additional income unit go to consumption, there are 0.2 units left for additional savings. We define the *marginal propensity to save* as the differential quotient dS/dY. The latter indicates how much savings rise due to a given small rise in income. By differentiating the budget constraint with respect to Y, it becomes obvious that the marginal propensity to consume and the marginal propensity to save must add up to one:

$$\frac{dY}{dY} = \frac{dC}{dY} + \frac{dS}{dY} \tag{83}$$

$$1 = \frac{dC}{dY} + \frac{dS}{dY}. \tag{84}$$

This follows from the simple fact that any income must be used in this way or another.

In order to simplify the figures, we assume a *linear* consumption function from now on. It looks like this:

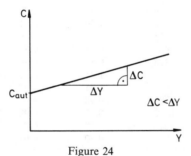

Figure 24

The assumption of a linear consumption function is made for simplification only; and all subsequent results are also valid for non-linear functions in so far as they satisfy the fundamental psychological law. The equation of a linear consumption functions reads:

$$C = C_{aut} + C' \cdot Y. \tag{85}$$

C is called *autonomous consumption*; this is the point of intersection of the consumption function and the ordinate. The constant marginal propensity to consume indicates the *slope* of the consumption function. A change in autonomous consumption causes a *shift* of the graph whereas a change in the marginal propensity to consume causes a *rotation*. Finally, we define the quotient

$$c := \frac{C}{Y} \tag{86}$$

as the *average propensity to consume*. It indicates the proportion of total income spent on consumption, whereas the marginal propensity to consume refers to the proportion of the last small income unit spent.

After these rather tedious explanations, we want to give a numerical impression of actual consumption and estimate a consumption function. The marginal propensity to consume must be calculated as a difference quotient since only discrete numbers are available from the statistics. The following schedule shows consumption, income, and the marginal and average propensities to consume[12]:

Year	Consumption	Income	$\Delta C/\Delta Y$	C/Y
	(Billion US dollars)			
1960	452	490	–	0.92
1961	461	504	0.64	0.91
1962	482	525	1.00	0.92
1963	501	542	1.12	0.92
1964	528	581	0.69	0.91
1965	558	616	0.86	0.91
1966	586	647	0.90	0.91
1967	603	674	0.63	0.89
1968	634	701	1.15	0.90
1969	658	723	1.09	0.91
1970	672	752	0.48	0.89
1971	697	779	0.93	0.89
1972	737	810	1.29	0.91
1973	769	865	0.58	0.89
1974	764	858	0.71	0.89
1975	780	876	0.89	0.89
1976	824	907	1.41	0.91
1977	864	940	1.21	0.92
1978	905	982	0.98	0.92
1979	931	1012	0.87	0.92
1980	932	1022	0.10	0.92
1981	951	1049	0.70	0.91

From this, a linear consumption function can readily be estimated. Using the method of least squares, we find the straight line which best approximates the above values[13]:

$$C = 0.61 + 0.91\,Y \quad \text{(Bill. \$)} \tag{87}$$

The following graph depicts the measured values and the estimated consumption function:

---

12 In our estimate, "consumption" is personal consumption expenditures, and "income" is total disposable income, both in bill. 1972 dollars. Source of figures: Department of Commerce (Bureau of Economic Analysis and Bureau of the Census).

13 The method of least squares is explained in any statistical textbook. In the above regression, the coefficient of determination amounts to 0.997. Thus, the regression line explains 99.7% of the variation in consumption. (For experts: F = 3.15, DW = 0.78, t = 0.07 and 81.63. THEIL's BLUS residuals indicate autocorrelation and heteroscedasticity.)

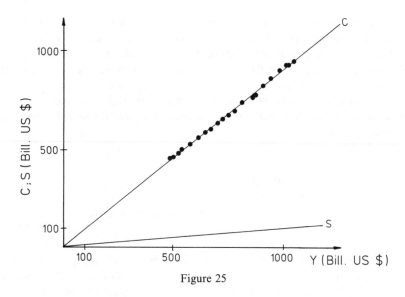

Figure 25

In addition, Figure 25 represents the corresponding savings function which can be calculated from (82) and (85):

$$Y = C_{aut} + C' \cdot Y + S. \tag{88}$$

$$\Leftrightarrow Y - C' \cdot Y - C_{aut} = S. \tag{89}$$

$$\Leftrightarrow S = (1 - C') \cdot Y - C_{aut}. \tag{90}$$

In our concrete example, the savings function reads

$$S = -0.61 + 0.09\,Y \quad \text{(Bill. \$)} \tag{91}$$

Over the years 1960–1981, a $1 increase in income obviously entailed a $0.91 increase in consumption on average since, according to equation (87), the marginal propensity to consume amounts precisely to 0.91. Similarly, savings increased by $0.09 as can be seen from (91). The above graph suggests that the set of measured values is described rather well by the regression line because all points lie in its close neighborhood. But this should not obscure the problems involved by such equation estimating: here, we only mention that the estimation does not (as theoretically required) refer to ex ante but to ex post magnitudes. And what is more, there is an spurious correlation because C is by far the greatest constituent of Y.

Let us add some words concerning *autonomous consumption*. This must not be interpreted as a subsistence level of consumption because this would require the stability of the consumption function even if income approached zero. But this is not conceivable; on the contrary, autonomous consumption can be called a statistical illusion for the following reasons: In Figure 25, the various points, all relating to rather high levels of income and consumption, were approximated by a straight line. This approximation is likely to serve well for forecasting consumption on the condition that income remains in this region. But it cannot serve for arbitrary extrapolation, because the consumption function will certainly change if income decreases significantly.

More fundamentally, it is hard to conceive of the poor inhabitants of a closed economy with zero production who try to make a bare living by *real* dissaving, that is by consuming the accumulated equipment. A single individual undoubtedly is able to subsist on his savings – but this does *not* hold for the economy as a whole. If, in the long run, production and income are zero, consumption must be zero, too; hence, any long-run consumption function has to intersect the origin. Therefore, we repeat, autonomous consumption is only to be considered a statistical residual and not to be interpreted in economic terms.

§34 Investment Demand

"Keynes without uncertainty is something like Hamlet without the Prince."
(HYMAN P. MINSKY)

Our next subject is investment as the second component of aggregate demand. The essential departure of Keynesian theory from the Classical doctrine of investment is the hypothesis that decisions to invest do not rest on current marginal productivity of capital: but on *expected future* returns to capital. This amounts to much more than a mere change of terminology.

Think of an investor who is considering the purchase of some capital good, and try to replicate his cost-benefit analysis: As a result of the purchase, the investor acquires a claim to an expected future flow of receipts which stem from the sale of additional output. But, simultaneously, he sacrifices the possibility of lending the money at the going interest rate i and takes additional costs on himself, such as they arise from the increased production. The question is, which investment decisions are optimal under the given circumstances?

Assume again that the capital good under consideration may have a life-span of n years, and that *expenditures* (E_j) and *receipts* (R_j) which are allocable to the investment accrue at the beginning of year j $(j \leq n)$. Hence, *net receipts* in year j amount to:

$$Q_j := R_j - E_j; \quad j = 1 \ldots n. \tag{92}$$

The sum of the n net receipts, Q_j, is counteracted by the investment outlay. However, it does not suffice to compare these two directly. As you know, "a dollar today" is not the same as "a dollar tomorrow" because it can be invested in the meantime and then yields interest. Hence, the future net receipts must be discounted. The sum of discounted net receipts is the *present value* of the investment, Q_0:

$$Q_0 = Q_1 + \frac{Q_2}{(1+r)} + \frac{Q_3}{(r+1)^2} + \ldots + \frac{Q_n}{(r+1)^{n-1}}. \tag{93}$$

As already stated, Q_1 accrues at the *beginning* of the first year and thus is not discounted. r is a properly chosen discount rate. Now, the *marginal efficiency of capital* is just that discount rate which equalizes present value and investment outlay. Hence, the marginal efficiency of capital, denoted by R, is defined by the following equation:

$$\text{investment outlay} = Q_1 + \frac{Q_2}{(1+R)} + \ldots + \frac{Q_n}{(1+R)^{n-1}}. \tag{94}$$

Example: A machine has a life span of two years and it costs $ 1.000. The investor is assumed to expect a net receipt of $ 500 that accrues at the beginning of the first, and a net receipt of $ 540 that accrues at the beginning of the second year. Thus, the marginal efficiency of capital can be calculated as

$$1.000 = 500 + 540/(1 + R) \Rightarrow \quad R = 8\%.$$

It is to be stressed that the investor deals with *expected* magnitudes; thus the marginal efficiency of capital is not purely determined by technology but also by psychology. The investor will buy the capital good if marginal efficiency of capital *exceeds the interest rate i*. This can easily be shown by the above example: Marginal efficiency of capital turned out to be 8%, i.e. the investment yields an annual "interest" of 8 per cent. If the market rate of interest amounts to 7% then the investor will buy the capital good; and if the market rate increases to 9%, he will not because a fincancial investment has now become more advantageous.

Up to now, we have only considered the decisions of an individual in order to explain the concept of marginal efficiency of capital. With respect to the total economy, KEYNES alleged that marginal efficiency *decreases* as the amount of investment *increases*. This indeed seems plausible because the most profitable investments are carried out first, the less profitable thereafter, and last of all those investments which are just profitatable at the prevailing rate of interest. Hence, marginal efficiency of capital is by definition independent of the interest rate, yet at any time converges towards the interest rate because investments are carried out up to this point.

Hence the interest rate determines the marginal efficiency of capital; but the latter, in turn, determines aggregate investment. Therefore, *investment demand* depends indirectly on the interest rate:

$$I = I \underset{(-)}{(i)}. \tag{95}$$

The negative sign can be explained as follows: A higher rate of interest entails a higher marginal efficiency of capital because the latter – as we saw above – always converges towards the interest rate. But since the marginal efficiency of capital decreases as investment increases, the rise in the interest rate causes a declining investment demand.

Comparing equations (33) (the Classical investment function) and (95) (the Keynesian investment function) does not highlight the difference between these two theories adequately: in both cases, there is a negative relationship between investment demand and the rate of interest. But, while the Classical investment function was derived from purely technical considerations, the Keynesian view employs psychological factors, too.

The consequence of this is decisive: A deterioration in the economic climate – production function and the rate of interest both remaining constant – can cause a sudden change in investment demand. This is because the entrepreneurs will expect lower values of the future net receipts, and that will diminish the marginal efficiency of capital and hence investment.

Moreover it is conceivable that the investors aim at a faster armortization when times become tough, because the more distant future appears too *uncertain* to them. The "n" of our equation (93) will then decrease, and this will cause the interest elasticity of investment to decrease, too. In the extreme case of $n = 1$, an immediate amortization is called for (because $Q_0 = Q_1$) and the interest elasticity of investment is equal to zero. Then, the interest rate does not influence investment at all.

Let us summarize. If expectations and the economic climate have such a strong impact on investment, then the investment function depicts no stable relationship. Investment is then likely to oscillate erratically; and it is even possible that interest elasticity falls to zero. The consequences of this will become obvious in the following analysis.

§35 The Income-Expenditure Model

"Every prodigal a public enemy and every frugal man a public benefactor."

(ADAM SMITH)

We are now in a position to explore the core of Keynesian doctrine: the *income-expenditure model*. Two assumptions are essential to this model:

– The amount of investment is given, and
– there exist idle resources.

Clearly, this is a case of *depression* where investment demand – due to extremely pessimistic expectations – does not respond to changes in the interest rate; and the economic resources (labor and capital) are not fully utilized. Adding the given amount of investment to our linear consumption function, (85), yields KEYNES' *effective demand*:

$$Y^d = C_{aut} + C' \cdot Y + I. \qquad (96)$$

According to KEYNES, an equilibrium in the commodity market prevails if and only if production equals effective demand. Note: We deliberately say *production* and not *supply*: this will be explained later on. Thus the equilibrium condition of the commodity market reads:

$$Y^d = Y. \qquad (97)$$

By means of this condition, the *equilibrium income*, Y, can be calculated if we substitute Y^d for Y in (96):

$$Y = C_{aut} + C' \cdot Y + I. \qquad (98)$$

Solving with respect to Y yields:

$$Y - C' \cdot Y = C_{aut} + I. \qquad (99)$$

$$\Leftrightarrow (1 - C') \cdot Y = C_{aut} + I. \qquad (100)$$

$$\Leftrightarrow Y_0 = \frac{1}{1 - C'} \cdot (C_{aut} + I). \qquad (101)$$

Equation (101) does not look very exciting – but from the Classical point of view it is truly revolutionary: There is only *one single* level of real income which satifies this equilibrium condition. This contradicts Say's law which assured us that *every* level of real income would be consistent with an equilibrium in the commodity market, and that the specific level would be determined by the *labor market*.

But here, only Y_0 constitutes equilibrium in the goods market; i.e. supply does *not* create its own demand. Moreover, it would be pure chance if Y_0 were identical to full employment income, Y^*, which is determined independently of commodity demand by the labor market and the production function.

This is the Keynesian explanation of involuntary unemployment: If Y_0 is less than Y^*, production and employment are decreased due to inadequate commodity demand and this also holds if the real wage rate is at its equilibrium level, $(w/P)^*$.

The income-expenditure model is usually depicted by the following figure:

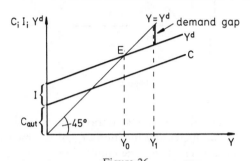

Figure 26
The income-expenditure model

The figure shows the consumption function which intersects the ordinate at C_{aut} and has the slope C', as explained in §33. Vertical addition of the constant level of investment yields the effective demand function Y^d.

Additionally, the bisector of the angle between ordinate and abcissa is drawn, called the 45°-line for short. This is the equilibrium condition (97) which requires effective demand and production to coincide. (On such a 45°-line lie points such as (1,1) or (3,3) since the dimensions of both axes are the same.)

The point of intersection, E, of the effective demand function and the 45°-line fulfills both the effective demand equation and the equilibrium condition. Thus, E depicts the solution of the model. If we suppose – as in Figure 26 – that autonomous consumption and investment are positive, then *just one* point of interesection exists. This is because the 45°-line has the slope 1 whereas the slope of the effective demand curve is equal to marginal propensity to consume, i.e. less than 1. Thus, the two lines can have only one point of intersection.

The income-expenditure model can be formulated in another way if we take the effective demand function

$$Y^d = C(Y) + I \tag{102}$$

together with the budget constraint

$$Y = C(Y) + S(Y). \tag{103}$$

By means of the equilibrium condition $Y^d = Y$, (102) and (103) can be equated; and after subtracting $C(Y)$ we are left with

$$S(Y) = I. \tag{104}$$

This equation is equivalent to (101), and we will use it in the following figure:

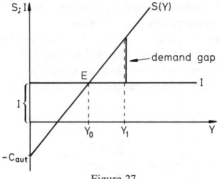

Figure 27

By means of this figure, we are able to unravel the previous rather bewildering conclusions: Savings are an increasing function of real income whereas the amount of investment is assumed given. Thus, the equilibrium point, E, is identical to the point E of Figure 26 and demonstrates that Y_0 is the only equilibrium income.

What happens if savings exceed investment? In such an instance, let us take Y_1, effective commodity demand falls short of production because savings are not fully absorbed by investment. There is a *demand gap* as depicted in both figures. But this is only a temporary situation since production will be *decreased* until $S(Y) = I$.

This adjustment process is so essential to Keynesian theory that we want to contrast it with the Classical adjustment via the interest rate. Considered purely mathematically, it is a small difference whether savings and investment are reconciled by an adjustment in *real income* or by an adjustment in the *interest rate*:

$$\text{Keynesian case: } S(Y) = I \tag{105}$$

$$\text{Neoclassical case: } S(i) = I(i) \tag{106}$$

But what an enormous difference in reality! In the latter case, the interest rate, as only one of several prices, has to change if savings exceed investment – but in the former, a depression arises: real income and employment decline. No matter how KEYNES is interpreted: this adjustment process of real income is the essence of the "General Theory".

These conclusions exerted a decisive influence on the reasoning of many economists. Saving was no longer considered economically beneficial for making investment and growth feasible but, quite on the contrary, it was judged as harmful for causing a decline in effective demand and thus depression and unemployment. Our introductory quotation from ADAM SMITH was precisely reversed. The impact of this change in attitude towards savings can hardly be underrated, especially in so far as the practice of financial management of the state is concerned. We will return to these matters later.

To conclude, we must point out that the equilibrium in the commodity market is *sui generis*: it does *not* mean a balance of supply and demand in the Classical sense. On the contrary, effective demand is insufficient and determines the level of production – supply is irrelevant. It may be that the firms originally planned to supply Y^*; but they only *produce* Y_0 and adjust employment accordingly, because only the amount Y_0 can actually be sold and the firms are assumed not to manufacture for stockbuilding. Hence, the reader must carefully distinguish between *supply* (i.e. the original plan) and *production* (i.e. the quantity actually sold).

In terms of § 4, we can state that in the commodity market there is an equilibrium in the methodical sense. Production and all other endogenous variables remain constant as long as all exogenous variables – most notably investment – remain constant, too. And this holds irrespective of original commodity supply.

§ 36 The Simple Multiplier

"Given the psychology of the public, the level of output and employment depends on the amount of investment." (JOHN MAYNARD KEYNES)

In the preceding section, we determined the *level* of equilibrium income. Now, we turn to the subsequent question of *changes* in income still maintaining all previous assumptions. Thus, we pass from statics to comparative statics.

The impact of a spontaneous change in *investment demand* can be derived directly by differentiating the equilibrium condition, (101), with respect to I:

$$Y_0 = \frac{1}{1 - C'} (C_{aut} + I) \quad \left| \frac{d}{dI} \right. \tag{107}$$

$$\Rightarrow \frac{dY_0}{dI} = \frac{1}{1 - C'}. \tag{108}$$

The term

$$m := \frac{1}{1 - C'} \tag{109}$$

is called the *simple multiplier*. It indicates how strongly real income reacts to a given small change in investment demand. The simple multiplier depends solely on the marginal propensity to consume, C'. If the latter is 0.8, for instance, the multiplier can be calculated as

$$m = \frac{1}{1 - 0.8} = 5. \tag{110}$$

That is, every additional unit of investment demand increases real income by *five* units[14].

This result appears rather astonishing. In order to give reasons for it we want to inspect the course of the multiplier process using a numerical example. The marginal propensity to consume is assumed to be 0.8 and additional investment to be 5 units.

---

14 The original idea of a "multiplier" is not due to KEYNES but (at least) to KAHN, R.F. (1931) The Relation of Home Investment to Underemployment. Economic Journal **41**, pp. 173–198. But even earlier fore-runners can be traced.

The following will happen:

1) Additional investment immediately increases effective demand and production. This primary effect is called dY_1 [15]

$$dY_1 = dI = 5.$$ (111)

2) This rise in production means a rise in real income for the households of exactly 5 units. Four fifths of this additional income ($0.8 = 4/5$) are spent on additional consumption. Hence, effective demand increases by four units:

$$dY_2 = 0.8 \cdot 5 = 4.$$ (112)

3) But this causes real income to snowball since production and real income increase once more, now by four units. Again, four fifth of the additional income are spent on consumption:

$$dY_3 = 0.8 \cdot 4 = 3.2 \quad (= (0.8)^2 \cdot 5).$$ (113)

Here we break off our consideration since it should have become clear that this process continues indefinitely. Consumption demand and real income amplify one another. In the "j-th round", additional income obviously amounts to:

$$dY_j = (0.8)^{j-1} \cdot 5.$$ (114)

By setting j to 1, 2, 3 our formulae (111) to (113) can be derived from this general expression. For arbitrary values of the marginal propensity to consume and additional investment, we get:

$$dY_j = (C')^{j-1} \cdot dI.$$ (115)

The total increase in real income can be calculated by adding the single effects given by (115), with j running from 1 to infinity. This is done by means of the well-known formula for infinite series

$$\sum_{j=1}^{\infty} k^{j-1} \cdot a = \frac{a}{1-k}, \quad \text{if } |k| < 1$$ (116)

which yields

$$dY = \sum_{j=1}^{\infty} dY_j = \sum_{j=1}^{\infty} (C')^{j-1} \cdot dI$$ (117)

$$\Leftrightarrow dY = \frac{1}{1-C'} \cdot dI.$$ (118)

This is an alternative way of deriving the elementary multiplier, (108). It might be imagined that the multiplier process "explodes" as real income goes up infinitely. But this is not true; on the contrary, real income converges towards a new equilibrium level as in every "round" a certain part of additional income is *saved* and does not increase effective demand. And the *more* is saved the *lower* becomes our multiplier. Conversely, if the marginal propensity to consume approaches one, the multiplier approaches infinity.

---

15 Instead of the differentials d(.) we could also use differences Δ(.).

For a graphical exposition of the multiplier process, we take Figure 26 and change it slightly:

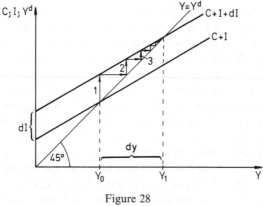

Figure 28
The multiplier process

In Figure 28, the effective demand curve is shifted vertically by the amount of additional investment, dI. The numbering of the arrows corresponds to the numbering of the above "rounds" of the multiplier process: Therefore, arrow no. 1 indicates the initial cause dI, arrow no. 2 the subsequent impact C' dI and so on. It is easily seen that real income converges towards the new equilibrium level, Y_1.

Let us conclude. Given a marginal propensity to consume of 0.8 the simple multiplier amounts to 5. According to this, an additional investment of $ 100 millions increases income by $ 500 millions if the assumptions of the model are met. The same holds for a decline in investment which decreases income drastically. Because investment is regarded as a very unstable magnitude by the Keynesians, we can understand their opinion that the amount of investment is crucial to the economic process.

It should be added that the simple multiplier can be elaborated in various ways, e.g. by taking income taxes into account.

§ 37 The Markets for Money and Bonds. The LM Curve

In the two previous sections the central role of effective demand in the Keynesian income-expenditure model was established. We recognized that the level of real income is determined here by effective demand and not by the labor market. Also, it seemed to be obvious that a sudden decrease of effective demand – say because of the entrepreneurs' expectations becoming pessimistic – would diminish both real income and employment. But were the explanations really satisfactory?

Reviewed critically, the income-expenditure model seems to obscure more than it clarifies. Are the firms really indifferent to the real wage rate? Do prices not influence effective demand? And, above all, why should the amount of investment be given? All in all, the income-expenditure model falls short of giving a full explanation; it is useful for pedagogical purposes, but of no use to a comprehensive macroeconomic analysis. Hence, we now move on to a more elaborate version of Keynesian economics.

Just a year after the appearance of KEYNES' "General Theory", JOHN R. HICKS published his now famous paper "Mr. Keynes and the 'Classics': A Suggested Interpretation"[16] and provided an interpretation of KEYNES that became generally adopted and belongs to the standard repertoire of contemporary macroeconomic textbooks. It is the *IS/LM model* which we now want to explain.

The abbreviation "LM" represents "liquidity = money supply" where "liquidity" means simply "demand for money". The LM curve is associated with the Keynesian explanation of the money market which replaces the quantity theory of money.

The crucial deviation from Classical theory is a different explanation of the demand for money, called the *liquidity preference theory*. In Chapter IV, we became aware of the fact that the demand for money – as viewed by the quantity theorists – derived from the transactions motive: people kept money in order to carry out their commercial transactions. A proper store-of-value function had already been assigned to money by the mercantilists but the Classics rejected this because money bears no interest.

In Keynesian theory, money serves for transactions purposes *and* as a store of value. The individuals are supposed to make two decisions:

– They select the *level* of savings and hence wealth. This is described by the saving and consumption function.
– They determine the *mode* of holding wealth by choosing between alternative assets: *bonds* and *money*.

The *nominal wealth*, W^n, of the individuals consists of the money stock, M, and the nominal stock of bonds, B:

$$W^n = M + B. \tag{119}$$

"Money" is some appropriately defined quantity of money which we take as given. "Bonds" are supplied by the firms (later by the state, too) and demanded by the households. We refer to the decision problem (119) as *portfolio choice* because, by selecting money and bonds, the individuals decide on the composition of their portfolio or stock of wealth. From the Classical point of view, such a choice simply does not come into question since money bears no interest and, hence, holding money instead of bonds would be unreasonable. Thus, KEYNES had to show why holding cash could be considered economically rational. In order to do so he developed, in chapter 15 of the "General Theory", two motives for using money as a store of value; and these two, together with the transactions motive, constitute the liquidity preference theory.

The *precautionary motive* derives from the individuals' wish to hold more money than required for current transactions because of *unforseeable* payments. We call this part of cash held *precautionary balances*. The size of precautionary balances is likely to increase as income rises because the amount of unforseeable payments will tend to increase. Furthermore, the precautionary balances tend to be reduced when the

---

16 HICKS, J.R. (1937) Mr. Keynes and the 'Classics': A Suggested Interpretation. Econometrica **5**, pp. 147–159.

interest rate increases, since this raises the opportunity costs of holding cash, i.e. the loss of interest. Thus, we arrive at the following equation for precautionary balances:

$$L_P = L_P(Y, \underset{(+) \, (-)}{i}) \tag{120}$$

The two signs indicate that precautionary balances are correlated positively with income and negatively with the rate of interest.

The explanation of the *speculative motive* is somewhat more involved. Consider a *fixed-interest bond* with an infinite duration and a face value (FV) of \$100 that yields 5% per annum[17]. The rate of interest refers to the face value; hence a *fixed* annual interest payment of \$5 accrues to the owner.

In the bonds market, the security described above is traded at its *market value* (MV), where the latter normally differs from the face value. The *effective rate* – as opposed to interest rate – refers to the bond's market value. Since the interest payment is constant, the effective rate varies inversely with the market value. This should become clear in the following examples. Interest rate and effective rate coincide if the market value is equal to \$100. If the latter increases to \$125 then the effective rate *decreases* to 4% because

$$\text{MV } \$125 \cdot 4\% = \$5 \text{ fixed interest payment} \tag{121}$$

If the buyer has to pay \$125 for the bond, then \$5 a year is a yield of merely 4% to him. In the following we suppose that the effective rate is the same for all bonds. In so far as we abstract from different risks and durations, this hypothesis is quite plausible because the bond market closely approximates the perfect market in the theoretical sense.

Now, let us suppose that the effective rate of all bonds rises to 10%. Due to this, the market value of our above bond will diminish to \$50 because only this market value implies an effective rate of 10%:

$$\text{MV } \$50 \cdot 10\% = \$5 \text{ fixed interest payment} \tag{122}$$

Thus, the *doubling* of the effective rate amounts to a *halving* of the bond's market value. Surely, this does harm to the owners because they originally had to pay \$100 for the bond. It is via the speculative motive that they take account of this danger.

In general, the market value of a bond yielding fixed interest of i_0 per cent amounts to

$$MV = i_0/i \cdot FV \tag{123}$$

at a prevailing effective rate, or market rate, i. In our example, it is equal to

$$\$50 = 5\%/10\% \cdot \$100 \tag{124}$$

Every market participant probably has an idea of the *normal* effective rate which he expects to prevail in the future. Hence, he expects a certain market value and at

_____

17 In order to maintain the following arguments we must assume that the security bears a fixed interest. The premise that we have a consol (security with infinte duration), however, may be altered. Finite durations will incur smaller changes in the market value when interest changes.

the same time a certain exchange profit or loss. The expected exchange loss is defined as the difference between current and expected market value:

$$\text{expected exchange loss} = MV - MV^e \tag{125}$$

The expected market value naturally depends on the normal, i.e. expected, future effective rate. According to formula (123), we can calculate the two market values of (125) by inserting the current and the normal effective rate, respectively:

$$\text{expected exchange loss} = i_0/i \cdot FV - i_0/i_n \cdot FV \tag{126}$$

This expected exchange loss is counteracted by the fixed interest yield

$$\text{interest yield} = i_0 \cdot FV \tag{127}$$

Now, under which circumstances will an individual hold bonds instead of money? Obviously he will do so if the interest yield *exceeds* the expected exchange loss. Thus, the condition for holding bonds can be written as

$$\text{interest yield} > \text{expected exchange loss}$$

$$i_0 \cdot FV > \frac{i_0}{i} \cdot FV - \frac{i_0}{i_n} \cdot FV \tag{128}$$

$$\Leftrightarrow 1 > \frac{1}{i} - \frac{1}{i_n} \tag{129}$$

$$\Leftrightarrow i > \frac{i_n}{1 + i_n}. \tag{130}$$

The rate which equalizes interest yield and expected exchange loss is termed the *critical rate*, (i_c). If this critical rate prevails, a market participant's choice is indeterminate since gain and loss just balance. If the effective rate is above the critical one then the gain exceeds the loss, and the invidual, choosing the best store of value, will hold bonds and nothing else. Finally, if the effective rate is below the critical one, the individual will prefer to hold only money.

Let us illustrate this by assuming that a certain market operator expects a future effective rate of 10%. From (130), the critical rate can readily be calculated as

$$i_c = \frac{0.1}{1 + 0.1} \doteq 9\% \,. \tag{131}$$

Hence, if the effective rate is less than 9%, he will not buy any bonds as the expected exchange loss exceeds the interest yield (the reader should check this by a numerical example). In other words, holding money is rational in this case. Generally, the *individual* demand for cash exhibits the shape depicted in Figure 29.

L_s denotes the liquidity demand for speculative purposes. As is clear from the figure, the individual holds only bonds, i.e. no money, if the effective rate is greater than i_c; and if the former is less than i_c, no bonds at all are held. Thus the liquidity demand curve is discontinuous – but this holds only with respect to the individual: Due to different expectations, the normal rate is not the same for all individuals. Hence, the aggregate demands for money and bonds do not change suddenly but there is a smooth shift from bonds to money as the effective rate diminishes. This is because –

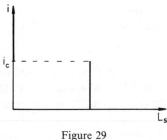

Figure 29

as the effective rate decreases – more and more individuals consider this rate to be below the critical one. Thus the aggregate speculative demand for money looks like this:

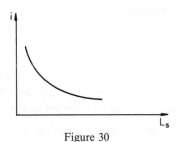

Figure 30

Expressed algebraically, aggregate speculative demand for money satifies the equation

$$L_S = \underset{(-)}{L_S(\,i\,)}. \qquad (132)$$

Liquidity preference theory has now been described completely, and we can summarize the results. The demand for money consists of transactions balances, familiar from the quantity theory of money

$$L_T = \underset{(+)}{L_T(Y)}, \qquad (133)$$

precautionary balances which depend on real income and the rate of interest

$$L_P = \underset{(+)\ (-)}{L_P(\,Y,\ i\,)}, \qquad (135)$$

and, finally, speculative balances which depend on the interest rate

$$L_S = \underset{(-)}{L_S(\,i\,)}. \qquad (136)$$

Clearly the analytical distinction between these three balances has no counterpart in reality: money is money or, as KEYNES put it: "Money is not ear-marked". Hence we can combine them to give the *aggregate demand for cash* which is a *stock*:

$$L = \underset{(+)\ (-)}{L(\,Y,\ i\,)}. \qquad (137)$$

Next, let us compare this liquidity preference theory with the quantity theory's explanation of the demand for cash, i.e. equation (60):

$$L^n = k \cdot P \cdot Y. \tag{138}$$

A minor difference between liquidity preference and quantity theory is that (137) represents *real* and (138) *nominal* demand for cash – but this is just a matter of form. By multiplying (137) by the price level, P, we can immediately transform it into nominal money demand.

The important difference is the following: In the quantity theory, the demand for real balances depends on real income and the constant k and thus is a function of real income only. In liquidity preference theory, on the contrary, demand for real balances is also determined by the *rate of interest*. This will prove to have important consequences.

An *equilibrium in the money market* prevails if and only if individuals hold their exogenous aggregate cash balances willingly, which can be written as

$$L(Y, i) = \frac{M}{P}. \tag{139}$$

Equation (139) defines the *LM curve*. In the IS/LM model, the aggregate stock of money as well as the price level are given; thus only real income and the interest rate can adjust in order to bring about an equilibrium in the money market:

The LM curve is the locus of all those combinations of real income and interest which equate demand and supply in the money market.

This is only one characterstic of the LM curve, since we already recognized, in equation (119), that total wealth consists of money *and* bonds. The stocks of money and bonds are not independent of one another: any particular stock of money – total wealth being given – implies a certain stock of bonds. And total wealth *is* given, since we consider stocks at the *beginning* of a certain period. The bond market is a reflection of the money market, and an equilibrium in the bond market prevails if and only if there is an equilibrium in the money market, too. Therefore we can state that the LM curve depicts *simultaneous* equilibrium in the money and bond markets[18].

The following figure depicts the LM curve:

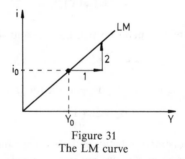

Figure 31
The LM curve

18 That follows immediately from the wealth constraint (119). Cf. FOLEY, D.K. (1975) On two Specifications of Asset Equilibrium in Macroeconomic Models. Journal of Political Economy 83, pp. 303–324. BUITER, W. (1980) Walras' Law and All That: Budget Constraints in Period Models and Continuous Time Models. International Economic Review 21, pp. 1–16.

It is certainly not a demand curve; rather, points *on* the LM curve indicate that there is equilibrium in the money market, and the points *off* the LM curve indicate that there is not. Our next question is why the LM curve – which is not necessarily a straight line – exhibits a *positive slope*. Let us start from an original position (Y_0, i_0) which implies an equilibrium in the money market:

$$L(Y_0, i_0) = \frac{M}{P}. \qquad (140)$$

What will happen if real income increases? Obviously, real money demand, owing to the transactions and precautionary motives, will increase also (arrow no. 1); hence an excess demand arises in the money market. In order to re-establish equilibrium, the rate of interest must rise, too. This causes a reduction in real money demand for precautionary and speculative purposes. The increase in the interest rate (arrow no. 2) will eventually offset the excess demand for money. Therefore, higher levels of real income require higher levels of interest in order to ensure an equilibrium in the money market: the LM curve has a positive slope.

Concerning its *position*, we assumed for the time being that the LM curve intersects the origin; but this assumption is not essential and will be removed soon as prices are allowed to vary.

Let us now analyze what happens if there is *disequilibrium* in the money market:

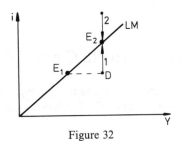

Figure 32

At point D, demand for money *exceeds* supply since real income – relative to E_1 – is too high; or the interest rate – relative to E_2 – is too low there. Both implies excess demand.

In order to understand the adjustment process, we have to remember that every excess demand in the money market is accompanied by an *excess supply* in the *bond market*. Since the market participants consider original real cash balances at D insufficient, they try to increase them by selling bonds. Of course, they cannot succeed in doing so because aggregate balances are given, and one individual's receipts are another's outlays. But there is excess supply in the bond market which will diminish the market values of bonds just as excess supply in any market would bid down the market price. *Declining* market values of bonds means the same as a *rising* rate of interest since we saw above that these two vary inversely.

The central feature of the adjustment process is that the rise in the interest rate (arrow no. 1) will last until there is a new equilibrium in the money market. Thus, the interest rate moves towards the LM curve. The same holds true for points above the

LM curve when the interest rate must decrease as illustrated by arrow no. 2. In this case, our arguments above simply have to be reversed. We can conclude that changes in the rate of interest bring about equilibrium in the money and bond markets, and, accordingly, that the LM curve represents a set of *stable* equilibria.

Let us outline the most significant differences between LM curve analysis and Classical theory: The former conceives of the interest rate as a *monetary magnitude*, in the sense that it brings about equilibrium in the money market, whereas Classical theory maintained that the rate of interest equalizes real investment and real savings. According to the latter, there is no relationship between interest rates and demand for money at all (remember: "Interest is commonly reckoned for Money ... but that is a mistake.") while, according to the Keynesians, money and interest are intimately connected.

Recollect the quantity theory of money. Because money is merely supposed to serve as a medium of payment, an increase in the quantity of money causes commodity expenditures to rise: *goods are substituted for money*. In Keynesian theory, on the other hand, money is also a store of value. An increase of the quantity of money disturbs the portfolio equilibrium, (119), *bonds are substituted for money*, and this diminishes the rate of interest.

The characterization of the interest rate as a monetary magnitude would be wrong, however, if we meant hereby that it does not influence real income and real investment. For the rate of interest, as will seen in the next section, determines investment now as before.

§38 The Capital Market. The IS Curve

The abbreviation "IS" represents "investment = savings" indicating that this is the equilibrium locus of the capital market[19]. The Keynesian savings function

$$S = S(Y) \tag{141}$$

and the investment function

$$I = I(i) \tag{142}$$

yield the equilibrium condition for the capital market:

$$S(Y) = I(i). \tag{143}$$

This is the equation of the IS curve:

The IS curve is the locus of all those combinations of real income and interest which equate demand and supply in the capital market.

---

19 Unhappily, the IS curve is frequently referred to as an equilibrium locus of the *commodity market*. From Walras' Law (cf. §24) it follows immediately that this is inconsistent if we regard "equilibrium" as a state were demand and supply match. RABIN and BIRCH have traced the inconsistencies in prominent macroeconomic textbooks which arise from treating the IS curve as an equilibrium locus of the commodity market. Our own interpretation involves no logical errors and is quite natural because savings and investment represent supply of and demand for claims. Cf. RABIN, A. and D. BIRCH (1982) A Clarification of the IS Curve and the Aggregate Demand Curve. Journal of Macroeconomics **4**, pp. 233–238.

Only certain combinations of real income and interest produce an equilibrium in the capital market as can be seen from (143) or from the following figure:

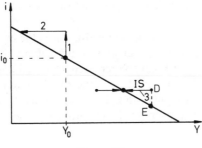

Figure 33
The IS curve

At this point we must explain why the IS curve exhibits a negative slope and why it intersects the ordinate at a positive interest rate. Let us start from an initial equilibrium at real income Y_0 and interest rate i_0:

$$S(Y_0) = I(i_0).\qquad(144)$$

If the rate of interest *rises* (arrow no. 1), investment declines and so must savings in order to establish a new equilibrium. But this means that income must *decline* (arrow no. 2), too, for savings are an increasing function of income. Hence, in order to maintain equilibrium in the capital market, interest and income have to move inversely: the IS curve exhibits a negative slope[20].

Second, consider the point of intersection of the IS curve with the ordinate where real income is equal to zero:

$$S(0) = I(i).\qquad(145)$$

According to our considerations of the consumption function, $S(0)$ is likely to be negative in the short run but certainly zero in the long run; in sum, it is probably never positive. But in order to reduce investment to such a low level, a very high rate of interest is obviously required. Thus, the IS curve intersects the ordinate at a positive rate of interest. Of course, the IS curve is not necessarily a straight line – it was only drawn as such to simplify the figure. The linear relationship neither follows from our previous assumptions nor is it essential to the following analysis. The only essential features are the negative slope and the positive point of intersection with the ordinate.

Using Figure 33 it is easy to study the adjustment processes that arise from disequilibrium in the capital market. At point D, the rate of interest – as compared to the equilibrium E – is to high and thus investment is too low, that is

$$S(Y) > I(i).\qquad(146)$$

---

20 In Subsection *4.4 of the Mathematical Appendix we derive the slope of the IS curve analytically.

It is absolutely essential to Keynesian theory that the rate of interest is *determined by the money market*; hence it cannot adjust in order to equilibrate investment and savings. Here investment does not fill the demand gap caused by savings. For this reason, production and real income must *decline* (arrow no. 3) until $S(Y) = I(i)$ holds anew.

It was already stated in §35 that we regard this as the core of Keynesian theory: the equilibrium of savings and investment is brought about by changes in income, not interest. Thus, arrow no. 3 of Figure 33 represents the well-known multiplier process.

Let us conclude. In Keynesian theory, the rate of interest does not equilibrate investment and savings: it equilibrates the money market. In the capital market – where the rate of interest is given – it is real income which adjusts in order to bring about an equilibrium.

§39 The IS/LM Model

Having finished the partial analyses of the money and capital markets, we move on to the determination of *simultaneous* equilibrium. For this purpose, we take the equations of the LM curve and IS curve:

$$\text{IS:}\quad S(Y) = I(i) \tag{147}$$

$$\text{LM:}\quad L(Y,i) = \frac{M}{P}. \tag{148}$$

These are two simultaneous equations with two endogenous variables, namely, real income and the rate of interest. Owing to our former assumptions, there exists just one solution (Y_0, i_0) which, in the graphical exposition, is the point of intersection of the two curves:

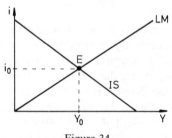

Figure 34
The IS/LM model

The exogenous real money supply and liquidity preference determine the LM curve, whereas the IS curve is determined by the savings and investment functions. Clearly, only the pair (Y_0, i_0) produces simultaneous equilibrium in the money and capital markets. Therefore, production is determined by the demand side, and this is the essence of the IS/LM model: *The price level being given, real income and employment are determined by aggregate commodity demand.*

What about the *stability* of this equilibrium? Only after answering this question can we be sure that our comparative static analysis is meaningful in the sense that real income and the rate of interest steadily converge towards their equilibrium values.

If there is *disequilibrium*, the following two adjustment processes, as explained in the previous sections, arise: Any excess demand in the capital market entails an increase in income via the multiplier process; and vice versa. Any excess demand in the money market entails an increase in the interest rate, and vice versa. Thus, these simultaneous adjustment processes can be illustrated in the following figure:

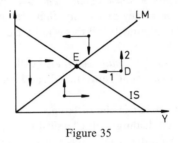

Figure 35

Point D, for instance, lies above the IS curve and below the LM curve. There is

- excess supply in the capital market because real income and real savings are too high, and
- excess demand in the money market, because interest is too low and, consequently, money demand for precautionary and speculative purposes is too high.

As a result,

- real income will diminish via the multiplier process, and
- the rate of interest will rise due to falling market values of bonds.

These two processes are indicated by the arrows no. 1 and 2. The reader should make sure that the three other sets of arrows all point in the correct directions. This is not difficult because the above reasoning need only be reversed where appropriate.

It is essential to the model that both adjustment processes take place simultaneously. It is obvious that these processes converge towards the universal equilibrium, although both linear and spiral paths are conceivable[21]:

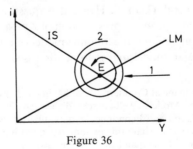

Figure 36

---

21 The local stability of the IS/LM model is proved in Subsection *5.5 of the Mathematical Appendix.

Thus the equilibrium of the IS/LM model proves stable, that is – other things being equal – the economy will tend towards the equilibrium, E.

Finally, let us explain the underlying logic of the Keynesian IS/LM model. It embodies three markets, namely

- the money market,
- the bond market, and
- the capital market.

The LM curve represents a *stock equilibrium*, also called *beginning of period equilibrium*. Those stocks of money and bonds that are given at the beginning of a certain period must be held voluntarily – if this is not the case, the rate of interest will adjust until they are.

The IS curve represents a *flow equilibrium*, also called *end of period equilibrium*. The flows "savings" and "investment" must match; and real income will adjust if they do not.

The reader may wonder what is the difference between a "bond market" and "capital market" since, when dealing with Classical theory, we maintained that just bonds are traded in the capital market. Yet, the two markets are fundamentally different in Keynesian theory since "equilibrium in the bond market" refers to a beginning of period equilibrium whereas "equilibrium in the capital market" refers to an end of period equilibrium. We do not pretend to consider it wise or appropriate to model the same market twice, applying two different notions of equilibrium to it at the same time but this is, as far as we can see, the only way to interpret the IS/LM model consistently.

It is in this respect that the IS/LM model is often criticized for embodying both stocks and flows. The resulting equilibrium is not a permanent one because – savings being positive – the stock of wealth increases over time. This causes the LM curve to shift, as its position depends on the stock of bonds. In order to avoid this problem, the best one can do is to choose a very special time period: long enough to allow for a full adjustment of real income and interest, and short enough to justify neglecting the changes in stocks[22].

Another criticicm of the IS/LM model is the objection that the two curves are not *steady* over time, but subject to permanent disturbances – especially due to changing expectations. This is the argument of those "disequilibrium theorists" who suppose erratic fluctuations in the marginal efficiency of capital and liquidity preference to be the essence of the "General Theory". Hence it is questionable whether the IS/LM model can be regarded as a proper representation of KEYNES' own model[23]. Nonetheless, it has become the most famous economic model of our century, and is the core of the complete Keynesian model that is to be discussed in the next section.

---

22 Cf. CHICK, V. (1973) Financial Counterparts of Saving and Investment and Inconsistencies in Some Simple Macro Models. Weltwirtschaftliches Archiv **109**, pp. 621–643. TOBIN, J. (1980) Asset Accumulation and Economic Activity. Oxford: Basil Blackwell.

23 The inventor himself seems to share this opinion when writing: "I must say that diagram is now much less popular with me than I think it still is with many other people. It reduces the General Theory to equilibrium economics." HICKS, J.R. (1976) Some Questions of Time in Economics. In: TANG, A.M. et al. Ed. Evolution, Welfare and Time in Economics. Lexington: Lexington Books.

§40 The Complete Keynesian Model

Now we have proceeded far enough to pass to the so-called *complete Keynesian model*, which is a comprehensive model of the total economy. This "Neoclassical synthesis", as it is also called, embodies the Neoclassical model of the labor market, the production function, and the IS/LM model as the demand sector of the economy. At first, the complete Keynesian model is described using simultaneous equations (K for Keynesian) and thereafter graphically.

$$N^d\left(\frac{w}{P}\right) = N = N^s\left(\frac{w}{P}\right) \quad \rightarrow N^*, \left(\frac{w}{P}\right)^* \tag{K.1}$$

$$Y = f(N) \quad \rightarrow Y^* \tag{K.2}$$

$$S(Y) = I(i) \left.\vphantom{\frac{M}{P}}\right\} \tag{K.3}$$

$$L(Y, i) = \frac{M}{P} \left.\vphantom{\frac{M}{P}}\right\} \rightarrow i^*, P^* \tag{K.4}$$

$$w = \left(\frac{w}{P}\right) \cdot P \quad \rightarrow w^*. \tag{K.5}$$

Like the Classical model of §27, the complete Keynesian model consists of six equations that are to determine six unknowns. We want to examine them in detail:

(K.1), from the classical model, are the two equations of the labor market that simultaneously determine employment and the real wage rate.

(K.2) represents the production function which, given full employment N^* by the labor market, yields equilibrium output Y^*.

(K.3) and (K.4) are the equations of the IS/LM model. However, in contrast to the IS/LM model proper, P figures as an *endogenous* variable. The graphical exposition will illustrate how the interest rate and the price level corresponding to given output Y^* are both determined.

(K.5), finally, determines the nominal wage, w^*, as in (C.5).

We immediately recognize the striking analogy between the Classical model and this one. Both give rise to the general equilibrium with full employment. Thus, we have to note that the Keynesian concepts of the consumption function, marginal efficiency of capital, and liquidity preference do not imply different results *per se*. This is one aspect of the Neoclassical synthesis: modifying the assumptions of the Classical model slightly does not change the essential results. Only in the following sections will it become clear what drastic deviations appear once additional complications are introduced.

The graphical exposition of the complete Keynesian model is as follows:

Quadrant I depicts the labor market, i.e. equation (K.1). The point of intersection of the demand and supply curves determines full employment N^* as well as the equilibrium real wage rate, $(w/P)^*$.

Quadrant II shows the production function, (K.2).

Quadrant IV is our IS/LM model of the previous section.

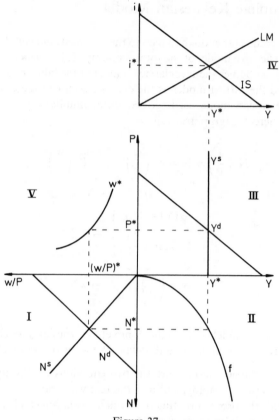

Figure 37

Quadrant V corresponds to (K.5). As in the same quadrant of the Classical model, it shows how the nominal wage rate w* is identified once real wages and the price level are given.

But, *Quadrant III* constitutes the model's core. This is the *commodity market* where supply of and demand for commodities meet and the equilibrium price level P* is inferred from the market clearing condition. The two curves Y^d and Y^s have to be explained next.

The *commodity supply curve*, Y^s, relates a certain commodity supply to any value of the price level. Why is this a vertical straight line? As we already know, commodity supply depends solely on the *real wage rate*, since the latter determines employment, and commodity supply is a direct function of employment. If we suppose, as does equation (K.5), that nominal wage rates adjust immediately if prices vary then any change in the price level has no influence on the real wage rate, and hence does not influence commodity supply. Thus, commodity supply is the same at any price level: and the commodity supply curve is a vertical straight line.

The *commodity demand curve*, Y^d, is not an ordinary demand function but an equilibrium locus. We have to bear in mind that – though the inverse relationship between price and demand is only too plausible for a single market – the same line of reasoning cannot be applied to the whole economy. For, if the price level rises, *all* commodities become dearer and there are no substitution effects. However, in Classical theory, we encountered an adjustment mechanism called the Cambridge-effect: A rise in the price level causes real cash balances to decrease, and thus entails diminishing demand for commodities. But here, this Cambridge-effect does not hold, and the explanation is somewhat more involved.

Let us assume a given IS curve and consider the equation of the LM curve in conjunction with a diagram:

$$L(Y,i) = \frac{M}{P}. \tag{149}$$

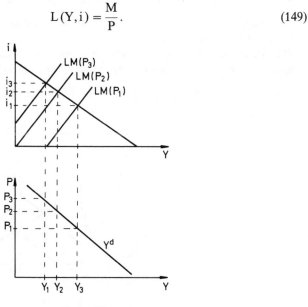

Figure 38
Derivation of the Y^d-curve

According to (149), any increase in the price level first causes real cash balances to decrease, since P is the denominator of M/P. In order to re-establish equilibrium in the money market, demand for real cash balances must also decrease.

But this implies either a decline in real income, or a higher rate of interest: both equivalent to a *shift* of the LM curve *to the left*. In Figure 38, the LM curve shifts from $LM(P_1)$ to $LM(P_2)$ because the price level increases. Now, the point of intersection of the IS and LM curves is to the left of the original one, and determines a *lower* real income. Therefore, as a rule, higher price levels entail lower levels of aggregate demand: Y^d is a declining function of P [24].

The Y^d curve can be constructed graphically in the following way. An arbitrary price level, P_0, is selected. This defines a certain position of the LM curve, and hence a certain point of intersection of the IS and LM curves. This latter point, in turn,

---

24 The slope of the Y^d curve is derived in Subsection *4.4 of the Mathematical Appendix.

determines real income, Y_0 and the pair (Y_0, P_0) constitutes one point on the Y^d curve. Repeating this procedure for every price level yields the whole commodity demand curve. The latter *shifts* if the position of the IS curve or nominal money supply change.

Let us return to Figure 37 which can now be explained in full: Quadrants I and II depict the *supply sector* of the economy which determines the aggregate commodity supply function, Y^s. Quadrant IV, on the other hand, constitutes the *demand sector* from which the aggregate commodity demand function, Y^d, can be derived. In Quadrant III, commodity demand and supply meet and the equilibrium condition yields a particular price level. One difficulty in understanding the model stems from the fact that its comparative static and its dynamic properties do not coincide:

– The price level *influences* the money market; but it is *determined* by demand and supply in the commodity market.
– The rate of interest *influences* investment and thus the commodity market; but it is *determined* by demand and supply in the money market.

This can be illustrated by means of the following figure:

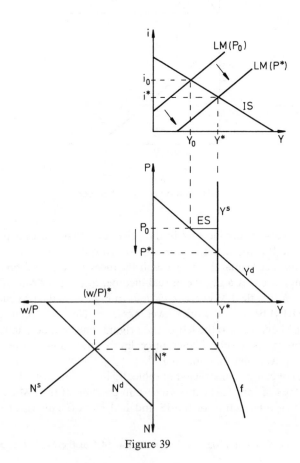

Figure 39

The original price level is above its equilibrium value and the LM curve is too far to the left. This implies a high interest rate and, accordingly, low investment demand. Hence, there is excess supply, ES, in the commodity market.

Due to the excess supply, prices will decline over time, causing the LM curve to move to the right. This, accompanied by decreasing interest, will stimulate investment and commodity demand. This process continues until there is equilibrium in the commodity market, at price level P*.

Consequently, we have eliminated the Cambridge-effect but substituted it with something that obviously works similarly. This is the *Keynes-effect*. The Keynes-effect represents an indirect link between commodity demand and the price level – a very indirect one. Declining prices, by increasing real cash balances, do *not* entail an immediate rise in commodity demand, as explained by the quantity theorists. On the contrary, it is the *demand for bonds* that rises, forcing the interest rate to decline. And this, finally, augments investment and hence commodity demand.

Beginning with an increase in the nominal quantity of money, the Keynes-effect works as follows:

Increased quantity of money (cash balances) → greater demand for bonds → increasing market values of bonds = decreasing rate of interest → increasing investment and commodity demand → rising prices.

At the same time, the quantity theory of money is affirmed by the *results*: a doubling of the quantity of money entails a doubling of the price level. Only if prices move in proportion to the quantity of money, does the position of the LM curve – depending on real cash balances – remain unchanged, ensuring that the point of intersection with the IS curve and hence commodity demand is unchanged too.

Owing to the Keynes-effect, the Classical dichotomy between the real and monetary sector survives in the sense that, *ultimately*, monetary disturbances result in price adjustments and nothing else. The principle of the neutrality of money is maintained. On the other hand, there is an important difference in that the adjustment is brought about by the interest rate. In Classical theory, we may recall, the interest rate was altogether unaffected by changes in the quantity of money – whereas, here, it is the crucial link between cash balances and commodity demand.

In this section, we have examined the Neoclassical synthesis from its Neoclassical angle. We established that its explanations are in detail different from that of Classical theory but that the outstanding results of the latter are maintained. In the following three "scenarios", we will present the more Keynesian aspects of the Neoclassical synthesis. In so doing, the meaning of the term "imperfectionism", which we attributed to the Neoclassical synthesis, will become plain: These authors proceed from the general conviction that the market mechanism does work in principle, and then ascribe the existence of real problems, like recessions, to certain "imperfections". In this respect, they differ from the "fundamentalists" who suppose the free market economy to be incapable of self-regulation.

§41 First Scenario: The Investment Trap

This and the following two scenarios are special cases of the complete Keynesian model. The *investment trap* is a situation where investment demand is perfectly interest inelastic. We have seen in §34 that interest inelasticity of investment can be traced back to extremely pessimistic expectations on the part of the entrepreneurs; and this case proved to be the foundation of the income-expenditure model. Of course, this is merely a theoretical construction though frequently regarded as a possible explanation of depressions.

Owing to the assumption of perfectly interest inelasticity, i.e.

$$S(Y) = I \tag{150}$$

the IS curve becomes a *vertical* straight line:

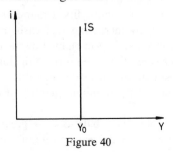

Figure 40

The verticality of the IS curve indicates that the interest rate does not influence investment demand; thus, by equation (150), real income is uniquely determined.

To analyze the economic consequences of such an investment trap, we substitute (150) into the complete Keynesian model and thus obtain the model K':

$$S(Y) = I \qquad \rightarrow Y_0 \tag{K'.1}$$

$$Y = f(N) \qquad \rightarrow N_0 \tag{K'.2}$$

$$\frac{w}{P} \overset{!}{=} \left(\frac{w}{P}\right)^* \qquad \rightarrow \left(\frac{w}{P}\right)^* \tag{K'.3}$$

$$L(Y,i) = \frac{M}{P} \qquad \rightarrow (P,i) \tag{K'.4}$$

$$w = \left(\frac{w}{P}\right)P \qquad \rightarrow w. \tag{K'.5}$$

(K'.1) represents the equation of the IS curve when there is an investment trap. Obviously, the equilibrium value of real income, Y_0, is determined by this equation. It need not be equivalent to full employment income Y^*.

(K'.2) is the production function which illustrates most clearly the core of the investment trap. Labor input does not determine production – but is determined by it! The firms, only able to sell the amount Y_0 in the commodity market, choose the required quantity of labor accordingly.

(K'.3) embodies the somewhat arbitrary postulate that the real wage rate is equivalent to its Classical equilibrium value. This hypothesis was employed only in order to show that in this case unemployment does *not* originate in an excessive real wage rate. According to some theorists, KEYNES himself alleged a function $w/P = (N^d)^{-1}(N)$ which depicts the firms as offering a real wage that is equal to the marginal productivity of labor. But this makes no essential difference.

(K′.4) is an equation with *two* unknowns, namely, the rate of interest and the price level. It cannot be solved uniquely; rather there is an infinity of pairs (i, P) which satisfy it.

(K′.5), finally, determines the nominal wage rate corresponding to a given price level.

Let us explore the most interesting features of this model. The dichotomy between the real and the monetary sector is immediately obvious: equations (K′.1) to (K′.3) determine the real variables Y, N, and w/P where there is no role for monetary influences. (K′.4) and (K′.5), on the other hand, define a *set* of consistent combinations of P, w, and i. Here, interest belongs to the monetary sector.

The capital market and the commodity market are the strategic markets of the model. By means of the multiplier process, production adjusts such that $S(Y) = I$. Therefore, we arrive at a *stable equilibrium with unemployment* if effective demand is slighter than full employment output.

Considered in purely static terms, there is also equilibrium in the monetary sector since any consistent combination of P, i, and w is as good as any other and has no influence on the real magnitudes at all. (Using the terms of § 4, this is an indifferent equilibrium.) But looked at dynamically, we recognize a disequilibrium for the following reason. Effective demand being insufficient, there occurs an excess supply in the commodity market which – in accordance with Classical reasoning – is likely to cause *deflation*, i.e. declining prices and wages. The rate of interest will diminish, too.

But the following point is of the utmost importance: The decline in prices, wages, and the rate of interest does not alleviate the depression; real income and employment are left *unchanged*. This is because investment demand does not increase due to the decline in interest rates since it is perfectly interest inelastic. In this respect, the dichotomy is remarkable because – even in the shortest run – the monetary variables have no impact on the real ones at all. Thus, the real sector exhibits a *stable equilibrium*, possibly with unemployment. Figure 41 on the next page will bring this home:

The IS curve, in Quadrant IV, is a vertical straight line and determines real income independently of the LM curve's position. Therefore, commodity demand is independent of the price level, too, and the Y^d curve is a vertical straight line. The decline in prices from P_2 to P_1, indeed, lowers interest to i_1 – but investment and commodity demand do not respond to this. One link in the chain of the Keynes-effect has been broken, and prices do not influence commodity demand.

Obviously, this is unfortunate because – commodity demand being unsufficient, i.e. Y^d to the left of Y^s – the commodity market can be cleared neither by means of price adjustment *nor in any other way*. Instead, the firms are confronted with a quantity constraint forcing them to diminish both production and employment. To put it in other words: the firms *wish* to produce full employment output, Y*, at the prevailing real wage (W/P)* as indicated by the broken line Y^s; but they actually produce only the amount Y_0. Owing to the quantity restriction, it is not possible to sell more[25].

---

25 Expressed in Neokeynesian terms (cf. Chapter XI), firms are rationed in the commodity market. Their commodity supply in the sense of Clower is represented by the broken line Y^s. Being rigorous, we ought to modify the decision model of the firms because they do not behave according to the marginal productivity rule here. But that task is postponed till Chapter XI.

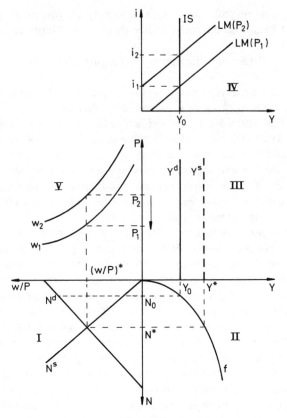

Figure 41
The investment trap

It is time to move on to the labor market. At the prevailing real wage rate, $(w/P)^*$, households supply N^* units of labor and the firms *would* buy precisely this amount *if* there were no quantity restriction in the commodity market. But, as matters stand, they only employ as much labor as is required to produce Y_0. In this case, N^d is not the labor demand function and was drawn for comparison only. Thus, there is underemployment, amounting to the distance $\overline{N_0 N^*}$. It may be that the real wage rate declines: but this would not alter labor demand. Real wages can decline to any positive value without stimulating the firms to employ one more man! If firms aim at profit maximization they do not employ more labor than is necessary to produce the given output Y_0.

Let us summarize the results:

- If investment demand is perfectly interest inelastic, a "demand gap" in the commodity market is possible because the Keynes-effect does not work. A supply gap is also conceivable.
- Such a demand gap certainly causes unemployment because labor demand is determined by commodity demand.

– The demand gap and unemployment cannot be removed by means of a general deflation: on the contrary, prices, wages, and interest may decline by any amount without stimulating effective demand.

Perhaps, the investment trap appears somewhat strange to the reader because of the vertical curves and the quantity constraints. But this model (together with the following couple) constitutes the core of Keynesian theory. What is more, we have employed no new assumptions, but only made *explicit* those already embodied in the income-expenditure model.

§42 Second Scenario: The Liquidity Trap

In the last section, it should have become clear that a perfectly interest inelastic investment demand may give rise to insufficient commodity demand, and thus to an equilibrium with unemployment. The consequences of a liquidity trap are basically the same.

A *liquidity trap* occurs when money demand becomes *infinitely interest elastic*: If the rate of interest is at an exceptionally low level, as compared to individual's subjective expectations, then the market participants will fear high exchange losses on their bonds. This is because they expect the rate of interest to rise and hence the market values of bonds to fall. Thus, individuals will prefer cash. If interest declines further, demand for money will rise rapidly until – in the theoretical extreme – it will respond infinitely to a given change in the interest rate. But this amounts to an infinitely interest elastic demand for money.

Due to this *absolute liquidity preference*, the rate of interest is bounded from below, the lower bound being called i_0:

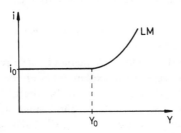

The figure suggests that the rate of interest cannot fall below i_0. Secondly, real income seems to exert no influence on money demand in the range $0 \leq Y \leq Y_0$: all these income levels correspond to the same rate of interest. Speculative demand for cash increases unboundedly, and transactions balances constitute but a negligible fraction of total balances. Therefore, the response of money demand with respect to changes in real income is very small or, in the extreme, zero [26].

---

26 Cf. Subsection *4.4 of the Mathematical Appendix for an analytical demonstration.

The liquidity trap involves the following danger. Assuming a normal (downward sloping) IS curve, there certainly *exists* a rate of interest that is consistent with full employment; but it is questionable if it can actually be *reached* since the LM curve defines a lower bound on the interest rate. If this lower bound, i_0, is *above* the full employment level of interest, i*, then investment and commodity demand fall short of their equilibrium levels – and, again, there is an equilibrium with unemployment. This may be illustrated by the model K″:

$$L(Y, i) = \frac{M}{P} \qquad \rightarrow i_0 \tag{K″.1}$$

$$S(Y) = I(i) \qquad \rightarrow Y_0 \tag{K″.2}$$

$$Y = f(N) \qquad \rightarrow N_0 \tag{K″.3}$$

$$\frac{w}{P} \overset{!}{=} \left(\frac{w}{P}\right)^* \qquad \rightarrow \left(\frac{w}{P}\right)^* \tag{K″.4}$$

$$w = \left(\frac{w}{P}\right) \cdot P \qquad \rightarrow (P, w), \tag{K″.5}$$

(K″.1) determines the rate of interest independently of the values of real income and the price level which – owing to the absolute liquidity preference – cannot exert any influence on it.

Thus, interest is given to the capital market, (K″.2). Real income adjusts, via the multiplier process, such that demand and supply in the capital market match. The resulting equilibrium income Y_0 will only by chance constitute full employment income Y*.

The other equations determine employment, the real wage rate, and pairs of P and w in the already familiar manner. Again, P and w are indeterminate while their ratio, w/P, is given by (K″.4).

The graphical exposition, except in quadrant IV, is identical to that of the investment trap – look at Figure 43.

Only the verticality of the commodity demand curve requires comment – apart from that we could merely repeat the explanations of the foregoing section. If, as depicted in Figure 43, prices decline from P_2 to P_1, the LM curve shifts to the *right* since real cash balances increase. But its horizontal range effectively does not shift. If there is an absolute liquidity preference, real cash balances simply do not matter because *any* quantity of money is demanded. It is for this reason that the decline in prices does not lower the rate of interest – and, consequently, both investment demand and real income remain unchanged.

With respect to the monetary sector, a permanent deflation is to be expected since there is excess supply in the commodity market. But this will not cure under-production and unemployment. On the contrary, commodity demand remains the same and the firms simply choose the quantity of labor required to produce this given output. Thus, employment amounts to N_0.

Essentially, the liquidity trap is caused by the inactivity of the *Keynes-effect*. In contrast to the investment trap, the problem is not that investment demand does not respond to declining interest – rather, a decline in interest is quite impossible if it is

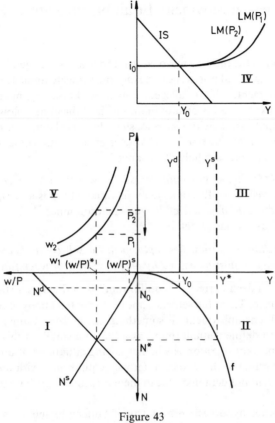

Figure 43
The liquidity trap

uniquely determined by absolute liquidity preference. Yet, both cases are similar in that excess supply in the commodity market, accompanied by declining prices, does not augment commodity demand. On the contrary, a theoretically unlimited deflation comes into being which is entirely ineffectual with respect to the real magnitudes. Employment is solely determined by commodity demand.

Let us summarize the results:

- Depending on the psychology of the public, a situation of absolute liquidity preference may arise. Then, the rate of interest cannot fall below a certain limit and this potentially creates a demand gap.
- Such a demand gap causes unemployment because labor demand is determined by commodity demand.
- The demand gap and unemployment cannot be removed by means of a general deflation. With respect to real magnitudes there is a stable equilibrium with unemployment.

§43 An Under-employment Equilibrium with a Flexible Real Wage?

Before moving on to the third scenario we want to discuss the age-old issue of whether assuming sticky wages and prices is a *necessary* prerequisite to the Keynesian explanation of unemployment. This is alleged, you must know, by many contemporary writers. KEYNES expressed his own opinion on the subject as follows:

"But this simplification, with which we shall dispense later, is introduced solely to facilitate the exposition. The essential character of the argument is the same whether or not money-wages, etc. are liable to change." [27]

Obviously, KEYNES did not consider sticky wages and prices essential to his argument. Moreover, JOHN R. HICKS demonstrated why this assumption was mistakenly taken as the *sine qua non* of Keynesian economics [28]. Let us consider two frequently stated assertions in detail:

1) *The term "equilibrium with underemployment" is self-contradictory.*
2) *Any unemployment must be caused by an excessive real wage rate.*

Ad 1): This is indeed correct if "equilibrium" is defined as a state where supply and demand balance. Then, the sentence above is true for purely logical reasons, and "equilibrium with unemployment" is something like a "round square". But we think it more suitable to define "equilibrium" as a "lasting state" in this context: for the economically important question is whether lasting situations of unemployment are conceivable. According to this choice of terms, "equilibrium with unemployment" is not merely consistent but demonstrable in theory; recollect the investment or liquidity trap.

Ad 2): The latter hypothesis proves true if "unemployment" is perceived as an excess supply in the labor market. This is because there is always a real wage rate which clears the labor market. Look at Figure 43: The real wage rate $(w/P)^s$ is so low that it forces labor supply down to N_0; and all resulting unemployment is voluntary. But we want to define *under-employment* as any negative deviation from full employment N^*, avoiding referring to "involuntary unemployment". This definition makes a great difference because, in Figure 43, there prevails underemployment in this sense but not in the former.

According to our definition, first suggested by PATINKIN, any level of employment below N^* is termed under-employment. N^* alone represents a level of employment which is considered optimal for society by Classical, Keynesian, and perhaps all economists. If $N < N^*$, an increase in employment would benefit *both* those individuals willing to work and those persons who want to consume more commodities; hence, such a situation cannot be Pareto-optimal. (A state is called Pareto-optimal if and only if it is impossible to improve the economic situation of one person without worsening that of another.)

---

27 "General Theory", op.cit., p. 27.
28 HICKS, J.R. (1974) The Crisis in Keynesian Economics. Oxford: Basil Blackwell, pp. 60 ff.

The investment trap and the liquidity trap cause an economic inefficiency ($N < N^*$) which is *not* remediable via changes in the real wage rate. Moreover, the resulting state is an *equilibrium* in the sense that there is no tendency to change.

To conclude, an equilibrium with under-employment is possible even if the real wage rate is perfectly flexible. When we assume sticky wages in the following section, this is an additional and quite independent assumption.

§ 44 Third Scenario: Sticky Wages

Our third scenario deals with the case most frequently cited in Keynesian literature. Assuming *sticky wages* sounds rather restrictive; but we do not mean by this a lasting exogeneity but rather that wage rates are independent of demand and supply to a certain degree, and that they do not adjust immediately.

Similarly, we could assume *sticky prices*, but this case does not require a special explanation since it is depicted by the pure IS/LM model. If prices are given, real balances remain unchanged and so does the position of the LM curve. Real production is determined by the point of intersection of the IS and LM curve, and this may give rise to a demand gap.

In order to establish the case for sticky wages or prices, perhaps the following arguments may be put forward.

Administered prices. A substantial number of prices are fixed or controlled by the state. In most contemporary economies, these cover freight tariffs, rates of broadcasting stations and public service corporations, rent rates and so on. Naturally, these prices do not necessarily respond to excess demands or supplies.

Fairness. In many cases, market participants do not merely desire a market-clearing price but one which is regarded as "fair", too. Though, in general, this is an impossibility because one variable is unlikely to accomplish two tasks at once, the economist has to take such desires into account when developing a positive theory.

Economic power. This argument is closely related to the previous one. In a real market economy, there is no benevolent auctioneer à la WALRAS whose sole interest consists in solving the allocation problem. Rather, there are strong interests concerned with distribution; economic power therefore exerts an important influence on pricing.

Market form. The former two arguments trace back to the fact that it is hard to find perfectly competitive markets in reality. On the contrary, oligopoly is the dominating market form; and it is known from the theory of oligopoly that the market participants behave very different from those in perfectly competitive markets.

Uncertainty. Transactions costs and imperfect foresight constitute an important cause of sticky prices. For instance, a firm faced with declining demand will not hectically alter prices but wait and see whether its marketing difficulties are *temporary* or *permanent*. In general, the firm will be justified in doing this, since price changes cause additional costs (e.g. printing of price lists), and customers are often interested in fairly constant prices.

Contracts. Finally, many prices are fixed by contract and cannot be altered in the short run. Wage rates are an example of this.

In the following model, we suppose that the nominal wage rate is exogenous in the short run – a premise that can be integrated into the complete Keynesian model without difficulty. As Keynesian theory primarily aims at explaining unemployment, we suppose that this wage rate, w, is above its equilibrium value. Thus we arrive at the model K''':

$$N = N^d\left(\frac{w}{P}\right) < N^s\left(\frac{w}{P}\right)$$ (K'''.1)

$$Y = f(N)$$ (K'''.2)

$$S(Y) = I(i)$$ (K'''.3)

$$L(Y,i) = \frac{M}{P}$$ (K'''.4)

$$\frac{w}{P} = \frac{\bar{w}}{P}$$ (K'''.5)

$$\rightarrow N_0, \left(\frac{w}{P}\right)_0, Y_0, i_0, P_0.$$

The model consists of five equations and five endogeneous variables, namely, N, w/P, Y, i, and P whereas the nominal wage rate is exogenous. In contrast to the previous models, it cannot be solved succesively.

(K'''.1) is the labor market. Because, due to our assumption, the nominal wage rate is too high, labor supply exceeds demand: there is unemployment. Hence, actual employment is determined by the firms whereas the households only succeed in selling some of their desired labor supply.

(K'''.2) represents the production function, which determines real output Y on the basis of labor input N_0.

(K'''.3) and (K'''.4) are the equations of the IS/LM model. Production Y_0 determines the rate of interest as well as the price level.

(K'''.5), finally, completes the circle: The real wage rate depends on the price level since the nominal wage rate is given. As a result, employment and production depend on the price level, too; thus it becomes obvious that the equations are interdependent and can only be solved simultaneously.

The graphical representation is better suited for illustrating the general solution.

In Quadrant III, the commodity demand curve, as in the complete Keynesian model, is downward sloping since neither an investment nor a liquidity trap was assumed. But, contrary to the complete Keynesian model, the commodity supply curve is upward sloping, a fact we must now substantiate.

An increase in prices from P_1 to P_0 lowers the real wage rate, as the hyperbola of Quadrant V suggests. This is because w is fixed and P is the denominator of w/P. Due to lower real wage rates, labor demand will *increase* and so will production. Hence, increasing prices correspond to an increasing supply of commodities: hence the commodity supply curve is upward sloping.

The point of intersection of the commodity demand and supply curves represents the solution of the model. Since this point is on the Y^s curve, it implies a consistent combination of prices and production; and since it is on the Y^d curve, it means

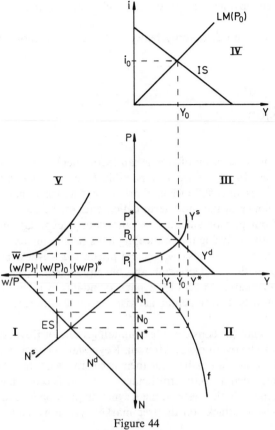

Figure 44
Sticky wage rates

simultaneous equilibrium in the capital and money market. The general equilibrium implies an excess supply, ES, in the labor market.

Remarkably, there is *no dichotomy* between the real and monetary sectors of this model: the price level influences both production and employment. The rigidity of the nominal wage rate causes the two sectors to be closely integrated. In this respect, the case of sticky wages is different from all previous models.

Of course, a fixed nominal wage too low in comparison to the equilibrium is also conceivable. The resulting situation would be similarly undesirable because employment is below its equilibrium level once more. Finally, we have to add that the commodity supply curve becomes backward bending if the price level exceeds a certain limit: then, the real wage rate falls short of its equilibrium value, $(w/P)*$ and now the laborers restrict employment since the wage rate appears unsufficient to them.

Let us conclude:

– Sticky wage rates incur either an excess supply or an excess demand in the labor market (except if they are by chance equal to $w*$).

- In both cases, employment and production fall short of their respective equilibrium values.
- Moreover, there is no dichotomy between the real and monetary sector in this model.

§45 Conclusion

Let us conclude our discussion of Keynesian theory here in order to review its most important features. In so far as it is possible to express the difference between Classical and Keynesian economics in short, we would argue that the latter is more inclined to take notice of the short-term deficiencies of the economic process.

Proceeding from phenomena such as uncertainty, expectations, and economic power, subsequently analyzing the connecting links such as interest inelasticity, absolute liquidity preference, or sticky wages and prices, the Keynesians finally arrive at a theoretical explanation of depression and unemployment. At the same time, they question the self-regulating forces of the market; and it is by no means surprising that their attitude towards governmental activism is quite different from that of the Classics.

On the other hand, the considerable common ground of Keynesian and Classical economics is not to be overlooked. After all, Keynesian theory merely demonstrated the possibility of certain crises but not their necessity. And, more important, these crises were not regarded as long-term tendencies towards economic collapse, but as temporary occurences. In this respect, the Keynesian position is fundamentally different from such frontal attacks on the free market system as made, for instance, by Marxist theory.

For the time being, we only want to mention two criticisms of Keynesian theory – besides the well-known general rejection of macroeconomics *per se* which, as we see it, is beneath contempt. First, the empirical relevance of investment and liquidity traps is doubtful. This is indeed a serious objection; and it is too often overlooked that these two extreme assumptions are necessary prerequisites for all that is truly revolutionary in Keynesian economics. The consequences of sticky wages and prices could have been, and in fact were, analyzed by Classical theory too; and that excessive nominal wages incur unemployment, as in our third scenario, is by no means surprising to any Classical economist – it is the very essence of his doctrine.

The second criticism comes from the Postkeynesians. They find fault with the fact that Keynesian economics is so strongly rooted in Classical theory and therefore reduces KEYNES' own economics to some insignificant special cases. Furthermore, they argue that this pseudo-Keynesianism is confined to the short run and hence irrelevant.

But, however that may be, Keynesian theory has become a second orthodoxy alongside Classical economics. In the next chapter, the reader will soon recognize that the political inferences of the two orthodoxies are more disparate than the theories themselves. Thus, the quarrel about KEYNES is especially important in economic policy.

Further Reading

KEYNES, J.M. (1936) The General Theory of Employment, Interest and Money. London. Reprinted 1964 New York etc.: Harcourt and Brace
KLEIN, L. (1966²) The Keynesian Revolution. New York: Macmillan
LINDAUER J. Ed. (1967) Macroeconomic Readings. New York etc.: The Free Press
MUELLER, M.G. Ed. (1967) Readings in Macroeconomics. New York etc.: Hilt, Rinehart and Winston

Chapter VI. Political Implications: A Comparison

All economic reasoning strives towards practical and especially political ends. *Positive* theories in this respect do not simply give "recommendations" to policy makers but show what measures must be taken in order to attain *given* goals; whereas the definition of these goals is left to government and to society as a whole.

It is questionable, however, whether *there is* any positive economic theory in this sense. Experience shows that the cold steel of analysis assumes a different temper when entering the field of economic policy. In economics more than in other sciences, knowledge and interest are closely related, and a truly positive theory must be considered an ideal.

With respect to the present chapter a second point must be emphasized. The models under discussion are by no means in an adequate form for immediate application; and it would be a blunder to employ them directly for deciding on practical matters. We deal with abstract theory, and abstract theory aims solely to supply the reader with an "apparatus of the mind". Beyond this, the present chapter is designed to compare the two former orthodoxies, namely, Classical and Keynesian theory, and a proper discussion of macroeconomic policy is not intended.

On the other hand it would be far from correct to think that the following simple, abstract models are of no practical relevance. Quite the opposite is true. At all times, it has been the most elementary models which, being understood by a tolerably large proportion of the public, have become the foundations of real policies: and never has a model exercised a stronger impact on governmental behaviour than our poor income-expenditure model of § 35.

§ 46 The Role of Government.
Goals and Means of Economic Policy

What economic tasks are the state's responsibility? Obviously, the answer to this question depends on the economic system; the question is only relevant to a *mixed economy*, since, in a pure market or planned economy, the responsibilities are uniquely determined. Now, all western economies are mixed economies in the sense that the prevalence of the market mechanism is supplemented by state interventions.

Let us start answering the above question by enumerating the possible *goals* of economic policy first. According to MUSGRAVE[1], these can be embraced under three headings, namely, the goals of

---

1 Cf. MUSGRAVE, R. (1959) The Theory of Public Finance. New York etc.: McGraw-Hill.

- allocation,
- distribution, and
- stabilization.

The government can try to change the *allocation* of scarce resources if it considers the given allocation undesirable. For instance, it can increase the supply of certain *merit goods*, such as education, by subsidizing them; or it may correct the allocation of goods when there are *external economies*.

Further, the *distribution* of income between the members of society is subject to governmental intervention if the original distribution is not desired by the majority. Means of changing the distribution are a progressive income tax or transfer payments.

Finally, *stabilization* policy concerns the performance of the total economy. It aims at attaining some "general equilibrium", which is often thought of as a state in which

- the price level is stable,
- full employment prevails,
- the country's balance of payments is in equilibrium, and
- the economy grows steadily.

Allocation and distribution are microeconomic problems by nature; hence we have to confine our debate to stabilization policy. Moreover, we exclude the goals of external equilibrium and steady growth since we deal solely with the static theory of a closed economy. However, the remaining economic problems, inflation and unemployment, are sufficiently important to justify a detailed analysis.

In order to make the two goals theoretically operational, we define *price stability* as a rate of inflation equal to zero and *full employment* as the absence of underemployment in our theoretical sense, i.e. the realization of N^*, the point of intersection of the labor demand and supply schedules.

In pursuing the above-mentioned goals, the government can employ three different sets of *means* or *instruments*, namely

- monetary policy,
- fiscal policy, and
- direct controls.

Monetary policy, broadly speaking, can be divided into means of influencing the quantity of money, or the rate of interest. In the former case, the central bank tries to control an appropriately defined quantity of money whereas, in the latter, it seeks to stabilize a representative rate of interest. The central banks of most Western countries are more or less independent of the government but always obliged to adopt the same general economic goals.

Fiscal policy covers all governmental actions in so far as they apply to the budgets of the central, regional, and local authorities. Frequently, this term is used in the narrower sense of those budgetary tools applied to the goal of stabilization. For the reasons outlined above, we will only deal with fiscal policy in this narrower sense.

Direct controls, finally, are the strongest set of instruments. The government, or parliament, directly intervenes individual decisions by dictating, for instance, certain prices or wages. In theory, however, this term can also be used in the sense of *price and wage policy*: Frequently, we will analyze the effects of price and wage adjustments without presuming that these are carried out by the state. This difference is important since in many Western countries, the state is not directly responsible for price and wage alterations.

With regard to the question posed at the outset – What economic tasks are the state's responsibility? – two fundamentally different attitudes can be distinguished: they are called *economic liberalism* and *activism*. On the issue of stabilization policy, these read as follows:

Attitude of economic liberalism:

– There is no need to stabilize a market economy, since it is stable in itself.
– Moreover, the government is *unable* to apply an efficacious stabilization policy.
– And if it tries, the result will be false, disproportionate, or lagged impacts which have *de*stabilizing effects.

Attitude of activism:

– A market economy must be stabilized since it is not stable at all times.
– The government alone is able to perform an effective stabilization.
– And it succeeds in doing so by applying monetary and fiscal tools as well as direct controls.

Obviously, the adherents disagree upon the three issues of whether stabilization is *necessary*, whether it is *theoretically possible* and whether it can be carried out *in practice*. Their diverging opinions result from differences both in ideology and theory. Here, we are chiefly interested in theory; thus, it will be shown in the following sections that Classical theory is somewhat connected with economic liberalism and Keynesian theory with activism.

This is the reason for the location of the present chapter: Having outlined Classical and Keynesian theory we are now able to compare these two doctrines and their respective political inferences. Those theories put foward in Part Three will yield important theoretical insight; yet the principal political issues remain unchanged. Therefore, a further chapter about policy is superfluous. Let us now discuss the effects of fiscal, monetary, and other policy tools in the Classical and Keynesian model.

§47 Fiscal Policy

As already indicated, the term *fiscal policy* comprises all governmental means that are directed towards the goal of stabilization. The governmental *budget* offsets receipts against expenditures in the manner of a balance sheet, but it depicts flows, not stocks. Disregarding its numerous entries, any budget exhibits the following form:

Expenditures	Receipts
Government expenditure (G)	Tax receipts (T) Deficit (D)

Figure 45
The Budget

Government expenditure, G, here denotes the value of those goods and services bought by the government; we neglect factor purchases and transfers. These goods and services are physically identical to those demanded by the private sector, that is, they constitute a part of real output Y.

The government is supposed to collect a single *lump-sum tax*, T: it requires the households to pay annual taxes irrespective of their income or economic activity. Therefore, we can assume that the tax does not induce any substitution effects but solely diminishes the disposable income of households. Put differently, the functions indicating private behaviour remain the same, though their values may change. Tax receipts, like government expenditure, are measured in commodity units.

In a certain period there is a *budget deficit*, D, if government expenditure exceeds tax receipts:

$$D := G - T. \tag{151}$$

The budget deficit is financed entirely by borrowing, that is, by issuing bonds. The alternative possibility of financing it by printing money is excluded since this is no "pure" fiscal policy but a mixed fiscal and monetary policy.

As suggested by equation (151), any choice of G and T simultaneously determines the budget deficit. When borrowing, the government enters our capital market and behaves there like any market participant: it does not issue forced loans. Assuming that the government bonds are considered identical to those issued by the private firms, we can assume a single rate of interest in the following.

By introducing the government, three modifications to the preceding models have to be made.

First, the household's *budget constraint* must be modified as the households are now obliged to pay taxes:

$$Y - T = C + S. \tag{152}$$

Comparison of this equation with (37) shows that real *disposable* income has been substituted for real income. Real disposable income is the term $Y - T$ which indicates what is left of real income, Y, after deducting real taxes, T.

Second, government expenditure must be added to consumption and investment demand when calculating aggregate commodity demand:

$$Y^d = C + I + G. \tag{153}$$

Third, we have already recognized that the government finances the budget deficit by issuing bonds. Therefore, the budget deficit, $D = G - T$, has to enter the equilibrium condition of the capital market:

$$S = I + (G - T). \tag{154}$$

In the following, these three changes must be taken into account in order to analyze the impacts of government behaviour.

§48 Fiscal Policy in the Classical Case

We are now about to undertake the analysis of fiscal policy in the Classical model. It has to be emphasized at the outset that this kind of policy is not *necessary* since the economy is bound to approach the full employment equilibrium by itself.

But what happens if the government employs fiscal measures all the same? We can suppose first that these will not alter the household's labor supply which is solely dependent on the real wage rate. Therefore, employment is unaffected and commodity supply remains at its original full employment level. Let us now examine the specific effects of government expenditure on aggregate demand. *Specific effects* are those that arise from isolated variations on the expenditure side disregarding variations in receipts. Of course this cannot happen really but it is analytically helpful.

Assuming that originally the government made no expenditures at all, and then raised them to G, aggregate commodity demand will increase by G, too:

$$Y^d = C + I + G. \tag{155}$$

In equilibrium, aggregate commodity demand must match aggregate supply which – as we saw above – is constant:

$$Y^d \stackrel{!}{=} Y^s = \text{const.} \tag{156}$$

These two equations already show that any increase in government expenditure necessarily crowds out an exactly equivalent amount of private expenditure. This is termed a *total crowding out*. The crowding out is called *total* because every unit of governmental purchases is a substitute for exactly one unit of private purchases.

But what are the economic forces that bring about such a crowding out? The answer to this question depends on the way of financing the government expenditure; and since the goverment has two options (taxes and debt) the answer must be twofold.

I. Loan Financing

Let us assume in the first instance that goverment expenditure is entirely financed by debt, and no taxes at all are collected:

$$G = D \quad \text{and} \quad T = 0. \tag{157}$$

Thus, the real budget deficit, D, is equivalent to the amount of government expenditure, G. Hence, there arises in the capital market an additional demand for capital of $D = G$:

$$S(i) = I(i) + G. \tag{158}$$

The following figure shows the consequences of this:

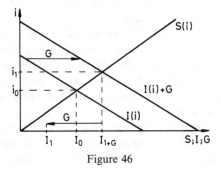

Figure 46

The capital demand curve is shifted to the right, its horizontal distance from the original curve being G, the additional capital demand. This incurs the following:

- The rate of interest rises from i_0 to i_1.
- Savings also increase because, according to the Classical assumption, a higher rate of interest induces people to save more.
- Investment demand declines as borrowing becomes more costly to the firms.
- Therefore, *total* borrowing, i.e. $I_1 + G$, increases, but less than G because I declines.

In sum, there is a *partial crowding out* in the capital market: partial because savings increase and, hence, investment does not decrease as much as government borrowing rises. Yet, with respect to the commodity market, the crowding out is nevertheless total: Any rise in savings means an equal reduction in consumption; and the *sum* of consumption and investment demand declines to the extent that government expenditure has risen.

The proportions in which the crowding out is distributed between investment and consumption depends on the interest elasticity of savings. If savings are perfectly interest inelastic (the capital supply schedule is vertical), consumption remains unchanged, and government debt only depresses investment. The greater is the interest elasticity of savings, the more consumption and the less investment will be crowded out. Because savings are usually considered to be fairly interest inelastic, we presume that primarily investment demand is crowded out. This worried the Classical economists who argued that "productive" private expenditure would be displaced by "unproductive" government expenditure. Stressing the importance of capital accumulation, they strongly opposed debt financing.

II. Tax Financing

If government expenditure is entirely financed by collecting taxes, we have

$$G = T \quad \text{and} \quad D = 0. \tag{159}$$

Real disposable income of households will decrease by an amount corresponding to the tax payments:

$$Y - T = C + S. \tag{160}$$

By means of this formula we immediately recognize that the burden of government expenditure is divided between consumption and savings because real income, Y, is the same as before. A total crowding out takes place, the distribution of which depends on the household's preferences.

The decrease in savings will diminish investment by the same amount. Therefore, in the case of tax financing too, both consumption and investment demand will decline. In this respect, the two ways of financing government expenditure are the same. But tax financing is likely to have a stronger impact on consumption and a weaker one on investment than loan financing; and this is one reason why the Classics were in favor of the first alternative.

Let us conclude. Within the Classical framework, any increase in government expenditure, be it financed by loans or taxes, crowds out an equal amount of private expenditure. This follows directly from the assumption that additional government spending does not stimulate households to work more: employment and output remain the same.

There will be changes in the distribution of production between the private and the public sector, the interest rate, savings, and consumption and investment demand. Whether such changes are desirable is a question of allocation policy; with respect to stabilization, government spending does neither good nor harm.

§49 Fiscal Policy in the Complete Keynesian Case

When disussing the complete Keynesian model, in §40, we soon became aware that its results do not diverge greatly from the Classical case notwithstanding that they are to some extend differently substantiated. Thus it is hardly astonishing that the political inferences are very similar, too. However, in order to prepare ourselves for the coming sections we want to discuss them in some detail. Again, we distinguish two methods of financing government expenditure.

I. Loan Financing

The government may finance expenditure by borrowing, such that

$$G = D \quad \text{and} \quad T = 0. \tag{161}$$

The equation of the IS curve is now to be modified since the government enters the capital market as an additional borrower:

$$\text{IS:} \quad S(Y) = I(i) + G. \tag{162}$$

G, government expenditure, is substituted for D, the public deficit, since we are assuming there is no taxation. A positive amount of public borrowing causes the IS curve to shift to the right:

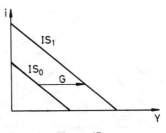

Figure 47

This can be easily explained: As capital demand is increased by $G = D$, real income must be *higher* at any given interest rate in order to stimulate savings. Or, at any level of real income, the corresponding rate of interest must be *higher* in order to reduce investment.

To calculate the horizontal distance between the original and the shifted IS curve, we employ the chain rule and differentiate equation (162) with respect to G (that is,

$S(Y)$ is first differentiated with respect to Y, and then Y^d with respect to G):

$$\frac{dS}{dY}\frac{dY^d}{dG}\bigg|_{dT=0} = 1 \tag{163}$$

$$\Rightarrow \frac{dY^d}{dG}\bigg|_{dT=0} = \frac{1}{\dfrac{dS}{dY}} = \frac{1}{1-C'} \quad \left(\text{since } \frac{dC}{dY}+\frac{dS}{dY}=1\right). \tag{164}$$

The index "$dT = 0$" means that government expenditure is solely financed by borrowing, not taxes. Formula (164) tells us that the IS curve shifts by the amount of additional government expenditure, multiplied by the simple multiplier $m = 1/(1 - C')$ which was derived in §36. Thus, additional government expenditure has the same impact as an increase in autonomous investment. However, this is but one chapter of the story because the rate of interest was kept constant.

In order to trace out the total impact we have to recollect that, in the complete Keynesian model, there is full employment; and aggregate production is determined solely by the labor market. Hence it must be expected that government expenditure, even if financed by loans, will incur a crowding out. This conjecture proves true:

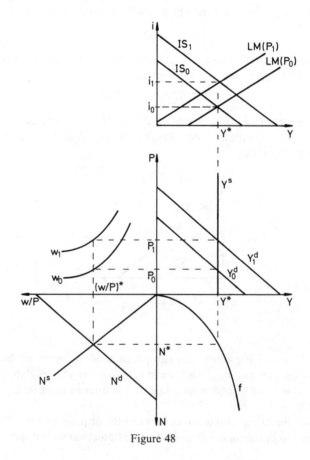

Figure 48

In Figure 48, the IS curve shifts to the right in the manner described above since the government creates an additional demand in the capital market. What is more, the aggregate commodity demand curve, Y^d, shifts as well because of the additional commodity demand that arises from government spending. These two effects are basically the same. Two adjustment processes will therefore take place:

First, the rate of interest increases owing to the rightward shift of the IS curve. This is a movement along the $LM(P_0)$ curve. Since the equilibrium value of Y increases, the individuals consider additional cash balances appropriate; they try to get them by selling bonds; and this raises the rate of interest. Consequently, investment demand will be reduced.

Second, the price level also increases since commodity demand, now increased by G, confronts a *constant* commodity supply which is equal to its full employment level. The equilibrium condition

$$Y^s = C(Y) + I(i) + G. \tag{165}$$

requires that prices rise. This, in turn, causes the LM curve to shift to the *left* because real cash balances decrease. The movement of the LM curve to the left entails still higher rates of interest and thus still lower levels of investment. And this process continues until the equilibrium condition for the commodity market, (165), is fulfilled. Then, the movement of the price level stops and the new equilibrium of the system is attained.

It should be noted that consumption demand is left *unchanged*, since real income is the same as before (i.e., equal to Y^*). From equation (165) it follows immediately that government borrowing crowds out investment demand only. And, again, the crowding out is *total*. Thus, the case of loan financing in the Keynesian model differs from the same situation in the Classical model in that only investment demand is depressed. This difference is due to the assumed interest inelasticity of savings in the Keynesian model.

II. Tax Financing

Let us assume now that government spending is entirely financed by taxes:

$$G = T \quad \text{and} \quad D = 0. \tag{166}$$

In this case, consumption and savings depend on *real disposable income*:

$$C = C(Y - T) \tag{167}$$

$$S = S(Y - T). \tag{168}$$

Demand in the capital market remains unchanged here because the government does not borrow, and investment demand is not altered by the household's tax payments. But capital *supply* diminishes since, according to (168), households will save less. Hence the IS curve has to be modified in the following manner:

$$S(Y - T) = I(i). \tag{169}$$

Looked at graphically, the IS curve shifts to the right by the amount of government spending (or taxing). This is because real income, Y, must exceed its previous level by $G = T$ in order to leave real disposable income, $Y - T$, at its former level:

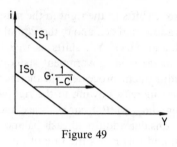

Figure 49

Note: Because we have assumed that government spending and taxation are originally equal to zero, the symbols G, dG, T, and dT can be used interchangeably.

Differentiating equation (169) with respect to G proves that the horizontal distance between the two IS curves is exactly equal to the amount of government spending:

$$\frac{dS}{d(Y-T)} \cdot \frac{d(Y-T)}{dG} = 0 \quad \text{with} \quad \frac{dS}{d(Y-T)} = \frac{dS}{dY} = \text{const.} \tag{170}$$

$$\Leftrightarrow \frac{dS}{dY} \cdot \left[\frac{dY^d}{dG}\bigg|_{dG=dT} - \frac{dT}{dG} \right] = 0 \tag{171}$$

$$\Leftrightarrow \frac{dS}{dY} \left[\frac{dY^d}{dG}\bigg|_{dG=dT} - 1 \right] = 0 \tag{172}$$

$$\Leftrightarrow \frac{dY^d}{dG}\bigg|_{dG=dT} = 1. \tag{173}$$

Since the multiplier equals 1, we recognize that the impact of government expenditure on the IS curve is *weaker* than in the case of loan financing where the multiplier was 1/(1-C′).

Despite this quantitative difference, the total impact of tax financed government expenditure is very similar to the former case of loan financing. This can be seen from Figure 50 on the next page.

In the first instance, the IS curve shifts to the right by the amount of government spending. This raises the rate of interest. The commodity demand curve, too, shifts to the right by the amount of government spending. The equilibrium condition for the commodity market differs from (165) in that consumption depends on real disposable income:

$$Y^s = C(Y-T) + I(i) + G. \tag{174}$$

In equilibrium, aggregate commodity demand must match aggregate supply which is given by the labor market and the production function. In the first instance, additional government expenditure will increase aggregate commodity demand by exactly dG. But since it is financed by taxes, consumption will decrease simultaneously because real disposable income is diminished. The former decrease can be calculated by means of the marginal propensity to consume; and because this pro-

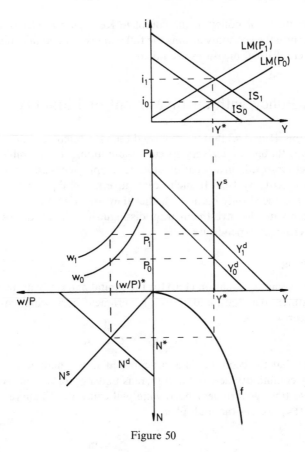

Figure 50

pensity is less than one, the reduction in consumption will not offset the increase in aggregate demand that is due to government expenditure:

$$dC = - C' \cdot dT \Rightarrow |dC| < dT. \tag{175}$$

Thus, we are left with an excess demand in the commodity market, which will cause prices to rise and the LM curve to shift to the left. The rise in prices, and the movement of the LM curve, continue until aggregate commodity demand matches the given supply. Then, general equilibrium is re-established.

Let us summarize the results. With respect to real income and employment, loan financing and tax financing are practically identical, since neither of these alternatives gives rise to any lasting deviation from the full employment levels. The rate of interest, the price level, and the nominal wage rate will increase in both cases. But the *difference* between the two methods of financing government expenditure is that the former *solely* crowds out investment demand while the latter causes *both* investment and consumption to decline because real disposable income of households is diminished. A second difference consists in the *stronger* impact of loan financing on prices, wages, and interest.

But, all in all, fiscal policy in the complete Keynesian model is *superflous* and *ineffectual* because the economy attains the full employment equilibrium itself; and is merely left there if fiscal measures are taken.

§ 50 Fiscal Policy with an Investment or Liquidity Trap

It was in sections 41 and 42 that we discussed the investment and liquidity traps. We discovered that, though under very special assumptions, it is possible for a market economy to get "trapped" in a situation of under-employment and under-production, which it cannot rectify by itself. In such a case, governmental policies are undoubtedly called for, and we need only discuss whether they are effective.

Let us begin with the investment trap, distinguishing again the two methods of financing government expenditure.

I. Loan Financing

Here we have to employ equation (150) for the capital market (with perfectly interest inelastic investment demand), adding to it government borrowing (equal to government expenditure):

$$S(Y) = I + G \quad (G = D). \tag{176}$$

We assume that the economy is in a depressed state where actual production is determined by commodity demand and there is under-employment. As explained in the previous section, government borrowing will cause the IS curve to shift to the right. From (164), we get the multiplier

$$\frac{dY^d}{dG}\bigg|_{dT=0} = \frac{1}{1 - C'} =: m. \tag{177}$$

Aggregate demand in the commodity market will rise by m times the amount of government expenditure, where m is the simple multiplier. So far that is nothing new. But we must recognize that here, increasing commodity demand means increasing *production* as well, since production is supposed to be constrained by demand. Thus, production will increase by m times the amount of government expenditure, and, consequently, employment will rise too.

When an investment trap prevails, government borrowing will indeed increase the rate of interest: but this will not reduce investment demand since the latter is perfectly interest inelastic. As the price level is indeterminate in this case, and as commodity supply exceeds demand, no crowding out can result. On the contrary, there emerges a *crowding in*! Let us suppose, for instance, that the marginal propensity to consume amounts to 0.8, which means that the simple multiplier is 5. Hence, if the government increases its expenditure by one unit, and finances this by borrowing, aggregate commodity demand and production will increase by *five* units. Deducting government expenditure, four additional units of private expenditure are left. In short, fiscal policy results in *pump-priming* of the economy.

Adjusting the budget in accordance with the economy's needs, the government is able to fill the demand gap completely, as shown in the following figure:

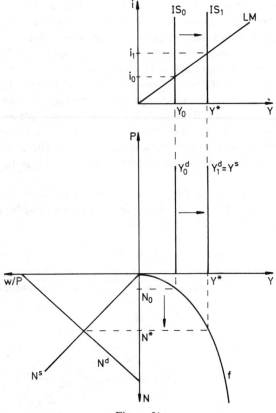

Figure 51

By government spending, production is raised from Y_0 to Y^*, and employment from N_0 to N^*, that is, a state of full employment is attained. This intriguing feature of fiscal policy makes it appear very attractive: for it is both necessary and effective when an investment trap prevails.

II. Tax Financing

When there is an investment trap, and the government finances its additional expenditure entirely by collecting taxes, we are inclined to suppose that this will have no favourable impact because the household's disposable income is reduced. But this conjecture is false. In order to prove that, let us recall the multiplier (173) which refers to tax financed government expenditure:

$$\left.\frac{dY^d}{dG}\right|_{dG=dT} = 1. \tag{178}$$

It tells us that an increase in government expenditure by one unit, if financed by taxes, will augment aggregate commodity demand by just one unit. Thus, when there is an investment trap with under-production and under-employment, production will

increase by one unit, too. Equation (178), first derived by the Norwegian TRYGVE
HAAVELMO, is termed the *Haavelmo-theorem*. According to the Haavelmo-theorem,
even tax-financed government expenditure is an appropriate measure for curing
depressions. As real income rises exactly by the amount of public spending, unemployment will decline, and there is no crowding out.

Let us consider this mathematical proposition in economic terms. Any dollar of
additional public spending will raise aggregate commodity demand in the first instance by one dollar, and it will diminish household's disposable income by the same
amount. Accordingly, consumption demand will decline – but by *less* than one dollar
since the marginal propensity to consume is less than one. Therefore, though smaller,
an expensionary impact remains, the ultimate reason for this being that the government does not save.

Finally, we turn to the *liquidity trap*, a case known to be very similar to the
investment trap. Here, the rate of interest is fixed by absolute liquidity preference,
although investment demand is interest elastic:

$$\text{IS:} \quad S(Y) = I(i) + G. \tag{179}$$

Governmental borrowing does not result in a crowding out because the rate of interest
will not rise, and there are idle resources. We confine ourselves to a graphical exposition:

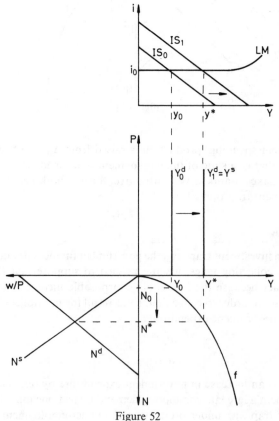

Figure 52

Let us summarize the results for an investment or liquidity trap. In these cases, the market economy cannot regain full employment, and that suggests the need for governmental measures. An appropriate remedy consists in increasing government expenditure, which brings about a rise in aggregate demand and thus a rise in production and employment. The manner of *financing* this expenditure does not make a difference with respect to the qualitative performance; but loan financed spending turned out to have a stronger impact than taxation. In the former case, the multiplier is equal to $1/(1 - C')$, that is, greater than one, whereas in the latter it is just one. Thus, in both cases there is no crowding out.

§ 51 Fiscal Policy with Sticky Wages

In the scenario of § 44, unemployment was not caused by extreme values of interest elasticity (of investment or liquidity demand), but by excessive real wages. The analytical treatment of this case is more difficult than the handling of the previous "traps", and we will confine ourselves to a graphical exposition[2]. For this purpose, the case

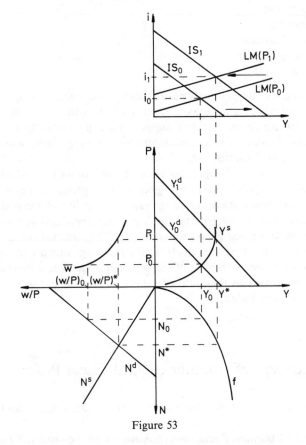

Figure 53

___
2 Cf. Subsection *4.6 of the Mathematical Appendix for an analytical derivation.

of loan financed government expenditure is selected, as it is clear from the explanations above that tax financing engenders the same, though weaker, effects.

Consider the following figure:

Clearly, the operation of fiscal policy with given nominal wage rates is rather complex since the values of all variables change. Therefore, we break it down into several steps:

- In the first instance, both the IS and the Y^d curve shift to the right, because the government exerts additional demand for capital and commodities.
- The rate of interest and the price level will rise as a consequence. Further, the impact of increasing prices is two-fold:
- First, the *real* wage rate, w/P, declines as w is fixed by assumption. Hence, labor demand, employment, and production increase.
- Second, the LM curve shifts to the *left* because real cash balances, M/P, diminish. This effect counteracts the original, rightward, shift of the IS curve.

Yet, as we show in the mathematical appendix, these opposing forces do not outweigh the original ones. In the end, an equilibrium is attained which exhibits

- higher employment,
- higher production,
- a higher rate of interest,
- a higher price level, and
- a lower real wage rate.

The multiplier, dY/dG, is strictly *positive* though not necessarily greater than one; therefore, a *partial crowding out* may arise. By partial crowding out we mean that the multiplier is between zero and one. For, suppose it is equal to 0.6: then, any additional unit of government spending will increase production by 0.6 units, while 0.4 units of privat expenditure are crowded out.

To summarize, if nominal wage rates are sticky and above their equilibrium levels, an expansionary fiscal policy produces higher levels of production and employment, a higher price level, and a *lower* real wage rate. The decline of the real wage rate is inevitable because there is no "demand gap", and only lower real wages will stimulate firms to hire more labor and so to produce more. Thus, an evaluation of this policy has to take into account that the effects on the real wage rate are identical to those which result from a direct lowering of the nominal wage. The important difference between the two measures is that, in the former, the government sector will increase, and there will be some inflation.

§52 The Concept of Counter-cyclical Fiscal Policy

"Things, left to themselves, turn from bad to worse."   (MURPHY's LAW)

The existence of business fluctuations has always been considered a serious problem; and this empirical fact stood in an odd relation to the Classical model of full employment. *Business fluctuations* are commonly regarded as oscillations in the general level of economic activity, as measured by certain indicators. If these fluctuations exhibit a fairly constant wavy shape, one of these waves is referred to as a *business cycle*:

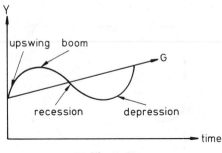

Figure 54

The slope of the straight line, G, in Figure 54 illustrates the path of long-term growth, while the actual performance staggers around this path. Production and employment increase in the *up-swing* (or recovery) until reaching their maximum in the *boom*. Then, *recession* sets in, finally giving rise to *depression* at the bottom of the business cycle. Thereafter, a new phase of prosperity comes into being.

In the climate of Keynesian theory the idea gained ground that business cycles were no inevitable fate, but could be mitigated, perhaps even obviated, by government action. Let us assume an *investment trap* in order to illustrate this. Owing to the interest inelasticity of investment demand, states of under-employment or over-employment are likely to arise according to whether effective demand falls short of, or exceeds, its full employment level. Effective demand itself depends primarily on the expectations of investors. Now we can construct a very simple theory of the business cycle proceeding from the hypotheses that investors' expectations will become more pessimistic in bad times, incurring a still further decrease in production. Then, in depression, a sudden change in expectations occurs (a political occurence? an invention?) – and from now on optimistic expectations accelerate, which is at once the consequence and the cause of the up-swing. Although the investment trap is of course an altogether impossible situation, something like this appears to be the Keynesian picture of the business cycle.

The idea of *counter-cyclical fiscal policy* rests on the notion that the government alone can swim against the tide. When there is a recession, government may pursue a policy of deficit spending, stimulating economic activity, and preventing a deep depression. If, on the other hand, a boom occurs, fiscal policy should be restrictive. Let us illustrate this by means of a figure (cf. the next page).

A hypothetical business cycle in the absence of governmental means is depicted in the topmost figure. During the first half of the cycle, the government pursues a restrictive buget policy, that is, tax receipts exceed government expenditure and are partly used to build up a reserve. Thereby, excessive effective demand is reduced, and an overheating can be avoided.

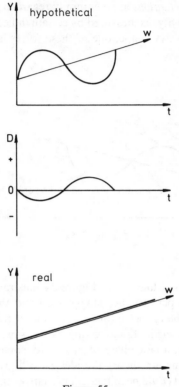

Figure 55
The workings of counter-cylical fiscal policy

During recession, the government disburses the reserves and creates additional commodity demand. The curve of the budget surplus, in the middle figure, is *flatter* than that of the notional business cycle because the effects of the budget are amplified by the multiplier process.

Thus, these are the characteristic features of an ideal counter-cyclical policy:

– It renders a constant economic performance possible as shown in the bottom figure;
– and no problem of public debt comes into being since reserves are amassed and disbursed alternately.

Looked at from this Keynesian point of view, no clumsier policy can be imagined than that of balancing the budget annually. If tax receipts decline in recession, and the government reduces its expenditure correspondingly, this will *reinforce* the business cycle according to the Haavelmo-theorem. Thus, the Keynesian recommendation reads: Use the budget to stabilize the economy and to prevent serious under-employment or inflation, by adjusting the surplus or deficit accordingly.

The concept of counter-cyclical fiscal policy remained by no means in the realm of pure theory. Quite on the contrary, it attained the utmost political importance all over the world from around the middle of our century. On the other hand, various problems concerning its performance arose in practice; and the concept was criticized on both theoretical and empirical grounds. The four essential criticisms of counter-cyclical fiscal policy – ranked according to their fundamentality – are the following:

The theoretical criticism: Keynesian theory is no adequate basis for making political inferences. It employs an utterly naive model, perhaps even involves logical errors, and ignores important aspects of reality.

The empirical criticism: Though Keynesian theory provides a consistent theoretical explanation, it is irrelevant empirically, since its essential assumptions, namely, the investment and liquidity trap, are never met in reality. Business cycles are caused by other, for instance monetary or structural, events.

The technological criticism: Granted that Keynesian theory is both theoretically consistent and empirically relevant, its prescriptions are nevertheless infeasible in practice. Diagnostic, decision-, and other lags are so significant that any measure, though adequate in principle, is likely to be taken at the wrong instant or in the wrong dosage. Therefore, "counter-cyclical" policy is apt to be destabilizing instead of stabilizing.

The political criticism: Even supposing that a counter-cyclical fiscal policy were feasible in practice, to be effective it imposes too strong a spending limitation in the boom. Politicians are unable to build up reserves in the face of public pressure, when this is theoretically necessary. Instead, they use the "expansionary" budget deficit as an *excuse* for increasing the public sector.

§ 53 Monetary Policy

We are now ready to move on to monetary policy as a further set of government policy measures. The theory of monetary policy is a broad subject. The main problems consist in

- finding an economically appropriate definition of money,
- determining which institutions are capable of controlling the money supply, and
- investigating the means by which the money supply can be effectively controlled.

These questions alone merit a whole book, and we are unable to answer them within our present introduction to macroeconomics. Instead, we want to analyze the *basic impact* of changes in the money supply, regardless of the measures that brought them about. In order to do this, three assumptions are made:

- The quantity of money is appropriately defined,
- the central bank *alone* is capable of controlling the money supply, and
- the *helicopter-effect* is assumed to be the only means of changing the money supply: We imagine that the central bank distributes fresh money by means of a "helicopter" in order to alter all individual cash balances proportionally. Thus there are no distributional effects.

§54 Monetary Policy in the Classical Case

The effect of a monetary change in the Classical model can be easily demonstrated by using the Cambridge equation, (61):

$$M = k \cdot P \cdot Y. \qquad (180)$$

Real income, Y, is determined by the labor market and the production function; thus, in the Cambridge equation, it is treated as *given*. The Cambridge k, depending on the individuals' propensity to hold cash, is assumed exogenous, too; most notably, it is independent of the interest rate. Hence, when the quantity of money increases, only the *price level* (and nominal wage rates) will increase whereas all other variables remain unchanged. The rise in prices lasts until *real cash balances* have declined to their original level. We termed this the Cambridge-effect:

Increasing quantity of money (cash balances) → increasing commodity demand → increasing prices → declining real cash balances.

Starting from general equilibrium any doubling of the quantity of money incurs an exact doubling of the price level because this alone leaves real cash balances, M/P, unchanged.

In sum, the *sole* effect of expansionary monetary policy is *inflation*; monetary policy is unable to influence the real variables of the model. Therefore, the Classical economists suggested that the monetary authorities should maintain a stable price level. An expansionary monetary policy was recommended for the case of economic growth only: If real income, Y, exhibits long-term growth, any constant money supply would force a permanent *deflation* which could easily be prevented by changing the quantity of money accordingly. But this is no *discretionary* stabilizing policy, but a fixed policy. We will return to this in Chapter IX (Monetarism).

§55 Monetary Policy in the Complete Keynesian Case

As remarked on several occasions, the complete Keynesian model is very similar to the Classical one; in particular full employment prevails. Thus, it is to be expected – and is indeed true – that monetary policy will entail no real changes at all, because there are no "rigidities" or "illusions". However, the transmission mechanism is somewhat different:

Due to an increase in the quantity of money, the LM curve will shift to the right, since the increased cash balances are required only if real income rises, or the rate of interest declines. In the first instance, the equilibrium rate of interest will thus fall to i_2 in Figure 56.

Investment demand will therefore increase, the aggregate commodity demand curve will shift to the right, and – commodity supply being given – we are left with an *excess demand* in the commodity market. Consequently, commodity prices will increase. With P rising, real cash balances, M/P, will decrease, which causes the LM curve to shift to the left. This process persists until excess commodity demand is eliminated or, equivalently, until the LM curve has shifted to its original position. Then a new equilibrium is established which differs from the previous one only in so far as nominal cash balances, nominal prices, and nominal wage rates have risen

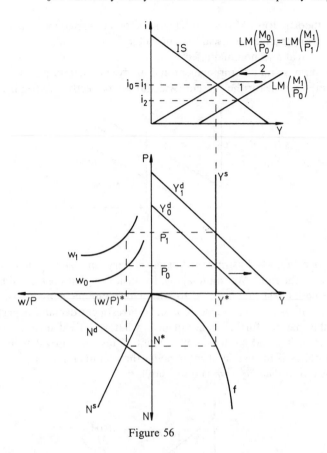

Figure 56

proportionally. Real cash balances M_1/P_1 and the real wage rate w_1/P_1 are the same as before.

The analogy between the Classical and the complete Keynesian model is striking: In both cases, any doubling of M merely incurs a doubling of P and w; the models differ only with respect to the transmission mechanism. In the Classical model, changes in the price level are brought about by the Cambridge-effect, which maintains a direct relationship between nominal cash balances and aggregate commodity demand. In the complete Keynesian model, on the other hand, the same rise in prices is due to the Keynes-effect, describing the indirect relationship between nominal cash balances, the rate of interest, and finally investment demand.

All in all, monetary policy in the complete Keynesian case is both superflous and ineffectual with regard to the real magnitudes.

§ 56 Monetary Policy with an Investment or Liquidity Trap

"Money doesn't matter."

Now we pass to the effects of monetary policy when there is an investment or liquidity trap. Hereby it will become clear how *Keynesianism*, a doctrine appealing to the monetary theorist JOHN MAYNARD KEYNES, soon converted into *fiscalism*, a position ascribing stronger effects to fiscal than monetary policy – and, in the extreme, denying the latter all real and nominal effects.

Let us suppose under-employment and analyze monetary policy by means of the IS/LM model which for the present case suffices perfectly. We begin with an *investment trap*:

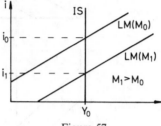

Figure 57

The above diagram illustrates an "expansionary" monetary policy, that is, the LM curve shifts to the right. We can imagine, for instance, that the central bank intended to reduce the interest rate in order to stimulate economic activity. The reduction in the interest rate is accomplished – but since investment demand is perfectly interest inelastic this has no further consequences whatever. Real income remains at the previous level, Y_0, and so does employment. Thus, in contrast to fiscal measures, monetary policy is incapable of influencing the real magnitudes.

The case of a *liquidity trap* is quite similar:

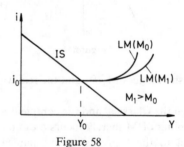

Figure 58

Owing to the greater quantity of money, the LM curve shifts to the right, again – but its horizontal section is effectively unmoved. Because of their absolute liquidity preference, the individuals are willing to hold any additional cash balances. They do not increase their demand for bonds, as is usual, in order to adjust their portfolios; and thus the rate of interest does not fall. Obviously, the central bank is not capable of reducing the rate of interest to its full employment level. Monetary policy is altogether ineffectual.

Let us conclude. When there is an investment or liquidity trap, monetary policy does not bring about any real effects whereas fiscal policy, as we saw above, is very efficient. Thus, by means of these two special cases, it is explicable why Keynesians generally judged fiscal measures superior to monetary ones and why monetary policy became almost entirely neglected for a considerable time. With respect to this issue, several remarks have to be added later on.

§ 57 Monetary Policy with Sticky Wages

Finally, we consider monetary effects when nominal wage rates are sticky – a precondition that is much more favorable to monetary policy:

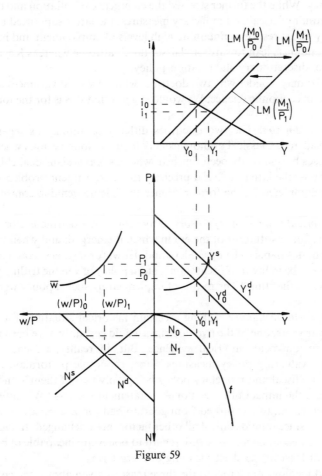

Figure 59

As a result of monetary expansion the LM curve shifts, as already seen, to the right. Because of this, the interest rate declines, and investment as well as commodity demand increases (the latter from Y_0^d to Y_1^d). Thus the price level rises. Owing to this, the LM curve shifts back to the left as real cash balances decrease, and commodity supply *increases*, because rising prices mean a reduction of the real wage rate when nominal wages are sticky. In the end, equilibrium income Y_1 is greater than the original income Y_0.

We can conclude that, nominal wages being given, an expansionary monetary policy will augment both production and employment. Simultaneously some inflation will occur, and the real wage rate will be reduced. Therefore, fiscal and monetary policy are *equivalent* in this case.

§ 58 Conclusion

In the present chapter we recognized that Classical theory on the one hand and Keynesian theory on the other arrive at rather different results with respect to stabilization policy. While the former stressed the emergence of inflation and crowding out as the sole result of fiscal and monetary measures, the latter supported the suitability of these very measures for maintaining high levels of employment and income. Thus, Classical economists lean towards a "laissez faire" attitude whereas Keynesians insist on an active, discretionary stabilization policy.

The reader may wonder why two doctrines which are so at variance can *both* stand their ground in economic science. We would suggest that this is for the following three reasons:

The Time Horizon. The two doctrines differ substantially as regards the time horizon considered. Classical authors usually focus on long periods where all adjustment processes have already been finished, whereas Keynesians deal chiefly with the short run. Thus, the latter analyzed precisely those adjustment problems which were regarded as completed by the former. Hence there is no genuine controversy in this respect.

The Historical Constraint of Theory. Any economic doctrine is closely related to the problems and institutions of the era in which it emerged: and when transferred to a later period, it is liable to be misunderstood. How, for instance, could an eighteenth century theorist be in favor of fiscal stabilization policy, given the trifling public sector share in GNP at that time? The means of implementing such a policy were simply not available.

The Empirical Testability. Taking a certain historical situation, for instance the early post-war years, one of the two doctrines would certainly have been rejected, had there been unequivocal empirical evidence. But, in reality, we encounter several problems in evaluating policy measures: First, economic performance depends on many factors – fiscal and monetary policy being only two of them – and it is impossible to isolate the impact of these alone. A statement such as "When fiscal measure X was implemented, things turned from good to bad (or vice versa)" is anything but definite proof, since it holds only if all other factors are unchanged. In fact, they never are. Therefore, recommendations with regard to policy are incapable of being falsified or verified, at least in the strict meaning of these terms.

If we add ideological factors to the three reasons given above, the co-existence of different orthodoxies seems perfectly inevitable. For the time being, any desire for a single economic doctrine remains unrealized, perhaps even unrealizable. Instead, we have to be content with several modes of economic reasoning.

Further Reading

LINDAUER, J. Ed. (1967) Macroeconomic Readings. New York etc.: The Free Press
MUELLER, M.G. Ed. (1967) Readings in Macroeconomics. New York etc.: Hilt, Rinehart and Winston

Part Three   New Macroeconomics

"All of importance has already been said by those who did not discover it."

(ALFRED N. WHITEHEAD)

§ 59 Introduction to Part Three

Under the heading "new macroeconomics" we include, broadly speaking, all those developments in macroeconomic theory that have taken place since the middle of the 1950s. Of course, such a labeling appears somewhat arbitrary; but it is suggested by the fact that, in the fifties, the Neoclassical synthesis was already established and served as point of departure and reference point for all future developments.

Whoever thought then that the Neoclassical synthesis could serve as a generally acceptable and accepted model of the economy was later to learn that he had been mistaken. Quite on the contrary, a steady interest in destroying or reformimg the Neoclassical synthesis has prevailed over the last three decades; and competing approaches have emerged which merit extensive attention and adopt a prominent position in current discussions.

But before passing on to these matters we have to consider the completion of the Neoclassical synthesis by DON PATINKIN. This is done in Chapter VII on the *real-balance effect*, where we show in more detail the features of the Neoclassical synthesis as a historical compromise between "KEYNES and the Classics".

In the subsequent chapter on the *theory of portfolio selection*, we continue to operate on the border-line between macroeconomic and monetary theory. It is intended first to introduce the theory of portfolio selection as an analytical device, and then to use it to examine fiscal and monetary policies. In doing so we orient ourselves by the Keynesian variety of portfolio theory as developed by JAMES TOBIN.

The most eminent attack on the Neoclassical synthesis is dealt with in the chapter on *Monetarism*. The Monetarist position is characterized there in its various aspects, and we show to what extent it can be regarded as a continuation of the Classical program.

In the chapter covering the *theory of Rational expectations*, in its special form of *New Classical theory*, we then discuss a theoretical foundation of monetarism: a theory that is frequently referred to as "Monetarism of the second kind". Furthermore, the *Phillips-curve*, as an important element of the Keynesian policy-program, is added in this chapter.

Our last chapter deals with *Neokeynesian theory*. The characteristic features of Neokeyesian theory are that it proceeds from a Neoclassical framework but occasionally yields "Keynesian" results by assuming sticky prices. Thus, this new, and promising, approach aims at a unification of theory, and at an elimination of the "Keynesian confusion".

The following books and articles provide suitable additional reading:

Further Reading

FITOUSSI, J.-P. Ed. (1983) Modern Macroeconomic Theory. Oxford: Basil Blackwell. (Read especially FITOUSSI's overview.)

GORDON, R.J. (1976) Recent Developments in the Theory of Inflation and Unemployment. Journal of Monetary Economics **2**, pp.185–219

STEIN, J.L. (1982) Monetarist, Keynesian and New Classical Economics. Oxford: Basil Blackwell

TOBIN, J. (1980) Asset Accumulation and Economic Activity. Oxford: Basil Blackwell

Chapter VII. The Real-Balance Effect

"Hence we find that the theory of money cannot be separated from the theory of relative prices." (OSKAR LANGE)

In this chapter we turn our attention to a discussion which is significant for both Keynesian and Neoclassical theory: the debate on the real-balance effect. The latter is by no means confined to a special problem of monetary theory; instead it constitutes the heart of the discussion on "KEYNES and the Classics" and for this reason deserves our undivided attention.

By a *wealth effect* we mean all those impacts on economic variables that result from a change in wealth. The *real-balance effect*, as a special wealth effect, covers all those economic impacts that can be traced back to a change in real cash balances, M/P. The latter term was first introduced by DON PATINKIN[1] who, proceeding from a criticism of Classical and Keynesian monetary theory, sought to integrate monetary and value analysis. In the following, the real-balance effect will prove to be the core of those economic adjustment mechanisms which arise from disequilibrium in the commodity market.

§ 60 A Criticism of Classical Monetary Theory

The segregation of the economy into a real and a monetary sector, mirrored by a segregation of analysis into monetary and value theory, had been, as we recall, a characteristic feature of the Classical doctrine. It was the task of value theory, chiefly represented by Walras' model, to determine *relative prices*, that is, the ratios at which commodities are exchanged. These depended solely on preferences, production technology, and initial endowments; indeed they merely represented the relative scarcities of goods once the "veil of money" was removed. Classical monetary theory (i.e. the quantity theory of money), on the other hand, was concerned with determining the price level: the *money prices*, and thus played a but supplementing role. In order to point out PATINKIN's critique we want to represent these ideas in a more formal manner.

Let us suppose an economy with G goods where good no. G, the last one, is *money*. Following the Classical line of reasoning, we first consider the real sector

---

1 PATINKIN, D. (1965) Money, Interest and Prices. New York: Harper and Row. Cf. also PATINKIN's fore-runner LANGE who first introduced the distinction between Say's law and Walras' law: LANGE, O. (1942) Say's law: A Restatement and Criticism. In: LANGE, O. et al. Ed. Studies in Mathematical Economics. Chicago: Chicago University Press.

which is represented by the first $(G - 1)$ equations. For each of these $(G - 1)$ commodity markets an *excess demand function* exists, which indicates the difference between demand and supply in this market:

$$E_g(\hat{\mathbf{p}}) := D_g(\hat{\mathbf{p}}) - S_g(\hat{\mathbf{p}}); \quad g = 1 \ldots G - 1. \tag{181}$$

In (181), $\hat{\mathbf{p}}$ denotes the vector of relative prices. If, for instance, we choose the $(G-1)$th good as numéraire, then

$$\hat{\mathbf{p}} := (\hat{p}_1, \hat{p}_2, \ldots, \hat{p}_{G-2}, 1). \tag{182}$$

Clearly the relative price of the numéraire is by definition equal to one. The other variables $\hat{p}_g$ – observe that there are $(G-2)$ of them – denote the exchange ratios of all other goods with respect to this numéraire. In Walras' model there is a general equilibrium if and only if all excess demands, (181), vanish. These $(G-1)$ equilibrium conditions, $(G-2)$ of them being independent, determine the $(G-2)$ relative prices simultaneously: and the problem of value theory is resolved.

Now let us assume that p_{G-1} is the *money price* of the numéraire. That is, if pears of a certain quality serve as numéraire, p_{G-1} denotes how much money one such pear costs. By means of this money price we can define the *vector of money prices* as

$$\mathbf{p} = (p_1, p_2, \ldots, p_{G-1}, 1). \tag{183}$$

Compared to (182), the vector of relative prices, this vector of money prices contains one extra element, namely, the price of money, p_G, which is identical to one. The p_g $(g \neq G)$ of (183) are the *money prices* of the goods, and any money price can be calculated as

$$p_g = \hat{p}_g \cdot p_{G-1}; \quad g = 1 \ldots G - 1. \tag{184}$$

An example should illustrate this. Good no. 1 may be apples of a certain quality, and good no. $(G-1)$, the numéraire, are pears. If one apple exchanges for two pears then $\hat{p}_1 = 2$. And if the money price of pears, p_{G-1}, amounts to \$5 then \$10 have to be paid for one apple, and p_1 can be calculated as $\hat{p}_1$ times $p_{G-1} = 2 \cdot 5 = 10$.

It was typical of many representations of value theory to assume, or prove, that excess demands are *independent* of money prices:

$$E_g(\mathbf{p}) = E_g(a \cdot \mathbf{p}); \quad g = 1 \ldots G - 1; \quad a > 0. \tag{185}$$

This equation served to paraphrase the assumption that none of the individuals is subject to "money illusion". If all money prices are doubled, for instance, the relative prices remain unchanged and so do, as it was thought, the excess demands. Thus, money prices were incapable of being determined by value theory.

Therefore, Classical real analysis was to be supplemented by the quantity theory of money. Let us begin with the Cambridge equation:

$$M = k \cdot P \cdot Y. \tag{186}$$

It should be added at this stage that the genuine variable of the Cambridge equation was not nominal income, PY, but nominal transactions, PT, that is the total volume of trade in all markets. It is quite obvious that the transactions demand for cash depends on this volume of trade; and assuming it to be a function of PY was justified only on the condition that transactions and income maintain a fixed ratio.

Thus we should substitute T for Y in the Cambridge equation, adjusting the cash balance coefficient, k, accordingly:

$$M = k' \cdot P \cdot T \quad \text{with} \quad k' = k \cdot \frac{Y}{T}. \tag{187}$$

Equation (187) states that demand for cash is proportional to the total amount of nominal market transactions, PT. The latter can be rewritten as the following sum:

$$M = k' \cdot \sum_{g=1}^{G-1} p_g \cdot D_g. \tag{188}$$

When there is a general equilibrium, demand and supply match in each market – so, $p_g D_g$, demand multiplied by the money price, denotes the nominal volume of trade that takes place in market no. g. Therefore, the sum in (188) represents the total amount of nominal transactions, and this equation itself can be regarded as a micro-economic formulation of the Cambridge equation.

Using our above definition of a money price, (184), we can separate the volume of trade into a monetary and a real part:

$$M = k' \cdot \sum_{g=1}^{G-1} \hat{p}_g \cdot p_{G-1} \cdot D_g \tag{189}$$

$$\Leftrightarrow M = k' \cdot p_{G-1} \cdot \sum_{g=1}^{G-1} \hat{p}_g \cdot D_g. \tag{190}$$

In this central equation, p_{G-1} is something like the price level[2], and the sum denotes real transactions. As the quantity of money, the propensity to hold cash, and real transactions are all *given* to the Cambridge equation, the latter determines solely the money price of the numéraire, p_{G-1}. As a result, *all* money prices are determined, too, as can be seen from (184).

After this brief review and restatement we can take up the criticism of PATINKIN who, following OSKAR LANGE, charges the Classical doctrine with some inconsistencies. PATINKIN proceeds from Walras' law – a proposition considered valid by him and the Classics alike. According to Walras' law, which we already derived in our § 28, the sum of the excess demands of all markets must always vanish:

$$\sum_{g=1}^{G} p_g \cdot E_g = 0. \tag{191}$$

Equation (191) extends our former formulation of Walras' law in that it embraces the money market, market no. G, too. The reader will immediately recognize that Walras' law, which was derived purely by means of budget constraints, holds if the money market is included: Any individual will only *plan* a demand for money if he simultaneously *plans* a supply of other goods; otherwise he would violate his budget constraint. Indeed, in this case the connection is even closer because *in supplying a*

---

2 This definition differs from the usual one where the price level is defined as a weighted average of money prices. The former is best suited for theory whereas the latter serves more for empirical measurement. If the price of the numéraire doubles, the weighted average must also double provided that there are no changes in relative prices.

good, an individual demands money – and vice versa. Thus if all other goods markets are in equilibrium, the money market must be in equilibrium, too:

$$\sum_{g=1}^{G-1} p_g \cdot E_g = 0 \quad \Leftrightarrow \quad E_G = 0. \tag{192}$$

Mathematically, (192) is directly inferred from (191): if $(G-1)$ terms of a zero sum vanish the Gth term must also vanish.

Now a logical contradiction becomes obvious if all money prices are doubled. Assume that prior to this a general equilibrium prevailed, such that both equations in (192) are valid. According to (185), the excess demands for goods $g = 1 \ldots G-1$ depend solely on relative, not money, prices. Thus a doubling of money prices leaves them unchanged. As a consequence. the left hand equation of (192) remains valid, and hence so does the right hand equation. In other words: the money market continues being in equilibrium. This is the result of value theory.

But what does the quantity theory of money tell us? According to (190), a doubling of money prices exactly doubles the demand for cash such that *disequilibrium* arises in the money market. This is in flagrant contradiction to the result of value theory.

Economically considered, the above contradiction can be explained as follows. Any doubling of money prices entails, according to the quantity theory of money, temporary excess demand in the money market accompanied by excess supply in the commodity markets. Only the latter brings about the fall in money prices which re-establishes equilibrium. But it is precisely this excess commodity demand that *cannot* arise in Walras' model since the excess demand functions are allegedly homogeneous of degree zero in money prices. Thus, Classical monetary theory proceeds from a phenomenon which, according to Classical value theory, is altogether impossible.

How is this contradiction to be resolved? PATINKIN's criticism proposed the suggestion that *real cash balances*, M/P, be included into the excess demand functions, where P is an appropriately defined price index:

$$E_g = E_g\left(\mathbf{p}, \frac{M}{P}\right). \tag{193}$$

Let us illustrate the Cambridge effect by means of this set of microeconomic equations. An increase in the quantity of money will at first cause excess demand in the commodity markets. Money prices will then increase up to the point where real cash balances are the same as before. Hence equation (185), purporting the homogeneity of degree zero in money prices, does not hold any more; and it has to be replaced by

$$E_g\left(\mathbf{p}, \frac{M}{P}\right) = E_g\left(a \cdot \mathbf{p}, \frac{a \cdot M}{a \cdot P}\right) \quad g = 1 \ldots G; \quad a > 0. \tag{194}$$

Thus a multiplication of all money prices by "a" leaves excess demands unchanged *if* the quantity of money is augmented by the same factor, because only then do real cash balances remain the same as before. This is by no means a "money illusion": on the contrary, the Classical postulate (185) implies money illusion since the individuals maintain their demand plans in the face of a change in all money prices, even though their real cash balances have been altered. (Similarly, the consumption function $C(Y)$ does not imply "absence of money illusion" but rather the very presence of money illusion.)

By embodying real cash balances into the excess demand functions, the integration of value and monetary theory is accomplished; and, strictly speaking, a separate monetary theory becomes superfluous. $(G-1)$ money prices are determined by the interaction of $(G-1)$ commodity markets, plus the money market. Owing to the usual assumptions, there is at least one vector of money prices which establishes a simultaneous equilibrium in all markets.

Far more important, the Classical theorem of the *neutrality* of money is maintained. Doubling the quantity of money at first incurs excess demand in the commodity markets, that is, there are *real* effects of this measure. Yet, the excess demands will cause a general rise in prices, which lasts until real cash balances have assumed there original values, as have all other variables except money prices. Thus the quantity theoretical *results* are reaffirmed, the "inconsistencies" cited above all referring to the *adjustment mechanism*. It is essential to understand that the *ultimate* neutrality of money implies *temporary* changes in the real variables: without the excess demands in the commodity markets, no money price would rise. At the same time the quantity theory of money proves false as regards those cases where a general excess supply of commodities prevails which prevents prices from increasing.

Let us finally consider PATINKIN's objections to some formulations of Say's law. In its original form, Say's law alleged an *identical* equivalence of aggregate commodity demand and supply. This assertion, frequently called *Say's identity*, holds for a barter economy without money. In this special case, it is equivalent to Walras' law, and merely states that all individuals plan according to their budget constraints.

Say's identity does *not* hold for a monetary economy; according to (192) it would hold only on condition that supply and demand in the money market are *identically* equivalent. This, of course, is not true: the Cambridge equation was not meant as an *identity* but as an *equilibrium condition*, and the latter term implies the possibility of disequilibrium. Thus, in a monetary economy, Say's law must be interpreted as an equilibrium condition, too. It asserts that at any time a price level *exists* which equilibrates aggregate demand for and supply of commodities. This version of Say's law is often referred to as *Say's equation*.

Let us conclude. Walras' model is untenable and incompatible with the quantity theory of money if excess demands are independent of (homogeneous of degree zero in) money prices. By introducing real cash balances as an argument in the excess demand functions, commodity demands and supplies will depend on money prices, too. Hence, money prices are already determined within the general equilibrium model; and a "supplementing" monetary theory becomes superflous. The theorem of the neutrality of money is maintained with respect to the original and new equilibrium but, during the adjustment process, real changes occur[3]. Finally, Say's law, as an identity, holds only for a barter economy. With regard to a monetary economy, however, it must be viewed as an equilibrium condition.

---

3 Cf. also the well-known critique from ARCHIBALD and LIPSEY which is essentially unjustified: ARCHIBALD, G.C. and R.G. LIPSEY (1958) Monetary and Value Theory: A Critique of Lange and PATINKIN. Review of Economic Studies **26**, pp.1–22.

§61 A Criticism of Keynesian Monetary Theory

In the previous section we recognized that the real-balance effect, in its special form of the Cambridge effect, is essential to the quantity theory of money. And moreover that it is also quite essential to value theory (if indeed there is still such a thing), for the real-balance effect alone guarantees the validity of Say's law in a monetary economy. But what role does the real-balance effect play within the Keynesian framework?

There is a sense in which the above question has already been answered in §40. There, we encountered the *Keynes-effect* according to which real cash balances exert an indirect impact on aggregate commodity demand via the bonds-interest-investment mechanism. With respect to the Keynes-effect, the assumption of substitutability between money and bonds proved to be the fundamental one; and we ensured that this allegation seemed reasonable by assuming money to be a proper store of value. But now we have to ask ourselves whether the more restrictive premise is acceptable: that bonds are the *only* substitute for money and that changes in the quantity of money only influence the demand for bonds, and not goods. Precisely this is a central premise of the IS/LM model.

It was ARTHUR CECIL PIGOU[4] who first tried to answer this question in his now celebrated article "The Classical Stationary State". To understand PIGOU's arguments two definitions are required. A *steady state* is a long run equilibrium, or a state of equilibrated growth. The existence and properties of such a steady state are the main concern of growth theory. Now, a *stationary state* is defined as a steady state where the growth rate is zero. This stationary state is attained finally if all variables such as technology, population, and preferences are constant. Its main properties consist in realization of the optimal stock of capital, K^*, and the optimal stock of wealth, W^*. Thus, in the stationary state, people do not save net, and also no net investment takes place[5].

Let us proceed from a stationary state and assume an exogenous increase in real cash balances. If money is perceived by the individuals as a component of their total wealth, the actual stock of wealth increases beyond its desired level, W^*. To re-attain the optimal stock of wealth, W^*, the individuals will be inclined to save less and thus to consume more. Hence, we arrive at the following modified savings and consumption functions:

$$S = S\left(Y, \underset{(-)}{\frac{M}{P}}\right) \quad \text{and} \quad C = C\left(Y, \underset{(+)}{\frac{M}{P}}\right). \tag{195}$$

This impact of real cash balances on savings and consumption is called the *Pigou-effect*. It states that increasing nominal cash balances *or* declining money prices will reduce savings and stimulate consumption because total wealth is increased.

The Pigou-effect becomes significant when there is an investment or liquidity trap – and it was designed precisely for these cases. PIGOU aimed at demonstrating the

---

4 PIGOU, A.C. (1943) The Classical Stationary State. Economic Journal 53, pp. 343–351.
5 In mathematical terms, we may assume two stock adjustment functions, $S = S(W^* - W)$ and $I = I(K^* - K)$ which are sign preserving and run through the origin.

impossibility of a stable equilibrium with under-employment. In Chapter V we saw that such a stable equilibrium may arise if investment is perfectly interest inelastic, or liquidity demand is perfectly interest elastic. In such cases, any fall in the price level would *not* stimulate commodity demand. But, if we take the Pigou-effect into account, the theoretical possibility of such a "trap" is invalidated. Consider the following liquidity trap:

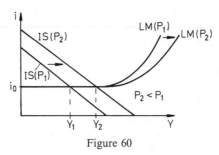

Figure 60

To repeat the original explanation, an excess supply in the commodity market lowers commodity prices – but, since the LM curve is horizontal within the relevant range, this incurs no decrease in the interest rate; investment remains the same; and hence the deflation is ineffectual. But the Pigou-effect implies a *rightward shift of the IS curve* because the deflation augments real cash balances and thus, according to (195), diminishes savings. Consequently, any rate of interest must be accompanied by a higher equilibrium income, and this means a rightward shift of the IS curve.

As a result, the liquidity trap – though theoretically possible – is not *stable*: prices will continue declining until *there is* full employment; and convergence towards the full employment equilibrium is "inevitable".

The majority of economists, however, including PIGOU himself, remained sceptical as to the strength of this Pigou-effect. Let us consider money as a fraction of wealth more thoroughly: With the exception of commodity money (e.g. gold), money is a promise to pay. Central bank money obliges the central bank to pay, cheques and deposits oblige the commercial banks to pay. If bills of exchange and the like are also regarded as money it becomes obvious that the *wealth* of the money owner is always faced with an equivalent *debt* of the issuer.

When prices decline, the wealth of the former increases but the debt of the latter does so, too. Therefore we have to ask which fraction of money constitutes *net* wealth.

On this score, a distinction between inside and outside money has been introduced by GURLEY and SHAW[6]. The attributes "inside" and "outside" refer to the domestic private sector. *Inside money* constitutes a claim of one member of this sector but a liability of another; hence, for the domestic private sector as a whole, it does not constitute net wealth. Bills of exchange and cheques are two typical examples of inside money. *Outside money*, on the other hand, represents the liability of an issuer who is not a member of the domestic private sector. Thus, in a closed economy, outside money consists of claims against the state, and of assets such as gold; and it is this

---

6 GURLEY, J.G. and E.S. SHAW (1960) Money in a Theory of Finance. Washington D.C.: The Brookings Inst.

fraction of the quantity of money only which constitutes the monetary net wealth of the domestic private sector [7].

In equations (195) we must not consider the total quantity of money, but only outside money, because it alone is capable of stimulating aggregate consumption demand by means of a real-balance effect. (*Remark*: Obviously, this base can be augmented by other parts of outside *wealth* as far as their nominal value is fixed. Then a more general real-wealth effect could be substituted for the real-balance effect. But for the time being we will confine ourselves to the former case.)

Since outside money constitutes but a tiny fraction of the total quantity of money, the base of the Pigou-effect is reduced; and if we add the tenacity of deflation to this, PIGOU's own rating that the Pigou-effect is rather an "academic excercise" has to be confirmed. Nonetheless, he had succeeded in showing that the investment and liquidity traps are no stable states; and, furthermore, it is questionable whether these traps are themselves more than "academic exercises".

Let us finally consider another argument, due to IRVING FISHER, which is directed against the stimulating effect of deflation. As already noted, any wealth consisting of inside money is faced with an equivalent debt. Now, let us suppose that the debtors' marginal propensities to consume are greater than those of the creditors'. The striking argument in support of this is: "How else would they be debtors?" Owing to a general deflation, the real values of claims and liabilities will increase at the same rate; and what the creditors gain is lost by the debtors. But – this would *reduce* aggregate demand because, as a result of the above assumption, the debtors will reduce their expenditures by more than the creditors will increase them. If this *Fisher-effect* [8] is strong enough it may outweigh the Pigou-effect. In this strange case, full employment equilibrium at lower prices does exist but cannot be attained via the dynamic adjustment process.

Three further arguments support the aforementioned objections to the "curing effects" of deflation.

- Because of debt overload, caused by falling prices, annual bankruptcies will increase; and these will in general mean a reduction in net wealth.
- Expectations of further deflation may induce people to postpone some purchases, since the real value of cash balances increases over time.
- Bankruptcies and the re-distribution of wealth are likely to cause a considerable change in the commodity demand pattern, requiring further adjustments.

All in all, a strong deflation is hardly bound to stimulate commodity demand immediately and smoothly, as in the models of Part II. Many economists are inclined to consider these problems as an important explanation of the Great Depression.

---

7 This proposition, again, has been contested and is subject to controversy up to the present. Cf. PESEK, B.P. and T.S. SAVING (1967) Money, Wealth and Economic Theory. New York: Macmillan. BUCHANAN, J. (1969) An Outside Economist in Defense of Pesek and Saving. Journal of Economic Literature 7, pp. 812–814.

8 Note that there are two "Fisher effects" in the literature. The first one is that explained above. The other refers to the distinction between nominal and real rates of interest. It states that the individuals add the prevailing rate of inflation to the real rate of interest such that nominal interest (the sum of both) varies with changes in the rate of inflation.

To conclude. PIGOU was right in criticizing the awkward Keynesian assumption that changes in real cash balances influence the demand for bonds only, and not that for commodities; that is, he was right in criticizing the Keynes-effect as being the sole adjustment mechanism. By means of the Pigou-effect he succeeded in showing that, even under the most extreme assumptions, there is a full employment equilibrium. Thus the Classical doctrine was rehabilitated, in spite of the well-founded objection that deflation may be a long lasting and grievous mode of equilibration.

§ 62 Conclusion

Following this "menu of effects" which is perhaps somewhat bewildering, we want to summarize and compare the various real-balance effects.

The *real-balance effect*, a special wealth effect, is the generic term. It states the relationship between real cash balances and other economic variables such as consumption or demand for bonds. The real-balance effect explains the adjustment processes towards general equilibrium.

The special real-balance effect of the quantity theory of money was called the *Cambridge-effect*. According to the Cambridge-effect, changes in real cash balances exert a *direct* impact on aggregate commodity demand where the term "commodity" is to be understood in its narrow sense, i.e. it does not include securities. Therefore, cash balances do not influence the interest rate.

In direct contrast, the *Keynes-effect* states that demand for securities alone is altered by changes in real cash balances. According to this second special real-balance effect, cash balances do not influence aggregate commodity demand directly. Thus the Classical adjustment process is exactly reversed; and the Classical dichotomy between the real and the monetary sector only holds to the extent that changes in aggregate demand are brought about by alterations in the interest rate.

In the Neoclassical synthesis, this Keynes effect is accompanied by the *Pigou-effect*, which asserts that cash balances have an impact on consumption demand, too. Yet the Pigou-effect is not to be understood as a rehabilitated Cambridge-effect. LLOYD A. METZLER rightly stressed that the Pigou-effect is un-Classical in spirit: First, it operates within the IS/LM framework and, second, in supporting the Keynes-effect it does not deny that interest depends on the quantity of money[9]. Hence the Pigou-effect has to be conceived as an independent feature of the Neoclassical synthesis.

Finally, the *Fisher-effect* suggests a force that opposes the Pigou-effect. Considered microeconomically, a deflation is not bound to cause an immediate increase in aggregate demand if one allows for the different propensities to consume of debtors and creditors. When the loss of net wealth which arises from bankruptcies, an increasing propensity to hoard, and structural shifts are taken into account, it is even conceivable that aggregate demand declines in the short run.

---

9 Cf. METZLER, L.A. (1951) Wealth, Saving and the Rate of Interest. Journal of Political Economy **59**, pp. 93–116. We must point out that this argument refers only to the main stream of Classical and Neoclassical thinking. Some authors, above all WICKSELL, not only perceived clearly that interest and money are closely connected but made that very fact the basis of their monetary theory.

With regard to a closed economy without non-monetary net wealth, the significance of the real-balance effect stems from the fact that it is absolutely indispensable for the equilibration of aggregate commodity demand and supply. In a single market, the pricing mechanism may always ensure an equilibrium: but with respect to the total economy it would entirely fail to do so if aggregate commodity demand were independent of real cash balances and thus independent of the price level. In this case, they would only match accidentally.

In sum, the weaker the real-balance effect the lengthier is the adjustment process towards general equilibrium; and, one could continue, the more obvious are governmental stabilization policies. With this line of reasoning, we have now established the essence of the Neoclassical synthesis. It constitutes a truce between "KEYNES and the Classics" that consists of three essential agreements:

- The Classics were right in describing the market economy's center of gravity as a state of full employment. The economy always approaches this equilibrium – even if there is an investment or liquidity trap.
- KEYNES' "General Theory" is in fact a special case of the Classical doctrine which results if more prominence is given to the adjustment problems and if the Pigou-effect is ignored.
- Yet, this "special case" is far more important than the "normal" one since the adjustment process, where the total economy is concerned, is much more complicated than that of a single market. Because the dynamic stability of full employment equilibrium is not guaranteed, and the adjustment may be lengthy, calls for governmental stabilization policy have to be approved.

With respect to policy, too, this must be considered a genuine "synthesis": The market mechanism is expected to provide an efficient allocation of resources, whereas the government aims at stabilizing the economy as a whole by means of demand management. At the same time, this "synthesis" is the basis of the economic policy that was for decades (and is?) actually practiced.

Further Reading

GRANDMONT, J.-M. (1983) Money and Value – A Reconsideration of Classical and Neoclassical Monetary Theories. Cambridge etc.: Cambridge University Press

GURLEY, J.G. and E.S. SHAW (1960) Money in a Theory of Finance. Washington D.C.: The Brookings Inst.

PATINKIN, D. (1948) Price Flexibility and Full Employment. American Economic Review 38, pp. 543–564. Reprinted in: MUELLER, M.G. Ed. (1967) Readings in Macroeconomics. Op.cit.

PATINKIN, D. (1956) Money, Interest and Prices. New York: Harper and Row. Second edition 1965 ibid.

PESEK, B.P. and Th.S. Saving (1967) Money, Wealth and Economic Theory. New York: Macmillan.

Chapter VIII. The Theory of Portfolio Selection

The *theory of portfolio selection* is an approach which derives the demands for money and other assets by means of individual maximization behaviour.

Let us briefly recollect the Classical theory in order to understand the novel features of this approach. It was characteristic of Classical theory to separate the economy into a real and a monetary sector; and this theoretical dichotomy, as we called it, was accompanied by a *methodological* one: The Classics deduced all *real* variables from individual optimization whereas, at the same time, they sought to derive the demand for *money* by means of an entirely different principle, which could be termed the principle of habit or necessity. The Cambridge k, or the circular velocity of money, v, were not derived from individual optimization but were explained in a more or less "mechanistic" manner. In this respect, monetary theory fell behind value theory.

The theory of portfolio selection overcomes this methodical dichotomy by applying the ordinary instruments of value theory to the demand for money. Thus it tackles with a difficult problem because the use of money depends chiefly on those imperfections which are assumed absent in value theory: on transactions costs and risks to mention but two. In sum, the theory of portfolio selection introduces the tools of value theory, as known from any microeconomic course, into monetary and macroeconomic theory. It was developed by HARRY M. MARKOWITZ[1] and JAMES TOBIN[2] in the 1950s, though its roots can be traced to a suggestion from HICKS[3] and KEYNES' work on liquidity preference.

In the following two sections, we deal first with the microeconomic foundations of portfolio theory; and then turn to its macroeconomic applications.

§ 63 Microeconomic Foundations

By a *portfolio*, we mean the total claims and liabilities of an individual. While we refer only to claims in what follows, the reader should keep in mind that all the principles are capable of being applied to liabilities, too. The *theory of portfolio selection* is

1 MARKOWITZ, H.M. (1959) Portfolio Selection. Second Edition New York 1970: Yale University Press. MARKOWITZ made his first contribution to portfolio selection in 1952.
2 TOBIN, J. (1958) Liquidity Preference as Behaviour Towards Risk. Review of Economic Studies **25**, pp. 65–86.
3 HICKS, J.R. (1935) A Suggestion for Simplifying the Theory of Money. Economica **2**, pp. 1–19.

concerned with the question of how a rational individual composes his given wealth when there are various assets. For instance, the individual's wealth may amount to $100. We then ask how much money, bonds, equities, and the like are held assuming that the individual makes a rational choice. Hereby, perfect competition is assumed while assumptions such as perfect foresight and absence of transactions costs are discarded. It will turn out that the demand for money depends on exactly these imperfections.

We want to begin with some general observations. Any asset taken into consideration by an investor has four properties, namely:

- the yield,
- the risk,
- the transactions costs that are involved by buying, keeping, and selling it, and
- how fungible the asset is, that is, how easily it can be obtained and resold in the market.

If we abstract from risks, transactions costs, and the fact that assets are imperfectly fungible then, clearly, the problem of an optimal portfolio composition can be solved easily. The investor will simply look for the asset which yields the *highest* income and – if it exists – he will buy *only* this one. In this situation, money would hardly have a chance.

But this is not the world in which we live. In reality, the yield of many assets is uncertain (for instance that of equities), there are transactions costs (brokerages, taxes), and it is often impossible to sell the asset instantaneously (because of notice terms). Therefore, a rational investor will weigh the respective advantages and disadvantages of several assets carefully. It is possible, for example, that he includes money in his portfolio because holding money, though not yielding an interest when prices are stable, is nearly riskless, involves trifling transactions costs, and can easily be undone.

Considered in this way, the existence of *transactions balances* is all but a passive, "inevitable" occurence; it is the outcome of a rational optimization that weighs the opportunity costs against the advantages of holding money. Without analyzing this mathematically[4], we want to retain as a first result of the portfolio approach: Transactions balances are due to an optimization, their amount being determined by the opportunity costs of holding money on the one hand, and the avoided transactions costs and risk on the other hand. Since opportunity costs depend on the rate on interest, they increase when the interest rate rises and, therefore, transactions demand for cash is dependent on the interest rate! Compared with the Classical and Keynesian approach, this is a novel result.

Having thus paid attention to transactions costs and imperfectly fungible assets, we want to abstract from these two determinants subsequently. Therefore, *yield* and *risk* remain as the sole distinguishing features of assets. In the following we examine portfolio choices by means of a very simple model with two assets only. Supposing

4 BAUMOL, W.J. (1952) The Transactions Demand for Cash: An Inventory Theoretic Approach. Quarterly Journal of Economics **66**, pp. 545–556. TOBIN, J. (1956) The Interest Elasticity of Transactions Demand for Cash. Review of Economics and Statistics **38**, pp. 241–247.

that the portfolio decision is independent of the *amount* of total wealth, we can confine our consideration to the shares of both assets:

$$x_1 + x_2 = 1. \tag{196}$$

x_1 and x_2 are the shares of the two assets, their sum being equal to 1 of course. Now our problem consists in finding a general rule according to which the investor chooses x_1 and x_2. Let us first have a look at the returns of the assets. In general, the investor is unlike to know them exactly, but he will have some expectation of the *probabilities* of different rates of return. These probabilities are purely *subjective* magnitudes, which does not exclude their being formed according to objective data of the past. If we suppose the returns to have a *normal distribution*, the expectations may be depicted by the following figure:

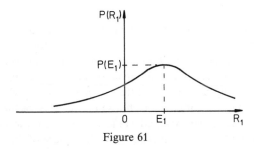

Figure 61

Here, R_1 denotes the return on asset no. 1, and $P(R_1)$ is the probability that R_1 will take place in the future. Since the normal distribution is symmetric its highest point is equal to the *expected value*, E_1. Thus our investor expects that on average a return equal to E_1 will accrue to him. It should be stressed that he might be wrong, because the distribution of Figure 61 is no objective one, but merely describes his conjectures. Yet, this is utterly unimportant since the investor behaves according to what he believes. The above reasoning can also be applied to the second asset. According to a mathematical theorem[5], the sum of two normally distributed variables is also normally distributed, and its expected value can be calculated as a weighted average of the expected values of the two variables:

$$E = x_1 \cdot E_1 + x_2 \cdot E_2. \tag{197}$$

E_1 and E_2 are the expected values of the returns on the two assets and x_1 and x_2 are the respective shares. Formula (197) shows how the expected value of the return of the *total* portfolio can be derived from these variables. To make this plausible: Suppose that the investor holds only the first asset, that is, $x_1 = 1$. Then, E is equal to E_1. And E is equal to E_2 if the portfolio is entirely made up of the second asset.

How would an investor decide on the two shares if he *only* took the expected returns into account? This question is very easily answered:

$$\text{choose} \begin{cases} x_1 = 1, & \text{if} \quad E_1 > E_2 \\ x_1 = 0, & \text{if} \quad E_1 < E_2. \end{cases} \tag{198}$$

---

5 This one and the following elementary theorems are discussed in almost any statistical textbook.

Thus the investor will keep only that asset with the higher expected return. In the following figure where E_1 is supposed higher than E_2, the optimum is on the very left:

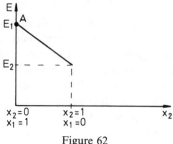

Figure 62

In order to maximize the expected return, the investor chooses point A, that is, he only includes the first asset into his portfolio. This was formally stated by (198).

Up to here, our approach seems a bit too simple for, in general, the investor will also pay attention to the *risk* that is involved by keeping a certain asset. If this were not so, one could hardly explain the different interest rates which are observed in reality. As a simple measure of risk, we choose the *variance* of the above distribution function. The variance is the expected value of the quadratic deviations from the mean; we denote it by S^2 because it is equal to the square of the standard deviation, S.

An investor may be *risk keen*, *risk averse*, or *risk neutral* according to whether risk yields positive, negative, or zero utility to him. It is in the latter case only that we could employ the above decision model; yet the following figure suggests that *declining marginal utility implies risk aversion*:

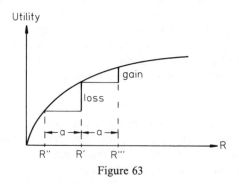

Figure 63

Here we have a Neoclassical utility function that obeys the law of declining marginal utility. Two possibilities are distinguished:

– Either the investor gets a *certain* return R', or
– he receives the returns R'' and R''' with probability 0.5 each.

The expected return is R' in both cases since R' is just the weighted average of R'' and R'''. Yet, the investor will *prefer* the first alternative. For, if he receives R''' instead of R′, the resulting gain in utility is obviously less than the loss of utility which results from receiving R″ instead of R′. Therefore, when declining marginal utility prevails, the investor will inevitably be risk averse – and this appears anyway as the relevant assumption outside gambling circles.

Let us suppose that S_1^2 and S_2^2 are the variances of our two assets, and ϱ is the correlation coefficient which indicates the correlation between the distributions of the two yields. Then, the risk of the total portfolio, measured by the variance S^2, is straightforwardly calculated as the following binomial:

$$S^2 = x_1^2 \cdot S_1^2 + 2 \cdot x_1 \cdot x_2 \cdot S_1 \cdot S_2 \cdot \varrho + x_2^2 \cdot S_2^2. \tag{199}$$

If the investor is risk averse, he will aim at *minimizing* this variance in order to run as small a risk as possible at least if we assume for the time being that the return on both assets is the same. The *risk minimizing* portfolio is simply obtained by setting $x_2 = (1 - x_1)$, differentiating the above expression with respect to x_1, and setting the derivative to zero:

$$x_1 = \frac{S_2^2 - \varrho \cdot S_1 \cdot S_2}{S_1^2 - 2 \cdot \varrho \cdot S_1 \cdot S_2 + S_2^2} \tag{200}$$

$$x_2 = \frac{S_1^2 - \varrho \cdot S_1 \cdot S_2}{S_1^2 - 2 \cdot \varrho \cdot S_1 \cdot S_2 + S_2^2}. \tag{201}$$

We should add that the second-order conditions for a minimum are met. Thus, the two formulas denote the investor's choice of x_1 and x_2 when he seeks to minimize the risk of his portfolio. There are some very interesting implications here. As the reader surely knows, the correlation coefficient measures the relation between the two risks S_1^2 and S_2^2 in the following way: It is equal to zero when the risks are independent of one another, positive (and ≤ 1) if they are correlated positively, and negative (and ≥ -1) if they are correlated negatively. Inserting the three typical values 0, -1, and 1 of the correlation coefficient into the above formulas, we obtain the following decision rules:

$$\varrho = 0: \quad \text{choose} \quad \frac{x_1}{x_2} = \frac{S_2^2}{S_1^2}, \quad \text{where} \quad S^2 = \frac{S_1^2 \cdot S_2^2}{S_1^2 + S_2^2} \tag{202}$$

$$\varrho = -1: \quad \text{choose} \quad \frac{x_1^2}{x_2^2} = \frac{S_2^2}{S_1^2}, \quad \text{where} \quad S^2 = 0 \tag{203}$$

$$\varrho = 1: \quad \text{choose} \quad \begin{cases} x_1 = 1, & \text{if } S_1^2 < S_2^2, \quad \text{where } S^2 = S_1^2 \\ x_1 = 0, & \text{if } S_1^2 > S_2^2, \quad \text{where } S^2 = S_2^2. \end{cases} \tag{204}$$

In the first two cases, *diversification* is the right strategy. When the risks are independent, i.e. $\varrho = 0$, the ratio of the shares x_1 and x_2 must be equal to the inverse ratio of the risks S_1^2 and S_2^2. Then, the resulting risk S^2 is *less than* both S_1^2 and S_2^2 if these two are positive. When the two risks are completely negatively correlated, i.e. $(\varrho) = -1$, the total risk is even capable of being reduced to *zero*.

On the other hand, total risk cannot be reduced when a complete positive correlation, i.e. $\varrho = 1$, prevails. In this case, only that asset with the lower risk is included into the portfolio; a strategy which might be termed *concentration*.

Hence, if an investor aims at running the smallest possible risk, and can choose from a wide variety of assets, he should select those whose risks are *negatively* correlated. Any expert will immediately recognize that this model depicts his very behaviour.

The above formulas are now to be supplemented by some figures which will clear up matters. To simplify the following graphs we will measure the risk by the standard deviations.

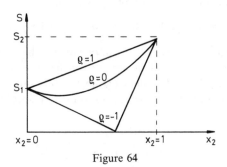

Figure 64

This figure depicts the variation of *total risk*, S, when the share of the second asset, x_2, is varied. $x_2 = 0$, that is, the portfolio consists solely of the first asset, implies that $S = S_1$; and $x_2 = 1$ obviously implies that $S = S_2$. This holds irrespective of the correlation coefficient. However, the latter determines the shape of the above *risk curves* between the two extremes. In accordance with formulas (202) to (204), three cases can be distinguished:

- $\varrho = 1$. Complete positive correlation implies that the risk curve is a straight line. The reader should prove this by inserting $\varrho = 1$ into (199) and then solving with respect to S_1.
- $\varrho = 0$. When the two risks are independent of one another, the risk curve is strictly below the afore mentioned straight line, except at the margin. Its minimum is *below* the minimum of the straight line.
- $\varrho = -1$. With complete negative correlation, the risk curve consists of two straight lines that touch the abscissa. Hence, total risk can be reduced to zero.

Following these preliminaries, we return to our original question: which choice is made by the investor if he takes both return and risk into account and if these two are generally different for each asset. In doing so we consider the especially interesting case in which *money* and *bonds* are the two assets in question. The graph depicted in Figure 65 shows the relation between return and risk of the total portfolio.

Money, whose share is measured by x_1, has an expected return and a risk of zero, which is true if prices are absolutely stable. Therefore, the locus of all possible combinations of return and risk, OL, runs through the origin. If the share of bonds, x_2, is gradually increased, both return and risk rise linearly; as a result, OL is a straight line. The linear relationship can be inferred from (197) and (199) with $E_1 = S_1 = 0$:

$$E = x_2 \cdot E_2 \quad \text{and} \quad S = x_2 \cdot S_2. \tag{205}$$

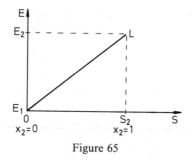

Figure 65

The investor is able to choose any point on OL. But which point will he choose? This obviously depends on his preferences, and these can be depicted by indifference curves. An *indifference curve* is the locus of all portfolios that are considered equally good by the investor:

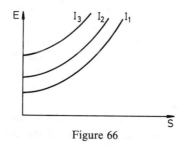

Figure 66

The indifference curves exhibit a positive slope since additional risk must be offset by higher returns if, as we assumed, the investor is risk averse. And they are convex because increasing risk has to be compensated for by progressively rising returns[6]. The investor seeks to attain as high an indifference curve as possible; thus, the decision problem is solved by combining Figures 65 and 66:

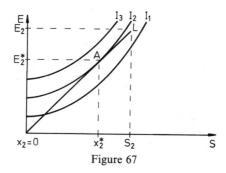

Figure 67

At point A, the indifference curve I_2 touches the locus, OL, of all possible portfolios. As I_2 is the highest indifference curve attainable under these circumstances, the

---

6 Cf. also TOBIN's analytical derivation: TOBIN, J. (1958) Liquidity Preference as Behaviour Towards Risk. Op.cit.

investor will choose precisely point A. Thus, the optimal share of money is x_1^*, and the optimal share of bonds $x_2^* = (1 - x_1^*)$. This is the general solution of the decision problem.

It is interesting to cast a glance at the *interest elasticity* of money demand using this approach, for, besides integrating monetary and value theory, TOBIN aimed chiefly at restating Keynesian liquidity preference theory. Was such a "restatement" indeed called for?

In § 37, we expended much effort on discussing KEYNES' speculative motive for holding cash; but did not mention then that his approach had already been subject to severe criticism since the 1940s. This criticisms referred to the allegation of certain and static expectations. Let us recollect that, according to KEYNES' liquidity preference theory, individuals formed some expectation of the "normal" interest rate on the basis of, say, past experience. If the market rate sunk below this normal value, they feared rising interest rates or, what is the same, falling market values of bonds, and thus were inclined to holding cash.

Strange that they did not adjust their conjecture about the normal interest rate if the lower market rate had prevailed for some time! Strange, too, that the individuals' expectations of the normal rate were held with certainty, and that the "portfolio choice" was thus reduced to an "all-or-nothing" decision. The two assumptions of *certain* and *static* expectations alone allowed the possibility of a lasting liquidity trap, and they were at variance with KEYNES' general concept of uncertainty as was manifest in precautionary balances.

Hence, TOBIN had every reason for restating the inverse relationship between money demand and the interest rate. For the afore mentioned reasons he dismissed the speculative motive, and founded his theory of the interest elasticity of cash balances on risk considerations (and transactions balances).

Let us discuss TOBIN's approach by means of the above model. A rise in the interest rate augments the return on bonds, our second asset in Figure 67. Therefore, other things being equal, the locus OL is rotated up to the left:

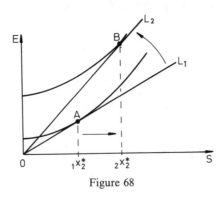

Figure 68

The figure shows that, due to the rise in the interest rate, money demand decreases and the demand for bonds increases. This result, KEYNES' own, however, is not the only conceivable one. The reader knows from the elementary microeconomic theory of the household that any rise in price incurs two effects, the substitution and the income effect, which possibly oppose one another. Here, the situation is very similar. Owing to the *substitution effect*, money demand must certainly decline when interest rises because the opportunity costs of holding money are increased. Yet, the *income effect* incurs an increase in the household's interest income what enables the household to run a lower risk for the same return as before. Thus, if risk is a superior and return an inferior good, the direction of the total impact cannot be inferred.

But, all things considered, it seems more plausible to proceed on the assumption that demand for money declines if the interest rate rises. This is suggested, too, by the consideration of the transactions demand for cash at the beginning of this section. Hence, KEYNES' liquidity preference has been substantiated in another manner. Holding cash balances turns out to be rational because

- money reduces the total risk of a portfolio,
- reduces transactions costs, and
- it is the most fungible one of all assets.

§ 64 Macroeconomic Applications

After discussing the more technical aspects of the theory of portfolio selection, we are now ready to apply it to our genuine subject: macroeconomics. We will recognize that portfolio theory is closely related to the so-called *asset approach* which can be characterized by two features. First, wealth is considered an important determinant of economic decisions; and second, the asset approach employs the concept of *stock equilibrium* which is already known from LM curve analysis. A stock equilibrium means that all given components of total wealth are willingly kept by the individuals, whereas a flow equilibrium implies that flows of, say, savings and investment match. In the first instance, the economic plans refer to the beginning, in the second, they refer to the end of some period.

The theory of portfolio selection provides a framework for examining fiscal and monetary instruments, and is especially designed to illuminate the transmission mechanism.

To begin with we require a definition of private wealth. Considered macroeconomically, five different components of wealth can be distinguished, which can in turn be assigned to the categories inside wealth and outside wealth. With *inside wealth*, every claim of a member of the domestic private sector corresponds to a liability of another member of this sector; thus it is no net wealth. *Outside wealth*, on the other hand, consists of claims (minus liabilities) against the state or against foreigners. Confining ourselves to the closed economy, the constituents of private wealth are the following:

Inside wealth:

- Money which is created by private banks, and
- all claims of individuals against other individuals, such as equities, bonds, and bills of exchange.

Outside wealth:

- Central bank money, as far as it is backed by public debt or gold,
- other components of public debt,
- all stocks of physical capital, which we suppose to be entirely owned by private domestic residents, and
- human capital.

For the time being, we abstract from human capital which is to be introduced in the following chapter, from gold, and from claims against foreigners. Because of the highly aggregative structure of the model, we can dispense with an analysis of inside wealth; for, what is the claim of one individual is the liability of another; and so far as we only examine the private sector *as a whole*, inside wealth is insignificant. This would be not so, however, if we were to disaggregate the private sector and take account of distributional effects.

Considering of outside wealth, the following "balance sheet classification" can be drawn up:

Government		Private Sector	
assets	total equity and liabilities	assets	total equity and liabilities
per contra item	M B	M B K	Capital of the private sector

Figure 69

M is the quantity of central bank money which, owing to our neglect of inside wealth, is identical to the total quantity of money. B is the stock of bonds issued by the government, and K the stock of physical capital. The latter is not necessarily owned by the households directly; but if we abstract from inventories and the like, K matches "total equity and liabilities" of the firms. And since the firms belong entirely to the domestic households, we can speak of "physical capital" or "equity interest" of the households synonymously. It is to be stressed that, in the following model, firms have *no liabilities*, but the right hand side of their balance sheets covers equity interest only. According to Figure 69, *real outside wealth* of the private sector can be reckoned as

$$W := \frac{M}{P} + \frac{B}{P} + q \cdot K. \qquad (206)$$

Hence, real outside wealth – or wealth, for short – consists of the real quantity of money, M/P, the real stock of bonds, B/P, and the stock of physical capital, K, multiplied by a factor (q) that is to be explained later on. We suppose that B represents bonds on a *floating rate* basis, that is, their return is instantaneously adjusted to the interest rate. Thus, changes in a bond's market value are excluded.

Tobin's q, also termed the *relative market rate of real capital*, denotes the exchange ratio between capital goods and goods. $q = 2$, for instance, means that one unit of capital goods exchanges for two units of goods. Let us assume for a moment that the value of a firm is equal to its *net asset value*, i.e. equal to the sum of its capital goods, valued at market prices (recollect that there are no liabilities of the firms which would otherwise have to be deducted). Consequently, the ratio q must be equal to 1, for capital goods and other goods are regarded as being *homogeneous*: capital goods are those goods used as means of production, and they are physically identical to consumption goods. This macroeconomic assumption was required for equations such as Y = C + I.

Therefore, a q *differing* from 1 must derive from the *earning capacity value* of a firm, i.e. to the sum of its discounted expected future profits. This becomes clear from the following definition:

$$q := \frac{R}{r_k}. \tag{207}$$

R represents the marginal efficiency of capital, and r denotes the *market rate of real capital*, also called the *supply price of capital*. The supply price of capital is the return on physical capital demanded by the public; or, more exactly, it is that rate of return on physical capital which induces the public to keep the given stock of physical capital willingly.

Suppose, for instance, that the households are ready to keep the given stock of capital at a return of 5%. Thus, the supply price of capital, r_k, is equal to 5%. If marginal efficiency of capital, R, amounts to 5%, too, then the households' requests are just matched. Therefore, a q equal to 1 (5%/5%) ensures the balance of capital supply and demand. If, on the other hand, R amounts to 10%, the return on physical capital is above the required level. In this case, q = 2, and the earning capacity value of a firm exceeds its net asset value. Of course, this is a disequilibrium. The households are now ready to keep *additional* equities of firms. As a result, investment continues until marginal efficiency of capital, R, has decreased to 5%, or, what is the same, q has become equal to 1. Hence, the marginal efficiency of capital will always tend towards the supply price of capital in due course.

Thus, Tobin's q is the decisive variable with respect to investment activity: Any q greater than one induces additional investment; any q less than one incurs disinvestment; and q = 1 gives rise to a stock equilibrium with respect to physical capital since the public is ready to keep just the given amount of physical capital – neither more nor less.

There is another, more vivid, way to define Tobin's q:

$$q := \frac{P_m}{P}. \tag{208}$$

In this equation, q is defined as a price ratio. P_m is the market price of real capital, and P are the costs of producing it. Formulas (207) and (208) are equivalent on the condition that capital has an infinite life span. This can be proved in the following manner. The present value of an infinite annuity A is equal to A/i where i is the discount factor. Thus, the present value of an investment, K, at a marginal efficiency of capital, R, amounts to

$$P \cdot K = \frac{P \cdot Y}{R}. \tag{209}$$

where P Y is the annual yield. Equation (209) is simply the definition of R. In order to calculate the market value of real capital we have to employ the supply price of capital, r_k, as the discount factor, obtaining

$$P_m \cdot K = \frac{P \cdot Y}{r_k}. \tag{210}$$

Formula (210) expresses the well-known fact that an investor, when calculating the present value of his investment, applies the required of return in discounting the future profits. The outcome is P_m as the highest price he is ready to pay; and P_m is smaller the greater the required rate of return. By dividing (209) and (210), we immediately obtain the desired relation:

$$\frac{P_m}{P} = \frac{R}{r_k} =: q. \tag{211}$$

Thus, Tobin's q can be defined as a ratio of rates of return, or as a price ratio. It is a magnitude which should not appear too unfamiliar because, when discussing other theories of investment, we repeatedly encountered two variables the difference or ratio of which determined investment activity. Within Classical theory, they were marginal productivity and the interest rate; in Keynesian theory, marginal efficiency of capital and the interest rate. These two approaches, however, differ from Tobin's in that the supply price of capital need not match the rate of interest. TOBIN's theory is to be considered as more general because the returns on physical capital and bonds are allowed to differ.

By equation (206) we stated that individuals could choose among three assets: money, bonds, and physical capital; and our next task consists in determining the choice actually made. In order to do this, we first want to examine these assets more closely:

Money serves for transactions purposes and as a store of value and is supposed to yield no return when prices are stable. Leaving state bankruptcies out of account, money is only subject to the risk of changes in the price level.

Bonds serve as a store of value and yield a return, r_B. Bonds are subject to the risk of changing prices, too, but additionally to the risk as regards yield because their return is steadily adjusted to the market interest rate.

Equities, equivalent to physical capital within our framework, serve as a store of value. Their value and yield are *not* subject to changes in the price level because any rise in the price level, according to (210), incurs a *proportional* rise in the market price of capital, and leaves the marginal efficiency of capital unchanged. Yet, equities are subject to other sorts of risk, which arise from shifts in relative commodity prices (caused by changes in technology or tastes) and the general economic performance which determines the marginal efficiency of capital.

The three assets have thus been characterized by "return" and "risk" since these two features, as known from the previous section, influence portfolio decisions. Now, the following assumption is essential to TOBIN's approach:

Money and bonds are subject to *similar* risks; and these *differ* from the risks associated with equities. Put differently, the risks of money and bonds are correlated *positively* with one another, and *uncorrelated* with the risk of equities.

Therefore, an investor is able to reduce the total risk of his portfolio by selecting appropriate shares of *financial assets* (money and bonds) and *real assets* (equities). Choosing financial assets only, his portfolio would be severly risky with respect to price changes – but by adding some equities he can reduce this risk considerably. Thus, holding both financial and real assets turns out to be the right strategy because in doing so the total risk can be reduced. In this case, *diversification* is the principle of avoiding risk.

If this is true, *and* if the investors are risk averse and tolerably clever, then financial assets will be *substitutes* for each other and *complements* for real assets [7]:

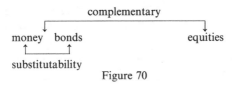

Figure 70

This implies: If the return on bonds rises, an investor is likely to substitute additional bonds for *money*, because these two are considered close substitutes. He is right in that the total risk of his portfolio will thus be only slightly augmented by the risk associated with the return on bonds. Therefore, the respective shares of finanancial assets respond strongly to changes in their relative rates of return.

On the other hand, our investor will not readily substitute bonds for *equities* since this would increase total risk considerably. In order to understand this, consider Figure 64 once more. If the risks of financial and real assets are independent of one another (i.e., $(\varrho) = 0$), there will be a certain ratio of them which minimizes total risk. We cannot expect that an investor will select precisely that ratio because risk is only one determinant of his choice. Yet, it has some significance, and complementarity between financial and real assets will be the stronger the greater is the risk aversion and the smaller is the value of the correlation coefficient. With absolute risk aversion (that is, where return is not taken into account) and a correlation coefficient less than 1, complementarity will be *complete*: the ratio of financial and real assets will remain the same irrespective of the returns.

As a further result, the supply price of capital, r_k, is not equal to the interest rate; this would only be the case if bonds and equities were considered perfect substitutes.

We are now ready to give a comprehensive account of total stock equilibrium in the financial sector. The *financial sector* is a sub-system, which means it is a part of the total macroeconomic model used for the analysis of fiscal and monetary measures.

---

7 The terms "substitutability" and "complementarity", known from basic microeconomic theory, refer to the response of a commodity ratio x/y to changes in the relative price p_x/p_y. This response is usually measured by the *elasticity of substitution*, $\sigma := \mathrm{d}(x/y)/\mathrm{d}(p_x/p_y) \cdot (p_x/p_y)/(x/x)$. With $\sigma = 0$ we have perfect complementarity (no response), and with $\sigma \to \infty$ we have perfect substitutability.

The equilibrium of this sector is defined by the following five equations:

$$M^s = M^d (Y, r_B, r_k, W) \tag{212}$$

$$B^s = B^d (Y, r_B, r_k, W) \tag{213}$$

$$K^s = K^d (Y, r_B, r_k, W) \tag{214}$$

$$W = \frac{M}{P} + \frac{B}{P} + q \cdot K \tag{215}$$

$$q = \frac{R(K)}{r_k}. \tag{216}$$

When a *stock equilibrium* prevails, the supply pattern of the three assets exactly matches the demand pattern. Then, money supply, bond supply, and physical capital are willingly kept by the investors. This is described by the first three equations. Adding the definition of wealth, (215), we recognize that only two of the above equilibrium conditions are independent of each other if W is the desired level of total wealth. Finally, (216) determines Tobin's q where R(K) indicates that marginal efficiency of capital depends on the capital stock given.

Since real income, Y, and the price level, P, are exogenous to the financial subsystem, four endogenous variables, namely, r_k, r_B, q, and W, are determined by four independent equations (we do not intend to enter the discussion of existence, uniqueness, and stability of the model). There are two connecting links between this financial sector and the rest of the model:

– First, real income and the price level, determined by the other markets and excerting an influence upon financial equilibrium, and
– second, Tobin's q, determined within the financial sector and influencing investment demand decisively.

By adding a commodity and a labor market, we could analyze the *stationary state* of this model, which exhibits the following features: There is a stock equilibrium within the financial sector; real income, employment, and prices have been adjusted to their equilibrium levels; the optimal capital and wealth stocks are realized such that neither investment nor savings take place any more; and the government's budget is balanced which incurs a constant supply of bonds. We refer the reader to the now prominent articles of BLINDER/SOLOW and TOBIN/BUITER[8] which deal with long-run effects of fiscal and monetary policy within this framework.

Our own aim is much less ambitious; we merely want to examine short-run impacts of fiscal and monetary measures, proceeding from a stock equilibrium of the financial sector which is disturbed by such a policy. The analysis is "partial" in so far as the commodity and labor markets are neglected. Consequently, we cannot decide whether an "expansionary" impact will increase output or prices – this depends on the condition of the latter markets.

---

8 BLINDER, A.M. and R.M. SOLOW (1973) Does Fiscal Policy Matter? Journal of Public Economics **2**, pp. 319–337. TOBIN, J. and W. BUITER (1976) Long-Run Effects of Fiscal and Monetary Policy on Aggregate Demand. In: STEIN, J.L. Ed. Monetarism. Amsterdam etc.: North-Holland.

I. Monetary Impact

The first case under consideration is that of a governmental budget deficit which is entirely financed by printing money. Thus, the government buys commodities and pays for them with money created by the central bank. Thereby, total monetary wealth of the private sector is augmented, and the original portfolio equilibrium is disturbed. Now we have to distinguish between a substitution and a wealth effect of this measure.

The *substitution effect* is due to the increased *share* of money in total wealth. If financial and real assets are perfect complements, the individuals will demand only additional bonds in order to establish a new portfolio equilibrium because these are the sole substitute for money. Consequently, the return on bonds, r_B, will decline – but no further substitution effect will come into being: there is no change in the demand for physical capital. If, on the other hand – and somewhat more realistically – financial and real assets are weak complements, the individuals will demand additional quantities of both bonds and equities. Therefore, r_B and r_k will decrease, and Tobin's q will increase. In this case, the substitution effect works in the "expansionary" direction because the supply price of capital, r_k, declines: marginal efficiency being unchanged, more physical capital will be demanded given the now smaller rate of return required of it.

Beside this substitution effect, there is a *wealth effect* which results from the fact that, other things being equal, any rise in M incurs a rise in total private wealth. Due to the wealth effect, demand for money, bonds, and equities will rise if these three are superior assets. When demand for bonds and equities rises, the rates of return of these assets, r_B and r_k, are bound to decline; and, applying the above line of reasoning, the decrease in r_k will stimulate investment activity.

To conclude, the *total effect*, being the sum of the substitution and the wealth effect, is definitely expansionary. This result coincides with that of Classical as well as Keynesian analysis: all three approaches imply that an expansion of the quantity of money will increase aggregate commodity demand. Whether this "expansionary effect" incurs more production or higher prices, however, cannot be decided on the basis of the present partial model.

II. Fiscal Impact

Government expenditure financed by borrowing is the more intriguing case – both as regards reasoning and results. Here, government is assumed to buy goods paying for them (indirectly) by issuing bonds. Let us examine the substitution and wealth effects once more.

Proceeding from an original portfolio equilibrium, the rate r_B is bound to rise in order to induce the individuals to keep more bonds. If financial and real assets are perfect complements nothing more will happen: The return on money was fixed at zero by assumption, and since real assets are not substituted for financial ones, r_k remains unchanged, the whole burden of adjustment being imposed on r_B.

This *contradicts* our former results. Because Classics and Keynesians considered financial and real assets to be perfect substitutes, they judged the impact of loan financing this way: Loans taken by the government will raise the interest rate, thereby crowding out private expenditures. In TOBIN's terminology this implies that the returns on bonds and equities, i.e. r_B and r_k, are identical or at least exhibit a constant relationship. Here, it is not so: since financial and real assets are perfect complements, r_k will not rise if r_B increases, and investment demand will not be reduced.

But let us now pass to the more moderate assumption of weak complementarity between financial and real assets. Investors will demand a higher return on physical capital if the return on bonds rises. Therefore, Tobin's q and, consequently, investment demand will decline when the government raises a loan; and they will decline the more, the weaker is the complementarity between financial and real assets.

The wealth effect is to be considered next. *In so far* as government bonds are perceived as net wealth by the private sector, the individuals will demand more money, bonds, and equities when B is increased by government borrowing. A higher demand for equities entails a lower supply price of capital; hence, Tobin's q as well as investment demand will increase. Thus, the wealth effect definitely works in the expansionary direction.

As regards the *total effect* no definite result emerges. If financial and real assets are perfect complements, loan financed government expenditures incur a "crowding in" since the wealth effect is positive, and the substitution effect is zero. Under the more moderate assumption of weak complementarity, however, the total effect is theoretically indeterminate as the wealth effect is positive, and the substitution effect negative. Yet, it is a general rule that crowding out becomes the more *probable* the *stronger* is the substitutability between financial and real assets.

Obviously, it makes a difference whether a budget deficit is financed by issuing money, or borrowing. In the first case, an expansionary impact emerges whereas, in the second, even a restrictive one proved to be possible. But what, we may ask, is the reason for the different performance of these two measures?

It is, the *fixedness of the return of money.* Consider the case of loan financing: Owing to government borrowing, the rate r_B rose; and thus a negative substitution effect emerged in the case of weak complementarity. We can state that this negative effect was due to the original rise in r_B.

The impact of money financing would be similar, in this model, if there were a rate of return on money which would rise in course of monetary expansion – but there is none. Because the yield of money was fixed at zero by assumption, the substitution effect even turned out to be positive.

§65 Conclusion

Finally, we want to compare Classical, Keynesian, and TOBIN's theory of money and wealth more closely, thereby summarizing the latter.

Classical theory. With respect to the Classical doctrine, it should first be noted that money serves as a medium of exchange and not as a store of one's wealth.

In the second place, bonds and real capital are perfect substitutes – a hidden assumption that will immediately become clear to the reader when considering Figure 46. There, we shifted the capital demand curve by the amount of governmental borrowing, which is only possible on condition that those assets issued by private firms, and those issued by the government, are homogeneous. Consequently, a uniform rate of return on these two assets was established, called the interest rate.

Third, government borrowing is analyzed within a flow equilibrium framework. Hence, no instantaneous "wealth effect" could arise; and the crowding out turned out to be inevitable.

Fourth, the expansionary impact of monetary policy depended solely on a wealth effect, the Cambridge effect. For well-known reasons ("Money is not a proper store of value."), no substitutability beween money and other assets is supposed.

Keynesian theory. The first difference with respect to the Classical doctrine is that money serves both as a medium of exchange and as a proper store of value.

Second, bonds and real capital were regarded as being perfect substitutes – as in Classical theory – which becomes obvious when looking at $S = I + G$: only if private (I) and public borrowing (G) are homogenous, are they capable of being added. And, again, a uniform rate of interest is established.

Third, there is no "wealth effect" because the analysis refers to a flow equilibrium.

Finally, we encounter another difference between Keynesian and Classical analysis. Monetary expansion causes a substitution effect (termed the Keynes effect) because bonds are a substitute for money. This was illustrated by shifting the LM curve to the right.

Tobin's theory. In the first place, Tobin maintains the Keynesian concept that money is a proper store of value.

Second, according to Tobin, money and bonds are close substitutes because they are subject to similar risks, and both are complements to equities (physical capital). As a result, the returns on bonds (r_B) and equities (r_k) usually differ, that is, there is no uniform interest rate common to all assets.

Third, Tobin applies the notion of a stock equilibrium to all asset markets. Due to this assumption, both money printing and government borrowing incur "wealth effects" which usually work in an expansionary direction.

As regards results, Tobin affirms both the Classical and the Keynesian analyis of monetary policy. At the same time, his theory of pure fiscal policy differs substantially from the former two since the specific effects of government borrowing are not necessarily restrictive. This difference is chiefly due to Tobin's concept of stock equilibria.

Naturally, Tobin's theory itself became subject to criticism; and the following four points seem worth mentioning:

- With regard to the microeconomic foundations, it has to be emphasized that only rather special distribution and utility functions yield the above results. In particular, the assumption of normally distributed yields is very important to Tobin's analysis.
- The second criticism, a more empirical one that is usually made by Monetarists, questions the complementarity of financial and real assets. Beyond that, some monetarists, and New Classics, oppose the assumption that government bonds are regarded as net wealth by the private sector.
- Third, Tobin's analysis of "liquidity preference as behaviour towards risk" suffers from the fact that there are assets, no riskier than money, which yield a positive return – short-term securities, for instance. Therefore, the proposition that money

is kept in order to reduce risk appears ill-founded[9]; and thus it seems more plausible that all money balances result from i) the fact that money is the most fungible asset and ii) the trifling transaction costs of exchanging it.

- Finally, the concept of stock equilibrium gives rise to some deep-seated problems. Though a now prominent and widely used approach, stock equilibria involve somewhat awkward modeling, since all changes in wealth have to be brought about by "helicopter-effects". Hence they are apt to obscure the fact that all money printing and borrowing actually takes place as flows – like the commodity flows which they are used to finance.

Further Reading

Hicks, J.R. (1967) Critical Essays in Monetary Theory. Oxford: Clarendon Press

Tobin, J. (1965) The Theory of Portfolio Selection. In: Hahn, F. and F.P.R. Brechling Ed. The Theory of Interest Rates. Op.cit.

Tobin, J. (1969) A General Equilibrium Approach to Monetary Theory. Journal of Money, Credit and Banking 1, pp. 15–29

---

9 Cf. Chang, W.H., D. Hamberg and J. Hirata (1983) Liquidity Preference as Behaviour Towards Risk is a Demand for Short Term Securities – Not Money. American Economic Review **73**, pp. 420–427.

Chapter IX. Monetarism

The Monetarist drama was somewhat confused from the outset – but what a staging! Seemingly, two camps of respectable scientists were battling against each other to the death, without the true cause of their disagreement becoming really obvious. This seems to be the impression the public has of the present state of macroeconomics, and the whole controversy is of course bound to remind one of the early days of the "Keynesian Revolution". Happily, the debate has become considerably de-emotionalized in the last decade, so that, today, a balanced account of the issues does not appear difficult.

It is difficult, however, to give a concise definition of "Monetarism". A first, tentative approach might read: *Monetarism* is a reformulated quantity theory of money, its essential allegation being that the evolution of national nominal income is dominated by changes in the money supply. This definition is common usage, brief, empty, and undoubtedly too narrow.

The ambiguity of the term under consideration is revealed more easily if we ask for its opposite: First, *Monetarism-Fiscalism* seems to fit best. In this case, Monetarism must be regarded as a pragmatic position which, for reasons to be explained later, prefers monetary to fiscal policy. This is indeed a first aspect.

Or is *Monetarism* the opposite of *Keynesianism*? The former would then be a theory whose adherents consider Keynesian theory fallacious, insufficient, or irrelevant. It is this definition that seems to be the prevailing one among economists.

Third, *Monetarism* is often conceived as anti-*Activism*, thus being a particular variety of economic liberalism. Guessing that the public considers this to be the essential feature of Monetarism, we want to accept it as an additional aspect.

Before discussing Monetarism in terms of these three aspects, some general remarks have to be made. It is important that the term "Monetarism" does not denote an economic school with a fixed doctrine, but rather a movement which started in the 1950s and has since developed and changed. Therefore, the following characterization of Monetarism cannot be applied to all so-called "Monetarists", that is, to KARL BRUNNER, PHILIP CAGAN, MILTON FRIEDMAN, DAVID LAIDLER, ALLAN H. MELTZER, and JEROME L. STEIN, to name a few. Moreover, Monetarists and Keynesians do not form two distinct and intransigent camps; rather, "pure Monetarism" and "pure Keynesianism" are the imagined extremes of a range, and most economists take their place somewhere in between. Notwithstanding that, our polarizing exposition is appropriate for bringing up the differences which actually exist.

Nowadays, Monetarism is interpreted as a "counter-revolution" to the "Keynesian revolution", primarily initiated by MILTON FRIEDMAN and advanced by him and his fellows until it has now attained the status of an orthodoxy. In our view three reasons were chiefly responsible for this "counter-revolution".

First, the "Keynesian revolution" had never achieved complete victory, in part for ideological reasons. "Fears" and "hopes" that the government sector would encroach as a result of this doctrine proved true; and the "fears" formed a fertile soil for any counter-revolution. One should be careful, however, not to consider the Monetarist-Keynesian-controversy as an essentially ideological debate. Matters are not so simple, and we will explain later why not.

A second important cause of the rise of Monetarism consisted in the devolopment of monetary theory. Yet, the increasing interest in money was not characteristic of Monetarism alone but of the major part of macroeconomic research since KEYNES: we have already mentioned HICKS, PATINKIN, TOBIN, and DAVIDSON. On the other hand, Monetarism took a very active part in connecting monetary theory (as an academic excercise) and monetary policy (as the totality of practical measures).

Real events, however, formed the most important cause of the counter-revolution. During World War II, many economists were afraid of a continuation, if not aggravation, of the pre-war depression. Influential Keynesians, such as ALVIN H. HANSEN or ABBA P. LERNER [1], predicted a lasting problem of deficient demand if the responsible authorities would not opt for active fiscal policy. Since they were anything but alone in this opinion, the chief stress of activist policy in the US as elsewhere was on *fiscal policy*. Monetary policy, on the other hand, was put last, its main task consisting in ensuring low interest rates to lessen the problem of the public debt and perhaps to stimulate investment demand. Changes in the *quantity of money* were almost entirely neglected.

Today we know that, in the post-war years, no diminution of aggregate demand arose; quite on the contrary, there was an unprecedented up-swing, and production as well as employment maintained high and stable levels for a long time. This being so, it is hardly astonishing that the problem of unemployment lost public interest and was replaced by the problem of *inflation*: then the most pressing one.

Consequently, the professional economists, or at least a considerable fraction of them, turned their attention from *employment* to *inflation*: the ground for Monetarism was prepared [2].

§ 66 The Theoretical Foundations, or: Monetarism versus Keynesianism

"Money is a veil, but when the veil flutters, real output sputters."   (JOHN G. GURLEY)

In this first section, we want to discuss Monetarist *theory* and explain in what respect it differs from that of the Classics and the Keynesians. The first milestone in the

---

1 HANSEN, A.H. (1941) Fiscal Policy and the Business Cycle. New York: W.W. Norton. LERNER, A.P. (1944) The Economics of Control. New York: Macmillan.

2 A formidable sociological analysis of the revolution and the counter-revolution is that of JOHNSON, H.G. (1971) The Keynesian Revolution and the Monetarist Counterrevolution. American Economic Review (PP) **61**, pp. 1–14.

evolution of Monetarist theory is MILTON FRIEDMAN's 1956 paper "The Quantity Theory of Money: A Restatement"[3]. FRIEDMAN's "restatement" combines Classical and Keynesian elements and is substantially a theory of money demand.

In order to understand FRIEDMAN's analysis, let us start with an explanation of the equivalence of wealth and income. If W^n denotes nominal wealth and r represents some rate of interest, then nominal income in a certain period amounts to:

$$Y^n = W^n \cdot r. \tag{217}$$

Conversely, wealth can be calculated when income and the interest rate are known:

$$W^n = \frac{Y^n}{r}. \tag{218}$$

Hence, "wealth" and "income" are just two aspects of the same thing since every kind of income can be regarded as a return on a stock of wealth. If interest is given, wealth yields a certain income; and, conversely, interest can be calculated by discounting the income flow. FRIEDMAN does not turn his attention to present wealth, or current income, but to the *permanent* magnitudes. To take the extreme case as illustration: W^n is wealth possessed by an individual during his whole life; and Y^n is the average (permanent) life time income. This novel definition of terms is closely connected to FRIEDMAN's research on the consumption function[4], and it is very significant to his theory.

Let us suppose for instance, in accordance with FRIEDMAN, that consumption does not depend on current but on permanent income. Therefore, current income determines consumption only in that it is a fraction of permanent income. KEYNES' *absolute income hypothesis* is thus rejected and replaced by FRIEDMAN's *permanent income hypothesis*. Now, when current income declines, the individuals will reduce their consumption only slightly, or even not at all, for they form up their consumption plans with respect to permanent income. If this is true, the Keynesian multipliers are utterly insignificant because a given reduction in real income does not diminish consumption very much. As a result of this permanent income hypothesis, the private sector seems much more stable than alleged by the Keynesians; and exogenous disturbances do not cause significant multiplier processes but merely trifling adjustments.

FRIEDMAN applies his concept of permanent income to the theory of money demand, too. Permanent income is the return on a rather widely defined stock of nominal wealth. The latter consists of

- *money*: a means of payment with a constant face value that does not yield interest;
- *bonds*: interest bearing securities with a constant face value;
- *equities*: claims on the profits of a firm;
- *physical goods*; and
- *human capital*.

3 FRIEDMAN, M. (1956) The Quantity Theory of Money: A Restatement. In: FRIEDMAN, M. Ed. Studies in the Quantity Theory of Money. Chicago: Chicago Press.
4 FRIEDMAN, M. (1957) A Theory of the Consumption Function. Princeton: Princeton University Press.

Thus, FRIEDMAN's idea of wealth embraces two elements that are new to us, namely, physical goods and human capital. Physical goods have much in common with equities for they are not subject to the danger of inflation. They differ from the latter because they do not yield payments in money, but in kind. FRIEDMAN's own examples of cars and condominiums illustrate that the "income" derived from physical goods does not consist in money but in direct utility.

Human capital is the totality of those abilities of an individual which yield labor income; it can be calculated in principle by adding the discounted labor income of the individual over his total life span. Thus we recognize again that any income can be regarded as stemming from an appropriately defined stock of capital. Human capital, however, is *sui generis*, in that it is incapable of being exchanged instantaneously for other stocks of wealth. Bonds can be exchanged for money without difficulty whereas the perfect fungibility of human capital exists only in a slave market. Finally, *permanent income* is the return on the above five assets.

We are now ready to introduce FRIEDMAN's money demand function:

$$L^n = f\left(P, r_B, r_E, \frac{\dot{P}}{P}, \frac{Y^n}{r}\right). \tag{219}$$

$$\underset{(+)(-)(-)(-)\ (+)}{}$$

Nominal demand for money depends on the following factors:

- The current price level. This is due to the fact (already familiar to us) that invididuals want to maintain a certain level of *real* cash balances.
- The rates of return r_B and r_E on bonds and equities, respectively. These two exert an influence upon the demand for money because bonds and equities are substitutes for cash balances. Any rise in r_B or r_E increases the opportunity costs of holding money balances and thus tends to reduce them.
- The rate of inflation, $\dot{P}/P$. $\dot{P}$ is the common shorthand for dP/dt, i.e. the change in P over time. Dividing this magnitude by P we obtain a growth rate which indicates the relative change in P. A positive rate of inflation causes a reduction in the real value of cash balances and hence augments the opportunity costs of holding cash. Therefore, as a rule, an increase in $\dot{P}/P$ will diminish the demand for money.
- The stock of wealth which, according to (218) can be calculated from permanent income and the *average rate of return*, r, on the five assets[5].

Two comments are called for. First we emphasize that changes in the *price level* and changes in the *rate of inflation* must be sharply distinguished. An increase in the former raises nominal cash balances whereas an increase in the latter reduces them. The first case is substantiated by the observation that the individuals want to maintain certain *real* cash balances. Therefore they will increase nominal cash balances if prices rise. To the second case we apply the principle of opportunity costs: the higher the rate of inflation, the more strongly do real cash balances diminish over time or, what is

---

5 In his paper, FRIEDMAN takes account of two further magnitudes, namely, the ratio of non-human to human capital (w) and the "preferences" (u). Since these two are both unmeasurable and are subsequently neglected by FRIEDMAN, we have not introduced them.

the same, the higher are the opportunity costs of keeping cash balances. Hence the latter will be deliberately reduced when inflation goes up.

Second, the somewhat mysterious rate, "r", must be explained. Above we enumerated five different assets any of which was supposed to yield some pecuniary or non-pecuniary return. Of the five corresponding rates of return, however, only two are *measureable*, namely, the returns of bonds and equities, r_B and r_E. Therefore, FRIEDMAN abandons an explicit account of the others, and assumes that r, as the weighted average of the five rates, varies "in some systematic manner" with r_B and r_E. The problem has thus been reduced to analyzing two rates of return, and an explicit account of r is unnecessary:

$$L^n = f\left(P, r_B, r_E, \frac{\dot{P}}{P}, Y^n\right). \tag{220}$$

In this equation, we have substituted permanent income for nominal wealth because their ratio, r, was assumed to be implied by r_B and r_E.

FRIEDMAN assumes next that individuals are not subject to any "money illusion" and that they aim to hold a certain amount of real cash balances. Thus, if prices and nominal permanent income are both multiplied by λ, nominal demand for cash will increase by λ, too:

$$\lambda \cdot L^n = f\left(\lambda \cdot P, r_B, r_E, \frac{\dot{P}}{P}, \lambda \cdot Y^n\right). \tag{221}$$

If prices and nominal income are doubled, for instance, nominal cash balances will also be doubled in order to maintain the level of real cash balances. Since (221) holds for *any* λ we can put $\lambda = 1/Y^n$ to obtain:

$$\frac{1}{Y^n} \cdot L^n = f\left(\frac{P}{Y^n}, r_B, r_E, \frac{\dot{P}}{P}, 1\right) \tag{222}$$

$$\Leftrightarrow L^n = f\left(\frac{P}{Y^n}, r_B, r_E, \frac{\dot{P}}{P}, 1\right) \cdot Y^n. \tag{223}$$

Now we ask the reader to compare (223) with (60), the money demand function of the quantity theory. Obviously, these two are quite similar, the only essential difference being that money demand is determined by a *constant* in (60), and by a *function* in (223). According to FRIEDMAN, the cash balance coefficient (k) is not a *numerically invariant* value but an *invariant function* of some variables. This is regarded as the most important difference between the Classical quantity theory of money and its restatement.

Since the circular velocity of money, termed v in equation (62), is just the reciprocal of the cash balance coefficient, we can define it in the following manner:

$$v\left(\frac{Y^n}{P}, r_B, r_E, \frac{\dot{P}}{P}\right) := 1/f\left(\frac{P}{Y^n}, r_B, r_E, \frac{\dot{P}}{P}, 1\right). \tag{224}$$

Neglecting the constant, "1", and replacing P/Y^n by its reciprocal, we obtained the circular velocity of money as a function of real permanent income, the rates r_B and r_E, and the rate of inflation. By means of the equilibrium condition for the money market, $M = L^n$, we immediately arrive at the final result, the restated quantity equation:

$$M \cdot v \left(\frac{Y^n}{P}, r_B, r_E, \frac{\dot{P}}{P} \right) = Y^n. \tag{225}$$

In view of the resemblance of (225) to (63), the expression "restatement of the quantity theory of money" seems quite apt. Now we have to investigate the specific "novelties" of FRIEDMAN's conception, and consider how it is related to the original quantity theory, to liquidity theory, and to portfolio theory.

The restatement differs from the original formulation of the quantity theory in that it conceives of the circular velocity of money as a dependent variable of the system, not as a constant. To be fair, however, we must add that many reflections on the determinants of v are to be found in the Classical literature though FRIEDMAN's analysis may be more explicit and systematic. The following inference is important to a proper appreciation of Monetarism: At the theoretical level, Monetarists do not argue that the circular velocity of money is an invariant magnitude but that it is a stable function[6] of the four variables enumerated in (225). Consequently, a change in v is conceivable *if* it results from a change in those variables. This formulation appears theoretically conclusive, and it is sharply at variance with the crude forms of the elder quantity theory. Beyond that, it cannot be falsified empirically since the determinants Y^n (permanent income) and r (the average rate of return) are not measurable.

FRIEDMAN's analysis differs from Keynesian liquidity preference theory which may be represented by the equation

$$M = L(Y, i) \cdot P \tag{226}$$

in at least three respects. First, the interest rate is replaced by five different rates of return, though only two of the latter are measurable and explicitly taken into account. This difference seems to be of minor significance.

A second deviation arises from the fact that the two approaches employ differing notions of income, namely, permanent income on the one hand and current income on the other hand. Keynesian demand for money is subject to spontaneous changes if current income varies, whereas FRIEDMAN's money demand is not, because it depends on permanent income. Since the determinant Y^n in (225) is nearly constant, FRIEDMAN's money demand turns out to be much more stable than the Keynesian one.

Third, the *rate of inflation* appears as a decisive determinant in equation (225); and it is a novel, dynamic, element. We will return to that matter when examining the problem of inflation.

Finally, what are the differences between FRIEDMAN's analysis and TOBIN's theory of portfolio selection? They are, again, FRIEDMAN's attention to the rate of inflation and his concept of permanent income. Save that, the two approaches are amazingly similar.

After these introductory remarks concerning the relations between the four theories of money demand, we are now ready to discuss FRIEDMAN's central allegations as

---

6 Here, we do not use the term *stability* in the theoretical sense (convergence towards an equilibrium) but in the statistical sense (invariance).

far as they relate to theory. This is undertaken using the restated quantity equation which, for short, may be written as

$$M \cdot v(.) = Y^n. \tag{227}$$

In his theoretical considerations, FRIEDMAN assumes an exogenous *nominal* money supply, M. Real cash balances, however, are determined by the individuals since their behaviour determines money prices. The impact of a monetary expansion may be analyzed first.

In the most simple example, the central bank distributes additional money via the "helicopter effect": M increases. Demand for real cash balances remains unchanged *for the present*, hence the individuals try to diminish their additional nominal balances by purchasing commodities, bonds, etc. Considered macroeconomically, they will not succeed in doing so because one individual's expenditure is another's receipt. But nominal income $Y^n := Y \cdot P$ will increase.

The point in question is whether the increase in nominal income consists in rising *real incomes* or in rising *prices*. Or, to put it another way, will an expansionary monetary policy result in rising output or inflation? This crucial issue can hardly be solved using FRIEDMAN's model above; he therefore habitually assumes that real income is determined within some kind of Walrasian system. Thus, monetary expansion will usually raise prices; however in some cases FRIEDMAN admits real effects of monetary policy. We will return to this matter later.

For the time being, let us assume that only price effects arise from the monetary expansion. Consequently, not only prices but also the *rate of inflation* will increase for some time. This causes the demand for money to diminish because the opportunity costs of holding money balances increase. Therefore, the average duration of holding money, k, *decreases* and the circular velocity of money, v, *increases*.

Now, consider equation (227). When v rises due to a monetary expansion, nominal income must rise more than in proportion to the quantity of money. Suppose, for instance, that the quantity of money is augmented by 5%. When v rises by 2% for a short time, then nominal income must rise by 7%. But only temporarily! For, when the price level has attained a level 7% higher than before, inflation stops and v decreases to its original value. Subsequently, a 2% *deflation* must take place. The equilibrium value of nominal income is only reached after some further deviations. It is 5% higher than the original one.

The description of this somewhat involved process yields an important result: Once-and-for-all changes in the quantity of money do not produce "well-behaved" effects but give rise to erratical, cyclical deviations. Discretionary policy appears to be destabilizing to a high degree.

The impact of monetary policy on *real magnitudes* is to be analyzed next. According to the Monetarists, real effects trace back primarily to lags in the forming of *expectations*. Let us consider an economy which has exhibited an annual rate of real economic growth of 3% for many years, and where the central bank has increased the quantity of money by 5% per year. Thus, circular velocity of money assumed constant, 2% inflation per year has been observed for a long time. The inhabitants of this economy are certainly accustomed to the annual rate of inflation: and when making longer-term contracts (about labor or credit, for instance), they take these 2% into account.

Now suppose that a spontaneous and unexpected increase in the quantity of money occurs. The resulting rise in inflation comes as a surprise to our individuals, and in the short run real wage rates and the real rate of interest (nominal rate minus rate of inflation) will diminish. If resources were not fully utilized at the outset, employment and production will rise. Thus we encounter *real effects* of monetary changes here. Yet, according to Monetarist opinion, employment and production will decline to their original, "natural" levels as soon as expectations of inflation have become fully adapted.

This consideration leads us on to the notion of a natural rate of unemployment. The *natural rate of unemployment* is that rate which is established by the market forces and which is incapable of being influenced permanently by fiscal or monetary measures. According to the Monetarists, the natural rate of unemployment is determined by frictional adjustment problems, the average real wage rate, and the pattern of real wages. Note that it is neither regarded as being given by "nature" nor meant as an "optimal" rate of unemployment. Rather, the natural rate of unemployment is defined analogously to the natural rate of interest we explained in Chapter IV.

The *existence* of such a natural rate of unemployment is a central issue in the controvery between Monetarists and Keynesians. Keynesians typically do not admit its existence but argue that government is able to remedy unemployment by means of fiscal or monetary policy – at least in principle. Monetarists, on the other hand, maintain that fiscal policy will alter the actual rate of unemployment not at all while monetary policy will do so only temporarily.

It should have become clear by the above example that the effects of monetary policy on the rate of unemployment are temporary in nature; but with regard to fiscal policy matters are somewhat more difficult. FRIEDMAN himself does not have an analytical apparatus at his disposal to examine fiscal impacts. He argues, however, that "pure fiscal policy" will always result in a total *crowding out*:

"It seems absurd to say that if the government increases its expenditures without increasing taxes, that may not by itself be expansionary. Such a policy obviously puts income into the hands of the people to whom the government pays out its expenditures without taking any extra funds out of the hands of the taxpayers. Is that not obviously expansionary or inflationary? Up to that point, yes, but that is only half the story. We have to ask where the government gets the extra funds it spends. If the government prints money to meet its bills, that is monetary policy and we are trying to look at fiscal policy by itself. If the government gets the funds by borrowing from the public, then those people who lend the funds to the government have less to spend or to lend to others." [7]

In short: tax-financed and loan-financed government expenditures entail a total crowding out. This result is clearly at variance with TOBIN's, which we discussed in the previous chapter. Unfortunately, FRIEDMAN's allegation is not based on an explicit analytical model; we can therefore only guess that he neglects the wealth effect of public loans and regards government bonds and money as complements.

---

7 FRIEDMAN, M. (1970) The Counterrevolution in Monetary Theory. London: Institute of Economic Affairs for the Wincott Foundation, Occasional Paper 33, p. 19.

It was left to FRIEDMAN's most prominent adherants, KARL BRUNNER and ALLAN H. MELTZER, to overcome this lack of analytical foundation. They developed a series of continuously modified models in order to give a thorough examination of the transmission mechanisms of fiscal and monetary policy and thus to clear away the partial theory-vacuum of Monetarism. Without discussing their comprehensive models [8] in detail, we want to point out the central features:

First, BRUNNER and MELTZER's models are based on the theory of portfolio selection. For this reason, their approach is also termed "price theoretic Monetarism" as opposed to the "neo-quantity theoretic Monetarism" of FRIEDMAN. It is particularly striking how minor are the differences between the Monetarist models à la BRUNNER/MELTZER on the one hand and the Keynesian models à la TOBIN on the other – at least with respect to their analytical instruments.

Second, the models of BRUNNER and MELTZER comprise a broad spectrum of assets. The authors struggle against attempts to define "Monetarism" as a theory assuming a vertical LM curve, i.e. assuming money demand to be perfectly interest inelastic. According to them, the IS/LM model cannot serve as a basis of comparison because it does not contain enough relevant information, namely, a whole spectrum of assets and rates of return. BRUNNER and MELTZER arrive at "Monetaristic" results even though the authors do not assume money demand to be perfectly interest inelastic – as did the Classics.

Third, BRUNNER and MELTZER's models cannot provide a total analysis of the economy because they do not contain a labor market and they take real income as exogenous. This fact shows once more that contemporary Monetarism is more a theory of inflation than a theory of the business cycle or even a theory of employment. Meanwhile, the problem of the "missing equation" of Monetarism (i.e. the one that determines real income) has become a winged word.

Due to the development of portfolio theory and its utilization by the Monetarists, a convergence of method between the two "schools" has taken place what is a benefit for all observers of the controversy because it facilitates comparison. This welcome development is somewhat marred, however, since both Keynesians and Monetarists do not always acknowledge the convergence. Especially when reading BRUNNER and MELTZER one tends to get the impression that the authors consider the theory of portfolio selection as an exclusively Monetaristic tool, whereas, when speaking of "Keynesianism", they seem to refer only to the income-expenditure model.

All in all it is safe to say that the differences in method between modern Keynesians and Monetarists have become trifling. In theory, the two central issues are

– the acceptance or rejection of a natural rate of unemployment, and
– diverging estimates of the kind and strength of relationships of substitution between various assets.

With regard to FRIEDMAN, the concept of permanent magnitudes must be added to this catalogue. But far more important than all this is the conviction of the

---

8 Cf. especially BRUNNER, K. and A.H. MELTZER (1972) A Monetarist Framework for Aggregative Analysis. In: Supplement 1 to Kredit und Kapital. BRUNNER, K. and A.H. MELTZER (1976) An Aggregative Theory for a Closed Economy. In: STEIN, J.L. Ed. Monetarism. Amsterdam etc.: North Holland.

Monetarists that the private sector is stable in itself – a conviction which is not shared by the Keynesians.

§67 The Empirical Investigations, or: Monetarism versus Fiscalism

"Inflation is always and everywhere a monetary phenomenon."

(MILTON FRIEDMAN)

FRIEDMAN's restatement of the quantity theory of money is a good example of SAMUELSON's dictum that the psychic impact of a theory is not invariant with respect to equivalent transformations. According to its algebraic structure, it seems to be more closely connected with the Classical quantity theory than, for instance, with liquidity preference theory. Yet this is not so; actually, it is more congenial with liquidity preference theory because it does not regard the circular velocity of money as a *numerical* constant.

Therefore, if FRIEDMAN fancies himself as being in the Classical tradition, *empirical* rather than theoretical reasons must be responsible for this opinion. In fact, the empirical differences between Monetarists and Keynesians are more important than the theoretical ones.

In a comprehensive study of the "Monetary History of the United States, 1867–1960", MILTON FRIEDMAN and ANNA J. SCHWARZ observed growth of the quantity of money, the price level, and income over more than a century. They arrived at the following results:

> "1. Changes in the behaviour of the money stock have been closely associated with changes in economic activity, money income, and prices.
> 2. The interrelation between monetary and economic change has been highly stable.
> 3. Monetary changes have often had an independent origin; they have not been simply a reflection of changes in economic activity." [9]

The first sentence is obviously a verbal formulation of the quantity theory of money but beyond that it states a relationship between the quantity of money on the one hand and prices and real income ("economic activity") on the other.

In the second sentence, the authors allege the *numerical* (!) stability of the circular velocity of money. This is a considerable intensification of FRIEDMAN's result that the circular velocity is a stable *function* of several variables. Only here does FRIEDMAN begin to be at variance with the Keynesians and nearer to the old quantity theorists. Specifically, FRIEDMAN and SCHWARZ estimate the interest elasticity of money to be − 0.15 on the average. This means, if interest declines from 10% to 9%, money demand will increase by only 1.5%.

---

9 FRIEDMAN, M. and A.J. SCHWARZ (1963) A Monetary History of the United States, 1867–1960. Princeton: Princeton University Press, p. 676.

Finally, FRIEDMAN and SCHWARZ establish in the third sentence that the quantity of money is generally *exogenous*. This relates to an issue we have not mentioned up to now: In the foregoing models, we always assumed the quantity of money to be given – an assumption that already caused feelings to run high in the last century. The dispute between the *currency school* and the *banking school* referred to this very issue. Contrary to the currency school, the banking school denied that the central bank could control the money supply. In support of this view, which has survived up to the present, the following arguments are put forward:

- First, monetary policy is conceived as a string. One could pull on it to diminish the money supply but one could not push it, because no one could be made to take money. Thus, monetary policy is capable of being restrictive but not expansionary.
- Second, a wide definition of "money" is proposed. If the quantity of money comprises cheques, bills of exchange, and the like, the central bank may possibly be unable to control the *total* money supply. If the authorities reduce some part of the money supply, say M1, the individuals can side-step this by using more bills, for instance. Thus, according to this view, the central bank cannot control the quantity of money.

Nowadays, this problem is well-known as the *reversed causation*. The adherants of the reversed causation-doctrine allege that the quantity of money is *endogenous* and merely reflects the level of economic activity. The third statement of FRIEDMAN and SCHWARZ opposes this reversed causation: the authors think that the money supply is chiefly exogenous. This exogeneity is a necessary prerequisite of Monetarism: because the proposition "Money doesn't matter" would be only too true if the quantity of money were entirely endogenous. Therefore, a Monetarist is necessarily a currency-theorist.

A further important Monetarist study is that by MILTON FRIEDMAN and DAVID MEISELMAN[10]. It concerns "The Relative Stability of Monetary Velocity and the Investment Multiplier". FRIEDMAN and MEISELMAN tried to find out whether Monetarism or Keynesianism is supported by the evidence. In order to do so they proposed an amazingly simple ground rule, reducing "Monetarism" and "Keynesianism" to one equation each:

$$Y^n = a + b \cdot M \qquad \text{"Monetarism"} \qquad (229)$$

$$Y^n = c + d \cdot A^n \qquad \text{"Keynesiasm"} \qquad (229)$$

Here, a, b, c, and d are the coefficients of the linear regressions which are to be estimated. The first equation represents the Monetarist proposition that nominal income is chiefly determined by the quantity of money. The second equation is meant to depict the income-expenditure model where "autonomous expenditure", A^n, i.e. investment and government demand, is the crucial determinants of nominal income. However, to avoid the problem of spurious correlation, FRIEDMAN and MEISELMAN

---

10 FRIEDMAN, M. and D. MEISELMAN (1963) The Relative Stability of Monetary Velocity and the Investment Multiplier in the United States, 1897–1958. In: the Commision on Money, Credit and Commerce Ed. Stabilization Policies. Englewood-Cliffs: Prentice-Hall.

did not estimate these two equations but the following two, in which income is replaced by consumption:

$$C^n = a + b \cdot M \qquad \text{"Monetarism"} \qquad (230)$$

$$C^n = c + d \cdot A^n \qquad \text{"Keynesianism"} \qquad (231)$$

They arrived at the result that the relationship between the quantity of money and nominal consumption is far closer than that between autonomous expenditure and consumption. Therefore, they inferred that

- the money demand function is much more *stable* than the consumption function;
- it is the quantity of money, and not autonomous demand, that exerts the decisive influence on consumption;
- and monetary policy must be expected to have a stronger impact than fiscal policy.

It is not surprising that these conclusions did not remain uncontested. Among the various criticisms[11], there are two especially important ones:

- The above approach does not depict Keynesian theory adequately whereas it fits Monetarism quite well. For the very reason that Keynesianism *cannot* be reduced to one equation, the estimation is bound to be in favor of Monetarism. In short, equations (230) and (231) support the Monetarist proposition from the outset.
- The close correlation between the quantity of money and nominal consumption is not sufficient to establish that the former determines the latter. On the contrary, an intimate relationship between these two variables will also result if the quantity of money is *endogenous*. It may even be true that, in (230), M is the dependent variable; at least the estimation is incapable of proving the opposite.

Thus the controversy between Keynesianism and Monetarism was not settled by the empirical investigations. The evidence as such was not doubted, but the conclusions inferred from it were. Up to now, most Keynesians do not consider their doctrine disproved by the Monetarists' empirical research.

To summarize, we may say that Monetarists draw the following conclusions from their empirical investigations:

- Nominal income and the price level are solely determined by the quantity of money in a systematic manner.
- Monetary policy thus exerts a strong impact on nominal income, but fiscal policy has a trifling and indirect effect because it possibly alters the circular velocity of money.
- The money demand function is more stable than the Keynesian consumption function. "Stability" is primarily meant as functional stability; but, from the evidence, a high numerical stability can also be established. The interest elasticity of money demand is relatively small.

---

11 ANDO, A. and F. MODIGLIANI (1965) The Relative Stability of Monetary Velocity and the Investment Multiplier. American Economic Review **55**, pp. 693–728. TOBIN, J. (1970) Money and Income: Post Hoc ergo Propter Hoc? Quarterly Journal of Economics **84**, pp. 301–317.

Of course, the judgement as to the instability of the consumption function refers to the *Keynesian* consumption function which employs the absolute income hypothesis. That consumption which depends on *permanent* income is regarded as stable, and so are investment and money demand. Therefore, as already mentioned, Monetarism proceeds from a considerable stability of the private sector as a whole. This is hardly an empirically assured result, however, but rather a basic proposition of Monetarism. And, in our opinion, it is the most important proposition separating Keynesians and Monetarists.

§ 68 The Political Inferences, or: Monetarism versus Activism

"A radical might even accept the constant monetary growth rule on the basis that this is the best one can do under capitalism." (THOMAS MAYER)

The hypothesis of an inherently stable private sector is essential to the political attitude of Monetarism. According to the Monetarist interpretation, a market economy, if left to itself, will be subject to only minor deviations in employment and production. It will by no means be exposed to such crises as imagined by the Keynesians. But – is this allegation not in flagrant contradiction to reality?

The Monetarists think that the actual depressions, which can hardly be denied, do not result from private behaviour, but from *interventions of the government*. The government weakens private enterprise by fiscal policies (taxes and debt), causes inflation by expansionary monetary policy, provokes unemployment by restrictive monetary policy, and in doing all this makes the individuals feel insecure, which destabilizes the economy additionally.

Thus, the Monetarists have an impression of economic performance which is utterly opposed to that of the Keynesians. While Keynesians consider the private sector to be (potentially) instable, so that government must assist in maintaining high levels of employment and production, Monetarists suppose the private sector to be inherently stable, though sometimes incapable of absorbing the disturbances caused by the state.

The *anti-activist* attitude of Monetarists is closely tied up with this view. According to them, government interventions are not only superflous but, beyond that, injurious. On the other hand, many Monetarists concede that the private sector may itself induce smaller fluctuations, and if they oppose government intervention even in this case, they must have good reasons. These reasons are, the *lags* of fiscal and monetary policy. Any "fine tuning" of the economy is possible only on condition that the impacts of fiscal or monetary tools result almost immediately. FRIEDMAN, for instance, estimated that the lag of a monetary stimulus amounts to some quarter of the length of a business cycle. It is clear that if discretionary measures are subject to such considerable lags, then it seems appropriate to dispense with them altogether, because they are apt to cause destabilization rather than stabilization.

With regard to the relative efficiency of monetary and fiscal policy, the Monetaristic position is not unique. On the one hand, FRIEDMAN emphasizes again and again that inflation is a purely monetary phenomenon. Fiscal policy would cause neither inflation – nor anything else, apart from re-distributing purchasing power between the private and the public sector. On the other hand, BRUNNER and MELTZER's models, based on the theory of portfolio selection, do assign *short-run* impacts to fiscal policy. Yet, these are transitory in nature; and in this respect, there is agreement among all Monetarists.

Hence, fiscal and monetary measures may be successful in the short run – but this disappears as soon as the individuals have adjusted their expectations. The Monetarist proposal consists in abandoning every discretionary policy. Hence we arrive at FRIEDMAN's *constant monetary growth rule*. FRIEDMAN suggested that the quantity of money be allowed to grow at a constant annual rate, amounting to 2–5 per cent. He emphasized that the numerical value of this rate is less important than its *constancy*. Such a monetary policy by rule would exclude any disturbance of the economic process arising from the central bank: The private sector would no longer be confused by measures which take place too early, too late, or to the wrong extent. Thus, the termination of discretionary monetary policy would be the best stabilization policy.

Monetarists have brought many more political proposals into prominence, we need only mention flexible exchange rates and the hundred per cent rule. These are less closely related to our main subject, and we cannot examine them here. Instead, we want to emphasize finally that Monetarism does not imply a certain ideological position. An example may illustrate this: *If* it is true that the private sector enjoys greater stability when discretionary policy is abandoned, then anyone must oppose such a policy, which does not exclude his favouring an increase of the public sector for other reasons. But *whether* this is true is a question of fact which is in principle independent of ideology.

§69 Conclusion

"Since we are all Keynesians now in the short run, those of us, who are not dead in the long run are at least near-monetarists." (A.M. BLINDER and R.M. SOLOW)

Finally we want to enumerate the various features which characterize Monetarism. This list is not intended to be exhaustive: we have neglected some more subtle properties which are dealt with in the advanced literature.

- Monetarism proceeds from a fundamental stability of the private sector.
- This attitude is supported by the theoretical concept of permanent magnitudes (such as permanent income) and the neglect of market imperfections.
- Its monetary theory is closely connected with liquidity preference and especially with TOBIN's theory of portfolio selection; but on the basis of *empirical* research, Monetarism arrives at the result of a numerically stable circular velocity of money.
- A distinguishing feature of the monetary theory of Monetarism consists in its incorporation of the rate of inflation as a determinant of money demand.
- The money supply is treated as an exogenous magnitude by Monetarists.
- The assumption of a natural rate of unemployment forms an essential part of Monetarist theory; it excludes the possibility that employment or production can be permanently altered by fiscal or monetary policy.

- Monetarists pay relatively more attention to the problem of inflation than to the problem of unemployment.
- Consequently, their theories tend to be theories of inflation rather than theories of employment.
- Monetarists fundamentally oppose discretionary policy. They think this policy is apt to work more in the destabilizing direction, especially because of lags.
- As a direct result, Monetarists are in favour of a constant monetary growth rule. They demand the growth rate to be fixed by law such that it is not at the discretion of the central bank.
- Finally, Monetarists are convinced that monetary policy is more efficient than fiscal policy[12].

These several theses do in fact form some coherent body of thought, so that the identification of a Monetarist position seems to be legitimate. They are interdependent in the sense that the affirmation of one tends to amplify the plausibility of the others; yet they do not imply one another. The postulate of abandoning any discretionary policy, for instance, can by no means be founded on the conjecture that monetary measures are more effective than fiscal ones. Therefore it is open to anyone to accept some of the above ten theses while rejecting others. Indeed, most contemporary economists are Monetarists with respect to at least one thesis – and this is the very meaning of the above quotation from BLINDER and SOLOW.

Further Reading

BRUNNER, K. and A.H. MELTZER (1976) An Aggregative Theory for a Closed Economy. In: STEIN, J. Ed. Monetarism. Op.cit.

FRIEDMAN, M. (1948) A Monetary and Fiscal Framework for Economic Stability. American Economic Review 38, pp. 245–264. Reprinted in LINDAUER, J. Ed. (1968) Macroeconomic Readings. Op.cit.

FRIEDMAN, M. (1968) The Role of Monetary Policy. American Economic Review 58, pp. 1–17. Reprinted in: FRIEDMAN, M. Ed. (1969) The Optimum Quantity of Money and Other Essays. Op.cit.

MAYER, Th. (1975) The Structure of Monetarism. Kredit und Kapital 8, pp. 191–218 and 293–316

MODIGLIANI, F. (1977) The Monetarist Controversy or, Should We Forsake Stabilization Policy. American Economic Review 67, pp. 1–19

STEIN, J.L. Ed. (1976) Monetarism. Amsterdam etc.: North Holland

---

12 In the subsequent chapter we will discuss the *Phillips curve* which forms another issue in the Monetarist controversy. The best and most comprehensive exposition of Monetarism is that of MAYER, Th. (1975) The Structure of Monetarism. Kredit und Kapital 8, pp. 191–218 and 293–316.

Chapter X. New Classical Economics

In this chapter we introduce a development of the 1970s, namely, the hypothesis of Rational expectations and the macroeconomic theories that rest on it. The theory of Rational expectations emerged from discontent with the prevailing doctrines: this discontent was two fold. First, we know that *expectations* either were not found in the theories at all, or were taken as exogenous. Since expectations not only influence the economic process crucially but are also a result of economic events, economists have for a long time sought to make the formation of expectations an endogenous part of their theory. Rational expectations are one result of this research as will be reported in the next section.

Second, the problem of stagflation began to bother most Western countries in the 1970s. *Stagflation* is an artificial combination of "stagnation" and "inflation". *Stagnation*, in turn, means properly a reduction in economic growth; yet a connotation of this term is "unemployment", and therefore we will mean by "stagflation" a simultaneous occurence of inflation and unemployment. In § 71 we will need to explain why the hitherto existing theories could not explain this phenomenon in full and what was undertaken to achieve this explanation.

As happens frequently, the term *Theory of Rational Expectations* become ambiguous as soon as it had been used for some years. Today, the adherents of this doctrine must be separated into two groups, typically referred to as New Classics and New Keynesians, respectively.

ROBERT J. BARRO, ROBERT E. LUCAS Jr., THOMAS J. SARGENT, and NEIL WALLACE, for instance, are reckoned among the *New Classics*. This group arrives at the Classical result of perfectly ineffective monetary and fiscal policy. Beyond this, the Monetarist allegations are partly founded analytically, partly modified, and even partly amplified. Therefore, New Classical economics are frequently called *Monetarism of the second kind*.

The *New Keynesians*, such as STANLEY FISCHER, EDMUND S. PHELPS, and JOHN B. TAYLOR, also employ the hypothesis of Rational expectations. But, since they allow for several "imperfections" of the Keynesian type, their results are more mediatory and, to a certain degree, "Keynesian". We will deal with New Keynesian economics only marginally, our main attention being directed towards New Classical economics.

The present chapter is structured as follows: First, we will introduce some theory on the formation of expectations, choosing a simple microeconomic framework for illustration. Thereafter, a brief summary of the discussion about the Philips-curve is given because this issue is closely related to the development of New Classical Economics. Having finished with these preliminaries, we are able to explain the New Classical "vision", the New Classical model, and the political inferences drawn from this approach. Finally, the results are summarized and the main criticisms of New Classical economics are listed.

§70 Expectations and Rational Expectations

In a world where the future is not known with certainty, i.e. in the real world, human behaviour is bound to depend on expectations to a considerable extend. Thus it is well known that phenomena such as the business cycle result, at least partly, from psychological factors. Keynesian theory, for instance, attributed deviations from full employment to enterpreneur's pessimistic expectations, or to certain expectations of asset holders. Yet these expectations were always treated as *exogenous*; in order to explain a business cycle, an appropriate change in expectations had to be *postulated*. In this section we want to demonstrate by means of a microeconomic model how expectations can be determined endogenously.

In doing so we want to refer to the famous *pig cycle*, i.e. the empirical observation that the production of pigs exhibits a steady up-and-down motion. The demand for pigs at time t may obey the linear equation

$$x_t^d = a - b \cdot p_t + u_t. \tag{232}$$

a and b are two positive constants, and the index "t" indicates that price and demand refer to a certain time period. Equation (232) comprises a feature new to us: the *stochastic variable*, u_t. u_t is a disturbance variable which cannot be predicted by the market participants. It has an expected value of zero and a finite variance and is independent of all other variables of the model[1]. Models containing such variables are called *stochastic models* as opposed to the more usual *deterministic models*. The purpose of a stochastic model consists in depicting those unpredictable deviations which occur in reality.

The supply of pigs obeys the linear equation

$$x_t^s = c + d \cdot {}_{t-1}p_t^e + v_t. \tag{233}$$

Here, c and d are also positive constants, and v_t is a stochastic variable with expected value zero and a finite variance which is independent of all other variables. In particular, there is no systematic relationship between u_t and v_t. Due to the assumption that the peasants need one period for breeding pigs, x_t does not depend on p_t, but on ${}_{t-1}p_t^e$, the pig's price which was expected by the peasants one period ago. Thus we define

$${}_{t-1}p_t^e := \text{the } subjective \text{ expectation of } p_t \text{ in period } t - 1. \tag{234}$$

The characteristic of this model is that demand and supply are subject to erratic deviations: whether it be that the number of peasants varies, or that culinary customs are subject to change. In the next step we *endogenize* the peasants' expectations via

---

1 Observe that it is by no means "restrictive" to assume that the expected value of u_t comes to zero. If u_t^* were a variable with expected value 5, for instance, and a^* were the corresponding coefficient, we could define $a := a^* + 5$ and $u_t := u_t^* - 5$, thus obtaining the above equation.

the premise of *static expectations*, the basis of the famous cobweb-theorem[2]:

$$_{t-1}p_t^e \overset{!}{=} p_{t-1}. \tag{235}$$

This equation states that, in period $t - 1$, the peasants expect that the then prevailing price will *continue* to prevail in the following period. Due to this premise, we immediately arrive at the "cobweb" which demonstrates the price adjustment process:

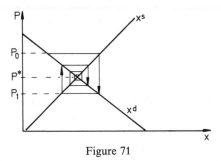

Figure 71

Obviously, the peasants' behaviour is not exceptionally shrewd since they either overrate the actual price and produce too much, or vice versa. In either case their expectations are systematically disappointed; and it is not even clear whether the above process converges at all: depending on the slopes of the curves it may also diverge.

At once the question arises as to why such divergent processes are *not* observed in reality. The most probable reason is that, in endogenizing the formation of expectations we neglected an important, specifically human, aspect: *learning*. It is extremely unlikely that all peasants will form their expectations according to (235) permanently. On the contrary, they will learn from their errors and take them into account in future. This can be modelled by the premise of *adaptive expectations*[3]:

$$_{t-1}p_t^e \overset{!}{=} {}_{t-2}p_{t-1}^e + h \cdot (p_{t-1} - {}_{t-2}p_{t-1}^e); \quad 0 < h < 1. \tag{236}$$

Let us explain this somewhat involved formula by means of a numerical example. Two periods ago, the peasants expected a price of $_{t-2}p_{t-1}^e = 5$ for the following period; but a price $p_{t-1} = 7$ was actually established in the market. Thus the estimation error, i.e. the term between the parantheses, amounted to 2. If we assume the constant h to be 0.5, the peasants will adjust their former estimation by $0.5 \cdot 2 = 1$ and expect a price of $5 + 1 = 6$ in the future. Thus, if h is 0.5, the new estimate is precisely half-way between the old estimate and the actual price; h can be interpreted as a constant indicating the intensity of learning. If $h = 1$, we are left with static expectations.

---

2 The cobweb theorem is discussed in any microeconomic textbook.

3 The assumption of adaptive expectations traces back to IRVING FISHER. CAGAN disseminated it and thus provided the expectation hypothesis of Monetarism. Cf. CAGAN, Ph. (1956) The Monetary Dynamics of Hyperinflation. In: FRIEDMAN, M. Ed. Studies in the Quantity Theory of Money. Chicago: Chicago University Press.

JOHN F. MUTH, when introducing the hypothesis of Rational expectations in 1961[4], was not quite satisfied with the above model of learning. He argued that in the community there exists some knowledge concerning the pricing problem: an economic theory and data are available which can be utilized for predicting the equilibrium price. Moreover, MUTH thought it very likely that the market participants would use this knowledge, because otherwise there would be unexploited profit possibilities. An economist could offer his proficiency for pay or make arbitrage dealings by himself. These unexploited profit possibilities would exist as long as subjective expectations were at variance with scientific prediction. Therefore, MUTH proposed the assumption of *Rational expectations*:

$$_{t-1}p_t^e \overset{!}{=} {}_{t-1}E(p_t).\tag{237}$$

$_{t-1}E(p_t)$ is the *expected value* of p_t at time $t-1$, which results from the economic model and the information available in period $t-1$. According to the hypothesis of Rational expectations, subjective expectations and mathematical prediction coincide[5].

Some comments on this are called for. If the peasants form Rational expectations, their expectations are on average fulfilled. It is not necessary that every peasant makes the required calculations himself – just as it is not necessary that one is a meteorologist to obtain a scientific prediction of the wheather. Rather, the peasants can listen, for example, to predictions made by experts in their unions – just as the citizen can listen to the weather report.

To understand the hypothesis of Rational expectations, it is very important to realize that the mathematical prediction is *not* necessarily correct. The expected value is called a *conditional expected value* since it depends on the information available in period $t-1$. The disturbance variables, u_t and v_t, can always cause the prediction to be wrong. Therefore, the thesis of Rational expectations is by no means equivalent to perfect foresight; these two coincide only in a deterministic model.

When thinking about the endogenization of expectations, one encounters a specific problem that may be stated as follows: The actions of the individuals depend on their expectations; but the latter, in turn, themselves depend on these actions. Is this not a vicious circle? Can an economic solution be found at all? In our case[6], the answer is in the affirmative. To show this, we assemble the demand function, (232), the supply function (233) and the hypothesis of Rational expectations (237) and add an equilibrium condition:

$$x_t^d = a - b \cdot p_t + u_t\tag{238}$$

$$x_t^s = c + d \cdot {}_{t-1}p_t^e + v_t\tag{239}$$

4 MUTH, J.F. (1961) Rational Expectations and the Theory of Price Movements. Econometrica **29**, pp. 315–335.
5 A broader definition of Rational Expectations is that the subjective expectation and the mathematical expected value differ by a stochastic term with expected value zero and finite variance. All further results are robust with respect to that broader definition.
6 "In our case" means: on condition that we have a linear model and Rational expectations. With static or adaptive expectations, we need to solve difference or differential equations in order to obtain the solutions.

$$_{t-1}p_t^e = {}_{t-1}E(p_t) \tag{240}$$

$$_{t-1}E(x_t^d) = {}_{t-1}E(x_t^s). \tag{241}$$

The equilibrium condition refers to expected values because the latter are used in an economic forecasting. The actual values, however, may be different. Thus, we have four simultaneous equations and four unknowns, namely, x_t, p_t, and the expected values of these two variables. The simultaneous equations can be solved uniquely. To do this, we calculate the expected values of demand and supply from (238) and (239):

$$_{t-1}E(x_t^d) = a - b \cdot {}_{t-1}E(p_t) + 0 \tag{242}$$

$$_{t-1}E(x_t^s) = c + d \cdot {}_{t-1}E(p_t) + 0. \tag{243}$$

The zeros result from our assumption that the expected values of the stochastic variables vanish. Because of the hypothesis of Rational expectations, $_{t-1}E(p_t)$ was substituted for $_{t-1}p_t^e$ in (243). By equalizing the expected values of demand and supply, we attain the expected value of the market price:

$$a - b \cdot {}_{t-1}E(p_t) = c + d \cdot {}_{t-1}E(p_t) \tag{244}$$

$$_{t-1}E(p_t) = \frac{a - c}{d + b}. \tag{245}$$

This is the scientific prediction of the market price p_t, formed in period $t - 1$. Substituting it into equations (238) and (239) yields the expected values of demand and supply. Thus, according to MUTH's hypothesis, the peasants will expect the price (245) to prevail in the next period. Their estimate will stand the test on the average but – because of the disturbance variables – not in every single instance. *Provided that the structure of the model is known and estimation incurs no costs, the expectation (245) is the only one that is economically rational, because it is the only one that does not imply systematic errors.*

Let us conclude. Undoubtedly, expectations play an important part in the working of an economy. If a theory takes them to be exogenous, not a lot can be explained, and forecasts are hardly possible because the "given" expectations are liable to change at any instant. There are several possibilities for endogenizing expectations: we discussed static, adaptive, and Rational expectations. Among these (and all others), Rational expectations are the only which do not incur *systematic* prediction errors. Forming Rational expectations is rational in the economic sense, at least if the required information is available without costs.

§71 The Phillips-Curve. Stagflation

The Phillips-curve is an aspect of the Monetarist-Keynesian controversy that we want to append now. This procedure may seem somewhat strange, for we have already finished with Monetarist and Keynesian theory. Hence a brief comment on the position of this section is in order: If we consider the Phillips-curve as one constituent of Keynesian theory, this is valid in so far as, in the 1960s and 1970s, most Keynesians took the existence of a Phillips-curve for granted; yet it is invalid in so far as this curve cannot easily be built into the Neoclassical synthesis – it even contradicts the latter in some sense. This very contradiction was the starting point of Monetarism and New Classical economics, so that the Philips-curve is well-suited for explaining the development of the latter doctrine. What is more, the discussion about the Phillips-curve depends chiefly on the assumptions one makes with respect to expectations; and this is a further reason to locate this subject here. We will begin by summarizing the arguments of the Keynesians and Monetarists, and afterwards discuss the New Classical position.

The issue of the Phillips-curve is rather extensive[7]. It began with an empirical paper of A.W. PHILLIPS, in 1958[8]. PHILLIPS' investigation was directed at the empirical relationship between *unemployment and the rate of change in money wages*. From a theoretical point of view, it is to be expected that, other things being equal, the smaller the rate of unemployment, the more money wage rates rise. This is exactly what was observed by PHILLIPS for the United Kingdom over the period 1862–1957. The figure below depicts that curve which – subject to a certain equational form – fitted the evidence best: it is the famous *Phillips-curve*:

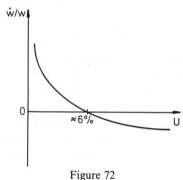

Figure 72

The three characteristic features of the curve are

– its negative slope,
– its hyperbolic shape, and
– its point of intersection with the abcissa at about 6% unemployment.

Thus, *stable* nominal wage rates are to be expected when the rate of unemployment amounts to 6%; in this case, the rate of change $\dot{w}/w$ is zero. If unemployment is below 6%, nominal wage rates are likely to rise, and vice versa. PHILLIPS' investigation was analytically refined by RICHARD G. LIPSEY[9] who essentially supported PHILLIPS' thesis. The significant allegation implied by the Phillips-

7 Cf. the overview of SANTOMERO, A.M. and J.J. SEATER (1978) The Inflation Unemployment Trade-Off: A Critique of the Literature. Journal of Economic Literature **16**, pp. 499–544.
8 PHILLIPS, A.W. (1958) The Relation between Unemployment and the Rate of Change of Money Wages in the United Kingdom, 1886–1957. Economica **25**, pp. 283–299.
9 LIPSEY, R.G. (1960) The Relation between Unemployment and the Rate of Change of Money Wages in the United Kingdom, 1886–1957 – A Further Analysis. Economica **27**, pp. 1–37.

curve is that of a relationship between unemployment and changes in money wages which is *stable in the long run*.

Thus far the discovery of the Phillips-curve does not appear very exciting. It gained its theoretical and political dynamite due to a paper of PAUL A. SAMUELSON and ROBERT M. SOLOW, in 1960 [10]. SAMUELSON and SOLOW replaced the rate of change of money wages with the *rate of inflation*. Their result, again depicted only qualitatively, is quite similar to that of PHILLIPS:

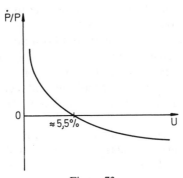

Figure 73

This is called the *modified Phillips-curve* where the prefix "modified" is dropped when no misreadings are to be feared. The modified Phillips-curve differs from the original one in that $\dot{P}/P$ is substituted for $\dot{w}/w$. It yields a highly interesting conclusion: Obviously, the desirable low rates of unemployment are accompanied by undesirable high rates of inflation. If one assumes that the government is able to alter the rate of inflation by fiscal or monetary means, it can choose between two evils, namely, high unemployment, or high inflation. There exists a *trade off* between these two.

Seemingly, the institutions responsible are in a position to decide on the precise combination of unemployment and inflation they prefer. "Leftish" governments will typically be in favour of a point to the left and upwards, whereas "conservative" governments are likely to decide on a point to the right and downwards [11]. Even nowadays we can recognize the conjecture of many politicians and journalists that we are faced with the alternative of unemployment or inflation in some kind of zero sum game.

It must be emphasized, however, that the Phillips-curve obtains scant theoretical support from the Keynesian model. The curve can only be derived from our model K''' (with sticky wages), but not at all from the other Keynesian scenarios. This is

---

10 SAMUELSON, P.A. and R.M. SOLOW (1960) Analytical Aspects of Anti-Inflation Policy. American Economic Review (PP) **50**, pp. 177–194. Reprinted in: MUELLER, M.G. Ed. (1967) Readings in Macroeconomics. New York etc.: Holt, Rinehart and Winston.
11 In 1976, GORDON stated: "It was common in the U.S. for economic advisers to Democratic Presidents to recommend the choice of a point on the curve northwest of the target of Republican advisers." GORDON, R.J. (1976) Recent Developments in the Theory of Inflation and Unemployment. Op.cit. p. 190.

because the other models exhibited a vertical commodity supply curve (Y^s curve), which means that production and employment are independent of the price level and its changes. Nor can the Phillips-curve be inferred from the Classical model. This is the theoretical aspect of the issue.

On the other hand, some empirical facts occurred in the 1970s which cast much doubt on the allegedly stable relationship between unemployment and inflation. The appearance of *simultaneously* high rates of unemployment and inflation contradicts the stability of the Phillips-curve and can be explained only by assuming arbitrary shifts of the curve. But if the Phillips-curve is subject to erratic shifts, it becomes a useless and somewhat tautological construct.

These difficulties led MILTON FRIEDMAN and EDMUND S. PHELPS to their *criticism* of the Phillips-curve[12]. FRIEDMAN and PHELPS essentially argued that the negatively sloped Phillips-curve presupposes some "money illusion" on the part of the laborers. But that this illusion would tend to be short-lived, and there would be no permanent trade off at all between unemployment and inflation. The long-run Phillips-curve would be *vertical*.

Let us consider this line of reasoning in some more detail. *Money illusion* means that workers adapt their wage demands to the expected, and not the actual, price level. If we take the expectation of P, or its rate of change, as *exogenous*, labor supply will depend solely on money wage rates:

$$N^s = N^s\left(\frac{w}{P^e}\right) \Rightarrow N^s = N^s(w), \quad \text{if} \quad P^e = \bar{P}^e. \tag{246}$$

Let us assume furthermore that the demand for labor depends on the *actual* price level:

$$N^d = N^d\left(\frac{w}{P}\right). \tag{247}$$

Given a general rise in commodity prices and constant nominal wage rates, the demand for labor will *increase* while the supply remains *unchanged*. Hence, the rate of unemployment will diminish if it was positive at the outset. Monetary policy is in a position to reduce unemployment by increasing the quantity of money and thus prices. Therefore, the modified Phillips-curve can be founded on *exogenous* expectations of laborers with respect to the price level. The latter assumption must be considered as a specifically Keynesian one, for the existence of a long-term Phillips-curve can hardly be derived otherwise.

However, this assumption did not seem appropriate to FRIEDMAN and PHELPS. They proceeded from the premise that, after some time, workers and their unions will perceive the rise in prices and learn from this observation. FRIEDMAN and PHELPS assumed *adaptive expectations*. The workers gradually adjust their expectations of the price level towards the actual one and demand corresponding increases in their wages

12 FRIEDMAN, M. (1970) The Role of Monetary Policy. American Economic Review **58**, pp. 1–17. Reprinted in: FRIEDMAN, M. Ed. (1969) The Optimum Quantity of Money and Other Essays. Chicago: Aldine. PHELPS, E.S. (1967) Phillips-Curves, Expectations of Inflation and Optimal Unemployment over Time. Economica **34**, pp. 254–281.

to make up the loss of purchasing power. As a consequence, there is no *permanent* trade off between unemployment and inflation, only a *temporary* one:

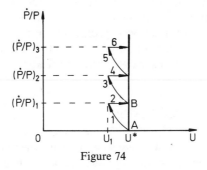

Figure 74

Point A in the figure shows the natural rate of unemployment[13] which is accompanied by stable prices. The central bank is capable of reducing the actual rate of unemployment below the natural level by expanding the quantity of money. Arrow no. 1 depicts such an expansionary monetary policy which raises the rate of inflation to $(\dot{P}/P)_1$ and reduces unemployment to U_1.

After some time, the laborers adjust their expectations and demand higher increases in their money wage rates. Thus the real wage rate rises to its previous level, and unemployment goes up to U^* as indicated by arrow no. 2. The rate of inflation remains unchanged provided that the central bank increases the quantity of money at the now higher rate. Therefore, the new equilibrium at point B exhibits a *higher* rate of inflation than before, but the *same* rate of unemployment.

Can the central bank exploit the short-run trade off again? Yes, but not by maintaining the now higher rate of monetary expansion but by *accelerating* it. At point B, the quantity of money must already be growing at the rate $\dot{M}/M = (\dot{P}/P)_1$, because expectations have become adjusted to this rate. Therefore, the central bank must force an even *higher* rate of monetary expansion in order to "fool" the workers again. This fact is referred to as the theorem of acceleration. The *theorem of acceleration* states that it is not changes in the quantity of money that matter but changes in the monetary *growth rate*.

This line of reasoning denies the existence of a permanent unemployment-inflation trade off since the natural rate of unemployment is consistent with *any* rate of inflation. There is no stable relationship between unemployment and inflation, but only between unemployment and *changes* in the rate of inflation.

According to the arguments of FRIEDMAN and PHELPS, discretionary monetary policy has few attractions. Unemployment can be reduced only temporarily at the cost of a permanently higher rate of inflation. If the authorities then try to reduce inflation, unemployment will *increase* for some time. Thus, according to the Monetarists, fighting inflation incurs social costs. For this very reason, FRIEDMAN proposed his constant monetary growth rule, which is aimed at guaranteeing a steady rate of inflation. Keynesians habitually oppose this proposal because they expect discretionary policy to smoothen the business cycle. At the same time they often deny the

---

13 This term was explained in § 66 above.

existence of a natural rate of unemployment and thus reject the core of the Monetarist reasoning.

Let us conclude. The existence of a modified Phillips-curve which is stable in the long run can be established by assuming that the workers have exogenous price expectations. If one assumes adaptive expectations, on the other hand, there is only a short-term trade off between inflation and unemployment. A discussion of the Phillips-curve when expectations are Rational is left until §73.

§72 The New Classical Vision

We can now move on to the New Classical approach. Due to our thorough acquaintance with Keynesian economics, this approach is not easy to appreciate; at the outset, therefore, we need to take a somewhat broader perspective.

In the realm of economic theory, the Classical doctrine, and especially Walras' model, formed the point of departure for all important developments that took place in our century. Walras' model – despite its shortcomings – provided an explanation of allocation, production, and distribution in a capitalist economy. Though this model was refined in various ways, its structure remained essentially static – and hence it was incapable of explaining a business cycle. In Walras' model, all resources are fully employed and optimally allocated in PARETO's sense at any instant. Thus analogy would tend to lead to the insight that these properties hold also over time, so that the economy exhibits a steady development at some growth rate. Yet, such an "insight" would be in flagrant contradiction to reality, and this is a fundamental problem of Classical theory. The attempts to solve this problem form three distinct lines of argument:

The first group is usually referred to as *fundamentalist criticism* of the Classical doctrine. Authors in this group infer the uselessness of Walras' model, and the uselessness of Classical theory as a whole, from the empirical observation of business cycles. We have already mentioned the Postkeynesians as an important school of this type.

In the second place, we encounter the *imperfectionists*, the outstanding example being the Keynesians. As we recognized in chapter V, Keynesian theory proceeds from a model that is Classical in spirit; but augments the Classical model by some "imperfections", and thus arrives at a possible explanation of the business cycle.

The third line, however, accepts the model of general economic equilibrium without imperfections as the basis of business cycle theory. This is the position of *New Classical* economics. These authors hold that Keynesian "imperfections" play such a trifling role in reality that they cannot serve to explain economic fluctuations. New Classics criticize Keynesians because of their "imperfectionism". They argue that Keynesianism *defines* the business cycle as a *disequilibrium phenomenon* without being able to prove this allegation[14]. In short, New Classical economists perceive the

---

14 LUCAS, R.E. Jr. (1976) Econometric Policy Evaluation: A Critique. In: Supplement 1 to the Journal of Monetary Economics. SARGENT, Th.J. (1976) The Observational Equivalence of Natural and Unnatural Rate Theories in Macroeconomics. Journal of Political Economy **84**, pp. 499–544.

business cycle as an equilibrium phenomenon: as a process in which markets are cleared at any instant and expectations are Rational[15]. Considered from the Keynesian point of view, this attitude appears strange; and one is apt to think that the New Classics have maneuvered themselves into a quite hopeless position. But we should not judge too hastily.

The New Classical model thus belongs to the species of general equilibrium models. Yet it deviates from them in an important aspect: Other models of the general equilibrium type are either static (and therefore useless for explaining business cycles), or dynamic but essentially deterministic[16]. In the deterministic world of ARROW-DEBREU, the individuals are in a position to make up contracts in the present which are conditional on all possible future events. Afterwards, these contracts are merely executed. Though this ingenious modeling widens the scope of Walras' model considerably, it does not shed any light on the existence of business cycles.

For this reason it seemed promising to the pioneers of New Classical economics to replace the deterministic environment by a *stochastic* one. Here, the individuals habitually suffer from expectation errors; and these errors serve to explain economic fluctuations. It is important, according to the New Classical view, that such errors do not imply some non-market-clearing. All markets are thought of as being cleared at every instant. Thus the New Classical model is charaterized by the following features:

- Prices are perfectly flexible, and all markets are permanently cleared. The individuals do not leave prices at a "false" level since this would incur some disadvantages: indeed those disadvantages which are implied by involuntary unemployment or other selling and buying restraints. Some authors, however, consider the market clearance assumption insignificant[17].
- Because present actions entail future consequences, all individuals deliberately form Rational expectations. They do so by exhausting all available information and adjust supplies, demands, and prices such that their plans are fulfilled optimally when the Rational expectations prove true.
- Yet, since the economic process is subject to stochastic disturbances, expectations typically do *not* prove true. Economic fluctuations thus arise which trace back to the voluntary deviations of supply and demand; "voluntary" with respect to the given exogenous shocks.

§ 73 The New Classical Model

In this paragraph, we want to discuss a typical, though extremely simple, New Classical model. It is a stochastic model of the *reduced form* type where only the

---

15 Cf. especially Lucas, R.E. Jr. (1977) Understanding Business Cycles. Supplement 5 to the Journal of Monetary Economics. Lucas, R.E. Jr. (1980) Methods and Problems in Business Cycle Theory. Journal of Money, Credit and Banking 12, pp. 696–715.

16 Here we refer to the model of ARROW and DEBREU. ARROW, K.J. (1964) The Role of Securities in the Optimal Allocation of Risk-Bearing. Review of Economic Studies 31, pp. 91–96. DEBREU, G. (1959) Theory of Value. New York: Wiley.

17 The New Classical results remain unchanged if quantity constraints are due to deliberate, rational behaviour. Cf. STEIN, J.L. (1982) Monetarist, Keynesian and New Classical Economics. Op.cit.

commodity market is depicted explicitly. All other markets work behind the scene. The first equation is that of aggregate commodity demand in period t:

$$Y_t^d = A_t + b \cdot (m_t - p_t) + u_t. \tag{248}$$

Here, A_t covers all those expenditures (including government demand) which are independent of real balances. b is a positive constant and u_t an independent stochastic variable with expected value zero and finite variance. m_t and p_t denote the natural logarithms of nominal cash balances and the price level. Hence the difference of m and p is equal to the logarithm of M/P [18]. Here we have a log-linear model where aggregate commodity demand depends on the logarithm of real cash balances. The real-balance effect (cf. Chapter VII) is essential to the working of this model.

Aggregate commodity supply is characterized by a so-called *Lucas aggregate supply function*:

$$Y_t^s = Y^* + c \cdot (p_t - p_t^e) + v_t. \tag{249}$$

Y^* represents the natural level of production which is associated with the natural level of unemployment. c is a positive constant and v_t an independent stochastic variable with expected value zero and a finite variance. The above supply function is based on the following premises: When price expectations are fulfilled ($p_t = p_t^e$) and stochastic disturbances are absent ($v_t = 0$), aggregate commodity supply takes its natural value, i.e. $Y_t = Y^*$. This is the state *preferred* by the private sector. Unemployment which prevails then is voluntary and due to the opportunity costs of leisure. All possible imperfections are ruled out by assumption.

Thus, the market participants aim at the realization of Y^*. Despite this, deviations from Y^* are conceivable, or even the rule, and result either from unanticipated changes in A_t or m_t, or from stochastic disturbances. These three instances all cause the price level to deviate from its expected value. But why does aggregate commodity supply depend on the difference between p_t and p_t^e? This question requires a thorough answer. It should be clear from the beginning that sticky wages or static price expectations and the like cannot provide an explanation since these do not exist in the New Classical model.

The meaning of the above supply function can be illustrated best by LUCAS' example of an artisan. Suppose that an artisan expects a rate of inflation of 5 per cent and that the price of the commodity he produces rises by 10 per cent. The artisan will interpret this as an increase in the *relative* price of his product, and he is likely to increase his effort since he believes the production to have become more profitable. The artisan will especially behave in this manner if he considers the perceived increase in the price to be temporary; in this case, an intertemporal substitution of work for leisure is advantageous.

Let us suppose further that the *actual* rate of inflation amounts to 10 per cent. Obviously, the artisan has mistaken the increase in the price of his product: there has not been any rise in the relative price, rather the price level has risen more than expected. Yet, the artisan does no recognize this fact before he has actually increased his output. We arrive at the result that, in our example, an *unexpected* rise in the rate of inflation raises real output.

---

18 Recollect that $\ln(a \cdot b) = \ln(a) + \ln(b)$ and $\ln(a^x) = x \cdot \ln(a)$.

One essential premise of New Classical economics is that all producers are fairly well informed about price changes in their respective markets, but less well about changes in the price level. If this holds, an unexpected rise in inflation will induce *all* producers to perceive rises in relative prices erroneously and will thus increase total production. Therefore, p_t^e being given, there is a positive relationship between p_t and aggregate commodity supply, as Formula (249) states. Note that this relationship is founded without assuming wage rate rigidities or money illusion. The behaviour of all producers is perfectly rational, although wrong indeed as a result of the lack of information.

After discussing the two constituents of the commodity market, we assume this market to be cleared at any instant. Prices are perfectly flexible:

$$Y_t^d = Y_t^s = Y_t . \tag{250}$$

Demand, supply, and actual production always match. Hence we can rewrite the above functions without "d" and "s" as follows:

$$Y_t = A_t + b \cdot (m_t - p_t) + u_t \tag{251}$$

$$Y_t = Y^* + c \cdot (p_t - p_t^e) + v_t . \tag{252}$$

On the basis of these two equations, we can not yet say which production level and which price level will result because the *expected* price level is unknown. In the New Classical model, we must assume Rational expectations so that all variables with index "e" are mathematical expected values. Let us first calculate the expected values from (251) and (252):

$$Y_t^e = A_t^e + b \cdot (m_t^e - p_t^e) \tag{253}$$

$$Y_t^e = Y^* . \tag{254}$$

The two disturbance variables are dropped because they have the expected value zero. Formulas (251) to (254) form four simultaneous equations with the four unknowns Y_t, p_t, Y_t^e, and p_t^e. The "political" variables A_t and m_t are given, and so are their expected values, A_t^e and m_t^e, since these cannot be inferred from an economic model. The first solution is given by (254): the expected value of Y_t matches the natural level of production. Substituting this into (253), we can immediately calculate the expected value of the price level:

$$p_t^e = m_t^e - \frac{Y^* - A_t^e}{b} . \tag{255}$$

Finally, Y_t and p_t are to be determined. Subtracting (253) from (251) and (254) from (252) yields:

$$Y_t - Y_t^e = (A_t - A_t^e) + b \cdot (m_t - m_t^e) - b \cdot (p_t - p_t^e) + u_t \tag{256}$$

$$Y_t - Y_t^e = c \cdot (p_t - p_t^e) + v_t . \tag{257}$$

By equalizing the right hand sides of these equations, we obtain p_t. Substituting the latter into (257) and setting $Y_t^e = Y^*$ yields the actual level of production:

$$Y_t = Y^* + \frac{c}{b + c} \cdot \left[(A_t - A_t^e) + b \cdot (m_t - m_t^e) + u_t + \frac{b}{c} \cdot v_t \right] \tag{258}$$

$$p_t = p_t^e + \frac{1}{b+c} \cdot [(A_t - A_t^e) + b \cdot (m_t - m_t^e) + u_t - v_t]. \qquad (259)$$

Now the solution is complete. The last two equations yield a series of interesting conclusions. First, the natural level of production is realized if unexpected disturbances and unexpected government actions are absent. In this case, Rational expectations concerning the price level are met also. Furthermore, any unanticipated monetary expansion ($m_t > m_t^e$) and any increase in government expenditure ($A_t > A_t^e$) incurs an increase in production *and* prices. This follows immediately from the formulas.

Erratic shifts in demand, caused by the variable u_t, also engender pro-cyclical price changes, i.e. p_t and Y_t move in the same direction. Due to a sudden increase in demand, both output and prices rise; and prices continue rising until the commodity market is cleared again.

Supply shocks however, caused by changes in v_t, incur anti-cyclical price behaviour. When there is an unexpected rise in v_t, output will increase whereas prices will decline. In the absence of government interventions, the level of production will oscillate around its natural level, Y^*, and prices will move pro-cyclically or anti-cyclically according to whether the disturbances are caused by u_t or v_t.

What attitude towards the *Phillips-curve* will a New Classical economist take? Let us state first that there is a negative relationship between output and unemployment. Now equation (258) says that an *unanticipated* monetary expansion will induce both production and prices to rise and will thus reduce unemployment. A fully *anticipated* monetary expansion, however, will not cause production, prices, and unemployment to deviate in the least from their natural levels. That is, production and unemployment will remain unchanged, the natural level of prices now being higher.

The New Classical explanation thus deviates from that of the Monetarists, who conceded short-run impacts of monetary policy. According to the New Classics it does not matter whether one considers the short or the long run but whether the monetary expansion was anticipated, or not. From the Monetarist view point, these two questions are one and the same, because of the hypothesis of *adaptive* expectations. We will return to this problem in the next section[19].

§74 Political Inferences

"It would be easy to produce a model in which prices adjust almost instantaneously to shocks, markets clear essentially all the time, and the correct policy is to do nothing." (ROBERT M. SOLOW)

Can a market economy be stabilized by means of discretionary fiscal and monetary policy? In order to give the New Classical answer to this question, let us reproduce

19 Cf. also LUCAS, R.E. Jr. (1973) Some International Evidence on Output-Inflation Trade-offs. American Economic Review **63**, pp. 326–334.

equations (258) and (259):

$$Y_t = Y^* + \frac{c}{b+c} \cdot \left[(A_t - A_t^e) + b \cdot (m_t - m_t^e) + u_t + \frac{b}{c} \cdot v_t \right] \qquad (260)$$

$$p_t = p_t^e + \frac{1}{b+c} \cdot [(A_t - A_t^e) + b \cdot (m_t - m_t^e) + u_t - v_t]. \qquad (261)$$

The essence of the issue can best be illustrated by the example of FRIEDMAN's constant monetary growth rule. Assume constant monetary growth at the rate k which is forced by law:

$$m_t = m_0 + k \cdot t \quad \text{or} \quad M_t = M_0 \cdot e^{k \cdot t}. \qquad (262)$$

Since the rule is known to the individuals, they anticipate the monetary growth fully:

$$m_t^e = m_0 + k \cdot t. \qquad (263)$$

Now consider equations (260) and (261). Because the monetary expansion is accurately predictable, the terms $(m_t - m_t^e)$ will vanish, and monetary policy will produce no real effects whatever. This is nothing new since it is exactly equivalent to the Monetarist result. A difference occurs when we suppose the quantity of money to grow *progressively*. Owing to the Monetaristic assumption of adaptive expectations, this rule will produce real effects; but, according to the New Classics, it will not provided that the rule has been made public. Indeed, the central bank may obey *any* arbitrarily constructed rule without changing the real variables, as long as the rule has previously been announced.

Therefore, the Monetarists' *theorem of acceleration* does not hold in the New Classical model. This is the core of New Classical analysis: It is perfectly irrelevant to the neutrality of money how a monetary growth rule is designed or indeed whether a Friedman-type rule is adhered to at all. Beyond that, accelerations or decelerations in monetary growth incur no real effects whatever on the condition that they are known beforehand. And, finally, it is a mistake to distinguish between short-term and long-term effects of monetary policy: the correct distinction is that between *antici-pated* and *unanticipated* measures. Any anticipated monetary action is ineffectual, and any unanticipated monetary action will produce real effects.

At the same time, New Classical theory solves an outstanding problem of Mone-tarism. In the previous chapter we recognized that Monetarists allege a close relation-ship between the quantity of money and nominal income, $P \cdot Y$; but the extremely important question of how the effect is split up between changes in P and changes in Y was not answered satisfactorily. Or, to put it another way: does an expansionary monetary policy produce prosperity, or inflation? New Classical theory has ready a clear answer: First, anticipated monetary expansion incurs pure inflation. Second, unanticipated expansion leads to rises in both prices and quantities, where the respec-tive changes can be calculated from (260) and (261).

Of course, New Classical theory does not state that Y^*, the natural and in some sense optimal level of production, can be maintained steadily. First, policy measures may cause deviations from it – which is reason enough for disallowing them. Second, the stochastic variables u_t and v_t may produce deviations. This leads us to the interesting question of whether economic policy is not in a position to alleviate at least *these* disturbances.

The New Classical answer to this question reads unequivocally: No, because the political authorities cannot foresee the disturbances either. This is a decisive issue, for if one supposes the authorities to be *better informed* than the private individuals there will be a case for discretionary policy even though expectations are Rational and though markets are cleared.

To illustrate this, let us suppose that the central bank is able to predict u_t and v_t with certainty whereas these variables continue being unpredictable by the private sector. Then, by means of a simple modification of the monetary growth rule, the disturbances can be ruled out completely:

$$m_t = m_0 + k \cdot t - \frac{u_t}{b} - \frac{v_t}{c}. \tag{264}$$

The individuals expect the quantity of money to grow according to the rule (263) because u_t and v_t cannot be forseen by them and have the expected value zero. By substituting (264) into (260) and (261) the reader should make sure that the "random" disturbances are fully absorbed so that production assumes its natural value at every instant. Rules of the type (264) are termed *active rules* (or "formula flexibility") because they prescribe an active, though automatic, response. They are thus different from the *passive rules* à la FRIEDMAN.

Yet this reasoning was meant for illustration only. It is by no means part of the New Classical doctrine but rather contradicts it because we supposed information to be distributed asymmetrically between the public and the private sector. According to New Classical theory, the individuals will obtain all information which is available to the public authorities. Thus they will be equally well informed.

Let us discuss next the case of *stagflation*. At an arbitrary instant, production may decline because of stochastical disturbances, and unemployment may rise. If the government or the central bank now try to increase production by an expansionary policy, the individuals will anticipate the result of such measures. If the policy has been announced or has otherwise become known to the individuals, production will not change even in the shortest run. The price level, however, will increase according to (255) and (261): and stagflation arises.

To summarize. From the New Classical point of view, neither active rules nor discretionary policies are capable of producing any beneficial real effects. If they produce any real effects at all because the measure was not anticipated, the real outcome will be *unfavourable* since the private sector is thrown out of the state it prefers. Stabilizing policy would be advantageous only if it absorbed an exogenous shock by chance. But this cannot be the basis of systematic intervention.

The logic of this theory can be formulated as a criticism of Keynesian economics: Keynesianism describes the economy by some simultaneous equations which assume private behaviour to be *invariant* under different government behaviour. Given an arbitrary change in the quantity of money, for instance, the consumption function (not its numerical value!), the investment function, and all other behavioural relationships remain unchanged. Therefore, this policy is likely to incur real results. Keynesian theory does not recognize that – when perceiving the monetary change – the individuals will possibly alter their behaviour so that the above-mentioned functions themselves are subject to change. New Classical theory destroys this constancy of behaviour by taking account of expectations: A monetary expansion will leave all real variables unchanged on the condition that it is anticipated.

Up to here, we have been primarily concerned with monetary policy. Next we have to consider an argumentation relating to fiscal policy which belongs to New Classical economics taken in a broad sense[20]. Assume that the government decreases lumpsum taxes in the current period only and finances the resulting gap by raising loans:

$$- \Delta T = \Delta B. \tag{265}$$

The tax reduction, ΔT, is equal in value to the loan, ΔB. As explained by Keynesian theory and the theory of portfolio selection, this measure *increases* aggregate commodity demand. According to the theory of portfolio selection, that result is due to the rise in *net wealth* of the private sector. Because owning additional government bonds, the individuals now consider themselves richer, and they increase consumption and other expenditures. Against this *fiscal illusion*, as it is sometimes called, the following argument can be advanced: In the subsequent periods, the government will have to pay interest on the additional debt and will have to repay it if the debt is of finite duration. In doing so, where government expenditures are given, the government is bound to raise higher taxes than would have been necessary in the absence of the additional debt. It is true that new loans could also be raised; but this would merely postpone the problem.

Since the market participants are fully aware of these facts – at least according to the New Classics – they will not consider ΔB as an increase in net wealth but subtract the present value of the future taxes from it. In order to calculate this present value, let us proceed from a bond of infinite duration. In every subsequent period, government has to pay interest on the debt and must raise additional taxes to cover this:

$$\Delta T_t = r \cdot \Delta B; \quad t = 1 \ldots \infty. \tag{266}$$

If government bonds and other assets are perfect substitutes, r, the rate of interest, is equal to the subjective discount factor (or the rate of time preference) of the individuals. The present value of the tax burden amounts to:

$$\Delta T_0 = \sum_{t=1}^{\infty} \frac{\Delta T_t}{(1 + r)^t} = \sum_{t=1}^{\infty} \frac{r \cdot \Delta B}{(1 + r)^t} = \Delta B. \tag{267}$$

$r \cdot \Delta B$ represents additional annual taxes, the sum of which is discounted at the rate r. It turns out that *the present value of the additional taxes is equal to the debt*. This result is downright trivial since the rate of interest and the subjective discount factor are identical. Thus, government borrowing incurs *no* increase in private net wealth. This conclusion, important to the crowding out debate, is called the *Ricardian equivalence theorem*. "Equivalence theorem" because the impacts of tax and loan financing are obviously the same.

The Ricardian equivalence theorem is subject especially to the following two criticisms. First it is pointed out that the life span of the individuals is finite: the latter

---

20 The following line of reasoning is due to BARRO, R.J. (1974) Are Government Bonds Net Wealth? Journal of Political Economy **82**, pp. 1095–1117.

will only reckon those taxes that are raised up to their expected date of death. Hence there is some increase in net wealth. BARRO tried to solve this difficulty by means of overlapping generations where every generation leaves a bequest to its successor. Under very special assumptions, the inhabitants of such an economy exhibit the same behaviour as if they lived infinitely.

Second, it may be argued that the individuals do not anticipate future taxes (fully) or that their subjective discount factor is somewhat above the interest rate of government bonds. The latter instance is met at least if government bonds are considered to be safer than a representative bond. It implies an increase in net wealth since ΔB exceeds the present value of future taxes, ΔT_0.

It must be noted additionally that fiscal policy is not bound to be altogether ineffective when the equivalence theorem holds strictly. For we can merely conclude from this theorem that tax financing and loan financing are equivalent: thus loan financing will be expansionary just when tax financing is expansionary. In the extreme Keynesian cases, the fiscal multiplier would be reduced from $1/(1 - C')$ to 1 (Haavelmo-theorem) – but not to 0.

The discussion of BARRO's argument should have illuminated the methodology of New Classical economics once more: The market participants strive towards the state *they prefer*; and when the state takes any action (here: by reducing taxes and raising loans), they immediately counteract that action (here: by increasing savings for repaying the additional taxes later). Thus the individuals alter their behaviour in order to regain the original, optimal state. In such a world: is there a case for government intervention?

Finally, it is not difficult to guess the concrete New Classical policy proposals[21]:

- The central bank should obey a passive monetary growth rule because the private sector is to be shielded from exogenous disturbances that are *primarily* due to discretionary policy.
- Discretionary fiscal policy should be dispensed with for the same reason. The budget should be balanced on the average.
- It should be announced that the authorities will not respond to the consequences of private price-setting. In this way, the individuals are forced to set market-clearing prices.

Obviously, the New Classical proposals correspond to those of the Monetarists quite well. Indeed, many of the New Classics consider their doctrine as a theoretical *foundation* of Monetarism. In this respect, New Classical economics is a direct continuation of Monetarism and its label "Monetarism of the second kind" seems quite fitting.

21 LUCAS, R.E. Jr. (1980) Rules, Discretion and the Role of the Economic Adviser. In: FISCHER, St. Ed. Rational Expectations and Economic Policy. Chicago: Chicago Press, p. 200.

§ 75 Conclusion

"Are truly rational expectations really adaptive after all?"   (BENJAMIN FRIEDMAN)

Now we want to summarize the essential elements of New Classical economics and supplement the most important criticisms of this doctrine. The significant assumptions turned out to be:

- the assumption of Rational expectations according to which the individuals know the correct economic model, use all information available, and thus form subjective expectations which coincide with the scientific prediction; and
- the basic principle of considering the business cycle and all other economic events as equilibrium phenomena.

Thus the New Classical theory of the business cycle is committed to HAYEK's program:

"(T)he incorporation of cyclical phenomena into the system of economic equilibrium, with which they are in apparent contradiction, remains the crucial problem of Trade Cycle Theory."[22]

Keynesian theory solved this problem by taking the general equilibrium model as starting point only, augmenting it by several "imperfections", and then interpreting business cycles as sequences of disequilibria. With New Classical theory this is not so: the business cycle is conceived as an equilibrium phenomenon, and the observable fluctuations are traced back to

- stochastic disturbances and changeable policy, accompanied by
- imperfect foresight.

Stochastic events, and policy, thus incur unanticipated deviations in demand, supply, and prices. Changes in the price level are mistaken for changes in relative prices by the individuals because market participants are informed solely about changes in the "own" market and perceive changes in the price level only after some lag. Therefore, increases in prices which are not due to supply shocks incur increments in economic activity. By means of this model, New Classical theory explains the *pro-cyclical* behaviour of prices and the *co-movements* of economic activity in different markets. These are, in fact, two typical features of the business cycle.

The New Classical view implies that unemployment in the recession is *voluntary* and the outcome of an optimization process which causes the individuals to substitute labor and leisure intertemporally. Since, given a mere change in the rate of inflation, this substitution rests on a deception, it results in a sub-optimal state. Consequently, business fluctuations are unwelcomed. It is quite natural that the New Classics suggest giving up any discretionary policy in order to remove at least one cause – according to them, the most important one – of business fluctuations. If this advice is followed they expect business fluctuations to diminish. The remaining deviations, however, are

---

22 HAYEK, F.A. von (1933) Monetary Theory and the Trade Cycle. London: Jonathan Cape, p. 33.

incapable of being mitigated by discretionary policy since the authorities cannot forecast exogenous shocks better than the private sector.

A significant aspect of this theory is that it serves as an analytical foundation of the policital inferences of Monetarism. As we already recognized, it is hard to oppose Monetarism from the Keynesian position since the former does not offer a genuine comprehensive analytical foundation. New Classical theory provides a "fully articulated, artificial model" (LUCAS) and thus raises the standard of the debate[23].

It is an outstanding advantage of explicit models that they provoke *criticism* – precisely because of their explicitness. We do not intend to withhold the most important criticisms from the reader:

1. Criticism. The hypothesis of Rational expectations is founded, as we already saw, on the premise that the individuals do not *waste* information. This must be conceded in principle – if one proceeds from utility maximizing behaviour at all – but it is sharply different from the premise that *all* information in existence will actually be used. In order to form a Rational expectation of the price level, for instance, the true economic model as well as information about the numerical parameter values are required. Of course, the acquisition of this information will incur some *costs* where the term "costs" must be interpreted in a broad sense. Indeed, it is not necessary that every individual undertakes some econometric research; but at least he must buy the results or read newspapers to obtain them.

It is true that a Rational expectation is useful; yet it must be acknowledged that the utility gained from such an expectation decreases when the variance of the disturbance variables increases: If those institutions making the predictions must leave too many factors out of account and are poorly informed about many relevant facts, the disturbance variables will exert a considerable influence, and the utility of the resulting forecast is trifling.

Therefore, when the costs of acquiring Rational expectations are high and the utility gained from them is low, an individual may arrive at the conclusion that forming Rational expections is inappropriate since marginal costs soon exceed marginal utility. In short, it may seem rational to dispense with Rational expectations.

Consequently, FRITZ MACHLUP has argued that the term "Rational expectation" in the New Classical sense represents a misuse of language[24]. In economics, "rationality" was always meant as coincidence of action and opinion but not as coincidence of action and "objective reality". In this sense, the word "Rational" shifts the original meaning of that notion – and this is the very reason why we write it with a capital "R".

2. Criticism. It may be concluded in advance that the New Classical inferences do not hold unless the individuals suppose the New Classical model to be true. If they proceed from a Keynesian model, they will Rationally expect the effectiveness of

---

23 Admittedly, the comprehensive character of the New Classical models has not become obvious in our simple exposition. Therefore, cf. SARGENT, Th.J. (1976) A Classical Macroeonomic Model of the United States. Journal of Political Economy **84**, pp. 207–237. LUCAS, R.E. Jr. (1975) An Equilibrium Model of the Business Cycle. Journal of Political Economy **83**, pp. 1113–1144.

24 "American Indians were perfectly rational if they, on the basis of their beliefs, performed a rain dance when they wanted rain, and they entertained 'rational expectations' when they expected their rites to have the desired effects." MACHLUP, F. (1983) The Rationality of 'Rational Expectations'. Kredit und Kapital **16**, p. 174.

discretionary measures. Also a Keynesian model can be self-fulfilling when Rational expectations prevail.[25]

3. Criticism: New Keynesian economics proceed from the second criticism. The New Keynesians[26] co-opt the traditional assumption of sticky wages[27] but assume Rational expectations at the same time. If wages or prices are fixed by contract and cannot be revised at any instant, there is some room for effective discretionary policy. STANLEY FISCHER, for instance, argues that contracts with price proviso clauses incur additional costs and are thus avoided by the market participants. If this holds, discretionary monetary policy can be employed to advantange since the central bank, in contrast to the private sector, is capable of responding immediately to exogenous disturbances. New Keynesian economics are a substantiation of the allegation that assuming Rational expectations does not *per se* imply policy ineffectiveness.

4. Criticism: A further objection is directed towards LUCAS' aggregate supply function – the centerpiece of New Classical economics. This supply function rests on the premise that the market participants are informed about prices in "their" markets only, but not about prices in the other markets or the general price level. In the context of New Classical theory, this lack of information appears extremely strange. All individuals are assumed to be fairly well informed about such difficult things as the structure of the true econometric model and even its parameter values: why should they not know the price level? After all, monthly changes in the price level are published in every quality newspaper; and information about the price level can be acquired so much easier than information about the econometric structure of an economy. Hence, this assumption – which is an indispensible prerequisite of LUCAS' aggregate supply function – seems to be inconsistent with the New Classical framework.

5. Criticism: The New Classical economy is apt to become rather uncomfortable for its inhabitants if it is not by chance log-linear. The reader certainly knows that even simple quadratic equations possibly involve multiple solutions. What should a rational individual expect when there are several Rational expectations?

6. Criticism: An important empirical objection should be mentioned finally. If unemployment results solely from serially uncorrelated disturbances, as stated by the New Classical theory, the rates of unemployment would have to be serially uncorrelated, too. But in fact, they are not.

It is our impression that nowadays the New Classical doctrine appears very questionable to the greater part of the economics profession though its contribution

---

25 "Agents brought up in Chicago will verify Chicago predictions and agents who grew up in the sober landscape of Cambridge (England) will verify the Cambridge prediction." HAHN, F.H. (1980) Unemployment from a Theoretical Viewpoint. Economica **47**, p. 291.

26 FISCHER, St. (1977) Long-Term Contracts, Rational Expectations and the Optimal Money Supply Rule. Journal of Politic al Economy **85**, pp. 191–205. PHELPS, E.S. and J.B. TAYLOR (1977) Stabilizing Powers of Monetary Policy under Rational Expectations. Journal of Political Economy **85**, pp. 163–190. TAYLOR, J.B. (1979) Staggered Wage Setting in a Macro Model. American Economic Review (PP) **69**, pp. 108–113.

27 Using the so-called theory of implicit contracts, New Keynesians derive wage rigidities from rational behaviour. Cf. AZARIADIS, C. (1975) Implicit Contracts and Underemployment Equilibria. Journal of Political Economy **83**, pp. 1183–1202.

to several deep-seated theoretical problems is generally acknowledged. With regard to its policy inferences, the aphoristic question of TOBIN remains essentially unanswered:

"Why is unemployment so high at full employment?"

After all, the majority of economists are not ready to interpret the Great Depression as a sudden rise in infectious laziness, i.e. as a voluntary intertemporal substitution of labor and leisure.

Further Reading

FISCHER, St. Ed. (1980) Rational Expectations and Economic Policy. Chicago: Chicago Press

FRIEDMAN, B. (1979) Optimal Expectations and the Extreme Information Assumptions of "Rational Expectations" Macromodels. Journal of Monetary Economics 5, pp. 32–41

LUCAS, R.E. Jr. (1975) An Equilibrium Model of the Business Cycle. Journal of Political Economy 83, pp. 1113–1144

LUCAS, R.E. Jr. (1977) Understanding Business Cycles. Supplement 5 to the Journal of Monetary Economics

MACHLUP, F. (1983) The Rationality of 'Rational Expectations'. Kredit und Kapital 16, pp. 172–183

PARKIN, M. (1983) Modern Macroeconomics. Scarborough: Prentice-Hall

SARGENT, Th.S. (1979) Macroeconomic Theory. New York: Academic Press

SHILLER, R.J. (1978) Rational Expectations and the Dynamic Structure of Macroeconomic Models – A Critical Review. Journal of Monetary Economics 4, pp. 1–44

SARGENT, Th.S. and N. WALLACE (1976) Rational Expectations and the Theory of Economic Policy. Journal of Monetary Economics 2, pp. 169–183

TOBIN, J. (1980) Are New Classical Models Plausible Enough to Guide Policy? Journal of Money, Credit and Banking 12, pp. 788–799

Chapter XI. Neokeynesian Theory

"To be a Keynesian, one need only realize the difficulties of finding the market clearing vector." (AXEL LEIJONHUFVUD)

The beginning of this chapter is devoted to terminology since "Neokeynesian theory" enjoys a variety of designations. But first, the theory itself must be defined. By *Neokeynesian theory* we mean a micro- or macroeconomic approach which is based on individual optimization behaviour, which – though Walrasian in spirit – does not insist on permanent market clearance and hence potentially arrives at "Keynesian" results. In short: it is a Walrasian theory without an auctioneer. The basic work on this subject was done by ROBERT J. BARRO, JEAN-PASCAL BENASSY, ROBERT W. CLOWER, JACQUES DRÈZE, JEAN-MICHEL GRANDMONT, HERSCHEL I. GROSSMAN, AXEL LEIJONHUFVUD, and EDMOND MALINVAUD while JOHN R. HICKS and DON PATINKIN are especially important fore-runners.

Sometimes, Neokeynesian theory is called "disequilibrium theory" which is at best misleading. Considered from the Classical point of view, this term may seem appropriate because "equilibrium" and "market clearance" are taken as one and the same (in § 4 we referred to this as equilibrium in the theoretical sense). Various authors, however, have insisted on interpreting "equilibrium" as a general notion of "rest" or compatibility of individual plans. In this respect, Neokeynesian theory is an equilibrium theory, and it is bound to be one because of its comparative-static character.

Furthermore, the term "Neowalrasian theory" is appropriate in principle, but ambiguous since it denotes some other branches of general equilibrium theory, too. And finally, "theory of temporary equilibrium with quantity rationing" is supremely exact but a bit too long-winded. Hence, we will speak of Neokeynesian theory on the grounds that it constitutes a development of Keynesian theory, a devolopment of the Neoclassical synthesis[1].

§ 76 The Evolution of Neokeynesian Economics

"In view of recent interest in non-tatônnement processes, such a disequilibrium interpretation of Keynes should be welcome as a nice extension of general equilibrium theory." (TAKASHI NEGISHI)

To the development of Neokeynesian theory, three endeavors were significant, not independent of one another but rather three aspects of a large-scale revision of theory.

---

1 Probably, BENASSY was the first to introduce this meaning of "Neokeynesian theory": BENASSY, J.-P. (1975) Neo-Keynesian Disequilibrium Theory in a Monetary Economy. Review of Economic Studies **42**, pp. 502–523.

This view is supported by the fact that all three derive from the same work, namely, "Value and Capital" by JOHN R. HICKS[2].

1) Re-interpretation of KEYNES. After the Neoclassical synthesis had become the prevailing doctrine of the 1950s, ROBERT W. CLOWER initiated a re-interpretation of the "General Theory" in 1962 which was later on given new impetus by AXEL LEIJONHUFVUD[3]. CLOWER, and especially LEIJONHUFVUD, reduced the difference between "KEYNES and the Classics" to a simple common denominator:

"In the Keynesian macrosystem the Marshallian ranking of price- and quantity-adjustment speeds is reversed: In the shortest period flow quantities are freely variable, but one or more prices are given..."[4]

This message was conveyed forcefully by LEIJONHUFVUD, and adopted enthusiastically by many economists. Was the cause of the issue now found, and KEYNES exposed as a heretical Classic? We do not intent to enter this KEYNES-exegesis but only remark that LEIJONHUFVUD soon had to retract his interpretation[5]: a fact that does not diminish the *analytical* significance of CLOWER's and his contribution. Their work induced a true deluge of publications, the best known being "Money, Employment and Inflation" by BARRO and GROSSMAN, and "The Theory of Unemployment Reconsidered" by MALINVAUD[6]. These works provided the macroeconomic groundwork of Neokeynesian theory.

2) Imperfectionist development of general equilibrium theory. As already mentioned, Walras' model was ignored for a long time, which was at least in part due to the barrier between him and the English-speaking world. Not before HICKS' publication of "Value and Capital", in 1939, did an increasing interest in general equilibrium theory emerge. Much was to be done: with the exception of the unknown mathematician ABRAHAM WALD, no one had actually proved the existence of a general economic equilibrium under the conditions of perfect competition, or even shown under which conditions such an equilibrium would be unique and stable. Thus, many able mathematicians and economists turned their attention to these problems, KENNETH J. ARROW, GÉRARD DEBREU, LIONEL McKENZIE, and PAUL A. SAMUELSON perhaps being the most prominent of them. By the 1950s, the most urgent problems were resolved[7].

Up to then, however, the authors had been chiefly busy with optimal conditions, i.e. perfect competition in a world with an auctioneer, which is quite natural to the devolopment of science. Now, the solution of the basic problems made way for

---

2 HICKS, J.R. (1939) Value and Capital. Oxford: Oxford University Press. Second edition 1946 ibid.

3 CLOWER, R.W. (1965) The Keynesian Counter-Revolution: A Theoretical Appraisal. In: HAHN, F.H. and F.P.R. BRECHLING Ed. The Theory of Interest Rates. London: Macmillan. (Our date 1962 refers to CLOWER's original lecture.) LEIJONHUFVUD, A. (1968) On Keynesian Economics and the Economics of Keynes. Oxford: Oxford University Press.

4 LEIJONHUFVUD, A. op.cit., p. 52.

5 "... it is not correct to attribute to Keynes a general reversal of the Marshallian ranking of relative price and quantity adjustment velocities." LEIJONHUFVUD, A. (1974) Keynes' Employment Function. History of Political Economy **6**, p. 169.

6 BARRO, R.J. and H.I. GROSSMAN (1976) Money, Employment and Inflation. Cambridge etc.: Cambridge University Press. MALINVAUD, E. (1977) The Theory of Unemployment Reconsidered. Oxford: Basil Blackwell.

7 A very good overview is WEINTRAUB, E.R. (1983) On the Existence of a Competitive Equilibrium: 1930–1954. Op.cit.

considering some imperfections. Beside the analysis of non-tatônnement, investigation of the consequences of rigid prices began, and so-called "disequilibrium theory" was founded. In this respect, JEAN-PASCAL BENASSY, JACQUES DRÈZE, JEAN-MICHEL GRANDMONT, GUY LAROQUE, TAKASHI NEGISHI, and EDMOND MALINVAUD [8] in particular are to be mentioned.

Their essentially microeconomic theories have fertilized the macroeconomic branch of Neokeynesian theory in many respects.

3) "Microfoundation of macroeconomics". The attempt to develop a microeconomic foundation of macroeconomics formed a third impetus [9]. Because of the microeconomic structure of reality, microeconomic theory appears, from an analytical point of view, as the unquestionably superior method, whereas macroeconomic theory is primarily employed for heuristic reasons such as simplicity, and uniqueness of solutions. Therefore, microeconomics had a much stronger attraction for many theorists than the clumsy macromodels, and it is by no means surprising that they aimed at a "microfoundation of macroeconomics" [10].

Our attitude towards these endeavors is somewhat ambiguous. If the "costs of aggregation", i.e. the loss of information, are unimportant with regard to the specific explanatory goal, a "microfoundation" is obviously *unnecessary* since the macroeconomic approach as such arrives at the correct explanation. But if a certain phenomenon cannot be dealt with macroeconomically, such a "microfoundation" is *impossible* since there is simply no macroeconomic theory to be "founded". Hence, micro- and macroeconomics may fertilize and complement each other, yet there is no way to found one by the other in the strict sense. On the contrary, both approaches are valid in their own right.

It was the foundation of macroeconomic theory on *optimization behaviour*, often confounded with the microeconomic foundation, that was actually achieved. We consider this to be the most significant feature of Neokeynesian theory. The Classical apparatus of decision-making – consisting of general assumptions such as utility maximizing behaviour – is applied to "representative" decision units and allows the derivation of behavioural relationships. The reader is already familiar with this procedure from our Chapter IV on Classical theory. But – by employing some different assumptions – rather un-Classical results emerge in Neokeynesian theory. The analyt-

8 BENASSY, J.-P. (1975) Neo-Keynesian Disequilibrium Theory in a Monetary Economy. Op.cit. BENASSY, J.-P. (1977) On Quantity Signals and the Foundations of Effective Demand Theory. Scandinavian Journal of Economics **79**, pp. 147–168. DRÈZE, J. (1975) Existence of an Exchange Equilibrium under Price Rigidities. International Economic Review **16**, pp. 301–320. GRANDMONT, J.-M. and G. LAROQUE (1976) On Temporary Keynesian Equilibria. Review of Economic Studies **43**, p. 53–67. SVENSSON, L.E.O. (1977) Effective Demand and Stochastic Rationing. Review of Economic Studies **44**, pp. 339–355.

9 WEINTRAUB, E.R. (1979) Microfoundations. The Compatibility of Microeconomics and Macroeconomics. Cambridge etc.: Cambridge University Press. HARCOURT, C.G. Ed. (1977) The Microfoundations of Macroeconomics. London: Macmillan.

10 This "supremacy-aspiration" of microeconomists led FITOUSSI to the judgement: "General equilibrium theory and Keynesian economics have always maintained an ambiguous relationship founded on a superiority complex on the part of the one and a conviction of greater empirical evidence on the part of the other." FITOUSSI, J.-P. (1983) Modern Macroeconomic Theory: An Overview. Op.cit.

ical instrument for their derivation is the so-called dual decision hypothesis which we want to introduce now.

§77 The Dual Decision Hypothesis

"When forming his demand for a particular good, an unemployed individual remembers, that he is unemployed." (EDMOND MALINVAUD)

Seldom has an apparently simple idea had such far-reaching consequences for economic theorizing as the dual decision hypothesis of ROBERT W. CLOWER. We cannot appreciate it properly, however, before knowing the problem underlying it.

In the 1950s, as mentioned on several occasions, a vast part of the economics profession was concerned with the construction of a "Neoclassical synthesis" and, finally, one was happy to have incorporated the contribution of KEYNES (or what one believed that to be) into Neoclassical theory. In the process, a profound basic problem was overlooked: The Keynesian consumption function is irreconcible with Classical reasoning according to which the individuals maximize their utility subject to a certain budget constraint. We remember that, in Classical theory, consumption does *not* depend on income but solely on the rate of interest and perhaps on the real wage rate; nothing else can be deduced from the Classical utility maximizing approach. Hence the question was to arise whether the integration of the Keynesian consumption function into the Classical model was not inconsistent; but all economists at that time have overlooked this problem. As an example, the prominent German economist ERICH SCHNEIDER wrote:

"The macroeconomic consumption function (C (Y)) is exactly the counterpart of the microeconomic, individual demand functions of the Walras-type which depict individual consumption as a function of prevailing commodity prices and income of the current period. Adding the individual demand functions of the Walras-type leads to the Keynesian consumption function."[11]

This sounds convincing but is simply not true. Let us demonstrate the error by means of a representative household which maximizes utility depending on consumption and leisure:

$$U = U(C, (1 - N)). \tag{268}$$

C denotes the quantity of consumption commodities, and N the working time. By appropriate choice of units, total available time amounts to 1. Therefore, (1-N) denotes leisure time. The utility function may exhibit strictly positive first derivatives and a decreasing marginal rate of substitution.

When forming its decisions, our representative household must observe the budget constraint which forces it to finance consumption expenditure by labor income:

$$P \cdot C - w \cdot N = 0. \tag{269}$$

---

11 SCHNEIDER, E. (1953) Der Streit um Keynes. Jahrbücher für Nationalökonomie und Statistik **165**, pp. 89–122, p. 102. Translation by the authors.

Here, P represents the price of consumption goods, and w the nominal wage rate. By the usual methods, we can derive a Classical consumption function as well as a labor supply function from (268) and (269):

$$C = C\left(\frac{w}{P}\right) \tag{270}$$

$$N^s = N^s\left(\frac{w}{P}\right). \tag{271}$$

Real labor income, in turn, is the product of labor supply and the real wage rate:

$$Y = N^s\left(\frac{w}{P}\right) \cdot \frac{w}{P}. \tag{272}$$

Contrary to the above statement of ERICH SCHNEIDER, consumption demand depends *solely* on the real wage rate – not on income. Income is determined by the supply of labor; it is an *endogenous* variable to the household and *not given*. If the household prefers to work 10 hours a day, at the given real wage rate of $ 10 per hour, it has at the same time determined its daily income of $ 100. In Walras' model, only prices are given to the individuals. But quantities, and income, they decide by themselves.

As a result of this simple model, we recognize that the Classical (or Walras-type) demand functions are irreconcilable with the Keynesian $C(Y)$ since the latter takes income as exogenous. In the following, we will name the Walras-type demand (and supply) functions *notional functions*. These notional functions depend solely on prices.

It was CLOWER's aim to demonstrate that – under certain circumstances – the Keynesian consumption function can be founded on the Classical approach. He argued as follows: In Classical theory, it is tacitly assumed that the household can *realize* its plans. The above notional functions are effectively answers to questions of the type: "Suppose you could carry out all your plans at given prices, what consumption pattern would you choose?" But what if the household is subject to a constraint, to rationing, in some market? If he cannot actually sell the supplied quantity of labor in the labor market, the budget constraint will *force* a reduction in consumption. This is seen from the following figure:

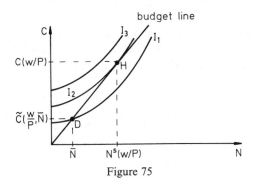

Figure 75

On the axes, you see the "good" consumption and the "ungood" labor. Therefore, the indifference curves are upward sloped. Additional labor incurs a loss of utility which must be compensated for by additional consumption in order to maintain the same utility level. The indifference curves are convex because we employ the usual assumption of a decreasing marginal rate of substitution between consumption and leisure. This means that additional labor must be offset by *increasing* additional consumption.

The budget constraint exhibits the slope w/P and restricts the households'possible choices to the points on and below it. At point H, the *equilibrium of the household*, the budget line becomes tangent to the highest attainable indifference curve. Thus, the household will decide for $C(w/P)$ and $N^s(w/P)$ as shown in the figure. Thereby it has simultaneously decided on its income.

Let us now consider a *selling constraint*, $\bar{N}$, which confronts the household in the labor market. The household is unable to sell more labor than $\bar{N}$ and the selling constraint forces it to reduce consumption to $\tilde{C}(w/P,\bar{N})$ owing to the fact that it cannot spend more money than it receives. Hence, the household must revise his notional consumption plan and realize point D. $\tilde{C}(w/P,\bar{N})$ is called the household's *effective consumption demand*.

This is the very meaning of the *dual decision hypothesis*: In the first step, the household forms its plans solely according to the price signals of the market, and decides for point H. But if confronted with quantity constraints, it must revise its plans in the second step, now taking *quantity signals* into account, too. Thus we have founded the Keynesian allegation that consumption depends on a quantity (Y) within an essentially Classical framework. Income becomes an exogenous variable to the household as soon as the household is faced with a constraint in the labor markt.

Note that the Classical core of the decision process remains unchanged. The household continues maximizing utility even when perceiving quantity constraints. Of course, it does not attain the utility level at H but "maximizing" can only mean striving for the best subject to given circumstances. This is no no different from Classical theory where the individuals have to observe their budget constraints. Thus, we have not altered the core of the decision process but specified the "given circum-stances" as less favorable[12].

What will household's effective demand in the commodity market be when obey-ing the dual decision hypothesis? This question is answered by the following formula:

$$\text{choose} \quad \min\left(C\left(\frac{w}{P}\right); \frac{w}{P} \cdot \bar{N}\right). \tag{273}$$

The household thus proceeds in the following manner: At first, it formulates the notional consumption plan, $C(w/P)$ and offers the notional quantity of labor, $N(w/P)$. If it is *not* restricted in the labor market, the decision is already complete. In this case, the constraint $\bar{N}$ can be viewed as being above the notional labor supply.

But if it perceives that it cannot succeed in selling the notional quantity of labor, the household must adjust consumption demand such that it matches *given* labor income, $w/P \cdot \bar{N}$. The household is subject to a binding constraint. (In general, we

---

12 We might wonder, of course, why the household does not change the wage rate in order to evade the quantity constraint. But this is to be discussed later on.

term a constraint *binding* if the effective demands in Clower's sense are restricted. From this it follows that, if an effective plan is below the notional one, and a constraint lies between these two, the constraint is *not* binding.)

By now, it should have become clear that the household diminishes its consumption demand if it perceives a binding constraint in the labor market. For the time being, we abstract from savings, consumer credit, and other sources of income. The next problem is how the household behaves in the *labor* market when faced with a selling constraint there. Two extreme cases are conceivable:

– The household may reduce its supply to the quantity constraint, or
– it may adhere to the notional supply, even though perceiving the constraint and adjusting consumption.

In the first case, the household obviously plans point D in the following figure:

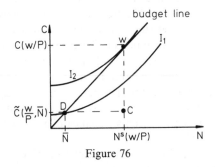

Figure 76

Such a "frustrated" household is said to offer an effective labor supply in the sense of Drèze. For short, we will speak of a *Drèze-demand*[13], whereby supply is conceived as a negative demand. Thus, a Drèze-demand is defined by the fact that a market participant reduces his plan to the quantity constraint. This behaviour is *rational* at given prices if

– the quantity constraint is known with certainty,
– the market participant believes he cannot alter it, and
– a demand exceeding the constraint incurs costs.

Let us consider the second possibility now, namely, that the household *maintains* his notional labor supply while adjusting its consumption demand according to the quantity of labor actually sold. Then, the household plans point C in the above figure. It is said to offer an effective labor supply in Clower's sense, termed *Clower-demand*[14] from now on. In general, a Clower-demand is defined by the fact that a market participant adheres to his notional plan in the market where he is constrained, but revises his plans relating to all *other* markets. The Clower-demand is possibly *rational* at given prices if

– the market participant does not know the quantity constraint for certain (*stochastic rationing*), or

13 This designation is due to BENASSY, J.-P. (1977) On Quantity Signals and the Foundations of Effective Demand Theory. Op.cit.
14 This designation is also due to BENASSY, op.cit.

– he believes in being able to alter the constraint by means of his demand (*manipulable rationing*), and
– a demand exceeding the constraint incurs no or trifling costs.

When stochastic rationing prevails, a market participant is likely to maintain his notional demand in order to exploit the market chances fully. He behaves similarly if he supposes that he is in a position to alter the constraint. For instance, the *individual* labor constraint may weaken if the constrained worker looks for a job very intensely. These two possibilities are the more significant the lower the costs involved in making the offer.

It must be pointed out that the household in our above example plans a point, C, *below* his budget constraint. Generally, a Clower-demand may violate the budget constraint in both directions. Nonetheless, this concept of demand cannot be dismissed as irrational. One must take cognizance of the fact that in the case of quantity constraints, *realized demand* can differ from the *demand signal*. In the above figure, point D will always be realized, though it may be rational to express a different demand signal, i.e. a Clower-demand, on the conditions enumerated above[15]. Of course, a full-fledged decision model would have to incorporate the weighing of costs and utility incurred by a Clower-demand; in this respect, out model is rudimentary.

Up to now we have dealt with the special case of rationing of households in the labor market – but just for illustration. Now we want to introduce the Drèze- and Clower-demand as two general concepts which can be applied to any individual and to rationing in any market.

In the general case, an individual maximizes some function $z = f(\mathbf{x})$, where z is some goal variable which depends on the n components of the vector $\mathbf{x}$. z can be interpreted as a utility index or as a firm's profit. The components of $\mathbf{x}$ are denoted with a positive sign if they represent supplies, and with a negative sign if they represent demands. The *Drèze-demand* with respect to x_i is given by the program:

$$\operatorname*{Max}_{x_i} z = f(\mathbf{x}) \quad (j = 1 \ldots n). \tag{274}$$

subject to   i) $\mathbf{p} \cdot \mathbf{x} \geq 0$

ii) $x_j \leq \bar{x}_j$ for all $x_j > 0$ (supplies)

iii) $x_j \geq \bar{x}_j$ for all $x_j < 0$ (demands).

Condition i) represents the budget constraint since the scalar product $\mathbf{p} \cdot \mathbf{x}$ is equal to "receipts minus expenditures". The two other conditions require the individual to observe all possible constraints which are marked by a bar. According to ii) and iii), the household never supplies or demands a quantity that exceeds the constraint in the respective market.

In contrast, the *Clower-demand* with respect to x_i is given by the program:

$$\operatorname*{Max}_{x_i} z = f(\mathbf{x}) \quad (j = 1 \ldots n). \tag{275}$$

subject to   i) $\mathbf{p} \cdot \mathbf{x} \geq 0$

ii) $x_j \leq \bar{x}_j$ for all $x_j > 0, \, j \neq i$ (supplies)

iii) $x_j \geq \bar{x}_j$ for all $x_j < 0, \, j \neq i$ (demands).

15 Cf. SVENSSON, L.E.O. (1981) Effective Demand in a Sequence of Markets. Scandinavian Journal of Economics **83**, p. 1–21.

The sole difference from the Drèze-demand is the supplement "j $\neq$ i" in ii) and iii). It means that the individual, when forming his demand for good x_i only observes the constraints in the *other* markets, but not that in market i itself. Given a binding quantity constraint in market i, the individual maintains the notional offer as long as he is not constrained in other markets.

In the following, Drèze-demands are denoted as $\hat{x}_i$, and Clower-demands as $\tilde{x}_i$. We can immediately infer the relationship between these two from the above maximization programs:

$$\hat{x}_i = \min(\tilde{x}_i, \bar{x}_i) \quad \text{for all } x_i > 0$$

$$\hat{x}_i = \max(\tilde{x}_i, \bar{x}_i) \quad \text{for all } x_i < 0. \tag{276}$$

If there is no binding constraint in market i, the two demand concepts coincide. But if there is such a constraint, the Drèze-demand will be smaller in its absolute value than the Clower-demand because the constraint in market i is also observed. Subsequently, we will proceed from a model without stochastic or manipulable rationing; and therefore all comparative static analyses will refer only to Drèze-demands. The Clower-demands, however, interpreted as a mere demand signal, will prove important when we turn to price dynamics.

Let us examine next what quantities are actually traded in a market when at least one market participant is rationed in this market. The quantities x^s and x^d are supplied and demanded, respectively, both being denoted with a positive sign. The above optimization programs imply that no market participant is compelled to trade more than he wishes: trade is *voluntary*. Consequently, the quantity x which is actually traded must not exceed x^d or x^s:

$$x \leqq \min(x^d; x^s). \tag{277}$$

In the second place we will assume that trade is *efficient*: it is not possible that *both* sides of the market are rationed at the same time. This postulate guarantees that only the participants on the "longer" side of the market are rationed whereas those on the "shorter" side can all carry out their plans. Therefore, x must not fall short of both x^s and x^d:

$$x \geqq \min(x^d; x^s). \tag{278}$$

Combining the last two equations, we arrive at the *minimum rule*. It states that realized transactions will be equal to the minimum of supply and demand provided that trade is both voluntary and efficient:

$$x = \min(x^d; x^s). \tag{279}$$

Let us finally discuss the concept of a *rationing scheme* which serves to answer questions such as: If labor supply exceeds labor demand, which workers are rationed to what degree? The rationing scheme is a function that assigns a certain quantity to any market participant on the long side of the market. Clearly, there are in principle countless conceivable rationing schemes. The following types are particularly important:

– *Proportional rationing*. Every demand (or supply) is cut by a certain percentage. This occurs, for instance, when an issue of equities is oversubscribed.

- *Uniform rationing.* Every demand (or supply) is met up to a certain maximum. An example of uniform rationing is food ration cards in war times.
- *0/1-rationing.* Every demand (or supply) is either satisfied fully, or not at all. The selection can be governed by economic efficiency (*efficient rationing*) or by criteria such as age or sex (*priority rationing*).

The prevailing type of the rationing scheme plays a central role in microeconomic models with quantity rationing because it influences the behaviour of the market participants. Proportional rationing, for example, invites "overbidding": An invididual who expects a proportional cut by ten percent of his demand is inclined to show an effective demand that exceeds the hypothetical one by some ten percent. He does not behave in this manner when faced with uniform or 0/1-rationing. Within our macroeconomic models, however, the prevailing rationing scheme is less important; where it is, this is due to several components of demand in the same market. We will return to this later.

§78 The Logic of the Fix Price-Method

In the preceding section we expounded the dual decision hypothesis without discussing the reason why quantity constraints might occur in a market economy. This reason is given by the *fix price assumption*. The fix price assumption is often misunderstood. In a sense, it merely states that there is no auctioneer[16]. Recollect Walras' model: All market participants were considered as price takers, nobody being in a position to alter prices except the imaginary auctioneer. The latter announces a certain price vector at the beginning of each period, collects the resulting demand and supply plans, and *prevents* the individuals from exchanging till the market clearing price vector is established. Viewed in this way, the auctioneer appears as a rather totalitarian institution, unparalled in reality.

The *fix price assumption* states that the market participants establish prices by themselves so that there are potentially situations of non-market-clearance. Hence, the fix price assumption does not necessarily refer to institutional obstructions or lasting price stickiness. It only states that quantity constraints must arise *first* in order to induce the individuals to alter prices; and that quantities react quicker than prices. As a result, fixed prices in this sense do not necessarily depend on monopolies but can also arise in perfect competition when there is no auctioneer.

The fix price assumption has not always been interpreted in this way, however. The more mathematically oriented Neokeynesians have tended to adopt this assumption without explaining it further, instead stressing the "short-run" character of their models. Hence many readers were bound to get the impression that this is a rather difficult, but happily uninteresting theory which refers only to extremely short periods. This opinion is ill-founded as should become clear from the following passages. Moreover, it is entirely beside the point to reproach Neokeynesian theory on the grounds that it does not offer a genuine theory of price formation. The latter accusa-

---

16 The fixprice-method was developed by HICKS. Cf. HICKS, J.R. (1965) Capital and Growth. Oxford: Clarendon Press, Chapter VII.

tion, appropriate as it is in principle, overlooks that the lack of a choice-theoretic approach to price setting applies to Walras' model and the rest of contemporary general equilibrium theory alike.

In short, we will proceed from given prices in the following; analyze the behaviour of the market participants; consider the resulting equilibria; and finally turn to the question of *price dynamics*. The fix price assumption requires that quantities react quicker than prices but not that the latter are exogenous.

Because of the complexity of this approach, we want to begin with an example in which all functions are numerically specified. Our model comprises a closed economy with a representative household and a representative firm, no government, and two commodities: a consumption commodity, and labor.

The representative household maximizes a utility function

$$U = C \cdot (1 - N). \tag{280}$$

were C denotes consumption and N labor. Since the household's total disposable time is standardized to 1, $(1 - N)$ represents leisure. The above utility function is strictly quasi-concave and exhibits strictly positive first derivatives; thus the indifference curves exhibit the usual shape. Our representative household receives wage income and all profits, and expends its income for consumption only. Hence the budget constraint reads:

$$P \cdot C - w \cdot N - \pi = 0. \tag{281}$$

The household has perfect foresight with respect to the profits that accrue to it in the current period. With prices given, it will adjust the quantities offered and demanded in order to maximize utility. The utility maximizing quantities can be calculated using the method of Lagrangean multipliers[17]:

$$L(\lambda, C, N) = C \cdot (1 - N) + \lambda(P \cdot C - w \cdot N - \pi). \tag{282}$$

Computing the three derivatives of this function, equalizing them to zero, and transforming the results somewhat yields the *notional functions*:

$$C(\alpha) = \frac{\pi + w}{2P} \tag{283}$$

$$N^s(\alpha) = \frac{w - \pi}{2w} \tag{284}$$

$$\alpha := (P, w, \pi). \tag{285}$$

The notional functions are determined by α, the vector of P, w, and π. They exhibit the following properties. Consumption increases when the wage rate or profit income rises but decreases when prices rise. Labor supply increases when wages rise but diminishes when profit income rises. Labor supply is independent of prices on the grounds that the income and substitution effects of a price change cancel out.

The representative firm seeks to maximize its profits

$$\pi = P \cdot Y - w \cdot N. \tag{286}$$

---

17 The Lagrange method is explained in Subsection 3.8 of the Mathematical Appendix.

which are defined as revenue $(P \cdot Y)$ minus labor costs $(w \cdot N)$. We abstract from fixed costs since they would not alter the firm's behaviour, but only complicate the exposition. The representative firm has to observe the feasable production set which is described by the production function

$$Y = N^{0,5}. \tag{287}$$

This concrete production function exhibits positive diminishing marginal returns which increase without bound as labor input approaches zero. In order to determine notional commodity supply and notional labor demand, we employ the Lagrange-function

$$L(\lambda, Y, N) = P \cdot Y - w \cdot N + \lambda(Y - N^{0,5}). \tag{288}$$

The usual procedure yields the following notional functions:

$$Y(\alpha) = \frac{P}{2\,w} \tag{289}$$

$$N^d(\alpha) = \frac{P^2}{4\,w^2} \tag{290}$$

$$\pi(\alpha) = \frac{P^2}{4\,w}. \tag{291}$$

These function show the expected reactions: Due to an increase in prices, commodity supply, labor demand, and profits increase; and due to an increase in wages, they diminish. The description of notional behaviour is thus complete, and we can move on to the complete model. The Walrasian working of the model is demonstrated first in order to analyze the Neokeynesian deviations from it thereafter.

Owing to the *Walrasian view* we have the following ground rules. First, there exists only one relative price in a model with two markets. Hence, we take the commodity price as numèraire $(P \overset{!}{=} 1)$ such that nominal and real wage rate coincide from now on. Second, Walras' law holds. It states that the sum of the excess demands in all markets is equal to zero. This is easily proved by adding the notional functions. After some transformations, we obtain:

$$P(C(\alpha) - Y(\alpha)) + w(N^d(\alpha) - N^s(\alpha)) = 0. \tag{292}$$

Thus, when demand and supply in the labor market match, demand and supply in the commodity market will match, too. When there is an excess demand in one market, the other will exhibit excess supply of the same value.

The model is completed by postulating a price-tatônnement in the labor market:

$$\frac{dw}{dt} = H(N^d(\alpha) - N^s(\alpha)); \quad H(0) = 0, \quad H' > 0. \tag{293}$$

The meaning of this price adjustment function, H, is best illustrated by Figure 77 on the following page.

The function H assigns a certain rate of change in the nominal wage to any excess demand (or supply) in the labor market. Because of the property $H(0) = 0$, nominal wages do not change in equilibrium. The assumption $H' > 0$ (for all excess demands)

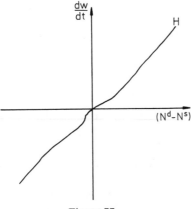

Figure 77

guarantees that H preserves the sign of its argument[18]: When there is a positive excess demand in the labor market, wages will rise and vice versa. Hence the function H is nothing but a mathematical representation of the auctioneer. We assume that the wage rate is adjusted according to the market conditions, and that no exchange takes place till equilibrium is reached. There can be no doubt that it will be reached, finally.

From the equations for labor supply (284) and labor demand (290), we can determine the market clearing nominal wage rate which, in turn, yields the other solutions of the model. The results are rounded to two places:

$$P^* = 1; \quad w^* = 0.87; \quad \pi^* = 0.29 \tag{294}$$

$$C(\alpha) = Y(\alpha) = 0.58 \tag{295}$$

$$N^d(\alpha) = N^s(\alpha) = 0.33. \tag{296}$$

Let us now turn to the *Neokeynesian view*. We discard the assumption that all market participants wait till general equilibrium is established. On the contrary, individuals trade from the outset, which means that they are potentially rationed and must alter their behaviour according to the dual decision hypothesis.

Let us assume, for instance, that the original wage rate amounts to one. In the first step, we want to calculate the notional plans. Substituting $w = P = 1$ into equations (289) to (291) yields the following notional magnitudes:

$$Y(\alpha) = 0.5; \quad N^d(\alpha) = 0.25; \quad \pi(\alpha) = 0.25. \tag{297}$$

Equations (283) and (284) give notional consumption demand and notional labor supply:

$$C(\alpha) = 0.63; \quad N^s(\alpha) = 0.38. \tag{298}$$

As one would expect, the notional plans of households and firms are not compatible at the prevailing wage rate. Consumption demand exceeds supply by 0.13 units,

---

18 The assumption that H′ is positive everywhere is far too restrictive and has only be employed for simplicity. It is sufficient to assume that sign (H(.)) = sign (.) for all (.) and that H is continuously differentiable on R.

whereas labor demand falls short of labor supply by the same amount. When exchange is voluntary and efficient, the *quantity constraints* can be calculated as the respective minima of supply and demand. This is the minimum rule introduced in the preceding section:

$$\bar{C} = \min(C(\alpha), Y(\alpha)) = 0.5 \qquad (299)$$

$$\bar{N} = \min(N^d(\alpha), N^s(\alpha)) = 0.25 \qquad (300)$$

Comparing the constraints with the notional plans, we recognize that the households are rationed in *both* markets whereas the firms are not constrained. The above quantity constraints match the firms' notional plans. Let us now apply the dual decision hypothesis to calculate effective commodity demand and effective labor supply in Clower's sense:

Faced with a constraint in the labor market amounting to $\bar{N} = 0.5$, households must revise their consumption plans. Effective commodity demand in Clower's sense follows simply from substituting $\bar{N}$ into the household's budget constraint:

$$\bar{N} = 0.25 \Rightarrow \tilde{C}(\alpha, \bar{N}) = \frac{w \cdot \bar{N} + \pi}{P} = 0.5. \qquad (301)$$

Due to the rationing in the labor market, consumption demand is thus reduced from 0.63 to 0.5; the notional plan is now economically irrelevant.

Conversely, the households are rationed in the commodity market and will thus adjust their effective labor supply in Clower's sense. For, why should they work when there are not enough commodities available to exhaust income? We obtain effective labor supply in Clower's sense by substituting $\tilde{C} = 0.5$ into the budget constraint and solving for N:

$$\bar{C} = 0.5 \Rightarrow \tilde{N}^s(\alpha, \bar{C}) = \frac{P \cdot \bar{C} - \pi}{w} = 0.25. \qquad (302)$$

As mentioned in the foregoing section, we must procede from the Drèze-demands within our comparative static analysis, because the constraints are assumed to be neither stochastic nor manipulable. According to the rule (276), we calculate the Drèze-demands as the respective minima of the Clower-demands and the quantity constraints. This is because, in its Drèze-demand, the household does not merely observe the constraints in the other markets but also those in the same market. Thus:

$$\hat{C} = \min(\tilde{C}, \bar{C}) = \min(0.5; 0.5) = 0.5 \qquad (303)$$

$$\hat{N}^s = \min(\tilde{N}^s, \bar{N}) = \min(0.25; 0.25) = 0.25. \qquad (304)$$

Obviously, the Drèze-demands are identical to the Clower-demands in this particular example; it is to be emphasized that this does not hold universally. By comparing (297) with (303) and (304) we recognize a second feature: The Drèze-demands are consistent with the notional plans of the firms because effective consumption matches commodity supply, and effective labor supply matches labor demand. Therefore, some kind of equilibrium is established.

We now want to put this more precisely. In the first place we should note that the notional plans of the firms also constitute a Drèze-demand: it is the special case of a Drèze-demand where there is no binding constraint. Thus, the above case is characterized by the fact that all Drèze-demands are consistent. We call this a *quantity equilib-rium*. The present quantity equilibrium is described by:

$$P = 1; \quad w = 1; \quad \pi = 0.25 \tag{305}$$

$$\tilde{C} = Y(\alpha) = 0.5 \tag{306}$$

$$N^d(\alpha) = \bar{N}^s = 0.25 . \tag{307}$$

Note that profits, employment, and consumption fall short of their Walrasian values. When binding constraints prevail, the resulting state is always *suboptimal* as compared to the Walrasian equilibrium in the sense that the household's utility index assumes a lower value. It is not necessarily pareto-inferior (i.e. everyone is worse off) since there may be distributional effects; yet the typical or representative inhabitant of such an economy attains his highest utility in Walrasian equilibrium.

Will the individuals be content with this suboptimal state, or will they alter their behaviour to attain the Walrasian equilibrium? The question is of course misleading since the individuals do not act according to the abstract Walrasian equilibrium unknown to them but according to the market signals. Hence we have to put the question differently: Will prices change as a result of the market forces? Thus we ask for *price dynamics*.

In order to give an answer, we must first take cognizance of the following two facts:

– In the general case, notional demands exert no influence at all on prices because they have become irrelevant in the case of quantity constraints.
– The Drèze-demands are also completely unsuited for price considerations. They imply that a rationed individual reduces his demand to the quantity constraint such that there is never any excess demand. Excess demand is zero by definition.

This suggests that our analysis of price dynamics must refer to Clower-demands. Indeed, the Clower-demand is appropriate here because it yields a *demand signal*. The demand signal induces a change in prices which is directed towards removing the quantity constraint. In our concrete example, we substitute the following equation for (293):

$$\frac{dw}{dt} = H(N^d(\alpha) - \tilde{N}^s(\alpha, \tilde{C})); \quad H(0) = 0, \quad H' > 0. \tag{308}$$

The difference between (293) and (308) seems trifling – but is indeed far-reaching. Both functions H comprise notional labor demand as one argument but, in (308), effective labor supply has been substituted for notional labor supply. Notional labor supply is effectively the answer to a question like: "Suppose, you could buy as many commodities as you could afford – what quantity of labor would you supply?" But in fact, matters are quite different: the households are rationed in the commodity market and will therefore not maintain their notional labor supply. They will offer no more labor than required to buy the available quantity of goods.

A further difference between (293) and (308) is that (308) employs a hypothesis about actual behaviour whereas (293) describes the working of the auctioneer. For, if effective labor supply exceeds notional labor demand, the nominal wage rate will decline because the households are interested in mitigating the labor market constraint. Or, it will decline because the firms are now in a *monopolistic* position and have thus become able to force a reduction in wages. In contrast, (293) does not describe the behaviour of the market participants, who by assumption cannot alter the wage rate. It must be added, however, that (308) has not been derived from an optimization calculus; hence it is a mere behavioural assumption.

In our specific model, as will be seen from (297) and (302), it happens that notional labor demand and effective labor supply in Clower's sense just match so that the difference term in (308) vanishes, and the "false" wage rate will remain unchanged. In other words, the quantity equilibrium is *inherently stable*, and there is no tendency for prices to change. It must be emphasized that the lack of any price movements is not due to an assumption of absolutely fixed prices. On the contrary, we allowed for changes in the wage rate by means of equation (308). The absence of an adjustment towards the Walrasian equilibrium is due to the lack of corresponding market forces. The obvious reason for this dilemma is that notional labor supply was replaced by effective labor supply. Hence it is not wishful thinking or abstract optima that determine market prices, but supplies and demands which actually manifest themselves. It may be interesting to the economic theorist that effective labor supply would be higher *if* the households were not constrained in the commodity market – but this matter does not concern the participants in the labor market. To them, there is no measurable or perceptible excess supply.

Thus we arrive at an *unemployment equilibrium* which exhibits the following properties:

– The *households* have maximized utility subject to the given constraints.
– The *firms* have maximized profits subject to the production possibilities.
– The effective Drèze-demands are compatible in each *market*.
– There is no tendency for *prices* to change.

According to the terminology suggested in § 43, we call this an unemployment equilibrium because employment and production fall short of their Walrasian values. Yet, the wage rate does not decline since the effective plans in Clower's sense match, so that there is no perceptible excess supply in the labor market.

Let us summarize the most important point of the present section. First, we considered the Walrasian working of the simple model at hand. It implied the crucial assumption – not that prices are "flexible" but – that exchange does not take place before general equilibrium is established. The outcome was the familiar pareto-optimal equilibrium. The "totalitarian" auctioneer, however, who forestalls any trading at false prices does not mirror the core of Classical reasoning, it is merely an *analogy*. The Classics thought rather that trading at false prices would incur some frictions but would not prevent the economy from approaching the Walrasian equilibrium. Neokeynesian theory challenges this conjecture, showing that the tendency towards the general equilibrium *may* be eliminated when one takes the effect of quantity constraints into account.

There is no reason, however, to shelve WALRAS now once and for all. The present model has been deliberately designed to yield drastic results. Our next task will consist in developing an extended model which is capable of being compared to the Classical one. Then we examine which of the present results will survive, and which have to be revised. The subsequent section will prepare us for this task.

§ 79 A Reconsideration of the Consumption Function

In § 77 we already mentioned that the Keynesian consumption function can obtain support from an essentially Classical-type optimization model by means of the dual decision hypothesis. This problem is now to be considered more closely. Up to here, our analysis has been rudimentary in that the households were not allowed to form savings [19].

Consider a representative household with the utility function

$$U = U\left(C, (1 - N), \frac{\Delta M_H}{P}\right) \tag{309}$$

and the budget constraint

$$P \cdot C + \Delta M_H = w \cdot N + \pi. \tag{310}$$

C denotes real consumption, $(1 - N)$ leisure, and ΔM_H nominal savings that take place in form of accumulating money. P, w, and π are the price level, the nominal wage rate, and profits. We have to analyze first why the household derives utility from money savings, other savings being excluded by assumption. The interest motive drops out since no interest is paid on money balances.

As a basis for the above utility function we may refer to a two-period-model. The household makes up its plans over two periods and maximizes its *intertemporal utility*, $U(C_1, C_2, (1 - N)_1, (1 - N)_2)$ where the indices denote the period concerned. In doing so, current prices and profits and expected prices and profits in the subsequent period are taken into account. In any period, the household must finance its expenditures by current income and past savings. If it intends to spend more in the following period than it will receive, positive savings in the first period are necessary. Thus, the utility function (309) can be regarded as being derived from an intertemporal utility function. It is strictly concave with strictly positive first derivatives.

The graphical determination of the utility maximum could be carried out in a three-dimensional figure, but we will take another approach. Current prices, wages, and profits being given, the household decides on consumption, labor supply, and savings. But, due to the budget constraint, it has only two degrees of freedom. A certain choice of consumption and labor, for instance, simultaneously determines savings. This is seen by solving the budget constraint for ΔM_H:

$$\Delta M_H = w \cdot N + \pi - P \cdot C. \tag{311}$$

The result can be substituted into the original utility function:

$$U\left(C, (1 - N), \frac{w \cdot N + \pi - P \cdot C}{P}\right) =: V(C, (1 - N)). \tag{312}$$

The function V, defined by the preceding equation, is termed a *utility function with an absorbed budget constraint*. Explicitly, utility depends only on C and $(1 - N)$ for

---

19 With respect to the following, cf. SVENSSON, L.E.O. (1977) Effective Demand and Stochastic Rationing. Op.cit. MUELLBAUER, J. and R. PORTES (1978) Macroeconomic Models with Quantity Rationing. Economic Journal **88**, pp. 788–821.

the very reason that these two determine savings uniquely. Maximizing U subject to the budget constraint is equivalent to maximizing V without the constraint.

The deviation from the usual procedure involves no additional assumptions whatever and is solely designed to simplify the exposition. Graphically, V exhibits the following shape:

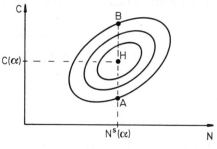

Figure 78

The indifference curves represent a "utility mountain" with the peak H. Thus, H is the *equilibrium of the household*, the utility maximum. Departing from H in any direction, utility will decrease, and thus an indifference curve consists of the set of all points that yield the same utility level.

The heuristic motivation of the above figure runs as follows[20]: First, H represents the household's equilibrium given by the point of tangency of the indifference surface and the budget surface in three-dimensional space. Owing to strictly decreasing rates of substitution, there is one and only one such point. Moreover, points such as A and B in the figure yield the same level of utility since they are on the same indifference curve. The amount of leisure is the same at both A and B, but consumption in B exceeds consumption in A. Nevertheless, resulting utility is the same because savings in B fall short of savings in A, which follows immediately from the budget constraint. Therefore, the fact that A and B are on the same indifference curve means that the consumption gain in B as compared to A yields additional utility which just offsets the loss of utility due to smaller savings.

Such a system of indifference curves differs from the usual schemes in that its position does not depend solely on preferences but also on the parameters P, w, and π. A change in prices, for instance, incurs a shift of the above "mountain".

We are now in a position to analyse the effects of *quantity constraints* in a very vivid manner. Let us start with two different constraints in the labor market.

The household is subject to the labor market constraints $\bar{N}_1$ and $\bar{N}_2$, whereas it is not rationed in the commodity market. In order to reach the highest attainable utility level, it seeks to approach point H as closely as possible. Thus, according to the

---

20 The proper proof runs as follows. First, the strict concavity of U implies the strict concavity of V. Second, the strict concavity of U guarantees the existence of a utility maximum in the positive orthant when prices are also positive. Hence, V has a maximum in the positive orthant. The special form of the "ellipses", finally, is due to the assumption that consumption and leisure are net substitutes. Strictly speaking, the results hold only in a neighborhood of H.

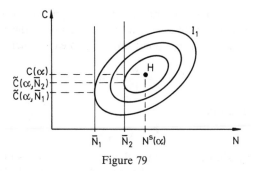

Figure 79

labor market constraint, $\tilde{C}(\alpha, \bar{N}_1)$ and $\tilde{C}(\alpha, \bar{N}_2)$ are the utility maximizing consumption quantities. Given the quantity constraint $\bar{N}_1$, for instance, I_1 is the highest attainable indifference curve.

In general, effective consumption demand is obtained as the point of tangency of an indifference curve and the vertical straight line which corresponds to the labor market constraint. Therefore, the slope of the indifference curve with respect to the consumption axis must vanish at the optimum point[21]:

$$\frac{\partial V(C, (1 - \bar{N}))}{\partial C} = 0.\tag{313}$$

This can be derived otherwise: Due to a quantity constraint in the labor market, the households can decide on consumption (and implicitly savings) only. Hence V becomes a function depending on only one variable, C. The necessary (and also sufficient) condition for a maximum is simply that the first derivative of V with respect to C vanishes. This is equation (313).

The effective *consumption function* is obtained by varying the constraint $\bar{N}$ over the entire range from zero to $N(\alpha)$. Analytically, the consumption function follows immediately from condition (313), which implicitly assigns the utility maximizing consumption to any labor constraint[22]:

$$\tilde{C} = \tilde{C}(\alpha, \bar{N}).\tag{314}$$

Graphically, we can construct the consumption function point-wise by varying $\bar{N}$ from zero to $N(\alpha)$:

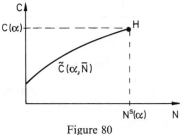

Figure 80

---

21 Implicit differentiation yields $dN/dC = - (\partial V/\partial C)/(\partial V/\partial N)$. Cf. the Mathematical Appendix, Subsection 4.2.
22 This follows from the implicit function theorem which is discussed in Subsection 4.3 of the Mathematical Appendix.

In other words, we obtain a straightforward Keynesian consumption function exhibiting the above shape. Recognizing that, at given prices, the constraint $\bar{N}$ and the household's real income, Y, correspond uniquely to each other

$$Y = \frac{w}{P} \cdot \bar{N} + \frac{\pi}{P},\tag{315}$$

it is clear that (314) can be rewritten as

$$\tilde{C} = \tilde{C}(\alpha, Y).\tag{316}$$

Hence it has been shown that KEYNES' concept of the consumption function can be founded on an essentially Classical approach to household behaviour provided that the household is rationed in the labor market. Furthermore, it is clear that the Keynesian consumption function only makes sense in that case. When there is full or even over-employment, (316) does not hold any more and must be replaced by the notional consumption function which depends on prices and profits only. Finally, the function (316) generalizes KEYNES' original hypothesis in so far as the consumption function continues to depend on prices, wages, and profits when there are quantity constraints.

Yet the most important result of the above analysis is the following one: If the household's income constraint is tightened by, say, five money units, consumption will be reduced by *less than* five money units because savings are also reduced. Thus, whereas the marginal propensity to consume in our model of §77 was equal to one, it is now positive but less than one. Savings work as a buffer when quantity constraints are intensified.

Let us extend the application of our graphical exposition somewhat to analyze households' rationing in the *commodity market*:

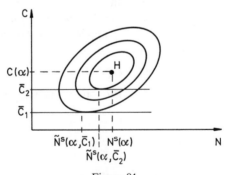

Figure 81

In Figure 81, households are rationed in the commodity market but not in the labor market. The quantity constraints $\bar{C}_1$ and $\bar{C}_2$ generate two reactions: First, the households reduce their labor supply, and second, they increase savings, since the latter, representing future consumption, are substitutes for present consumption. Put differently, the households side-step the current constraint in the commodity market by augmenting the funds for future consumption. The utility maxima are depicted in the figure as the points of tangency of the indifference curves and the horizontal straight lines corresponding to the respective commodity market constraints. Analogous to (313), the formal conditions for a utility maximum read:

$$\frac{\partial V(\bar{C}, (1 - N))}{\partial N} = 0. \tag{317}$$

This, in turn, yields effective labor supply as a function which assigns a certain labor supply to every feasable constraint in the commodity market:

$$\tilde{N}^s = \tilde{N}^s(\alpha, \bar{C}). \tag{318}$$

By combining the two previous figures, we obtain the so-called *wedge-diagram*:

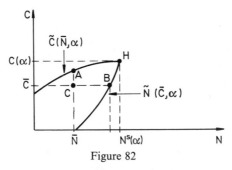

Figure 82

The wedge-diagram depicts the household's behaviour for all possible constraints in the labor or commodity market:

- In the Classical case, there are no quantity constraints, and the household attains point H.
- Given a constraint in the *labor market* only, households choose their consumption according to the effective consumption function. They attain, for instance, point A.
- Given a constraint in the *commodity market* only, households choose their labor supply according to the effective labor supply function. They attain, for instance, point B.
- Given constraints in *both markets*, there is no degree of freedom left to the households, and the resulting points lie in the interior of the wedge. Consider, for instance, point C.

Let us summarize the most important result of the present section. Due to the formation of savings, a quantity constraint in the labor market does not incur an equivalent reduction in consumption. The income loss partly reduces consumption, and partly savings. In contrast, consumption constraints do not incur an equivalent reduction in effective labor supply because in this case savings are augmented. Therefore, savings work as a buffer; without them, the wedge of Figure 82 would be reduced to a ray running through the origin and point H.

§80 The Neokeynesian Model

After the more introductory considerations of the preceding sections, we are now able to discuss the Neokeynesian model in full[23]. We commence by describing the behav-

23 Cf. the similar models of BARRO/GROSSMAN op.cit. and MALINVAUD, op.cit.

iour of households, firms, and the government in order to argue through the total model afterwards. The role of stabilization policy is saved for the next section.

Households. Our representative household demands consumption commodities, supplies labor, forms monetary savings, receives profits, and has to pay taxes. "Money" in this model is the instrument for transferring purchasing power from one period to the next. It can be conceived of as a non-interest bearing security which is issued by the government and demanded by the households. From two-period utility maximization we obtain a utility function

$$U = U\left(C, (1 - N), \frac{\Delta M_H}{P}\right). \tag{319}$$

Utility depends on consumption, leisure, and savings. It exhibits the usual properties, i.e. strictly positive first derivatives and diminishing marginal rates of substitution. Solutions at the margin are excluded. The household maximizes utility subject to a budget constraint

$$P \cdot C + \Delta M_H = w \cdot N + \pi_0 - T^n. \tag{320}$$

Consumption expenditures ($P \cdot C$), savings (ΔM_H), and nominal tax payments (T^n) must be financed by labor income ($w \cdot N$) and nominal profit income (π_0). π_0 are the profits of the *preceding* period which are distributed at the beginning of the current period. Since desired cash balances (M_H^d) and initial cash balances (M_0) are both stocks,

$$\Delta M_H := M_H - M_0 \tag{321}$$

is a *flow*.

For the representative household, being by definition an average household, we can rule out some "pathological" kinds of behaviour without restricting the generality of our approach too much. It is assumed, first, that consumption, leisure, and savings are *absolutely superior*, which means that the demand for them rises when exogenous (profit) income increases. Absolute inferiority is quite likely to be valid for some *single* consumption commodity, but not for the bundle of *all* consumption commodities. Note that we do not rule out relative inferiority which means, for instance, that the share of consumption expenditures diminishes when income rises. In the second place we suppose consumption, leisure, and savings to be *net substitutes*. This means that the pure substitution effects are all positive. Third, the substitution effect of a change in the real wage rate is assumed to outweigh the income effect. Hence there is a positive relationship between the real wage rate and labor supply. And finally, the relationship between the price level and the demand for *nominal* cash balances is positive. These assumptions imply the households' *notional demands*:

$$C(\alpha) = C \underset{(-)(+)\ (+)\ (+)\ \ (-)}{(P, w, \pi_0, M_0, T^n)} \tag{322}$$

$$N^s(\alpha) = N^s \underset{(-)(+)\ (-)\ (-)\ \ (+)}{(P, w, \pi_0, M_0, T^n)} \tag{323}$$

$$M_H^d(\alpha) = M_H^d \underset{(+)(+)\ (+)\ (+)\ \ (-)}{(P, w, \pi_0, M_0, T^n)} \tag{324}$$

$$\alpha := (P, w, \pi_0, M_0, T^n) \tag{325}$$

Notional demand curves depend only on the price variables and the exogenous parts of income, which are combined as the vector α.

Household rationing may occur in the commodity market, the labor market, or both. These three instances yield the *effective Clower-demands*:

$$\tilde{C} = \tilde{C}(\alpha, \bar{N}) \quad \text{and} \quad \tilde{M}_H^d = \underset{(+)}{\tilde{M}_H^d}(\alpha, \bar{N}) \tag{326}$$

$$\underset{(+)}{\tilde{N}^s} = \tilde{N}^s(\alpha, \bar{C}) \quad \text{and} \quad \tilde{M}_H^d = \underset{(-)}{\tilde{M}_H^d}(\alpha, \bar{C}) \tag{327}$$

$$\tilde{M}_H^d = \underset{(-)\ (+)}{\tilde{M}_H^d}(\alpha, \bar{C}, \bar{N}) . \tag{328}$$

The three equations represent household behaviour with quantity rationing as derived in the preceding section: A relaxation of the labor market constraint raises income and thus consumption expenditure and savings (equation (326)). A relaxation of the commodity market constraint will increase labor supply and diminish savings (equation (327)). With constraints in both markets, however, savings are simply obtained by solving the budget constraint for them; and the response turns out to be that of equation (328).

Finally, we define the *nominal marginal propensity to consume* and the *nominal marginal propensity to work*:

$$c' := \frac{\partial P\tilde{C}}{\partial w\, \bar{N}} \tag{329}$$

$$n' := \frac{\partial w\, \tilde{N}^s}{\partial P\bar{C}} . \tag{330}$$

The nominal marginal propensity to consume states how much consumption expenditure will rise due to an increase in exogenous labor income; clearly, this magnitude presupposes a quantity rationing of households in the labor market. Nominal marginal propensity to consume is denoted by "c" in order to distinguish it from the real marginal propensity to consume, $C' := dC/dY$, we encountered in Keynesian theory.

Conversely, the nominal marginal propensity to work indicates the increase in labor supply when a quantity constraint in the commodity market is relaxed. Owing to our previous assumptions, we have

$$0 < c' < 1 , \tag{331}$$

$$0 < n' < 1 . \tag{332}$$

Let us suppose for illustration that households are rationed in the labor market at a prevailing nominal wage rate $w = 2$. If the labor market constraint is relaxed by 1 unit, labor income will increase by 2 units. According to equation (326), these two units are used partly for consumption, and partly for savings. Hence, the increase in nominal consumption expenditures must lie somewhere between 0 and 2, and as a result, the term $\partial P\tilde{C}/\partial w\, \bar{N}$ of equation (329) is in the interval $(0; 1)$. The argument relating to the nominal marginal propensity to work runs analogously. Note that n' is not simply the reciprocal of c'.

Firms. The representative firm acts as a price taker and tries to maximize profits defined as

$$\pi = P \cdot Y - w \cdot N \tag{333}$$

We assume a Neoclassical production function with strictly positive, strictly diminishing marginal returns which increase without bound as N approaches zero:

$$Y = f(N). \tag{334}$$

Using Lagrange's method we immediately obtain the *notional demands*

$$Y(\alpha) = Y(P, w) \atop (+)\,(-) \tag{335}$$

$$N^d(\alpha) = N^d(P, w). \atop (+)\,(-) \tag{336}$$

Here, the vector α is again used in order to shorten the exposition. Of course, the firms do not respond to changes in π_0, M_0, or T^n. When they are constrained in the labor or commodity market, firms revise their plans according to the *effective Clower demands*:

$$\tilde{Y}(\bar{N}) = f(\bar{N}) \tag{337}$$

$$\tilde{N}^d(\bar{Y}) = f^{-1}(\bar{Y}). \tag{338}$$

In contrast to the households, the firms cannot be rationed bindingly in both markets. $\bar{N}$ and $\bar{Y}$ together can fall short of the notional plans but not of the effective plans. This asymmetry traces back to the fact that, in the firms sector, there is no equivalent to households savings. Only if we allowed for inventories, would binding quantity rationing of the firms in both market be possible.

It follows immediately from (338) that the Classical labor market theory becomes irrelevant when the firms are rationed in the commodity market. As you know, the existence of unemployment in the Classical macro-model always resulted from an excessive real wage rate. You will remember the labor market diagram which served to substantiate this proposition. From a Neokeynesian point of view, however, unemployment is also possible at the "correct" or even at "too low" a real wage rate:

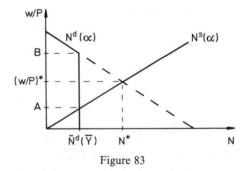

Figure 83

Due to the quantity constraint $\bar{Y}$, the firms require only $\tilde{N}^d(\bar{Y})$ workers, these being demanded *independent* of the real wage rate, provided that it is below the level "B". The real wage rate may even decline to the level "A": this will not incur any increase in employment. And at the "market clearing" real wage rate, $(w/P)^*$, it is not N^* laborers that are employed, but only $\tilde{N}^d(\bar{Y})$. Hence, the Neokeynesian approach substantiates the Keynesian allegation that inadequate commodity demand entails unemployment. The dual decision hypothesis describes the firm's behaviour when there is an investment or liquidity trap. Of course, the construction of a figure such as Figure 83 is simplistic, and the question of the stability of such a case arises immediately. But this would anticipate the later analysis.

The firm's demand for money is defined as the difference between accrued and distributed profits:

$$\Delta M_F^d := \pi - \pi_0. \tag{339}$$

This equation completes the model. The firm's money demand does not stem from maximization behaviour, but is simply a bookkeeping necessity: If actual profits (π), exceed distributed profits (π_0), for instance, the difference is hoarded and distributed at the beginning of the next period[24].

Government. We can conceive of the "government" as a homogeneous unit that also represents the central bank and acts subject to the bugdet constraint

$$P \cdot G = T^n + \Delta M^s. \tag{340}$$

Thus, nominal government expenditure, $P \cdot G$, is financed by nominal taxes, T^n, and the issue of money, ΔM^s. In the commodity market, government competes with the households and we must ask in what way the commodities are distributed when there is an excess demand in that market. We assume *priority rationing*: the government succeeds in satisfying its notional demand, and only households are subject to rationing.

Markets. The economic activities of the households, the firms, and the government can now be combined into a model which comprises a commodity market, a labor market, and a money market. For the notional plans, we have the equilibrium conditions:

$$C(\alpha) + G = Y(\alpha) \tag{341}$$

$$N^d(\alpha) = N^s(\alpha) \tag{342}$$

$$\Delta M_H^d(\alpha) + \Delta M_F^d(\alpha) = \Delta M^s. \tag{343}$$

The Walrasian properties of the present model are obvious. We choose money as numéraire, neglect the money market, and specify the price adjustment rules:

$$\frac{dP}{dt} = H_1[C(\alpha) + G - Y(\alpha)]; \quad H_1(0) = 0, \quad H_1' > 0 \tag{344}$$

$$\frac{dw}{dt} = H_2[N^d(\alpha) - N^s(\alpha)]; \quad H_2(0) = 0, \quad H_2' > 0. \tag{345}$$

The H_i are sign preserving functions as explained in §78. Due to excess demand (supply) in the commodity market, nominal prices rise (fall). Similarly, nominal wages

---

24 We assume that, due to an increase in nominal wages, the decrease in firms' money demand is less than the increase in housholds money demand. This amounts to assuming gross substitutability which ensures the local stability in the Walrasian case.

increase (decrease) due to an excess demand (supply) in the labor market. According to Walras' law, the money market is cleared at least if the other two markets are cleared too. The dynamic properties of our model are illustrated in the following figure[25]:

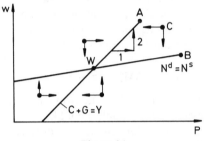

Figure 84

The *equilibrium locus* $C + G = Y$ is the set of all price-wage combinations which entail equilibrium in the commodity market. The positive slope of this locus – which need not be a straight line – is due to the following: Proceeding from an original equilibrium in the commodity market, rising prices incur an excess supply in this market as depicted by arrow no. 1. In order to re-establish equilibrium, nominal wage rates must rise (arrow no. 2). Hence, there is a positive relationship between those prices and nominal wage rates which imply an equilibrium in the commodity market[26].

The same is true for the *equilibrium locus* $N^d = N^s$ which is the set of all price-wage combinations which entail equilibrium in the labor market: Rising prices, causing labor demand to rise and labor supply to diminish, must be compensated by rising wage rates in order to re-establish equilibrium.

The four double-arrows of Figure 84 indicate the dynamic properties of our model. At point C, for instance, there is excess supply in both markets, which causes a reduction in prices and wages. Because of the stability of the Walrasian equilibrium, the economy – starting from an arbitrary point not too far away from W – will finally attain the Walrasian equilibrium, W. There, the commodity market, the labor market, and the money market are cleared in the sense that the notional plans are consistent.

So much for the Walrasian view. The decisive novelty of the Neokeynesian approach is that the *notional equilibrium loci* are replaced by *effective equilibrium loci*. For the time being, let us confine our consideration to the locus WA of Figure 84. Along WA, notional commodity demand and notional commodity supply match. *But*: WA is to the left of WB, the equilibrium locus of the labor market. On the left of WB, there is *excess supply* in the labor market because, in that region, wages are higher or prices lower than their equilibrium values. Therefore, along WA households are

---

25 The underlying assumptions of the figure are i) existence and ii) uniqueness of the general equilibrium. In subsection *5.6 of the Mathematical Appendix we demonstrate the stability of the model and show that the relative slopes of the two equilibrium loci follow from that property.

26 In Subsection *4.4 of the Mathematical Appendix we derive the slopes of the equilibrium loci.

rationed in the labor market, and they will express not their notional but their effective commodity demands.

In short: Since along WA we are to the left of WB, and households are rationed in the labor market, equation (341) which defines the equilibrium locus of the commodity market must be replaced by the equation

$$\tilde{C}(\alpha, \bar{N}) + G = Y(\alpha) \tag{346}$$

if we take quantity rationing into account. As a result, the Neokeynesian equilibrium locus will generally differ from the Walrasian one.

We have thus arrived at the core of Neokeynesian analysis: The equilibrium conditions of a market cannot be specified independently of the prevailing circumstances in the other markets. If the households are rationed in the labor market (as they are along WA), they do not express their notional commodity demand, and the locus WA becomes irrelevant. This is termed a *spill-over*: if individuals are rationed in one market, they will alter their behaviour in the other markets.

Applying analogous argument to the other equilibrium loci, we obtain the following *effective classification*[27]:

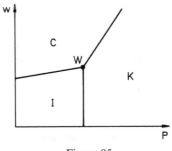

Figure 85

The effective equilibrium loci indicate those price-wage combinations which incur a coincidence of the effective demands. They divide the price-wage space into three regions (or regimes) which are usually called[28]:

Classical unemployment (C): In this region, the households are rationed in both markets. There is excess demand in the commodity market and excess supply in the labor market.

Keynesian unemployment (K): Here, we encounter excess supply in both markets. Hence, the firms are rationed in the commodity market, and the households are rationed in the labor market.

Repressed inflation (I): In this region, there is excess demand in both markets. Therefore, the firms are rationed in the labor market, and the households are rationed in the commodity market.

---

27 The properties of the effective equilibrium loci are derived in Subsection *4.4 of the Mathematical Appendix. The slope of the border line of regions I and K is indetermined.

28 The figure is due to BENASSY, J.-P. (1973) Disequilibrium Theory. Unpubl. Diss. CRMS Working Paper No. 185. Berkeley: University of California and MALINVAUD, E. (1977) The Theory of Unemployment Reconsidered. Op.cit.

The three designations should be interpreted as *termini technici*, that is, they are only suggestive. It is neither correct that this sort of "Classical unemployment" traces back to the Classical writers, nor is it right that the region K depicts KEYNES' own thinking. (It may be, however, that the latter region gives a proper interpretation of the Keynesians.) The regions are *defined* by the following equations:

$$C: \quad \tilde{C}(\alpha, \bar{N}) + G > Y(\alpha) \quad \text{and} \quad N^d(\alpha) < \tilde{N}^s(\alpha, \bar{C}) \tag{347}$$

$$K: \quad \tilde{C}(\alpha, \bar{N}) + G < Y(\alpha) \quad \text{and} \quad \tilde{N}^d(\bar{Y}) < N^s(\alpha) \tag{348}$$

$$I: \quad C(\alpha) + G > \tilde{Y}(\bar{N}) \quad \text{and} \quad N^d(\alpha) > \tilde{N}^s(\alpha, \bar{C}). \tag{349}$$

The three regions are thus defined by the respective excess demands or supplies in the markets. Note that it is not correct to argue that an excessive real wage rate implies Classical unemployment; it may also result in Keynesian unemployment[29].

Moreover, the above equations suggest that there is a fourth U, *Underconsumption*[30], with the following properties:

$$U: \quad C(\alpha) + G < \tilde{Y}(\bar{N}) \quad \text{and} \quad \tilde{N}^d(\bar{Y}) > N^s(\alpha). \tag{350}$$

But here, the firms would be rationed in both markets, which, as we saw above, is impossible. If the equality sign in (350) is admitted, U becomes a limiting case which coincides with the boundary of regions K and I.

Let us consider Figure 85 more thoroughly. At point W, we have the Walrasian equilibrium. This is the only point which has survived from the foregoing Figure 84, for it incurs no quantity rationing. At all point other than W, at least one market participant is rationed in at least one market, so that the notional equilibrium loci must be replaced by the effective ones.

Any point in the price-wage space of Figure 85 represents a *quantity equilibrium*. That is, prices and wages given, the individuals adjust their plans until the effective demands match in every market. We now have to explain this *adjustment process* of quantities, which eventually incurs equilibrium. The adjustment processes are different in each region.

When *Classical unemployment* prevails, households are rationed in both markets, and firms not at all. Because of the labor market rationing, households will reduce their commodity demand, and because of the commodity market rationing, they will diminish their labor supply. Thus, the quantity equilibrium is attained by a two-fold revision of the households' plans whereas the firms maintain their notional plans. They are not rationed. In quantity equilibrium, all Drèze-demands are consistent.

The case of *Keynesian unemployment* is somewhat more involved because households and firms are both rationed. Therefore, a special adjustment process, called *quantity tatônnement*, is required. Consider the following diagram:

The figure depicts the firm's production function and the houshold's effective consumption function, which was derived in the previous paragraph. Government

---

29 In this respect, MALINVAUD has pushed his interpretation too far. The facts that excessive real wage rates do not necessarily correspond to Classical unemployment, etc. have been pointed out by HILDENBRAND, K. and W. HILDENBRAND (1978) On Keynesian Equilibria with Unemployment and Quantity Rationing. Journal of Economic Theory **18**, p. 255–277.

30 That term is due to MUELLBAUER and PORTES, op.cit., who employ a model with inventories.

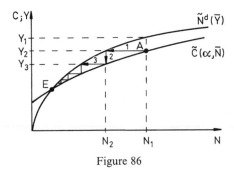

Figure 86

demand is set to zero without restricting the generality of the argument, since it does not influence the adjustment process. Let us start with point A where employment is N_1. Given this effective demand for labor, households' commodity demand, according to the effective consumption function, amounts to Y_2. On the other hand, firms supply the amount Y_1 in accordance with the production function. These effective demands are not consistent: there is no quantity equilibrium.

Because the firms are rationed in the commodity market they reduce their effective Drèze-supply of commodities to Y_2 and their effective labor demand to N_2 (arrow no. 1). Only N_2 labor units are required to produce the quantity Y_2. Now, the effective Drèze-plans referring to the commodity market are consistent – but not the plans referring to the labor market because households' rationing in the labor market amounts to N_2. Again, there is no quantity equilibrium.

The quantity constraint N_2 will induce the households to diminish their effective Drèze-supply to N_2 and to diminish consumption to Y_3. Thus, the interplay of mutual rationing starts anew. It will continue until point E, the quantity equilibrium, is reached. At point E, the effective Drèze-plans for both markets are consistent.

Such a quantity tatônnement is likely to be a long-lasting process. In Neokeynesian analysis, however, we have to assume that the quantity adjustment is terminated before prices vary.

Repressed inflation, finally, also requires a quantity tatônnement because mutual rationing of households and firms will occur here, too. The explanation is anologous to that above. Thus we can conclude that a quantity tatônnement is necessary in the cases of mutual rationing (regions K and I) but not if only one sector is constrained (regions C and U).

Up to here, the analysis was limited to quantity equilibria with given prices. Now we want to ask about *price dynamics*. In order to deal with that problem, we consider the current period with a constant money stock and reproduce Figure 85 with some minor alterations[31]:

---

31 Another possible dynamization of the model is to investigate the adjustment of the money stock when prices are given. Cf. BÖHM, V. (1978) Disequilibrium Dynamics in a Simple Macroeconomic Model. Journal of Economic Theory **17**, p. 179–199. To the price dynamics within a single period, cf. also BENASSY, J.-P. (1978) A Neokeynesian Model of Price and Quantity Determination in Disequilibrium. In: SCHWÖDIAUER, G. Ed. Equilibrium and Disequilibrium in Economics. Dordrecht: Reidel.

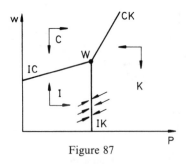

Figure 87

The arrows indicate the directions of price and wage movements. For instance, in region K we have simultaneous excess supply in both markets, and prices and wages will thus decline if we employ the usual price adjustment rules. The simple figure above yields four interesting observations.

First observation: If the Drèze-demands alone are expressed in the markets, there will be no price movement whatever; any point in Figure 87 will represent a *stable equilibrium*. Consider a point in region K, for instance. The households are rationed in the labor market, and the firms are rationed in the commodity market. Thus, with respect to the Clower-demands, there is excess supply in both markets. Yet we mentioned that a rationed seller reduces his Drèze-supply to the constraint. As a result, the price movements induced by the Drèze-demands read

$$\frac{dP}{dt} = H_1 [\hat{C}(\alpha, \bar{N}) + G - \hat{Y}] = 0 \tag{351}$$

$$\frac{dw}{dt} = H_2 [\hat{N}^d(\bar{Y}) - \hat{N}^s] = 0. \tag{352}$$

The functions H_i are assumed to be the same as in the Walrasian case. In spite of this, prices will not change because the arguments of the H_i vanish identically. Commodity supply is always reduced to the constraint and so is labor supply. Let us try to give an economic interpretation to this. The "quantity adjustment in the commodity market" may cause the *bankruptcy* of some firms which are more heavily rationed or whose financial funds are weaker. After the bankruptcies, there is simply no excess supply which could induce prices to decline. This is a conceivable method of attaining an "equilibrium" of supply and demand. (In the longer run, though, new firms are likely to enter the market when profits exceed their usual level due to the higher prices.)

Similarly, it is possible that those households rationed in the labor market refrain from searching for a job because, in their eyes, the trifling chance of getting one does not justify the costs incurred by searching[32]. The pure desire for a job on the part of such a "frustrated" laborer survives, but it is not expressed in the *market*. Hence, there is no pressure on wages. Notice that this does not involve a logical circle of the kind

---

32 Cf. also VARIAN's elaborated argument where the costs of job searching influence household's utility: VARIAN, H.R. (1975) On Persistent Disequilibrium. Journal of Economic Theory 10, p. 218–228.

in which sticky prices are explained by sticky prices. Rather, *short-run* stickiness serves to establish the possibility that "false" prices last *permanently*.

The above examples are probably somewhat exaggerated. But if we accept that they are not altogether irrelevant, they may give an additional explanation as to the tenacy of recessions.

Second observation. With regard to the Clower-demands, the price dynamics in region C, compared with those in the Walrasian case, are weaker but not absent. When Classical under-employment prevails, the households are rationed in both markets so that – from the Walrasian view – prices should rise and wages should decline. Taking account of the dual decision hypothesis, however, households' effective consumption demand falls short of its notional level since households are rationed in the labor market. Because commodity supply maintains the Walrasian level, *excess demand* in the commodity market falls short of its Walrasian value, too. Therefore, the rise in prices will take place slower than in the Walrasian case. Vice versa, excess demand in the labor market also falls short of its Walrasian level since housholds' effective labor supply is smaller than notional labor supply, and the firms' labor demand is the same in both cases. Hence, the pressure on wages is diminished. Considered with the aid of equations

$$\frac{dP}{dt} = H_1 [\tilde{C}(\alpha, \bar{N}) - Y(\alpha)] \tag{353}$$

$$\frac{dw}{dt} = H_2 [N^d(\alpha) - \tilde{N}^s(\alpha, \bar{C})] \tag{354}$$

it is obvious that the adjustment of wages and prices will last longer than in the Walrasian case provided that the functions H_i are the same. Yet, the adjustment is not entirely suspended – and this fact distinguishes the present model from that of § 78. Quantity equilibria apart from W are generally not stable because households have an additional degree of freedom in that they can form savings. As a result of the labor market constraint, households diminish consumption as well as savings, so that the reduction in consumption is smaller. The tendency of prices to change will thus diminish with increasing nominal marginal propensity to consume but it will not vanish entirely if $c' < 1$. In the limiting case $c' = 1$, effective consumption demand will exactly match commodity supply, and prices will not change. This was the result of § 78: any original combination of prices and wages produces a stable equilibrium.

Third observation. The assumption of an auctioneer is not required when replacing the notional plans by the effective ones. In the Classical model of perfect competition, no market participant is in a position to influence the market price so that we must have recourse to the auctioneer. KENNETH J. ARROW remarked early on that "perfect competition" and "quantity rationing" are two irreconcilable facts[33]. For, if a price falls short of its equilibrium level, some sellers, being on the short side of the market, become monopolists in the sense that their price-demand curves are no longer horizontal but have a negative slope. Due to quantity rationing, the buyers' reactions, as

33 ARROW, K.J. (1959) Toward a Theory of Price Adjustment. In: ABRAMOVITZ, M. Ed. The Allocation of Economic Ressources. Stanford: Stanford University Press.

viewed by the individual seller, are not infinitely price elastic, which gives some price-setting power to the sellers. Thus, the price adjustment functions do not represent the working of a "deus ex machina" but can be derived from the market participants' behaviour: *Price changes are employed in order to remove the quantity constraints*[34]. Though the problems involved here are anything but adequately solved, this may be one of the most interesting aspects of Neokeynesian theory.

Fourth observation. Conventional stability theory cannot be applied to the boundaries of regions C, K, and I since there are discontinuities in the differential equations. Without intending to enter into the mathematical difficulties involved[35], we want to direct the reader's attention to the boundary of regions I and K. Consider Figure 87 and the arrows along the boundary between I and K. Obviously, the arrows are opposed to one another, which traces back to the missing region "U". This implies: if the price-wage vector were to converge towards IK, it is bound to move along this line, either upwards or downwards. This is merely an illustration of the stability problems that arise when employing the dual decision hypothesis.

So much for the logic of the fix-price method. We have seen that, in Neokeynesian theory, "false" prices do not trace back to irrationality or ill-will on the part of the market participants but rather to *problems of information* that are inherent in any market economy without an auctioneer. When behaving according to the dual decision hypothesis, the individuals generally express in the markets demands and supplies which do not represent their notional plans.

§81 Political Inferences

In Chapter VI we recognized that the political recommendations for removing unemployment made by the Classics and the Keynesians are rather clear-cut. The former proposed wage-cuts whereas the latter demanded increases in government demand or in the quantity of money. In the present sections it will be shown that the impact of policy measures, in Neokeynesian theory, depends on the respective *region* in which the economy is located. This holds at least with respect to fiscal and monetary policy. Concerning wage and price policy, matters are a bit different, as will be explained at the end of this section.

Let us turn to fiscal policy first and investigate its impacts in the cases of Classical and Keynesian unemployment. According to the government's budget constraint, additional government expenditure may be financed by additional taxes (*pure fiscal policy*) or by issuing money (*mixed policy*).

Classical unemployment. A quantity equilibrium with Classical unemployment is defined by the simultaneous equations

$$\hat{C} + G - Y(\alpha) = 0 \tag{355}$$

34 Note that this behavioural hypothesis is better than the auctioneer but has not been derived from optimization behaviour. Cf. GORDON, D.F. and A. HYNES (1970) On the Theory of Price Dynamics. In: PHELPS, E.S. Ed. Microeconomic Foundations of Employment and Inflation. New York: W.W. Norton.

35 Cf. HONKAPOHJA, S. and T. ITO (1983) Stability with Regime Switching. Journal of Economic Theory **29**, p. 22–48.

$$N^d(\alpha) - \hat{N}^s = 0. \tag{356}$$

We already know that such a quantity equilibrium is defined by the consistency of the Drèze-demands. Since firms are not rationed, their effective Drèze-demands are identical to the notional demands whereas households' Drèze-demands are identical to the quantity constraints. Government demand is exogenous, and we assume $G < Y(\alpha)$. Because of priority rationing, effective consumption demand in Drèze's sense is solely determined by commodity supply and government demand; it is equal to $Y(\alpha) - G$ and does not depend on employment. This may sound strange at first, but is easily proved by defeating the opposite. If effective consumption demand in Drèze's sense depended on employment, there would be no binding rationing of the housholds in the commodity market but then we would have no Classical unemployment which is defined by this phenomenon. Therefore, the above equations suffice to define a quantity equilibrium with Classical underemployment.

How will *mixed fiscal policy* influence this quantity equilibrium? Assuming no departure from region C, we obtain the answer by differentiating the above equations with respect to G:

$$\frac{d\hat{C}}{dG} + 1 - 0 = 0 \tag{357}$$

$$0 - \frac{d\hat{N}^s}{dG} = 0. \tag{358}$$

The derivatives of Y and N^d with respect to G vanish since these variables depend only on α and since the firms are not rationed. We obtain immediately

$$\frac{d\hat{C}}{dG} = -1 \tag{359}$$

$$\frac{d\hat{N}^s}{dG} = 0. \tag{360}$$

As Classical theory stated, expansive fiscal policy entails a total crowding out and does not produce any change in output or employment. This is precisely what is expressed by the two equations. Every unit of additional government expenditure crowds out one unit of private expenditure and leaves production and employment unchanged.

Obviously, fiscal policy is *unsuited* to the case of Classical unemployment, and this holds both for pure and mixed fiscal policy whose effects are virtually identical. They are virtually identical because an increase in taxes will not alter consumption expenditures or effective labor supply in Drèze's sense as long as we have Classical unemployment. Thus, Classical theory is affirmed with respect to its results.

Keynesian unemployment. Let us now consider the impact of fiscal policy when Keynesian unemployment prevails. The respective quantity equilibrium is defined by

$$\hat{C}(\alpha, \hat{N}) + G - \hat{Y} = 0 \tag{361}$$

$$\hat{N}^d(\hat{Y}) - \hat{N}^s = 0. \tag{362}$$

Effective commodity supply in Drèze's sense equals effective commodity demand because there is excess supply in the commodity market. Similarly, effective labor supply in Drèze's sense equals effective labor demand because excess supply exists in the labor market, too. Let us now analyze mixed fiscal policy assuming that the economy stays in region K. Differentiation of the simultaneous equations with respect to G yields:

$$\frac{\partial \hat{C}}{\partial \hat{N}} \cdot \frac{d\hat{N}}{dG} + 1 - \frac{d\hat{Y}}{dG} = 0 \tag{363}$$

$$\frac{d\hat{N}^d}{d\hat{Y}} \cdot \frac{d\hat{Y}}{dG} - \frac{d\hat{N}}{dG} = 0. \tag{364}$$

The multipliers we need are obtained by solving the second equation for $d\hat{N}/dG$ and substituting the result into the first equation:

$$\frac{d\hat{Y}}{dG} = \frac{1}{1 - \partial \hat{C}/\partial \hat{N} \cdot d\hat{N}^d/d\hat{Y}} \tag{365}$$

$$\frac{d\hat{N}}{dG} = \frac{d\hat{N}^d}{d\hat{Y}} \cdot \frac{d\hat{Y}}{dG}. \tag{366}$$

At first sight, these multipliers appear novel. We can simplify them by defining the *real marginal propensity to consume* analogously to the Keynesian procedure:

$$C' := \frac{dC}{dY} = \frac{\partial \hat{C}}{\partial \hat{N}} \cdot \frac{d\hat{N}^d}{d\hat{Y}}. \tag{367}$$

This is a simple application of the chain rule. The response of effective consumption demand to changes in real income turns out to be the product of the response of consumption demand to changes in employment, and the response of employment to changes in production. Substituting (367) into the above multiplier formulas immediately yields:

$$\frac{d\hat{Y}}{dG} = \frac{1}{1 - C'} \tag{368}$$

$$\frac{d\hat{N}}{dG} = \frac{1}{1 - C'} \cdot \frac{d\hat{N}^d}{d\hat{Y}}. \tag{369}$$

Obviously, equation (368) gives us the *elementary multiplier* of Keynesian theory which we already encountered in § 36. But it is somewhat differently substantiated here. In the income-expenditure-model, an increase in real income produced a *direct* change in consumption because of the hypothesis $C = C(Y)$. In the Neokeynesian approach, two steps must be distinguished. First, labor demand increases due to a rise in production; and second, consumption demand increases due to augmented labor income. The Keynesian multiplier, dC/dY, has thus become broken down into a "technical" coefficient, $d\hat{N}^d/d\hat{Y}$, and a "psychological" coefficient, $d\hat{C}/d\hat{N}$.

Can we be sure under these circumstances that the real marginal propensity to consume is between 0 and 1? This question is important to the numerical value of the multiplier and to the stability of the adjustment process. The answer is in the affirmative, which can be shown in the following manner. First, we reduce the multiplier (367) to higher terms:

$$C' = \frac{\partial P \hat{C}}{\partial w \hat{N}} \cdot \frac{w}{P} \cdot \frac{d\hat{N}^d}{d\hat{Y}}. \tag{370}$$

The first factor is the nominal marginal propensity to consume which takes values between 0 and 1 according to equation (328):

$$0 < c' = \frac{\partial P\hat{C}}{\partial w\bar{N}} < 1 . \tag{371}$$

Therefore, C′ is in the intervall (0; 1) at least if the second factor in (370) is in this intervall, too:

$$0 < \frac{w}{P} \cdot \frac{d\hat{N}^d}{d\hat{Y}} < 1 . \tag{372}$$

The first relation is certainly met; the second one can be rearranged to

$$\frac{dY}{dN} > \frac{w}{P} . \tag{373}$$

This condition proves true in the case of Keynesian unemployment. If the marginal productivity of labor does not exceed the real wage rate, firms would not be rationed in the commodity market and would behave according to the marginal productivity rule. Therefore, marginal productivity of labor must exceed the real wage rate when Keynesian unemployment prevails, and this guarantees a real marginal propensity to consume less than 1.

Owing to this fact, the multiplier of equation (368) is greater than 1. Mixed fiscal policy, in the case of Keynesian unemployment, works just as described by Keynesian theory. The impact on employment is also definitely positive as we see from (369). The numerical value of this multiplier, however, is indeterminate because it depends on the dimensions of N and Y.

Up to here, we have been concerned with mixed fiscal policy where all government expeditures are financed by new money. In the case of *pure* fiscal policy, expenditures are financed by additional taxes, and matters are different because an increase in taxes diminishes housholds' disposable income. We must differentiate (361) again, setting $dT^n = P \cdot dG$:

$$\frac{\partial \hat{C}}{\partial T^n} \cdot P + \frac{\partial \hat{C}}{\partial \hat{N}} \cdot \frac{d\hat{N}}{dG} + 1 - \frac{d\hat{Y}}{dG} = 0 . \tag{374}$$

Compared with (363), there is one additional term (the first one), whereas equation (364) has remained unchanged. P is the derivative of T^n with respect to G. In order to evaluate the first term, $\partial\hat{C}/\partial T^n \cdot P$, consider the following line of reasoning. With Keynesian unemployment, labor income is an exogenous variable to the household as are taxes. Therefore, the houshold will respond to increases in labor income just as it does to tax reductions. Put differently, the nominal marginal propensities to consume with respect to labor income and with respect to taxes are equal in value but have the opposite sign:

$$\frac{\partial P\hat{C}}{\partial T^n} = -\frac{\partial P\hat{C}}{\partial w\hat{N}} = -c' . \tag{375}$$

Substituting this and $d\hat{N}/dG$ from (364) into equation (374) we obtain some sort of *Haavelmo-theorem*:

$$\frac{d\hat{Y}}{dG}\bigg|_{P \cdot dG = dT^n} = \frac{1 - c'}{1 - C'} . \tag{376}$$

In the Keynesian model, numerator and denominator were the same, so the multiplier amounted to 1. This result does not hold here, because the marginal propensities to consume, c' and C', are different. From (367), we know that C' is less than c'. Therefore, the multiplier (373) is positive but less than 1:

$$0 < \left. \frac{d\hat{Y}}{dG} \right|_{P \cdot dG = dT^n} < 1 . \qquad (377)$$

This result derives from the fact that the real marginal propensity to consume, C', comprises both "technical" and "psychological" factors as seen from (370). The ultimate reason for the multiplier being less than 1 is thus that the firms do not increase their labor demand by P/w but, as (373) tells us, by an amount less than P/w. In Neokeynesian theory, the original Haavelmo-theorem holds only along the boundary of regions C and K where the firms are not rationed in the commodity market. Along the locus CK, the market clearing locus for the commodity market, equation (370) holds with the equality sign; marginal propensities to consume, c' and C' are the same; and the multiplier is 1 [36].

Finally, we want to move on to *wage and price policy*, asking whether a certain "false" wage level implies a certain type of unemployment. To analyze this matter, we first need an important theorem: CK, the boundary of regions C and K, is above the ray which runs through the origin and the Walrasian equilibrium:

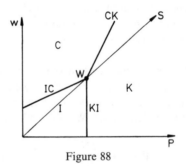

Figure 88

The ray S has the slope $(w/P)^*$ because it runs through the Walrasian equilibrium, W, which is associated with the market clearing real wage rate, $(w/P)^*$. Hence, S depicts the set of all equilibrium real wage rates in the Walrasian sense. Saying that CK is above S implies that if we proceed from the Walrasian equilibrium W and multiply prices and wages by the same factor, Keynesian unemployment will result. This is essentially due to the *real-balance effect*. The firms do not respond to a proportional increase in P and w, whereas housholds will diminish consumption and increase their labor supply, because the real value of their initial real wealth, M/P, has been diminished. Therefore, Keynesian unemployment will arise [37]. Now, we can infer from the above figure:

---

36 Interestingly, some authors think that KEYNES had had just that special case in mind: household's rationing in the labor market, accompanied by identical Clower plans with respect to the commodity market. Cf. BARRO, R.J. and H.I. GROSSMAN (1976) Money, Employment and Inflation. Op.cit. , Chapter 2, Footnote 40. Note, however, that the locus CK is a set with measure zero.

- If the real wage rate falls short of its Walrasian value *and* if there is unemployment, the latter must be of the Keynesian type.
- Given Classical unemployment, the real wage rate must be too high – but the reverse is not true.
- The occurence of Keynesian unemployment is more probable the higher are price and wage levels.

These three assertions can be substantiated by means of Figure 88. *First*: If the real wage rate falls short of its Walrasian value, we have a point below line S: and such a point is bound to lie either in K, or in I. Thus, if we encounter unemployment, it must be of the Keynesian type. Note, however, that Keynesian unemployment may be associated with real wage rates which exceed, or fall short of, their Walrasian equilibrium levels.

Second: Classical unemployment implies an excessive real wage rate since all points in region C are above the line S[38]. In this case, a decline in real wages is definitely advisable.

Third: If, starting from an arbitrary point in wage-price space, wages and prices are proportionately increased without bound, Keynesian unemployment will eventually be attained. The real cause of Keynesian unemployment is that both nominal wages and nominal prices are too high, it being less important whether the real wage rate exceeds its Walrasian value, or falls short of it. As a consequence, the appropriate remedy is a reduction in both wages and prices, which will augment demand via the real-balance effect.

In sum, we have recognized in the present section that both Classical and Keynesian proposals for economic policy gain some support from the Neokeynesian approach. The latter approach can be said to be more general because it allows for different causes of economic problems and facilitates an analysis of them by means of one and the same model.

§82 Walras' Law with Quantity Constraints

"Either Walras' law is incompatible with Keynesian economics, or Keynes had nothing fundamentally to add to orthodox economic theory."   (ROBERT W. CLOWER)

So states CLOWER in his vigorous re-interpretation of KEYNES. The question of Walras' law, its significance for economic theory, and its validity within the Keynesian model has concerned economists as has hardly any other problem of detail. And rightly so: whoever speaks of an "equilibrium in all markets, except the labor market"

---

37 The formal derivation reads: CK is defined by the equation $\tilde{C}(\alpha,\bar{N}) + G - Y(\alpha) = 0$. It comprises the point W where $\bar{N} = N(\alpha)$, i.e. $W \in CK$. For all $\lambda > 1$ we have $\tilde{C}(\lambda P^*, \lambda w^*, \lambda \pi^*, \bar{N}) < \tilde{C}(P^*, w^*, \pi^*, \bar{N})$ and $N^s(\lambda P^*, \lambda w^*, \lambda \pi^*) > N^s(P^*, w^*, \pi^*)$. On the contrary, $Y(\alpha)$ and $N^s(\alpha)$ are homogeneous of degree zero in (P, w). And finally, π is homogeneous of degree one in (P, w). Therefore, $W = (P^*, w^*) \in CK$ implies $(\lambda P^*, \lambda w^*) \in K$ for all $\lambda > 1$.
38 Analogously to the previous footnote, we could show that the border line of regions C and I is necessarily above the ray S.

contradicts this theorem. But this was precisely the standard allegation of the Keynesians. On the other hand, we remember that Walras' law is simply derived from an addition of budget constraints. Therefore, its disproof turned out to be a hard nut to crack – apparently too hard for Keynesian theory. And moreover, in nearly all models some market is neglected because – as we learn – it depends on the other markets according to Walras' law. Memorably, this procedure was also employed by Keynesian authors, which raises the question of whether this involved a contradiciton.

Let us consider the issue with the aid of the previously developed apparatus. Adding up households' and government's budget constraints and the profit definition, we immediately obtain:

$$P[C + G - Y] + w[N^d - N^s] + [\Delta M_H^d + \Delta M_F^d - \Delta M^s] = 0. \tag{378}$$

This equation states that simultaneous equilibrium in the commodity and labor market implies equilibrium in the money market. The equation is not to be misunderstood as an *ex post* identity; rather, it refers to the individuals' *notional plans* and is due to the simple fact that individuals neither plan to expend more than they plan to receive, nor conversely. Since in Walras' model, the individuals always succeed in carrying out their plans, we can at once eliminate one market. Thus, Walras' law *holds* with respect to the notional plans.

Let us proceed with the effective demands in the sense of Drèze. In the case of Keynesian unemployment, for instance, we have the following quantity equilibrium:

$$P[\underset{(=0)}{\hat{C} + G - \hat{Y}}] + w[\underset{(=0)}{\hat{N}^d - \hat{N}^s}] + [\underset{(=0)}{\Delta \hat{M}_H^d + \Delta \hat{M}_F^d - \Delta M^s}] = 0. \tag{379}$$

The firms are rationed in the commodity market; they reduce their effective commodity supply to the quantity constraint. Similarly, households face a quantity rationing in the labor market; and they reduce their effective labor supply in Drèze's sense to the quantity constraint. Hence, excess demand vanishes in both markets. The money market, however, is defined such that no quantity rationing occurs there. Effective money demand and money supply match. Therefore, Walras' law holds with respect to the effective demands in Drèze's sense. It was legitimate to neglect one market when analyzing a quantity equilibrium with Keynesian unemployment. With respect to the realized transactions, i.e. the Drèze-demands, anyone spends as much as he receives.

Finally, we demonstrate, by means of an example showing the opposite, that Walras' law does not hold universally with respect to the effective demands in Clower's sense. Let us again refer to Keynesian unemployment:

$$P[\underset{(<0)}{\tilde{C} + G - \tilde{Y}}] + w[\underset{(<0)}{\tilde{N}^d - \tilde{N}^s}] + [\underset{(=0)}{\Delta \tilde{M}_H^d + \Delta \tilde{M}_F^d - \Delta M^s}] < 0. \tag{380}$$

The firms maintain their notional commodity supply in the commodity market regardless of the quantity constraint; thus, there is excess supply in the commodity market. Similarly, the housholds maintain their notional labor supply, which incurs excess supply in the labor market. The clearance of the money market, however, is motivated by the following consideration: First, there are no binding constraints in this market. Hence, as we know from our formula (276), the Drèze- and Clower-plans are *identical*. Therefore, the third term in (380), depicting the money market, is identical to the third term in (379) and must exhibit the same sign. It is necessarily equal to zero. Since the first two terms in (380) have a negative sign, and the third one vanishes, the total sum must be negative: Walras' law does not hold with respect to the effective demands in Clower's sense.

In spite of this, it remains legitimate to eliminate the money market because the latter is cleared and because no binding quantity constraints can occur there. The technique of analysis employed in the previous sections is thus justified.

To summarize, the notorious Keynesian allegation that an equilibrium in all markets – except the labor market – is conceivable is not false because Walras' law does not hold with respect to the Clower-demands. However, we may eliminate one market without obtaining an inconsistent model.

The most important outcome of this re-examination of Walras' law is a qualification of Say's law. Recollect that Say's law, the fundamental proposition of Classical macroeconomics, stated:

"Every supply creates its own demand."

MILL's explanation on p. 58 according to which commodities are bought by commodities does not provide a sound basis because it essentially involves ex post considerations; the proper substantiation of Say's law is Walras' law which says that no one *plans* to supply more than he *plans* to demand. From this latter proposition we immediately infer that supply and demand must also coincide for the whole community.

When taking equation (380) into account, however, we are forced to modify Say's law. It seems appropriate to restate it as

"Every *realized* supply creates its own demand."

which amounts to saying that only those supplies which do find a buyer will incur an equivalent demand on the part of the seller. A laborer who succeds in selling labor worth $ 20.000 will certainly exert a demand that amounts to that value; but when constrained in the labor market he will possibly demand nothing at all. As the same holds for any entrepreneur, it seems to be a general principle that only realized supplies will entail an equivalent demand.

§ 83 Conclusion

Finally, we want to summarize the most important points of this chapter, and add some of the criticism to which Neokeynesian theory is subject.

The original impetus for the development of Neokeynesian theory stemmed from the interest in a clarification of the relationship between "KEYNES and the Classics" – a subject which has kept economists busy for half a century. CLOWER has argued conclusively that the so-called "Neoclassical synthesis" is not likely to contribute much to such a clarification: Its consumption function (and not only its consumption function!) contradicts Classical theory, and this contradiction is incapable of being eliminated by however many plausibility considerations. The "re-interpretation" of Keynes' has at least succeeded in giving a convincing interpretation of the *Keynesians*; and it is not an exaggeration to say that only Neokeynesian theory can count as a true "Neoclassical synthesis".

Quantity rationing, the dual decision hypothesis, and the phenomon of "spill-overs" form a base for Classical and Keynesian results which are both founded by optimization behaviour. Yet, perhaps more important than the feature of utility and profit maximization is the thorough treatment of the *budget constraints*. Here, we encounter the genuine problem of the Neoclassical synthesis: What economist has never asked himself why money demand in a liquidity trap is allowed to rise infinitely without affecting consumption expenditures? Of course, the question is put wrongly since the LM-curve depicts a stock equilibrium and there is no flow-money demand within the Keynesian model, capable of affecting the budget constraints. But that such questions (and similar ones which are justified) should arise is the inherent short-coming of any model which is constructed by placing diverse behavioural assumptions side by side. How much of the "Keynesian confusion" could possibly have been avoided if CLOWER had written twenty years earlier! Independent of the attitude one takes towards Neokeynesian theory one has to appreciate that this approach is much more transparent than the Neoclassical synthesis, even if the latter may appear more intelligible at first sight.

Beyond these more academic questions, we must note that Neokeynesian theory may incur the more policy-oriented economists to change their view to some degree. It is no longer required to accept either the Classical or the Keynesian analysis and then take to heart their respective recommendations. Instead, Neokeynesian theory indicates that, with respect to unemployment, there is a diagnostic problem. Hence, it yields no unconditional but conditional proposals for policy, and the possible dissension is transferred from the theoretical to the empirical level. In connection with the Neoclassical synthesis, we have spoken of a "compromise" between the theorists. Such a compromise on the basis of Neokeynesian theory would consist of the following items:

1) Classical optimization theory is and remains the basis of theory. It facilitates the development of a consistent model involving no "leakages" or "injections", since any individual is subject to a budget constraint.

2) The "market law", that is, the Classical dynamic of prices, is accepted *in principle*. But, in reality, there is no auctioneer. Changes in prices are generated by rationing, since only rationing induces the market participants to alter prices in "perfect" competition without perfect foresight.

3) There is some reason to assume that quantities react quicker than prices. Hence, not the notional but the effective plans are relevant. Trading at false prices takes place for at least some time.

4) The case of Keynesian unemployment is theoretically conceivable, though the economy will probably move towards the Walrasian equilibrium. In the static model, the usual fiscal measures as well as promotion of price flexibility turn out to be effective.

Finally, we want to supplement the most important criticisms, separated into three groups.

1. Criticism: The first caveat refers to the fix price assumption. Several shadings of this objection must be carefully distinguished. The first one, stating that Neokeynesian theory is a theory with exogenously fixed prices, is perfectly immaterial which, after our §§ 78 and 80, requires no further explanation. Second, BARRO considers as typical of the Neokeynesian model that the market participants renounce mutual advantagenous exchanges if they do not remove quantity constraints at once by changing prices instantaneously. This seems to be beside the point. The proper question is that concerning the relationship between the costs involved in changing prices at once and the costs incurred by quantity constraints. Only the absence of transaction and information costs of altering prices can be expected to ensure permanent market clearing.

The third shading of this objection is more significant. It refers to the extremely questionable assumption that all quantity tatônnements have been terminated *before* any price changes occur. This assumption is implied if we analyze the quantity equilibria in region K first, and use the emerging Clower-demands as inputs of the price adjustment function. As already shown, a quantity tatônnement is a complicated and perhaps long-lasting process so that we cannot expect price reactions to be absent throughout. The radical reversal of the Classical price adjustment velocities is equally unsatisfactory.

2. Criticism: The Neokeynesian model is of a very short-term nature, not as a result of the fix price assumption (when properly interpreted), but of the confinement of the analysis to one period, which is required by the derivation of household behaviour from a two-period-optimization calculus. Because of this, the model is incapable of giving insight into long-run phenomena such as stationary states, for instance. However, this is not a problem of Neokeynesian theory as such but a problem of our simple exposition.

3. Criticism: With regard to its *richness*, our Neokeynesian model can hardly compete with the previous theories; it is rudimentary through and through. Of course, we could built markets for capital and bonds into the model as before; but then it would become very difficult. Thus, it is a disadvantage of Neokeynesian models that they must be extremely simple in structure in order to be intelligible.

Hence, for the time being we must regard Neokeynesian theory only as a contribution to the "pure logic of the market"; it cannot replace the other theories yet. We must wait and see what developments emerge from it in the future.

Further Reading

Barro, R.J. (1979) Second Thoughts on Keynesian Economics. American Economic Review (PP) **69**, pp. 54–59

Barro, R.J. and H.I. Grossman (1976) Money, Employment and Inflation. Cambridge etc.: Cambridge University Press

Benassy, J.-P. (1982) The Theory of Market Disequilibrium. New York etc.: Academic Press

Clower, R.W. (1965) The Keynesian Counter-Revolution: A Theoretical Appraisal. In: Hahn, F.H. and F.P.R. Brechling Ed. The Theory of Interest Rates. Op.cit.

Drazen, A. (1980) Recent Developments in Macroeconomic Disequilibrium Theory. Econometrica **48**, pp. 283–304

Kahn, R.F. (1977) Malinvaud on Keynes. Cambridge Journal of Economics 1, p. 375–388. Reprinted in: Eatwell, J. and M. Milgate Ed. (1983) Keynes' Economics and the Theory of Value and Distribution. Op.cit.

Leijonhufvud, A. (1967) Keynes and the Keynesians: A Suggested Interpretation. American Economic Review (PP) **57**, pp. 401–410

Leijonhufvud, A. (1968) On Keynesian Economics and the Economics of Keynes. Oxford: Oxford University Press

Malinvaud, E. (1977) The Theory of Unemployment Reconsidered. Oxford: Basil Blackwell

Mathematical Appendix

If you do some acrobatics
with a little mathematics
it will take you far along.

If your idea's not defensible,
don't make it comprehensible
or folks will find you out,
and your work will draw attention
if you only fail to mention
what the whole thing is about.

Your must talk of GNP
and of elasticity
of rates of substitution
and undeterminate solution
and oligonopopsony.

(KENNETH E. BOULDING)

Introduction

Economics has not always been so thoroughly mathematical in its formulation as it is today; rather, the application of mathematical methods has only become important within the last hundred years. Thus economics progressed as did physics and several other sciences which became mathematized during their advance, according to KANT's maxim that any science requires a "pure component". While the advent of the mathematical mode in economics was subject to some controversy, it is clear that mathematical methods have now become an accepted part of economic tradition and hold their ground in both research and teaching. A fact we do not want to evaluate but only recognize.

When writing the present textbook we aimed at a simple, easily grasped exposition unburdened by mathematical formalism. But this strategy demanded two sacrifices: In the first place, some steps in the text had to remain unsubstantiated; let us only mention Figure 85 whose deeper sense we could not explain in twenty pages. Second, the authors of advanced contributions to macroeconomics habitually employ an abundance of those mathematical techniques which were not made accessible to the reader within the present book (and similar introductions). Hence there is a *schism* between textbooks and specialized books, the consequences of which often become only too marked to writers of university papers or even doctoral dissertations.

For these two reasons, we designed the present mathematical appendix, which is separated accordingly into two parts. The *purely mathematical sections* serve to diminish the above cited schism. They are by no means intended as a comprehensive introduction to mathematics, but explain those techniques important to macroeconomics (and only those) in a concentrated manner.

In addition, the appendix comprises some sections, marked by an asterisk (*), in which *economic examples* are given, and where some problems are solved whose answer could not be given in the current text.

1. Calculus of Functions of a Single Variable

Economic analysis in terms of marginal changes, referred to as *marginalism*, was a characteristic feature of Neoclassical economics. By virtue of this innovation, mathematics, and especially calculus, became introduced into economics, since derivatives and differentials provide the natural medium for marginalistic considerations.

1.1 Functions of a Single Variable

The notion of a real function is essential to the following. By a *real function* we mean a mapping f: $\mathbb{D} \to \mathbb{R}$ which assigns one and only one element of $\mathbb{R}$ to *every* element of $\mathbb{D}$. $\mathbb{R}$ is the set of real numbers, and $\mathbb{D}$ is called the *domain* of f. We write

$$f: \quad \mathbb{D} \to \mathbb{R} \quad \text{where} \quad y = f(x); \quad x \in \mathbb{D}, \ y \in \mathbb{R}. \tag{1}$$

The *range* of such a real function is the set of all real numbers y for which $y = f(x)$; in the general case, the domain is a subset of $\mathbb{R}$. In this section we consider only such functions whose domain is the set of the real numbers, that is:

$$f: \quad \mathbb{R} \to \mathbb{R} \quad \text{where} \quad y = f(x); \quad x, y \in \mathbb{R}. \tag{2}$$

For simplicity, in the present section we always refer to functions of this type when we speak of a "function".

A function is called *continuous* iff $\lim_{x \to a} f(x) = f(a) \ (x \neq a)$ for all $a \in \mathbb{D}$. (Mathematicians use the word "iff" to denote the more complicated expression "if and only if".) A vivid circumscription of continuity is that the graph of f has no "gaps" or "isolated points". We define

$$C^0 := \text{set of all continuous functions} \tag{3}$$

Thus if we want to presume the continuity of a function we can conveniently write $f \in C^0$.

1.2 Derivatives

A function as defined by (2) can serve to describe a causal relationship such as the dependence of consumption on income, if we take y as consumption and x as income. The economic theorist often has insufficient information, however, to specify a relationship such as $y = 0.8 \, x + 20$. He is more interested in general results which hold independently of the ever changing numerical values. Therefore, we seek for the *qualitative* properties of functions; we ask, for instance, whether a function is increasing or decreasing. The derivative of a function is a very helpful instrument in answering such questions.

Consider the graph of a function f and its slope at some point a:

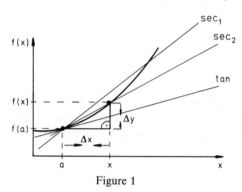

Figure 1

The graph's slope at a is obviously equal to the slope of the tangent line (tan). On the other hand, the slope of one of the secant lines (sec) can be conceived of as the *average* slope of the graph in some interval. According to a well-known formula, the slope of sec_2 can be calculated as

$$m_{sec_2} = \frac{\Delta y}{\Delta x}\left(:= \frac{f(x) - f(a)}{x - a}\right). \tag{4}$$

But how do we obtain the slope of the tangent line? As suggested by the figure, the secant lines approach the tangent line as Δx approaches zero:

$$m_{tan} = \lim_{\Delta x \to 0} \frac{\Delta y}{\Delta x}. \tag{5}$$

The slope of the tangent line which is equal to the slope of the function's graph at a is called the *derivative of f at a*. We write

$$f'(a) := \lim_{\substack{x \to a \\ x \neq a}} \frac{\Delta y}{\Delta x}. \tag{6}$$

Other symbols frequently used to denote derivates are the differential quotient, dy/dx or the differential operator (D) applied to a function f: D f(a). Moreover, the "point", $\dot{y}(a)$, is habitually used to denote derivatives with respect to time. The *differential quotient* (or *derivative*) is thus defined as the limit of *difference quotients*. A function is termed *differentiable in a* iff the limit (6) exists at a. It is important to understand that the *local* derivative defined by (6) is just a number. In contrast, the *global* derivative,

$$f'(x) \quad \text{or} \quad \frac{dy}{dx} \tag{7}$$

is itself a function. f is called *differentiable* iff it is differentiable in a for all a of the domain.

Example: Assume $y(x) = x^2$.
The global derivative is calculated according to the usual rules as

$$f'(x) = 2x.$$

From this we obtain some local derivative by inserting a certain number for x. The number "3", for instance, yields:

$$f'(3) = 6.$$

The slope of a function is easily inferred from the sign of its derivative: If the derivative is strictly positive for all elements of the domain, then f is *strictly increasing*; conversely, if the derivative is strictly negative for all elements of the domain, then f is *strictly decreasing*.

The *second derivative of f* is simply defined as the derivative of the (global) first derivative:

$$f''(x) := (f'(x))' \tag{8}$$

or

$$\frac{d^2 f}{dx^2} := \frac{d}{dx}\left(\frac{df}{dx}\right). \tag{9}$$

Both symbols mean the same. This definition becomes clear when one realizes that the global first derivative is a function *itself* and hence capable of being differentiated. f is called *2-times differentiable* if the expression (8) exists. In general, the *n-th derivative* of a function is defined as

$$f^{(n)}(x) := (f^{(n-1)}(x))'. \tag{10}$$

and f is called *n-times differentiable* if this expression does exist. To have a convenient short-hand, we define

$$C^n := \text{set of all n-times continuously differentiable functions.} \tag{11}$$

Continuous differentiability requires that the derivative is a continuous function. Hence, the statement "$f \in C^1$" means that the first derivative of f exists and is continuous. In this case, f is itself continuous so that continuous differentiability implies continuity (but not vice versa!). Put differently, C^1, the set of all continuously differentiable functions, is a subset of C^0, the set of all continous functions; and likewise, C^n is a subset of C^{n-1}.

In economic theory we frequently encounter the problem that a variable (y) depends on another one (x) while the latter, in turn, depends on a third one (t). Then, a typical question is "How does y respond to changes in t?". The answer is given by the

Chain rule: Let f, g: $\mathbb{R} \to \mathbb{R}$; $y = f(x)$ and $x = g(t)$ be two elements of C^1. Then, there is a function

$$h: \quad \mathbb{R} \to \mathbb{R}; \quad y = h(t) \quad \text{of} \quad C^1,$$

whose derivative is

$$h'(t) = f'(g(t)) \cdot g'(t) \quad \text{or} \quad \frac{dy}{dt} = \frac{dy}{dx} \cdot \frac{dx}{dt}. \tag{12}$$

Example: A firm's revenue (y) may depend on the number of product units sold (x):

$$y = f(x) = 5 \cdot x \Rightarrow f'(x) = 5.$$

To produce the good, t workers are hired each of whom produces four units:

$$x = g(t) = 4 \cdot t \Rightarrow g'(t) = 4.$$

How does revenue respond to a change in the number of workers? The answer is given by (12):

$$\frac{dy}{dt} = 5 \cdot 4 = 20.$$

Thus, revenue will rise by 20 units if one additional worker is employed.

1.3 Taylor's Theorem

To us, Taylor's theorem is the most important theorem in differential calculus because many further results can be substantiated by it. Let us begin with a function

$$y = 3x + 2. \tag{13}$$

and its graph

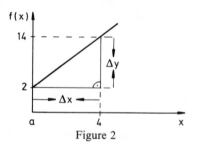

Figure 2

The basic idea of the so-called *Taylor-expansion* is to calculate the values of the function by proceeding from a certain point, a. Let us take a = 0, for instance. The slope of the above straight line obeys:

$$f'(x) = \frac{\Delta y}{\Delta x} \tag{14}$$

$$\Leftrightarrow \Delta y = f'(x) \Delta x. \tag{15}$$

Hence, changes in the function's value can be calculated by multiplying the corresponding changes in x and the constant f'(x). Proceeding from a = 0 and assuming a change of "four", we obtain according to (15):

$$f(4) - f(0) = f'(0) \cdot (4 - 0). \tag{16}$$

The value of f(0) may be known. Then, f(4) can be calculated as

$$f(4) = f(0) + f'(0) \cdot (4 - 0) \tag{17}$$

$$f(4) = 2 + 3 \cdot 4 = 14. \tag{18}$$

Thus, we can compute $f(4)$ when $f(0)$ and the derivative of the linear function f are known. This is described by saying "f has been expanded at $a = 0$". In general, linear functions obey

$$f(x) = f(0) + f'(0) \cdot (x - 0). \tag{19}$$

Let us now pass on to a somewhat more complicated function

$$y = x^2 + 5. \tag{20}$$

Considering its graph it can immediately be seen that the simple rule (19) *cannot* be applied here:

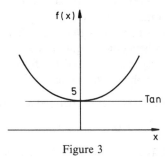

Figure 3

We want to try to expand this function at $a = 0$ where the tangent exhibits a horizontal trend: $f'(0) = 0$. Applying (19), we arrive at the result that f does not respond at all to changes in x! This error is certainly due to the fact that the graph is not a straight line. Yet, f is capable of being expanded correctly at $a = 0$ if we take the second derivative into account:

$$f(x) = f(0) + f'(0) \cdot (x - 0) + \tfrac{1}{2} f''(0) \cdot (x - 0)^2. \tag{21}$$

This formula is not immediately obvious; but we can show that it is correct. In order to do this, let us calculate $f(4)$ by expanding f at $a = 0$:

$$f(4) = 5 + 0 \cdot (4 - 0) + \tfrac{1}{2} \cdot 2 \cdot 4^2 = 21. \tag{22}$$

This is true because $4^2 + 5 = 21$. Being satisfied with our new formula (21) and applying it, we would soon have to recognize that it too does not hold for all functions. (It will hold only for polynomials of degree 2 or less.) Hence, mathematicians have looked for another formula that holds for *all* differentiable functions, and they have found it in

Taylor's theorem: Let $f: \mathbb{R} \to \mathbb{R}$; $y = f(x)$ be an element of C^{n+1}. f may be expanded at a according to

$$f(x) = f(a) + f'(a) \cdot (x - a) + \tfrac{1}{2} f''(a) \cdot (x - a)^2 + \dots$$

$$+ \frac{1}{n!} f^{(n)}(a) \cdot (x - a)^n + R_{n+1}, \tag{23}$$

where

$$R_{n+1} := \frac{1}{(n+1)!} f^{(n+1)}(z) \cdot (x - a)^{n+1} \quad \text{with} \quad z \in [a, x]. \tag{24}$$

Taylor's theorem states that every (sufficiently differentiable) function can be written as a *polynomial*, as shown in equation (23). The polynomial consists of n + 1 terms which involve f(a) and the function's derivatives, *all calculated at a*. Additionally, there is a "rest term", R_{n+1}, which differs from the other terms only in that the derivative is calculated at a point z which is *between* a and x. Taylor's theorem states that there is always such a z. Note that the polynomial in (23) is not an approximation but yields the *exact* value when z is chosen appropriately.

Our formula (21) turns out to be a special case of (23). Insert a = 0 and it can be recognized that, with a polynomial of degree 2, all derivatives or degree 3, 4, ... vanish. Then, the first three terms in (23) are sufficient to calculate the exact value of f, and they are identical to the terms in (21).

Moreover, Taylor's theorem ensures that the expansion may be stopped at any arbitrary term of the sum, it being only required that the last one is taken as the "rest term". Since, in the following, we only need the formulas where the rest term is of order one or two, let us state these two explicitly:

Corollary 1 (Mean Value Theorem): If f is defined as above and $f \in C^1$, then we have

$$f(x) = f(a) + f'(z) \cdot (x - a) \quad \text{where} \quad z \in [a, x]. \tag{25}$$

Corollary 2: If f is defined as above and $f \in C^2$, then we have

$$f(x) = f(a) + f'(a) \cdot (x - a) + \tfrac{1}{2} f''(z) \cdot (x - a)^2 \tag{26}$$

where $z \in [a, x]$.

1.4 Differentials

In economic publications, differentials are used frequently, and often they are interpreted incorrectly as "infinitesimal magnitudes". Again, the problem is to calculate a function's values proceeding from a certain point, a. In contrast to Taylor's formula, however, differentials are *linear approximations*. By neglecting the rest term in (26), we obtain

$$f(x) = f(a) + f'(a) \cdot (x - a) + \varepsilon. \tag{27}$$

This approximation is *not* equivalent to the Taylor expansion (25) where the derivative is calculated at z rather than a. The error term (ε) is equal to the rest term of formula (26). We can now define the *differentials* dy and dx in the following manner:

$$dy := f(x) - f(a) - \varepsilon \tag{28}$$

$$dx := x - a. \tag{29}$$

In the figure below, the variable x, starting at a, is changed by the *finite* amount dx or Δx. These two symbols mean the same. The value of the function, however, changes by Δy whereas equation (30) yields the approximation dy:

$$dy = f'(a) \cdot dx. \tag{30}$$

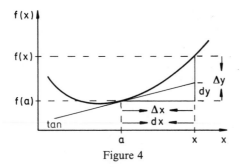

Figure 4

Thus we conclude that the differentials represent finite changes, dx is the same as Δx, and dy is an approximation of Δy. It follows immediately that the expression

$$\Delta y = \frac{dy}{dx} \cdot \Delta x \qquad (31)$$

is wrong in the general case. It is correct only if f is a linear function, or if dy/dx is regarded as the rest term of the first order and is evaluated at some $z \in [x, a]$.

Formulas (26) and (30) indicate that the error of the approximation, ε, is simply the rest term of the second order:

$$\varepsilon = \tfrac{1}{2} f''(z) \cdot (x - a)^2. \qquad (32)$$

If x approaches a, ε will converge towards zero. Hence we can say quite precisely that the error becomes sufficiently small when dx becomes sufficiently small.

Example: Let $y = f(x) = x^2 + x \Rightarrow f'(x) = 2x + 1$.
The differentials of this function at a = 2 are to be calculated. First, we have

$$f'(2) = 5.$$

Then dx = 2 (which means, x = 4) yields the approximation

$$dy = 5 \cdot 2 = 10.$$

Let us examine the quality of this approximation by evaluating the original function at points 2 and 4:
$$f(2) = 6 \quad \text{and} \quad f(4) = 20 \Rightarrow \Delta y = 14.$$

The actual change in y is 14; hence the error amounts to 4.

1.5 Concavity and Convexity

Viewed geometrically, a function is called strictly concave iff its graph is always above an arbitrary secant line. In the reverse case, the function is called strictly convex.

To arrive at a precise analytical definition, we want to consider the graph in Figure 5, which is obviously strictly concave. There are two arbitrarily chosen points x and x'. The function's values at all points between these two are described by the term

$$f(tx + (1 - t)x'), \qquad (33)$$

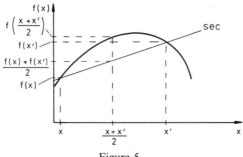

Figure 5

where t is a real number between zero and one. On the other hand, the secant line is obtained as the set of linear combinations

$$t\,f(x) + (1 - t)\,f(x'),\tag{34}$$

t being again between zero and one. $t = 0.5$, for instance, yields the mean value of $f(x)$ and $f(x')$, $t = 0$ yields $f(x)$, and $t = 1$ yields $f(x')$. To recall, (33) represents the function's graph, and (34) represents the secant line. If the function is to be strictly concave, we said that the points on the graph must be above those on the secant line. This means that the values (33) must be greater than the values (34). Hence, we obtain the following definition:

Definition 1: A function f: $\mathbb{R} \to \mathbb{R}$ is called *strictly concave* in an interval iff for all x, x' (x ≠ x') of this interval and all t, $0 < t < 1$, we have

$$f(t\,x + (1 - t)\,x') > t\,f(x) + (1 - t)\,f(x').\tag{35}$$

The function is *concave* iff we replace "<" by "≦"; it is *strictly convex* iff we replace "<" by ">"; and *convex* iff we replace "<" by "≧".

The criterion (35) is rather tiresome when testing a specific function for concavity etc. A criterion with narrower scope, but much greater power, is given by

Theorem 1: Let f: $\mathbb{R} \to \mathbb{R}$ be twice differentiable in the interval $I = [a, b]$. Then, f is

– strictly concave in I if $f''(x) < 0$ for all $x \in I$;
– strictly convex in I if $f''(x) > 0$ for all $x \in I$;
– concave in I iff $f''(x) \leqq 0$ for all $x \in I$;
– convex in I iff $f''(x) \geqq 0$ for all $x \in I$.

Note that the first two conditions involve "if" whereas the last two use "iff". Thus, the former conditions are only sufficient whereas the latter are both necessary and sufficient.

Let us assume for illustration that the second derivative is strictly negative on I. Since f'' represents the slope of the function f', f' must be strictly decreasing. But since f' represents the slope of the function f, this means that the slope of f diminishes everywhere on I. Recollecting Figure 5, it is immediately obvious that f is strictly concave in this case: the slope of f diminishes.

1.6 Maxima and Minima

How often we encounter in economics the problem of maximizing or minimizing some function. In this context, the aid of mathematics is two-fold. First, she provides methods for finding a maximum or minimum and thus helps to determine an optimum. But second, this procedure sheds light on the comparative static or dynamic characteristics of an economic system, if we assume that the individuals do indeed optimize. This second fact is less obvious than the first; but we will have occasion to demonstrate it.

Definition 2: A function f: $\mathbb{R} \to \mathbb{R}$ assumes at a $\in \mathbb{R}$

- a *local maximum* iff there is a neighborhood I of a where $f(x) \leq f(a)$ for all $x \in I$;
- a *local minimum* iff there is a neighborhood I of a where $f(x) \geq (a)$ for all $x \in I$.

The minimum or maximum is called *locally unique* iff the strict inequalities hold in the definition above for all $x \neq a$.

In the following figure, the function f exhibits a local maximum at a and a local minimum at b. But the maximum at a, in contrast to the minimum at b, is locally unique:

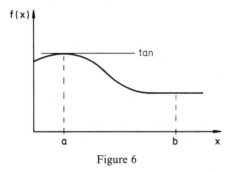

Figure 6

Whether unique or not, it is characteristic of such a local maximum or minimum that the slope of the tangent *vanishes* at the respective point. Hence it is *necessary* for a local optimum that the first derivative (provided that it exists) is zero. This is not *sufficient*, however. The well-known parabola of degree three ($f(x) = x^3$), for instance, has a *saddle point* at $a = 0$ though the first derivative vanishes at this point.

Therefore, $f'(x) = 0$ is called the necessary or *first order condition* for a local maximum or minimum. The *second order conditions* require the function to be concave or convex in a neighborhood of a. In the first case, we have a maximum and in the second one, a minimum. This is obvious from Figure 6.

Theorem 2: A function f: $\mathbb{R} \to \mathbb{R}$, $f \in C^2$, $a \in \mathbb{R}$

- assumes a local maximum at a iff $f'(a) = 0$ and f is concave in some neighborhood of a;
- assumes a local minimum at a iff $f'(a) = 0$ and f is convex in some neighborhood of a.

The first order and second order conditions taken together are both necessary and sufficient for all differentiable functions.

Yet Theorem 2 is somewhat unsatisfactory because, first, we are primarily interested in *unique* optima; and, second, it is often difficult to determine the concavity or convexity of a function. Because of this the following corollary is more helpful:

Corollary 3: Given the prerequisites of Theorem 2,

- the local maximum is unique iff f is strictly concave in some neighborhood of a, which is always true if $f''(a) < 0$;
- the local minimum is unique iff f is strictly convex in some neighborhood of a, which is always true if $f''(a) > 0$.

The second order conditions, involving the function's second derivative at a, are sufficient for locally unique optima when taken together with the first order conditions. But they are not necessary. The function $f(x) = x^4$, for instance, exhibits a locally unique minimum at a = 0, though we have $f''(0) = 0$. We call this an *irregular optimum*. The following analysis is confined to *regular optima*. With them, the above conditions are both necessary and sufficient.

It is simple to show by means of Taylor's theorem that $f'(a) = 0$ and $f''(a) < 0$ are sufficient conditions for a locally unique maximum. At a, the strict inequality

$$f(x) < f(a) \tag{36}$$

must hold for all $x = a$ in some neighborhood of a. The Taylor expansion (20) with the rest term of order one reads

$$f(x) = f(a) + f'(z) \cdot (x - a). \tag{37}$$

The necessity of the first order condition is proved first. Assume $f'(a)$ be positive. Then there is a neighborhood of a where f' is also positive, because $f'(a)$ is a continuous function. By an appropriate choice of x, the "z" of (37) will be in this neighborhood, so that $f'(z)$ is also positive. But then we have $f(x) > f(a)$ for $x > a$ which contradicts the definition of a maximum. Hence, $f'(a)$ cannot be positive. Conversely, an analogous contradiction would result if we assumed $f'(a)$ be negative. Consequently, $f'(a)$ must vanish.

By taking the Taylor expansion with the rest term of order two, we show that $f''(a) < 0$ is sufficient for a maximum, provided that $f'(a) = 0$: Recall equation (26):

$$f(x) = f(a) + f'(a) \cdot (x - a) + \tfrac{1}{2} \cdot f''(z) \cdot (x - a)^2. \tag{38}$$

As $f'(a) = 0$, this formula simplifies to

$$f(x) = f(a) + \tfrac{1}{2} \cdot f''(z) \cdot (x - a)^2. \tag{39}$$

Now $f(x) < f(a)$ for all $x = a$ in a certain neighborhood, as the definition of a maximum requires, iff the second term of the sum above is negative. Since its quadratic component is positive for all real $x \neq a$, the term's sign depends solely on $f''(z)$. This must be negative.

Observe that z may be on the left or on the right of a and may approach this value arbitrarily, according to which x has been chosen. If $f''(a)$ is *negative*, then there must be some neighborhood of a where f″ (z) is negative, too, because the second derivative is a continuous function. Thus we have shown that f′ (a) = 0 and f″ (a) < 0 guarantee the existence of a locally unique maximum.

*1.7 Profit Maximization

Let us demonstrate maximization by means of an economic example. A firm, producing one good with one factor may behave as price-taker and may attempt to maximize its annual profits

$$\pi = p \cdot y - q \cdot x. \tag{40}$$

Here, p, q, y, and x denote output, input, and their respective prices. The firm must observe the production possibilities, which are described by a production function

$$y = f(x) \tag{41}$$

f exhibits strictly positive marginal returns which diminish strictly and grow unboundedly as x approaches zero. The last of these assumptions is made in order to exclude a solution at the border. (This may occur if the factor price is very high relative to output price and factor productivity: the firm will produce nothing.) After substituting the production function (41) into the profit definition (40), profits depend solely on x:

$$\pi(x) = p \cdot f(x) - q \cdot x. \tag{42}$$

According to Theorem 2, the first order condition for a profit maximum is:

$$\frac{d\pi(x)}{dx} = p \cdot f'(x) - q \overset{!}{=} 0 \tag{43}$$

$$\Leftrightarrow \quad p \cdot f'(x) = q. \tag{44}$$

Thus, it is necessary for a profit maximum that marginal productivity times output price is equal to the factor price. What about the second order condition? From (44), the second derivative is straightforwardly calculated as

$$\frac{d^2\pi}{dx^2} = p \cdot f''(x). \tag{45}$$

Output price being positive, the sign of this second derivative depends only on f″ (x). Thus, our theorems of the previous subsection support the following statements:

- We have a local profit maximum at a ∈ ℝ iff the production function is concave in some neighborhood of a.
- This local profit maximum is locally unique iff the production function is strictly concave there.
- And this holds at least if f″ (a) < 0; then we have a regular maximum.

Beyond that it can be shown that there is just one regular profit maximum if the production function is strictly concave everywhere, that is, if f″ (a) < 0 for all a ∈ ℝ. This last requirement is met by the assumption of a Neoclassical production function.

With a *Classical* production function, however, f" is first positive and then becomes negative (the production function is first strictly convex and then becomes strictly concave). In this case, we will typically encounter two solutions of equation (43). One of them will correspond to a minimum, and the other to a maximum. When maximizing profits, the firms will simply *ignore* that range where f" > 0, i.e. where there are increasing marginal returns. In this sense, the assumption of a Neoclassical production function involves no loss of generality: firms will always produce within the range where marginal returns diminish.

2. Linear Algebra

The range of application of functions of a single variable is, of course, rather restricted. Functions of several variables are much more useful to us. For an adequate handling of the notorious "n dimensions", we must provide some devices from linear algebra first.

2.1 Vectors

A (real) *n-component vector* is an ordered n-tuple of real numbers. We write it as

$$\mathbf{x} := (x_1, x_2, \ldots, x_n) \quad \text{where} \quad x_i \in \mathbb{R}, \quad i = 1 \ldots n. \tag{46}$$

The x_i are called the components of the vector. Any vector may be written as a row or as a column of numbers; these two representations are equivalent. Real numbers can be regarded as 1-component vectors. In the following, we will designate vectors by *lower-case boldface* letters.

Some simple properties of vectors are certainly already known to the reader. Two n-component vectors $\mathbf{x}$ and $\mathbf{x}'$ are *equal* iff all their i-th components are pairwise equal ($i = 1 \ldots n$). Two n-component vectors are added (subtracted) by adding (subtracting) the i-th components ($i = 1 \ldots n$). The *null vector*, or zero vector, is defined as $\mathbf{0} = (0, 0, \ldots, 0)$. A vector is called *positive* iff none of its components is negative and at least one is strictly positive.

The *scalar product* of two n-component vectors $\mathbf{a}$ and $\mathbf{b}$ is the real number

$$c = \mathbf{a} \cdot \mathbf{b} = a_1 b_1 + a_2 b_2 + \ldots a_n b_n. \tag{47}$$

Note that $\mathbf{a}$ and $\mathbf{b}$ are two n-component vectors but their scalar product, c, is a real number.

Example: Let $\mathbf{a} = (2; 1; 5)$ and $\mathbf{b} = (10; 4; 2)$.
The scalar product of $\mathbf{a}$ and $\mathbf{b}$ is calculated as:

$$c = (2; 1; 5) \cdot (10; 4; 2) = 20 + 4 + 10 = 34.$$

Scalar products are conveniently employed for writing complex phenomena in a very simple and enlightening manner. Assume a firm produces n different goods, their respective quantities denoted by $\mathbf{x} = (x_1, x_2, \ldots, x_n)$ and their prices denoted by $\mathbf{p} = (p_1, p_2, \ldots, p_n)$. Then, total revenue may be written as

$$\text{revenue} = \mathbf{p} \cdot \mathbf{x} \, (= p_1 x_1 + \ldots + p_n x_n). \tag{48}$$

Thus by using the definition of a scalar product, revenue is written as if only one good were produced.

Now consider a set of m vectors of $\mathbb{R}$. One of these vectors is said to be *linearly dependent* iff it can be represented as a *linear combination* of the others, that is, iff there exist real numbers r_i such that

$$\mathbf{x_i} = r_1 \mathbf{x_1} + \ldots + r_m \mathbf{x_m}, \tag{49}$$

The sum on the right hand covers all $\mathbf{x_j}$ except $\mathbf{x_i}$ itself. The vector $\mathbf{x}$ is *linearly independent* if no such real numbers do exist. The set of m vectors is linearly independent iff *every* vector of the set is linearly independent.

2.2 Matrices and Determinants

A rectangular ordered array of real numbers is called a (real) *matrix*:

$$\mathbf{A} = \begin{pmatrix} a_{11} & a_{12} & \cdots & a_{1n} \\ a_{21} & a_{22} & \cdots & a_{2n} \\ \multicolumn{4}{c}{\dotfill} \\ a_{m1} & a_{m2} & \cdots & a_{mn} \end{pmatrix}; \quad \mathbf{A} \in \mathbb{R}^m \times \mathbb{R}^n. \tag{50}$$

In the following, matrices are denoted by *upper-case boldface* letters. The real numbers a_{ij} are the *elements* of the matrix. We can conceive of such a matrix as consisting of n column vectors $\mathbf{a} \in \mathbb{R}^m$ or of m row vectors $\mathbf{a} \in \mathbb{R}^n$. Hence two matrices are *equal* iff they have the same numbers of rows and columns and all their elements are pairwise equal.

A matrix is *square* iff m = n, that is, if the number of rows is equal to the number of columns. A square matrix is *symmetric* iff $a_{ij} = a_{ji}$ for all i, j = 1 ... n. The *main diagonal* of the matrix (which runs from the upper left to the lower right) is the set of all elements a_{ii}. The *trace* of a matrix, written as Tr (**A**) is the sum of all elements of the main diagonal.
Examples:

$$\mathbf{A} = \begin{pmatrix} 1 & 3 & 9 \\ 2 & 4 & 1 \\ 6 & 8 & 6 \end{pmatrix} \quad \mathbf{B} = \begin{pmatrix} 1 & 2 & 3 \\ 2 & 5 & 4 \\ 3 & 4 & 9 \end{pmatrix}.$$

Both matrices are square. But only **B** is symmetric, which can be seen by the mirroring of the elements "2", "3", and "4" about the main diagonal. The main diagonal of **B** consists of the elements "1", "5", and "9". Its trace is thus $1 + 5 + 9 = 15$.

Two matrices are added (subtracted) by adding (subtracting) their corresponding elements; of course, they must have the same numbers of rows and columns. The *transpose* $\mathbf{A}^T$ of a matrix $\mathbf{A} = (a_{ij})$ is the matrix (a_{ji}), obtained by interchanging the indices i and j. A symmetric matrix is equal to its transpose.

Let us now define matrix multiplication.

Definition 3: Let $\mathbf{A} \in \mathbb{R}^l \times \mathbb{R}^m$ and $\mathbf{B} \in \mathbb{R}^m \times \mathbb{R}^n$. Moreover, let $\mathbf{a_i}$ (i = 1 ... l) the i-th row vector of $\mathbf{A}$ and $\mathbf{b_j}$ (j = 1 ... n) the j-th column vector of $\mathbf{B}$. Then, the matrix

$\mathbf{C} \in \mathbb{R}^1 \times \mathbb{R}^n$ with elements

$$c_{ij} = \mathbf{a_i} \, \mathbf{b_j}$$

is called the *scalar product* of **A** and **B**.

Hence, every element of **C** is calculated as the scalar product of two vectors.

Example: Let $\mathbf{A} = \begin{pmatrix} 1 & 3 \\ 2 & 4 \end{pmatrix}$, $\mathbf{B} = \begin{pmatrix} 9 & 8 \\ 2 & 3 \end{pmatrix}$.

Matrix multiplication is facilitated by the following scheme (compute "1 times 9 plus 3 times 2 etc.):

$$
\begin{array}{cc|cc}
 & & 9 & 8 \\
 & & 2 & 3 \\
\hline
1 & 3 & 15 & 17 \\
2 & 4 & 26 & 28 \\
\end{array}
$$

The *identity matrix* **E** is a matrix with the following properties: The matrix is square; all elements along its main diagonal have the value one; and all other elements are zero. Multiplying a matrix **A** with the corresponding identity matrix leaves **A** unchanged.

Example: Let **A** be defined as before and **E** be the corresponding identity matrix. Multiplication shows that $\mathbf{A} \cdot \mathbf{E} = \mathbf{A}$:

$$
\begin{array}{cc|cc}
 & & 1 & 0 \\
 & & 0 & 1 \\
\hline
1 & 3 & 1 & 3 \\
2 & 4 & 2 & 4 \\
\end{array}
$$

Matrices may be multiplied by vectors also because a row vector is a matrix of $\mathbb{R}^1 \times \mathbb{R}^n$, a column vector is a matrix of $\mathbb{R}^n \times \mathbb{R}^1$. In the literature, row vectors are usually represented by the superscript "T", and thus represented as the transpose of the corresponding column vector. We do not want to maintain that convention but denote both as **x**.

Determinants are real numbers which are assigned to square matrices in a certain manner. We write the *determinant* of $\mathbf{A} \in \mathbb{R}^n \times \mathbb{R}^n$ as $|\mathbf{A}|$ and define it as

$$|\mathbf{A}| := \sum_{j=1}^{n} a_{ij} (-1)^{i+j} |\mathbf{A_{ij}}| \quad \text{und} \quad |a_{ij}| := a_{ij}. \tag{51}$$

$\mathbf{A_{ij}}$ is that matrix obtained from **A** by eliminating **A**'s i-th row and its j-th column. (51) is one of those notorious recursive definitions which are not intelligible at first sight: The determinant of a matrix is defined as some expression which itself involves determinants. Yet, this is not a vicious circle since the determinant of a real number is defined as that real number itself. Hence, the determinant of a matrix $\mathbf{A} \in \mathbb{R}^n \times \mathbb{R}^n$ traces back to determinants of matrices belonging to $\mathbb{R}^{n-1} \times \mathbb{R}^{n-1}$; and this procedure will be repeated till we arrive at matrices of $\mathbb{R}^1 \times \mathbb{R}^1$, that is, real numbers.

Example: Let $\mathbf{A} = \begin{pmatrix} 2 & 3 \\ 4 & 5 \end{pmatrix}$.

By applying definition (51) we obtain:

$$|\mathbf{A}| = 2 \cdot (-1)^2 \cdot |\mathbf{A_{11}}| + 3 \cdot (-1)^3 \cdot |\mathbf{A_{12}}|.$$

$\mathbf{A_{11}}$ consists of those elements of $\mathbf{A}$ which remain after eliminating $\mathbf{A}$'s first row and its first column: it is simply the element "5". Likewise, $\mathbf{A_{12}}$ is "4", and we obtain

$$|\mathbf{A}| = 2 \cdot 5 + (-3) \cdot 4 = -2.$$

In general, we have for a 2×2 matrix:

$$\begin{vmatrix} a & b \\ c & d \end{vmatrix} = ad - bc. \tag{52}$$

The determinant of a 3×3 matrix is calculated, for instance, by multiplying the elements of its first row and the determinants of the remaining 2×2 matrices, taking notice of the alterations in the signs.

Example: Let $\mathbf{A} = \begin{pmatrix} 3 & 2 & 0 \\ 3 & 4 & 1 \\ 4 & 6 & 2 \end{pmatrix}$

"Expanding by the first row" yields:

$$|\mathbf{A}| = 3 \cdot \begin{vmatrix} 4 & 1 \\ 6 & 2 \end{vmatrix} + 2(-1) \cdot \begin{vmatrix} 3 & 1 \\ 4 & 2 \end{vmatrix} + 0 \cdot \begin{vmatrix} 3 & 4 \\ 4 & 6 \end{vmatrix} = 2.$$

For simplicity, we call the term

$$(-1)^{i+j} |\mathbf{A_{ij}}| \tag{53}$$

the *cofactor* of element a_{ij}. Therefore, the determinant can be represented as the sum of one row's elements, each multiplied by the corresponding cofactor.

Finally, we will discuss a kind of "matrix division". The *inverse* of a matrix $\mathbf{A}$, denoted $\mathbf{A^{-1}}$, is that matrix which yields the identity matrix when multiplied by $\mathbf{A}$:

$$\mathbf{A^{-1}} \text{ is the inverse of } \mathbf{A} \Leftrightarrow \mathbf{A} \cdot \mathbf{A^{-1}} = \mathbf{E}.$$

The inverse is thus the "reciprocal value" of $\mathbf{A}$.

Theorem 3: Let $\mathbf{A}$ be a quadratic matrix. An inverse of $\mathbf{A}$ exists iff the determinant of $\mathbf{A}$ does not vanish. Then, there is just one inverse. It comes to

$$\mathbf{A^{-1}} = (a_{ij}^{-1}) \quad \text{where} \quad a_{ij}^{-1} = \frac{(-1)^{i+j} |\mathbf{A_{ji}}|}{|\mathbf{A}|}. \tag{55}$$

Example: Let $\mathbf{A} = \begin{pmatrix} 2 & 4 \\ 2 & 5 \end{pmatrix}$.

In order to calculate its inverse, we must first compute the determinant and the four cofactors:

$$|\mathbf{A}| = 2, \quad |\mathbf{A_{11}}| = 5, \quad -|\mathbf{A_{12}}| = -2, \quad -|\mathbf{A_{21}}| = -4, \quad |\mathbf{A_{22}}| = 2.$$

Assembling the cofactors, each divided by the determinant, and interchanging rows and columns yields:

$$\mathbf{A}^{-1} = \begin{pmatrix} 5/2 & -2 \\ -1 & 1 \end{pmatrix}.$$

The reader may ascertain, by carrying out the multiplication, that $\mathbf{A} \cdot \mathbf{A}^{-1}$ yields the identity matrix.

2.3 Simultaneous Linear Equations

Simultanous linear equations are given by

$$\begin{aligned} a_{11}x_1 + a_{12}x_2 + \ldots + a_{1n}x_n &= b_1 \\ a_{21}x_1 + a_{22}x_2 + \ldots + a_{2n}x_n &= b_2 \\ \ldots\ldots\ldots\ldots\ldots\ldots\ldots\ldots\ldots\ldots\ldots\ldots \\ a_{m1}x_1 + a_{m2}x_2 + \ldots + a_{mn}x_n &= b_m. \end{aligned} \tag{56}$$

The *coefficients* a_{ij} and b_i are given numbers, and the variables x_j are sought. In the following, we only consider the case where m = n, that is, the number of equations and the number of variables are the same. By using matrix notation, the simultaneous equations can be written in a much more compact form:

$$\mathbf{A} \cdot \mathbf{x} = \mathbf{b} \quad \text{where} \quad \mathbf{A} \in \mathbb{R}^n \times \mathbb{R}^n; \quad \mathbf{x}, \mathbf{b} \in \mathbb{R}^n. \tag{57}$$

Carrying out the matrix multiplication in (57) yields (56). The simultanous linear equations are called *homogeneous* iff $\mathbf{b} = \mathbf{0}$, otherwise they are called *inhomogeneous*. Consider the following simple example

$$\begin{aligned} 2x_1 + 4x_2 &= 2 \\ 2x_1 + 5x_2 &= 3. \end{aligned} \tag{58}$$

or, with matrix notation,

$$\begin{pmatrix} 2 & 4 \\ 2 & 5 \end{pmatrix} \begin{pmatrix} x_1 \\ x_2 \end{pmatrix} = \begin{pmatrix} 2 \\ 3 \end{pmatrix}. \tag{59}$$

The most simple method of solution is to solve the first equation in (58) for $2 \cdot x_1$ and then insert the result into the second equation:

$$2x_1 = 3 - 5x_2. \tag{60}$$

$$(3 - 5x_2) + 4x_2 = 2 \tag{61}$$

$$x_2 = 1; \quad x_1 = -1. \tag{62}$$

This method seems to work well; but with more extensive simultaneous equations, it turns out to be rather ineffective since we have to proceed differently each time. A more powerful procedure is given by

Cramer's rule: Assume equation (57) and $|\mathbf{A}| \neq 0$. Then,

$$x_i = \frac{1}{|\mathbf{A}|} \begin{vmatrix} a_{11} \ldots b_1 \ldots a_{1n} \\ \ldots\ldots\ldots\ldots \\ a_{n1} \ldots b_n \ldots a_{nn} \end{vmatrix} \tag{63}$$

$$\Leftrightarrow x_i = \frac{1}{|\mathbf{A}|} \sum_{j=1}^{n} b_j (-1)^{i+j} |\mathbf{A}_{ij}|. \tag{64}$$

Put verbally, we obtain the solution for the i-th variable by calculating the determinant of that matrix which emerges from substituting the i-th column of $\mathbf{A}$ by $\mathbf{b}$; and then dividing this value by $|\mathbf{A}|$. Equation (64) is just another way of expressing the same: there, the first determinant is calculated by "expanding by the i-th column".

Let us solve the simultaneous equations (59) by means of Cramer's rule. In order to compute x_1, the first variable, we must replace the first column of $\mathbf{A}$ by $\mathbf{b}$. Its determinant amounts to

$$\begin{vmatrix} 2 & 4 \\ 3 & 5 \end{vmatrix} = -2. \tag{65}$$

Because $|\mathbf{A}| = 2$, we immediately obtain $x_1 = -1$. x_2 can be calculated similarly.

The last, and most powerful, method of solving the simultaneous equations (57) is simply, to invert $\mathbf{A}$. Multiplying both sides of (57) by $\mathbf{A}^{-1}$ yields at once:

$$\mathbf{x} = \mathbf{A}^{-1} \cdot \mathbf{b}. \tag{66}$$

We have to multiply $\mathbf{A}^{-1}$ by $\mathbf{b}$, and not vice versa, because matrix multiplication is not universally commutative, that is, the order of the factors must not be interchanged. Let us demonstrate this method, too. The inverse of matrix $\mathbf{A}$ has already been calculated at the end of Subsection 2.2. Inserting this solution yields

$$\begin{pmatrix} x_1 \\ x_2 \end{pmatrix} = \begin{pmatrix} 5/2 & -2 \\ -1 & 1 \end{pmatrix} \begin{pmatrix} 2 \\ 3 \end{pmatrix}. \tag{67}$$

and by carrying out the multiplication we obtain

$$\begin{pmatrix} x_1 \\ x_2 \end{pmatrix} = \begin{pmatrix} -1 \\ 1 \end{pmatrix}. \tag{68}$$

Again, we have arrived at the solutions (62). The time required for the inversion, however, was much greater. Indeed, the method of inversion and Cramer's rule are not very attractive if specific numerical values are given. In this case, the method of Gaussian elimination, and perhaps even the method of inserting, are more efficient. In economic theory, however, we often have only qualitative information but not numerical values, and in this case, Cramer's rule is called for. The method of inversion is primarily required for a later proof; it also serves as a very simple proof of Cramer's rule, which the reader may try for himself.

2.4 Characteristic Value Problems

By a *characteristic value problem*, we mean the task of determining real numbers which satisfy the equation

$$\mathbf{A} \cdot \mathbf{x} = \lambda \cdot \mathbf{x} \quad \text{where} \quad \mathbf{A} \in \mathbb{R}^n \times \mathbb{R}^n, \ \mathbf{x} \in \mathbb{R}^n, \ \lambda \in \mathbb{R} \tag{69}$$

In these simultaneous equations, $\mathbf{A}$ is a *given* square matrix, and both λ and $\mathbf{x}$ are unknowns. The trivial solution $\mathbf{x} = \mathbf{0}$ is excluded. Real numbers λ satisfying (69) are the *characteristic values* (or eigenvalues, or characteristic roots) of (69). The vector $\mathbf{x}$ associated with such a characteristic value is called a *characteristic vector*. Let us transform (69) by multiplying both sides by the identity matrix

$$\mathbf{A} \cdot \mathbf{x} = \mathbf{E} \cdot \lambda \cdot \mathbf{x}. \tag{70}$$

substracting

$$\mathbf{A} \cdot \mathbf{x} - \mathbf{E} \lambda \mathbf{x} = \mathbf{0} \tag{71}$$

and factoring out $\mathbf{x}$

$$(\mathbf{A} - \mathbf{E} \lambda) \mathbf{x} = \mathbf{0}. \tag{72}$$

Now, (72) are *homogeneous* linear equations because the right hand side is zero. The matrix of coefficients is $(\mathbf{A} - \mathbf{E} \cdot \lambda)$. Homogenous linear equations always have the *trivial* solution $\mathbf{x} = \mathbf{0}$; they have *non-trivial* solutions $\mathbf{x} \neq \mathbf{0}$ iff the determinant of the matrix of coefficients vanishes. Recognizing this fact provides the first step towards solving the characteristic value problem. The reader should realize that the matrix of coefficients $(\mathbf{A} - \mathbf{E} \lambda)$ is not given because it is precisely the λ that we are seeking. We have non-trivial solutions iff the determinant of that matrix vanishes:

$$|\mathbf{A} - \mathbf{E} \lambda| = 0. \tag{73}$$

This is the *characteric equation* of matrix $\mathbf{A}$. One such characteristic equation is associated with any square matrix $\mathbf{A}$. The matrix $(\mathbf{A} - \mathbf{E} \lambda)$ is

$$(\mathbf{A} - \mathbf{E} \lambda) = \begin{pmatrix} a_{11} - \lambda & a_{12} & \cdots & a_{1n} \\ a_{21} & a_{22} - \lambda & a_{2n} \\ \cdots\cdots\cdots\cdots\cdots\cdots\cdots \\ a_{n1} & a_{n2} & \cdots & a_{nn} - \lambda \end{pmatrix} \tag{74}$$

because the identity matrix $\mathbf{E}$ consists of "1"s along its main diagonal and of "0"s elsewhere. The determinant of the matrix (73) is a *polynomial of degree n in* λ. For instance, when calculating the determinant of a 2×2 matrix, we obtain a polynomial of degree 2.

Now, a polynomial of degree n has exactly n zeros (not necessarily different) which are either real or complex. A *complex number* z is defined as the sum of a real number and another real number multiplied by i, the root of -1:

$$z = a + bi \quad \text{with} \quad a, b \in \mathbb{R} \quad \text{and} \quad i := \sqrt{-1}. \tag{75}$$

The complex number consists of a *real part* (a) and an *imaginary part* (b · i). If one of the characteristic values happens to be complex, the associated characteristic vector must be complex, too, since $\mathbf{A}$ is a real matrix.

Thus we have solved the characteristic value problem because the characteristic values can be determined as the zeros of a polynomial, the coefficients of this polynomial consisting of combinations of **A**'s components. For every characteristic value there is an infinite set of associated characteristic vectors which are all linearly dependent. This is due to the fact that if **x*** is a non-trivial solution of some homogeneous linear equations, $k \cdot \mathbf{x^*}$, $k \in \mathbb{R}$, is also a solution.

Example. Let $\mathbf{A} = \begin{pmatrix} 3 & 1 \\ 4 & 3 \end{pmatrix}$.

What are the characteristic values and the characteristic vectors of **A**?
    At first, we construct the characteristic equation according to (73):

$$\begin{vmatrix} 3 - \lambda & 1 \\ 4 & 3 - \lambda \end{vmatrix} = 0.$$

Calculating the determinant yields:

$$\lambda^2 - 6\lambda + 5 = 0.$$

This is a simple quadratic equation. By means of the "p/q formula" we obtain its solutions

$$\lambda_{1/2} = 3 \pm \sqrt{9 - 5} \Rightarrow \lambda_1 = 1 \quad \text{and} \quad \lambda_2 = 5.$$

Finally, let us calculate the characteristic vectors associated with λ_1. Formulating an equation like (72) and substituting the value $\lambda_1 = 1$ into it yields:

$$\begin{pmatrix} 2 & 1 \\ 4 & 2 \end{pmatrix} \begin{pmatrix} x_1 \\ x_2 \end{pmatrix} = \begin{pmatrix} 0 \\ 0 \end{pmatrix}.$$

Of course, these two equations are linearly dependent. Solving the first one with respect to x_2, we obtain the solutions belonging to λ_1:

$$\mathbf{x_1} = (x_1, -2x_1).$$

x_1 may be replaced by any real number ($\neq 0$). For λ_2, we obtain the solutions $\mathbf{x_2} = (x_1, 2x_1)$.

2.5 Quadratic Forms

A *quadratic form* is an expression

$$\mathbf{x} \cdot \mathbf{A} \cdot \mathbf{x} \quad \text{where} \quad \mathbf{x} \in \mathbb{R}^n; \quad \mathbf{A} \in \mathbb{R}^n \times \mathbb{R}^n, \tag{76}$$

where **A** is a given matrix of coefficients and **x** is the vector of variables. To facilitate the multiplication, the **x** on the left hand side must be written as a row vector and that on the right hand side as a column vector. The following example shows why (76) is referred to as a "quadratic" form.

Example: Let $\mathbf{A} = \begin{pmatrix} 1 & 1 \\ 1 & 1 \end{pmatrix}$ be the matrix of coefficients of (76). The quadratic form associated with $\mathbf{A}$ is

$$\mathbf{x} \cdot \mathbf{A} \cdot \mathbf{x} = (x_1, x_2) \begin{pmatrix} 1 & 1 \\ 1 & 1 \end{pmatrix} \begin{pmatrix} x_1 \\ x_2 \end{pmatrix}$$

$$= (x_1, x_2) \begin{pmatrix} x_1 + x_2 \\ x_1 + x_2 \end{pmatrix}$$

$$= x_1^2 + 2 x_1 x_2 + x_2^2 .$$

The last equation shows that all variables occur with the second power, which justifies the designation "quadratic form". Of special interest to us are those quadratic forms which assume a certain sign for *all* $\mathbf{x}$. This is expressed by the term "definiteness".

Definition 4: A quadratic form (or the associated matrix) is *positive definite* iff $\mathbf{x} \cdot \mathbf{A} \cdot \mathbf{x}$ is a strictly positive number for all $\mathbf{x} \neq \mathbf{0}$. The quadratic form is *negative definite* iff $\mathbf{x} \cdot \mathbf{A} \cdot \mathbf{x}$ is a strictly negative number for all $\mathbf{x} \neq \mathbf{0}$. It is *positive semi-definite* iff $\mathbf{x} \cdot \mathbf{A} \cdot \mathbf{x}$ is never negative, and *negative semi-definite* iff $\mathbf{x} \cdot \mathbf{A} \cdot \mathbf{x}$ is never positive.

These definitions may refer to a quadratic form or to a square matrix, since these two are uniquely related to each other. The matrix $\mathbf{A}$ of the previous example is clearly positive semi-definite because a binomial $(x_1 + x_2)^2$ resulted in the last transformation. It is not positive definite, however, because the binomial assumes the value zero for all $x_1 = -x_2$. It is true that definiteness is by no means an obvious property of a matrix, such as symmetry, but there are necessary and sufficient conditions for it, given without proof by

Theorem 4: A symmetric matrix $\mathbf{A} \in \mathbb{R}^n \times \mathbb{R}^n$ is

– positive definite iff

$$|a_{11}| > 0 \quad \text{and} \quad \begin{vmatrix} a_{11} & a_{12} \\ a_{21} & a_{22} \end{vmatrix} > 0 \quad \text{and} \ldots \text{and} \quad |\mathbf{A}| > 0 .$$

– negative definite iff

$$|a_{11}| < 0 \quad \text{and} \quad \begin{vmatrix} a_{11} & a_{12} \\ a_{21} & a_{22} \end{vmatrix} > 0 \quad \text{and} \ldots \text{and} \quad (-1)^n |\mathbf{A}| > 0 .$$

– positive semi-definite or negative semi-definite iff the respective first $(N - 1)$ conditions above hold and $|\mathbf{A}| = 0$.

Determinants of this kind are called *principal minors*. Thus, pricipal minors of a square matrix $\mathbf{A}$ are determinants of submatrices which are symmetric around the main diagonal and are obtained by eliminating k i-th rows and columns in $\mathbf{A}$ where $k \leq n$. The number of rows and columns is called the *order* of a principal minor. Hence, a_{11} and all other elements on the main diagonal are principal minors of order one. $\mathbf{A}$ itself is the only principal minor of order n. According to Theorem 4, not all principal minors have to be considered, but only those on the "upper left". We call them *leading* principal minors.

Put verbally, the above conditions read: With a positive definite matrix, all leading principal minors are positive; and with a negative definite matrix, they are alternatingly positive and negative, starting with the negative sign.

Example: Is the matrix $\mathbf{A} = \begin{pmatrix} 1 & 2 & 3 \\ 2 & 5 & 3 \\ 1 & 3 & 1 \end{pmatrix}$ definite?

According to Theorem 4, the leading principal minors have to be examined:

$$|1| > 0 \quad \text{and} \quad \begin{vmatrix} 1 & 2 \\ 2 & 5 \end{vmatrix} > 0 \quad \text{and} \quad \begin{vmatrix} 1 & 2 & 3 \\ 2 & 5 & 3 \\ 1 & 3 & 1 \end{vmatrix} > 0.$$

Since they are all positive, $\mathbf{A}$ is positive definite.

3. Calculus of Functions of Several Variables

Owing to the notorious property of "interdependence", nearly every magnitude depends on every other in reality. But in theory, we are urged to select only some relations which are considered especially important. Habitually, however, this simplification cannot be pushed so far that any economic magnitude is determined by only *one* other; such monocausalities are unlikely to survive. It is for this reason that we have to deal with functions of several variables.

3.1 Functions of Several Variables

A real function of several variables is a mapping

$$f\colon \ \mathbb{R}^n \to \mathbb{R} \quad \text{where} \quad y = f(x); \quad y \in \mathbb{R}, \quad x \in \mathbb{R}^n. \tag{77}$$

It assigns just one real number, y, to every vector $x \in \mathbb{R}^n$. A function (77) is called *continuous* iff $\lim_{x \to a} f(x) = f(a)$ $(x \neq a)$ for all $a \in \mathbb{R}^n$, and we denote this by saying $f \in C^0$.

3.2 Partial Derivatives. Gradients

In Subsection 1.2 we defined the derivative of a function of a single variable as the limit of a difference quotient and interpreted it as the slope of the function's graph. With functions of, say, two variables, the term "slope" does not designate something specific since such a "mountain-like" function exhibits "slopes" in infinitely many directions. Yet, the slopes in the directions of the axes are of special interest. With a function of n variables, there are precisely n of them. They are given by the partial derivatives of the function. $\partial y / \partial x_1$, for instance, denotes the function's slope in the direction of the x_1-axis. Put differently, it denotes the rate of change in y if x_1 is varied and all other arguments are kept constant. In this case, we encounter virtually a function of just one variable; thus, partial derivatives trace back to the "usual" derivatives.

Definition: Let $f\colon \mathbb{R}^n \to \mathbb{R}$, $y = f(x)$ and $h\colon \mathbb{R} \to \mathbb{R}$, $y = h(x_i)$ such that $f(x) = h(x_i)$ if all $x_j \neq x_i$ are constant. Then, the *partial derivative* of f with respect to x_i is defined as

$$f_i = \frac{\partial f}{\partial x_i} := \frac{dh}{dx_i}. \tag{78}$$

The partial derivative is nothing other than a "usual" derivative when all variables but one are kept constant. Partial derivatives are written with a stylized d (∂) and not with a greek delta (δ). Function (77) is called *differentiable with respect to x_i at* **a** iff the expression (78) exists at that point. It is called *differentiable with respect to x_i* iff this expression exists for all **a** of the domain. Finally, it is called *differentiable* iff it is differentiable with respect to x_i for all x_i. If a function f is differentiable and the derivatives are continuous, we write $f \in C^1$.

Partial derivatives of higher orders are defined as partial derivatives of partial derivatives. If all derivatives of order n do exist, we write $f \in C^n$. A function $f \in C^2$ of two variables has two first derivatives, and four second derivatives which are obtained by differentiating the first derivatives:

$$f_{11} := \frac{\partial^2 f}{\partial x_1^2}, \qquad f_{12} := \frac{\partial^2 f}{\partial x_1 \, \partial x_2}$$

$$f_{21} := \frac{\partial^2 f}{\partial x_1 \, \partial x_2}, \qquad f_{22} := \frac{\partial^2 f}{\partial x_2^2}. \tag{79}$$

Derivatives of the kind f_{ij} or f_{ji} where $i \neq j$ are called *cross derivatives*. f_{ij} denotes the rate of change in the slope with respect to x_i when x_j is varied.

Fundamental theorem on partial derivatives: Let f: $\mathbb{R}^n \to \mathbb{R}$, $f \in C^2$. Then, $f_{ij} = f_{ji}$ for all i, j = 1 ... n.

This theorem states that it is immaterial whether you differentiate first with respect to x_i and then with respect to x_j (obtaining f_{ij}) or vice versa (obtaining f_{ji}). Because partial derivatives were traced back to derivatives, all well-known techniques of differentiation apply to them, too.

For later purposes, we define the *gradient* of a function f: $\mathbb{R}^n \to \mathbb{R}$, $f \in C^1$ as the vector of all partial derivatives:

$$\text{grad}\,(f) := \left(\frac{\partial f}{\partial x_1}, \frac{\partial f}{\partial x_2}, \ldots, \frac{\partial f}{\partial x_n} \right). \tag{80}$$

Example: Let $y = x_1^2 + 5 \cdot x_2$.
Then, we have grad (f) = $(2 x_1, 5)$.

Is such a gradient a function itself? Obviously, one vector of $\mathbb{R}^n$ is assigned to any vector $\mathbf{x} \in \mathbb{R}^n$ whereas, up to here, we defined a function to be real-valued. But there is no difficulty in replacing real numbers by real vectors. Thus we want to extend the notion of a function:

Definition 5: A *vector-valued function* is a mapping f: $\mathbb{R}^m \to \mathbb{R}^n$, which assigns just one real vector of $\mathbb{R}^n$ to every vector of $\mathbb{R}^m$.

Therefore, our gradient is a vector-valued function. Vector-valued functions facilitate a convenient notation of simultaneous functions:

Example: Let
$$y^1 = f^1 (x_1, x_2) \quad y^2 = f^2 (x_1, x_2)$$

be two arbitrary simultaneous functions. They form a vector-valued function which may be written:
$$\text{f:} \quad \mathbb{R}^2 \to \mathbb{R}^2 \quad \text{where} \quad y = f(x); \quad y, x \in \mathbb{R}^2.$$

In the following, we will denote vector-valued funtions by *boldface* symbols for the function, that is, **f** instead of f. Their components are written with superscripts (f^i) in order to distinguish them from partial derivatives which are written with subscripts (f_j). A vector-valued function may be employed, for example, to denote a production technology with n outputs and m factors in very compact form.

3.3 Chain Rule

With function of several variables, too, there occur "indirect" relationships which are to be analyzed. Thus, a firm's total revenue depends on the quantities and prices of all goods produced and sold whereas these quantities, in turn, depend on the factors employed. Happily, a chain rule for this more complex case is also available.

Theorem 5: Let f: $\mathbb{R}^n \to \mathbb{R}$; $y = f(\mathbf{x})$ be a function of C^1 and let g: $\mathbb{R} \to \mathbb{R}^n$; $\mathbf{x} = \mathbf{g}(t)$ be a vector-valued function whose components g^i are all functions of C^1. Then, there is a function

$$\text{h: } \mathbb{R} \to \mathbb{R}; \quad y = h(t) \quad \text{of } C^1,$$

whose derivative is

$$\frac{dy}{dt} = \text{grad}(f) \cdot \frac{d\mathbf{x}}{dt}. \tag{81}$$

Let us explain this verbally: The variable y depends on n variables which are combined to form the vector **x**. This is described by the function f. Any component of **x**, in turn, depends on a variable t. This is described by the vector-valued function **g** which assigns just one vector **x** to any real number t. Clearly, y depends indirectly on t, as is indicated by the function h. The derivative of h is calculated according to (81) as the *scalar product* of f's gradient and the derivatives of **g**. With n = 1 we obtain the ordinary chain rule (12) as a special case. With n = 2, carrying out the scalar product in (81) yields:

$$\frac{dy}{dt} = \frac{\partial y}{\partial x_1} \cdot \frac{dx_1}{dt} + \frac{\partial y}{\partial x_2} \cdot \frac{dx_2}{dt} \tag{82}$$

This expression is frequently called the *total derivative* of f with respect to t. It consists of two "partial effects". The first term of the sum gives the change in y caused by a change in t and "mediated by x_1"; and the second term is that effect "mediated by x_2". Addition of them yields the "total effect".

Example: Let $y = 2x_1 + 4x_2$; $x_1 = t^2$; $x_2 = 3 \cdot t$.
According to (81) the total derivative is:

$$\frac{dy}{dt} = 2 \cdot 2t + 4 \cdot 3 = 4t + 12.$$

However, there remain some problems important to us which cannot be solved by means of the already powerful Theorem 5. Therefore, we want to proceed a step further and replace the function f of Theorem 5 by a *vector-valued function*:

$$y^1 = f^1(x_1, \ldots, x_n)$$
$$y^2 = f^2(x_1, \ldots, x_n)$$
$$\ldots\ldots\ldots\ldots\ldots$$
$$y^n = f^n(x_1, \ldots, x_n). \tag{83}$$

Definition 6: Let f^i $(i = 1 \ldots n)$ of (83) be elements of C^1. Then, the matrix

$$\text{Jac}(f) := \begin{pmatrix} f_1^1 & f_2^1 & \cdots & f_n^1 \\ f_1^2 & f_2^2 & \cdots & f_n^2 \\ \cdots\cdots\cdots\cdots\cdots \\ f_1^n & f_2^n & \cdots & f_n^n \end{pmatrix}$$

is termed the *Jacobian* matrix of this vector-valued function. It is itself made up of vector-valued functions.

The Jacobian consists simply of all partial derivatives of the functions (83). It is a *square* matrix. The Jacobian can be regarded as a vector of gradients since its i-th row represents the gradient of f^i.

Example: Let $y^1 = 3x_1^2 + 5x_2$; $y^2 = x_1^3 + 1$ be a vector-valued function. Its Jacobian is

$$\text{Jac}(\mathbf{f}) = \begin{pmatrix} 6x_1 & 5 \\ 3x_1^2 & 0 \end{pmatrix}.$$

By means of the Jacobian we can extend Theorem 5 to cover vector-valued functions.

Theorem 6: Let $\mathbf{f}: \mathbb{R}^n \to \mathbb{R}^n$; $\mathbf{y} = \mathbf{f}(\mathbf{x})$ and $\mathbf{g}: \mathbb{R} \to \mathbb{R}^n$; $\mathbf{x} = \mathbf{g}(t)$ be two vector-valued functions with all f^i, $g^i \in C^1$. Then, there is a vector-valued function

$$\mathbf{h}: \mathbb{R} \to \mathbb{R}^n; \quad \mathbf{y} = \mathbf{h}(t); \quad \mathbf{h} \in C^1$$

whose gradient is

$$\frac{d\mathbf{y}}{dt} = \text{Jac}(\mathbf{f}) \cdot \frac{d\mathbf{x}}{dt}. \tag{84}$$

This theorem becomes immediately obvious when the matrix multiplication for the i-th total derivative is carried out:

$$\frac{dy^i}{dt} = \text{grad}(f^i) \cdot \frac{d\mathbf{x}}{dt}. \tag{85}$$

This equation results from the fact that the i-th row of the Jacobian is simply the gradient of f^i. Equation (85) is equivalent to (81) of our Theorem 5. Thus, (84) is virtually a vector of solutions (81). Theorem 6 can easily be extended to the case where $\mathbf{x}$ depends on m variables combined to the vector $\mathbf{t}$; then, we must multiply two Jacobians to obtain $d\mathbf{y}/dt$, the result being a Jacobian.

3.4 Taylor's Theorem

In Section 1, Taylor's theorem turned out to be a very important device for introducing differentials and substantiating the conditions for maxima and minima. The same applies here. Let us commence in a somewhat heuristic manner with a linear function

$$y = f(x_1, x_2) = 2x_1 + 3x_2 + 4. \tag{86}$$

The function's values can be calculated by expanding at point $(0, 0)$, for instance:

$$f(x_1, x_2) = f(0, 0) + f_1(0, 0)x_1 + f_2(0, 0)x_2 \tag{87}$$

This expression corresponds to formula (19) but involves changes in two variables. The partial derivatives are constant here ($f_1 = 2$ and $f_2 = 3$). Hence, calculating $f(1, 5)$ by means of (87) yields the accurate result

$$f(1, 5) = 4 + 2 \cdot 1 + 3 \cdot 5 = 21. \tag{88}$$

An equation such as (87) will produce exact results provided that f is a linear function; in this case, the partial derivatives are constant and indicate the actual rates of change in y. With non-linear functions, on the other hand, the graph of f will generally deviate from the tangent plane (or hyperplane) so that (87) is but an approximation.

Taylor's theorem for functions of several variables is perfectly analogous to that for functions of a single variable. It states the existence of exact solutions for rest terms of arbitrary order, being so complicated, however, that we want to confine ourselves to the formulas with rest terms of the first and second order.

Theorem 7: Let $f: \mathbb{R}^n \to \mathbb{R}$; $y = f(x)$ be a function of C^1. f may be expanded at $a \in \mathbb{R}^n$ with the rest term of the first order, according to

$$f(x) = f(a) + \text{grad}(f(z)) \cdot (x - a), \tag{89}$$

where $z \in [a, x]$.

Equation (87) is merely a special case of this formula when $n = 2$ and $a = (0, 0)$.

To state Taylor's theorem with the rest term of the second order, we must provide some analogue of the second derivative:

Definition 7: Let $f: \mathbb{R}^n \to \mathbb{R}$ be a function of C^2. Then, the matrix

$$\text{Hess}(f) := \begin{pmatrix} f_{11} & f_{12} & \cdots & f_{1n} \\ f_{21} & f_{22} & \cdots & f_{2n} \\ \multicolumn{4}{c}{\cdots\cdots\cdots\cdots\cdots} \\ f_{n1} & f_{n2} & \cdots & f_{nn} \end{pmatrix}$$

is called the *Hessian* matrix of f. Due to the fundamental theorem on partial derivatives, the Hessian is *symmetric*.

Thus, as the gradient comprises the n first derivatives of a function of n variables, the Hessian comprises its second derivatives which are n^2 in number. The reader should not be discouraged by this abundance of novel terms but recognize that the Hessian is only a rectangular format consisting of second partial derivatives. With the aid of the last definition, we can write Taylor's theorem with the rest term of the second order in a very convenient form.

Theorem 8: Let $f: \mathbb{R}^n \to \mathbb{R}$; $y = f(\mathbf{x})$ be a function of C^2. f may be expanded at $\mathbf{a} \in \mathbb{R}^n$ with the rest term of the second order, according to

$$f(\mathbf{x}) = f(\mathbf{a}) + \text{grad}(f(\mathbf{a})) \cdot (\mathbf{x} - \mathbf{a}) + \tfrac{1}{2} \text{Hess}(f(\mathbf{z})) \cdot (\mathbf{x} - \mathbf{a})^2, \qquad (90)$$

where $\mathbf{z} \in [\mathbf{a}, \mathbf{x}]$.

Carrying out the matrix multiplication for the case of two variables

$$
\begin{aligned}
f(x_1, x_2) = {} & f(\mathbf{a}) + f_1(\mathbf{a})(x_1 - a_1) + f_2(\mathbf{a})(x_2 - a_2) + \\
& + \tfrac{1}{2}[f_{11}(\mathbf{z})(x_1 - a_1)^2 + f_{12}(\mathbf{z})(x_1 - a_1)(x_2 - a_2) + \\
& + f_{21}(\mathbf{z})(x_2 - a_2)(x_1 - a_1) + f_{22}(\mathbf{z})(x_2 - a_2)^2].
\end{aligned}
\qquad (91)
$$

and noting that $f_{ij} = f_{ji}$ (according to the fundamental theorem on partial derivatives), we recognize that the rest term of the second order is a binomial.

3.5 Partial Differentials

Let us begin with a function of several variables which is continuously differentiable. Its *partial differential* is an expression

$$\delta f = f_i \cdot dx_i. \qquad (92)$$

written with a lower-case greek delta (δ). The partial differential is a linear approximation of that change in y which results from a change in x_i, all other variables being constant. Hence, the partial differential resembles the "ordinary" differential just as partial derivatives resemble "ordinary" derivatives.

What approximate change in y will a simultaneous change in all x_i produce? Even heuristically it should be clear that this change is given by adding the partial differentials. The resulting sum is called the *total differential*:

$$
\begin{aligned}
& df = f_1\, dx_1 + f_2\, dx_2 + \ldots + f_n\, dx_n \\
& \Leftrightarrow dy = \text{grad}(f) \cdot \mathbf{dx}; \quad \mathbf{dx} := (dx_1, \ldots, dx_n).
\end{aligned}
\qquad (93)
$$

Taylor's formula with the rest term of the second order basically makes the same statement. When neglecting the rest term in (90), we obtain (93) where $dy = f(\mathbf{x}) - f(\mathbf{a}) - \varepsilon$ and $dx_i = x_i - a_i$. In formula (93), the partial derivatives are evaluated at $\mathbf{a}$. Because the rest term in Taylor's formula (90) approaches zero when $\mathbf{x}$ approaches $\mathbf{a}$, the approximation (93) will be better the smaller are the dx_i.

Example: Let $y = f(x_1, x_2) = x_1^2 + 3x_2$.
The function's total differential at $(1, 2)$ is

$$dy = f_1(1, 2) \cdot dx_1 + f_2(1, 2) \cdot dx_2.$$

Computing the partial derivatives gives

$$dy = 2 \cdot dx_1 + 3 \cdot dx_2.$$

Let us suppose $dx_1 = 1$ and $dx_2 = 3$, for instance:

$$dy = 2 \cdot 1 + 3 \cdot 3 = 11.$$

The true change in y is obtained by calculating $f(1, 2)$ and $f(2, 5)$ and then calculating their difference:

$$\Delta y = 19 - 7 = 12.$$

Thus, the approximation error ε amounts to 1.

3.6 Concavity and Convexity

These notions, introduced in Subsection 1.5, can be transferred to functions of several variables. Thus, the Neoclassical production function depending on labor and capital (on p. 37) is obviously strictly concave, that is, curved outward. Referring to functions of more than two variables, however, concavity and convexity are incapable of being represented geometrically since intuition fails when more than three dimensions are involved. Yet, concavity and convexity can be defined as general analytical properties of functions.

Definition 8: A function f: $\mathbb{R} \to \mathbb{R}^n$ is called *strictly concave* in an interval iff for all x, x' (x $\neq$ x') of this interval and all t, $0 < t < 1$, we have

$$f(t\mathbf{x} + (1 - t)\mathbf{x}') > t f(\mathbf{x}) + (1 - t) f(\mathbf{x}'). \tag{94}$$

The function is *concave* iff we replace ">" by "$\geq$"; it is *strictly convex* iff we replace ">" by "<"; and *convex* iff we replace ">" by "$\leq$".

As in Subsection 1.5, we have here a convenient criterion for testing whether a function exhibits one of these properties.

Theorem 9: Let f: $\mathbb{R} \to \mathbb{R}^n$ be twice differentiable in $\mathbf{I} = [\mathbf{a}, \mathbf{b}] \subset R^n$. Then, f is

- strictly concave in $\mathbf{I}$ if Hess $(f(\mathbf{x}))$ is negative definite for all $\mathbf{x} \in \mathbf{I}$;
- strictly convex in $\mathbf{I}$ if Hess $(f(\mathbf{x}))$ is positive definite for all $\mathbf{x} \in \mathbf{I}$;
- concave in $\mathbf{I}$ iff Hess $(f(\mathbf{x}))$ is negative semi-definite for all $\mathbf{x} \in \mathbf{I}$;
- convex in $\mathbf{I}$ iff Hess $(f(\mathbf{x}))$ is positive semi-definite for all $\mathbf{x} \in \mathbf{I}$.

Example: $y = x_1^{0.4} x_2^{0.4}$ is a standard production function of the Cobb-Douglas type with positive, decreasing marginal returns. Is it strictly concave?
The gradient of f is

$$\text{grad}\,(f) = (0.4 x_1^{-0.6}\, x_2^{0.4};\ 0.4 x_1^{0.4} x_2^{-0.6})$$

and the function's Hessian is thus

$$\text{Hess}\,(f) = \begin{pmatrix} -0.24 x_1^{-1.6} x_2^{0.4} & 0.16 x_1^{-0.6} x_2^{-0.6} \\ 0.16 x_1^{-0.6} x_2^{-0.6} & -0.24 x_1^{0.4} x_2^{-1.6} \end{pmatrix}.$$

According to Theorem 9, f will be strictly concave if the Hessian is negative definite. By means of Theorem 4 on definiteness we calculate the leading principal minors:

$$|f_{11}| = -0.24\,x_1^{-1.6}\,x_2^{0.4} < 0$$

$$|\text{Hess}(f)| = 0.032\,x_1^{-1.2}\,x_2^{-1.2} > 0\,.$$

The Hessian is thus negative definite for all strictly positive x_1, x_2. Therefore, the production function is strictly concave in $\mathbb{R}_+^2$.

3.7 Maxima and Minima

Most of the topics discussed up to here have been in preparation for the present subsection; it is optimization of functions of several variables that we are basically interested in. The definition of optima and their classification as local, unique, and regular optima runs as in Subsection 1.6. We need not repeat that here.

Theorem 10: A function $f: \mathbb{R} \to \mathbb{R}^n$; $f \in C^2$; $a \in \mathbb{R}^n$

- assumes a *local maximum* at a iff grad$(f(a)) = 0$ and f is concave in some neighborhood of a;
- assumes a *local minimum* at a iff grad$(f(a)) = 0$ and f is convex in some neighborhood of a.

Corollary 4: Given the prerequisites of Theorem 10,

- the local maximum is unique at least if Hess$(f(a))$ is negative definite;
- the local minimum is unique at least if Hess$(f(a))$ is positive definite.

The first order conditions for a local optimum require that the gradient vanishes at a. Viewed geometrically, this means that all tangent lines are horizontal at this point:

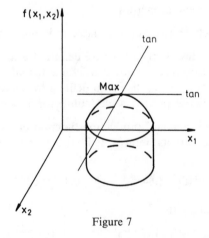

Figure 7

The second order conditions of the corollary appear somewhat far-fetched; but we can illustrate them in a very simple manner. First, observe that the negative definiteness of Hess$(f(a))$ means that the function is strictly concave in some neighborhood of a.

From the figure it follows immediately that this, together with the horizontal tangent lines, implies a local maximum which is locally unique.

To prove the first order conditions, let us take Taylor's formula with the rest term of the first order:

$$f(x) = f(a) + \text{grad}(f(z)) \cdot (x - a). \tag{95}$$

When there is a unique maximum at a we have

$$f(x) < f(a) \tag{96}$$

for all $x \neq a$ of a certain neighborhood of a. Let us assume that some components of $\text{grad}(f(a))$ are positive. Then, x could be chosen such that $\text{grad}(f(z))$ is also positive. This is due to the fact that the gradient consists of n continuous functions, and if at least one partial derivative is positive at a, it must be positive in a neighborhood of a. But then, the scalar product in (95) would be positive for some $x > a$, which contradicts the definition of a local maximum. Hence, $\text{grad}(f(a))$ cannot be positive. Conversely, it cannot be negative because this implies an anologous contradiction. Hence, $\text{grad}(f(a))$ must be 0.

For the proof of the second order conditions, we take Taylor's formula with the rest term of the second order:

$$f(x) = f(a) + \text{grad}(f(a)) \cdot (x - a) + \tfrac{1}{2} \cdot \text{Hess}(f(z)) \cdot (x - a)^2. \tag{97}$$

As just shown, the gradient must vanish at a. Therefore, the formula simplifies to

$$f(x) = f(a) + \tfrac{1}{2} \cdot \text{Hess}(f(z)) \cdot (x - a)^2. \tag{98}$$

In order to meet the definition (96) of a local maximum, the rest term of (98) must be negative. Neglecting the positive factor $1/2$ we can rewrite it as

$$(x - a) \cdot \text{Hess}(f(z)) \cdot (x - a). \tag{99}$$

This expression is a quadratic form! When $\text{Hess}(f(z))$ is negative definite, the quadratic form will assume negative values for all $x \neq a$ thus satisfying the requirement for a local maximum.

If, as supposed in Corollary 4, $\text{Hess}(f(a))$ is negative definite, $\text{Hess}(f(z))$ will also have that property when z comes sufficiently close to a. This is because the second partial derivatives which form the Hessian were assumed to be continuous functions. Hence, the negative definiteness of $\text{Hess}(f(a))$ together with $\text{grad}(f(a)) = 0$ is sufficient for a locally unique maximum. This proves the first half of the corollary. The remaining half, on minima, is simply proven by reversing the signs in the above reasoning.

Example: Has the function $y = f(x_1, x_2) = x_1^2 + 2x_2^2$ local optima?
    First, we calculate the gradient

$$\text{grad}(f) = (2x_1; 4x_2) \stackrel{!}{=} 0.$$

Hence, the first order condition is only met at $(0, 0)$. The Hessian is

$$\text{Hess}(f) = \begin{pmatrix} 2 & 0 \\ 0 & 4 \end{pmatrix}.$$

Using Theorem 4, we recognize that it is positive definite:

$$|f_{11}| = 2 > 0 \quad \text{and} \quad |\text{Hess}(f(\mathbf{0}))| = 8 > 0.$$

According to Corollary 4, f exhibits a unique local minimum at $(0, 0)$. (Try to imagine the function's graph, whose shape is obtained by rotating $y = x^2$ around the ordinate.)

3.8 Maxima and Minima under Constraints

In economics, we often encounter the problem of maximizing a function subject to one or more constraints. In the simplest but most important case, the constraints are equations: then, we can apply the method of Lagrangean multipliers. We must consider this method as a mere technology for finding optima in the case of constraints. The trick is to form an artificial function, the Lagrangean, from the function which is to be optimized and the constraints; and then optimize this Lagrangean along the conventional lines:

Theorem 11: Let $f: \mathbb{R} \to \mathbb{R}^n$; $y = f(\mathbf{x})$; $f \in C^2$ be a function which is to be optimized subject to the m constraints

$$g^i(\mathbf{x}) = 0 \quad \text{where} \quad g: \mathbb{R}^n \to \mathbb{R}; \quad g^i \in C^2 \quad \text{and} \quad i = 1 \ldots m.$$

Assume $m < n$ and the constraints to be linearly independent. The *Lagrangean* function is defined as

$$L(\boldsymbol{\lambda}, \mathbf{x}) = f(\mathbf{x}) + \lambda_1 g^1(\mathbf{x}) + \ldots + \lambda_m g^m(\mathbf{x}), \tag{100}$$

where $\boldsymbol{\lambda} := (\lambda_1, \ldots, \lambda_m)$.

f assumes at $\mathbf{a} \in \mathbb{R}^n$ subject to the constraints

– a regular maximum iff $\text{grad}(L(\bar{\boldsymbol{\lambda}}, \mathbf{a}) = \mathbf{0}$ and $\text{Hess}(L(\bar{\boldsymbol{\lambda}}, \mathbf{a})$ is negative definite;
– a regular minimum iff $\text{grad}(L(\bar{\boldsymbol{\lambda}}, \mathbf{a}) = \mathbf{0}$ and $\text{Hess}(L(\bar{\boldsymbol{\lambda}}, \mathbf{a})$ is positive definite.

Lemma 1: For testing the definiteness of $\text{Hess}(L)$ one is to consider its leading principal minors of order k where k runs from $2m + 1$ to $n + m$. $\text{Hess}(L)$ is

– negative definite iff those principal minors alternate in sign, the minor of order $2m + 1$ having the sign $(-1)^{m+1}$;
– positive definite iff those principal minors all have the sign $(-1)^m$.

Thus, these are the steps for applying the Lagrangean method:

Step 1: Rewrite the given constraints in the form $g^i(\mathbf{x}) = 0$.

Step 2: Add all constraints to the function which is to be optimized, multiplying each constraint by an unknown, λ_i. The outcome is the Lagrangean (100), which depends on n unknowns $\mathbf{x}$ and m unknowns λ_i.

Step 3: Now, the point is that f exhibits an optimum under constraints if the artificial function L satisfies the conventional conditions! This does not imply that L itself assumes an optimum (but, after all, what L does is perfectly uninteresting.) Hence, the gradient of L must be **0** as stated by Theorem 10. Because L is a function of $n + m$ variables, we obtain $n + m$ equations.

Step 4: Let the point $(\bar{\lambda}, \mathbf{a})$ satisfy the first order conditions. Calculate the Hessian of L by differentiating its gradient, and then insert the values $(\bar{\lambda}, \mathbf{a})$. The definiteness of the resulting Hessian evaluated at $(\bar{\lambda}, \mathbf{a})$ indicates whether this point is a regular maximum, a regular minimum, or neither.

Step 5: With a function f of two variables which is to be optimized subject to one constraint, the Hessian would look like this:

$$\text{Hess}(L) = \begin{pmatrix} 0 & g^1 & g^2 \\ g^1 & f_{11} & f_{12} \\ g^2 & f_{21} & f_{22} \end{pmatrix}$$

This is easily seen from differentiating the gradient of L with respect to λ, x_1, and x_2. Testing for definiteness is here *easier* than in the case of unconstrained optimization since according to Lemma 1, not all leading principal minors have to be considered but only $n - m$ of them. In our example, where $n = 2$ and $m = 1$, only one minor, the determinant of the Hessian itself, must be computed. By investigating its sign, the problem is solved.

The conditions for definiteness, given in Lemma 1, differ from the usual ones because the g^i of the Hessian cannot assume arbitrary values but must satisfy the first order conditions. The reader may ascertain, however, that the conditions in Lemma 1 are equivalent to those of Theorem 4 if $m = 0$ (no constraints).

Example: The function $y = f(x_1, x_2) = x_1 \cdot x_2$ is to be optimized subject to $2 \cdot x_1 + 3 \cdot x_2 - 12 = 0$. At first, we form the Lagrangean (100):

$$L(\lambda, x_1, x_2) = x_1 \cdot x_2 + \lambda \cdot (2x_1 + 3x_2 - 12)$$

Calculating the gradient and setting its components equal to zero yields:

$$L_\lambda = 2x_1 + 3x_2 - 12 \overset{!}{=} 0$$
$$L_1 = x_2 + 2\lambda \overset{!}{=} 0$$
$$L_2 = x_1 + 3\lambda \overset{!}{=} 0$$

The derivative with respect to λ is simply the constraint, which holds universally. Eliminating λ from the last two equations yields $x_1 = 3/2 \cdot x_2$. By substituting this into the first equation we obtain the solutions

$$x_1 = 3 \quad \text{and} \quad x_2 = 2.$$

Finally, we have to examine the definiteness of the Hessian. The Hessian is obtained by differentiating the three derivatives above with respect to λ, x_1, and x_2. In this simple example, the Hessian is constant:

$$\text{Hess}(L) = \begin{pmatrix} 0 & 2 & 3 \\ 2 & 0 & 1 \\ 3 & 1 & 0 \end{pmatrix}.$$

Let us apply Lemma 1. We have $2m + 1 = 3$ and $n + m = 3$. Thus, only the leading principal minor of order 3 must be considered. It is the determinant of the Hessian itself:

$$|\text{Hess}(L)| = 12 > 0.$$

Since the sign is that of $(-1)^{m+1}$ the Hessian is negative definite. Therefore, f assumes a regular maximum at point $(3; 2)$ subject to the constraint.

*3.9 Profit Maximization

We want to demonstrate the optimization of functions of several variables by a well-known example from economics. Consider a firm that produces a single commodity using two factors. Its production function reads

$$y = f(\mathbf{x}); \quad \mathbf{x} = (x_1, x_2). \tag{101}$$

This production function attributes a certain quantity of output, y, to any input vector, $\mathbf{x}$. Besides being twice continuously differentiable, the production function exhibits the following properties:

$$f_i > 0; \quad f_{ii} < 0; \quad \lim_{x_i \to 0} f_i \to \infty; \quad i = 1, 2. \tag{102}$$

For the time being, we assume nothing with respect to the cross derivatives. At a given price p, revenue is $p \cdot y$. Total costs amount to $\mathbf{q} \cdot \mathbf{x}$, where $\mathbf{q}$ is the given vector of factor prices. Profits are defined as revenue minus total costs. Substituting the production function for y, we thus obtain:

$$\pi(x_1, x_2) = p f(x_1, x_2) - \mathbf{q}\mathbf{x}. \tag{103}$$

This is a function of two variables. According to Theorem 10, the first order condition for a profit maximum is that the gradient of the profit function vanishes:

$$\frac{\partial \pi}{\partial x_1} = p f_1(x_1, x_2) - q_1 \overset{!}{=} 0 \tag{104}$$

$$\frac{\partial \pi}{\partial x_2} = p f_2(x_1, x_2) - q_2 \overset{!}{=} 0. \tag{105}$$

This amounts to the common rule that a profit maximum requires marginal revenue and marginal costs to coincide for every factor. Put differently, marginal productivity of any factor must match the factor's "shadow price", q_i/p. Yet, these conditions are not sufficient for a profit maximum. According to Theorem 10, the profit function must be concave, its Hessian must be negative semi-definite. The Hessian is easily computed by differentiating the gradient with respect to x_1 and x_2:

$$\text{Hess}(\pi) = \begin{pmatrix} p f_{11} & p f_{12} \\ p f_{21} & p f_{22} \end{pmatrix}. \tag{106}$$

This may be rewritten as

$$\text{Hess}(\pi) = p \begin{pmatrix} f_{11} & f_{12} \\ f_{21} & f_{22} \end{pmatrix}. \tag{107}$$

As Theorem 4 states, this Hessian is negative semi-definite iff

$$f_{11} < 0$$

$$\begin{vmatrix} f_{11} & f_{12} \\ f_{21} & f_{22} \end{vmatrix} = 0. \tag{108}$$

These two equations imply that the *production* function is negative semi-definite. Therefore, the properties of the production function imply the properties of the profit function. A *concave* production function guarantees the existence of a local profit maximum at a point **x** inferred from (104) and (105). But, of course, this profit maximum is not necessarily unique.

If the Hessian of the production function is negative definite, the production function will be *strictly concave* and the profit maximum will be *unique* and *regular*. Beyond that it can be shown that if the Hessian of the production function is negative definite *everywhere*, the profit maximum is *globally unique*. Then, for any given price vector there is just one regular profit maximum.

We could also consider the economic problem of this subsection as one of optimization subject to a constraint. The Lagrangean is formed from the profit function and the constraint, the production function:

$$L(\lambda, \mathbf{x}) = p \cdot y - \mathbf{q}\mathbf{x} + \lambda \cdot (y - f(\mathbf{x})) \tag{109}$$

The reader should work out this problem for himself, applying the above algorithm.

4. Implicit Functions

Comparative static analysis is very important to economic theory. After discussing the theory of implicit functions we will be in a position to deal with the former problem in a truly general manner; and we will be able to show its purely logical relationship to the problem of optimization.

4.1 Explicit and Implicit Functions

Assume that there are real numbers x_1, x_2 which satisfy

$$F(x_1, x_2) = 0. \tag{110}$$

F is an arbitrary *explicit function*. It is termed "explicit" because it has been solved for the "independent" variables x_1 and x_2. Moreover, F has been assumed to be constant, the constant being taken to be zero. Now, consider the following: If $F(x_1, x_2)$ must be zero, its arguments are not really "independent" (which causes many mathematicians to reject this term altogether). Instead, it seems that x_2 is already determined by a certain choice of x_1. Thus, we conjecture the existence of an *implicit function* f:

$$x_2 = f(x_1) \quad \text{such that} \quad F(x_1, f(x_1)) = 0. \tag{111}$$

Two questions arise. First, does such an implicit function actually exist? Second, if it does, what are its properties? These questions may appear trivial since nothing is easier than solving the explicit function

$$F(x_1, x_2) = 4x_1 - 2x_2 = 0 \tag{112}$$

for x_2:

$$x_2 = f(x_1) = 2x_1. \tag{113}$$

In this example, an implicit function (113) does exist, and it can be computed in a very simple manner. Yet, this does not hold universally. Consider

$$F(x_1, x_2) = x_2 \cdot \sin(x_1) - x_1 e^{x_2} = 0. \tag{114}$$

which cannot be solved for x_2 using elementary transformations, though it is possible that an implicit function exists. With $x_1 + 0 \cdot x_2 = 0$, there is certainly no implicit function at all. Therefore, we need

– a criterion ensuring the existence of implicit functions;
– and some method of examining the properties of that implicit function *without* solving explicitly.

These are the problems addressed by the present section.

4.2 Implicit Differentiation with Two Variables

Let us commence with the above function

$$F(x_1, x_2) = 0, \tag{115}$$

which is defined for certain vectors of $\mathbb{R}^2$ and is continously differentiable. In order to arrive at rules concerning the existence and properties of the implicit function, we differentiate (115) with respect to x_1 in accordance with Theorem 5:

$$\frac{\partial F}{\partial x_1} + \frac{\partial F}{\partial x_2} \frac{dx_2}{dx_1} = 0. \tag{116}$$

The left-hand side is differentiated according to the chain rule, whereas the derivative of the right-hand side is obviously zero. The application of the chain rule is due to the fact that we *conjecture* the existence of an implicit function

$$x_2 = f(x_1) \tag{117}$$

and the existence of its derivative

$$\frac{dx_2}{dx_1} = f'(x_1). \tag{118}$$

If these conjectures hold, dx_2/dx_1 is the first derivative of the implicit function. We obtain it by solving (116) for it:

$$\frac{dx_2}{dx_1} = -\frac{\partial F/\partial x_1}{\partial F/\partial x_2}. \tag{119}$$

This procedure is referred to as *implicit differentiation*. The output of formula (119) is the derivative of the implicit function, the input being the derivatives of the explicit function. Hence, we can compute dx_2/dx_1 without knowing the functional equation of the implicit function! Note, however, that this procedure makes sense only if the existence of a differentiable implicit function is already established. This problem will be tackled in the next subsection.

Example: Let $x_1^2 - 6 \cdot x_2 = 0$.
According to (119), we obtain the derivative of the implicit function:

$$\frac{dx_2}{dx_1} = -\frac{2x_1}{-6} = x_1/3.$$

The same result is obtained by computing the implicit function first

$$x_2 = x_1^2/6$$

and then calculating its derivative along the conventional lines.

4.3 Implicit Function Theorem

In this subsection we present a theorem of the utmost importantance which establishes the conditions for the existence of implicit functions and extends the foregoing examples to the case of functions of n variables. Consider a vector-valued function depending on n variables **x** and a parameter t. The distinction between variables and parameters is arbitrary and must be made according to the problem at hand. In economics, **x** are the *endogenous* variables and t is an *exogenous* variable. The vector-valued function is assumed *constant*:

$$\mathbf{F}(\mathbf{x}, t) = \mathbf{0}. \tag{120}$$

The Keynesian model of Chapter V, for instance, exhibits this structure. It consists of n (= 5) equations. By simple subtraction of the right-hand terms, it may be arranged such that there are only zeroes on the right-hand side. It comprises n endogenous variables. And, moreover, there is an exogenous variable, say government demand, whose *impact* on the endogenous variables is to be examined. Expressed mathematically, we look for n implicit functions **x** = **g**(t) or for their properties.

Assuming the existence of such implicit functions, let us differentiate (120) with respect to t, applying Theorem 6:

$$\frac{d\mathbf{F}}{dt} = \mathrm{Jac}_{\mathbf{x}}(\mathbf{F}) \cdot \frac{d\mathbf{x}}{dt} + \frac{\partial \mathbf{F}}{\partial t} = \mathbf{0}. \tag{121}$$

$\mathrm{Jac}_{\mathbf{x}}(\mathbf{F})$ denotes the Jacobian of **F** with respect to the vector **x**. The subscript 'x' is required because **F** also depends on t, its derivative with respect to t being the vector $\partial \mathbf{F}/\partial t$. Equation (121) states that the total change in **F** produced by changes in t consists of two factors: First, **F** varies in accordance with variations in **x**, and **x**, in turn, varies according to variations in t. This is denoted by the Jacobian and the vector $d\mathbf{x}/dt$. Second, changes in t influence **F** directly. This is denoted by the vector $\partial \mathbf{F}/\partial t$. The resulting total change, denoted by $d\mathbf{F}/dt$, is bound to vanish because we assumed **F** to be *constant*.

Casting a further glance at (121), we recognize immediately that it exhibits the structure of *simultaneous linear equations*. The Jacobian is the matrix of coefficients; $d\mathbf{x}/dt$ is the vector of unknowns that we are seeking; and $\partial \mathbf{F}/\partial t$ is a constant vector. These expressions are thus equivalent to **A**, **x**, and − **b** of our equation (57). Subtracting the righthand constant vector and inverting the Jacobian (under the favourable assumption that inversion is possible), we obtain the solutions:

$$\frac{d\mathbf{x}}{dt} = -\mathrm{Jac}_{\mathbf{x}}(\mathbf{F})^{-1} \cdot \frac{\partial \mathbf{F}}{\partial t}. \tag{122}$$

Regarding the Keynesian model, (122) gives us the impact of government expenditures (t) on all endogenous variables (**x**) because **F** and its derivatives are known. The advantage of this method is that solving explicitly for Y or i is not required in order to calculate their derivatives dY/dG and di/dG. Instead, these multipliers may be inferred *directly* from the model.

Up to here, we have confined ourselves to illustration because the *existence* of implicit functions has not yet been established. This, and more, is achieved by the following powerful theorem.

Implicit function theorem:

Let $\mathbf{F}: \mathbb{R}^{n+1} \to \mathbb{R}^n$; $F^i \in C^1$ $(i = 1 \ldots n)$;

$$\mathbf{F}(\mathbf{x}, t) = \mathbf{0} \quad \text{for some } \mathbf{x} \in \mathbb{R}^n; \; t \in \mathbb{R}$$

be a vector-valued function. Let $\text{Jac}_{\mathbf{x}}(\mathbf{F})$ denote the matrix of partial derivatives $\partial F^i / \partial x_j$, and let the determinant of this matrix

$$|\text{Jac}_{\mathbf{x}}(\mathbf{F}(\mathbf{x}_0, t_0))| \neq 0$$

for some point $(\mathbf{x}_0, t_0)$ where $\mathbf{F}(\mathbf{x}_0, t_0) = \mathbf{0}$. Then, there is just one implicit vector-valued function $\mathbf{g}: \mathbb{D} \to \mathbb{W}(\mathbb{D} \subset \mathbb{R}, \mathbb{W} \subset \mathbb{R}^n)$;

$$\mathbf{x} = \mathbf{g}(t) \quad \text{or} \quad x_i = g^i(t) \quad (i = 1 \ldots n)$$

which satisfies $\mathbf{F}(\mathbf{x}, t) = \mathbf{0}$ in a certain neighborhood of $t_0 \in \mathbb{D}$.

The partial derivatives $\partial x_i / \partial t = \partial g^i / \partial t$ do exist in this neighborhood and amount to

$$\frac{d\mathbf{x}}{dt} = -\text{Jac}_{\mathbf{x}}(\mathbf{F})^{-1} \cdot \frac{\partial \mathbf{F}}{\partial t} \tag{123}$$

$$\Leftrightarrow \frac{dx_i}{dt} = -\frac{|\text{Jac}_{\mathbf{x}}^i(\mathbf{F})|}{|\text{Jac}_{\mathbf{x}}(\mathbf{F})|} \quad (i = 1 \ldots n). \tag{124}$$

$\text{Jac}_{\mathbf{x}}^i(\mathbf{F})$ is the matrix that emerges from $\text{Jac}_{\mathbf{x}}(\mathbf{F})$ when the latter's i-th column is replaced by $\partial \mathbf{F}/\partial t$.[1]

If the impact of m different parameters on the n endogenous variables is to be analyzed (for instance: impacts of fiscal *and* monetary policy), the implicit function theorem has to be applied m times. This is not too troublesome since the inverse remains unchanged and only the vector $\partial \mathbf{F}/\partial t$ must be replaced.

The implicit function theorem yields the solution to virtually all problems in comparative statics. This should be shown by some applications.

*4.4 The Slope of Equilibrium Loci

Implicit differentiation with two variables, the most simple case, proves useful when investigating the slope of equilibrium loci. An equilibrium locus was defined as the set of variables $\mathbf{x}$ which establish a market equilibrium. Since equilibrium loci were always used in two-dimensional space, we can apply the rule (119) which is the simplest special case of the implicit function theorem:

$$F(x_1, x_2) = 0 \Rightarrow \frac{dx_2}{dx_1} = -\frac{\partial F / \partial x_1}{\partial F / \partial x_2} \quad \text{iff} \quad \frac{\partial F}{\partial x_2} \neq 0. \tag{125}$$

In order to determine the slope of an equilibrium locus, you must proceed in the following manner:

---

1 According to a deeper theorem due to GALE and NIKAIDÔ, one can infer the *global* existence of implicit (or inverse) functions under more restrictive assumptions. Specifically, it is required that the Jacobian is a P matrix, i.e. that all its principal minors are strictly positive. Cf. GALE, D. and H. NIKAIDÔ (1965) The Jacobian Matrix and Global Univalence of Mappings. Mathematische Annalen **159**, pp. 81–93.

Step 1: Rewrite the market equilibrium condition in the form $F(x_1, x_2) = 0$.

Step 2: Take x_1 and x_2 as those variables which are on the axes of the diagram that represents the equilibrium locus.

Step 3: Differentiate implicitly according to (125).

Slope of the IS curve. The equation of the IS curve reads:

$$S(Y) = I(i) + G. \tag{126}$$

In the first step we rewrite it as

$$S(Y) - I(i) - G = 0. \tag{127}$$

Step 2: On the axes are the variables Y and i.
Step 3: Hence, (127) must be differentiate implicitly with respect to Y and i:

$$\frac{di}{dY}\bigg|_{IS} = -\frac{dS/dY}{-dI/di} = \frac{dS/dY}{dI/di} < 0. \tag{128}$$

Using the general rule (125), we differentiated (127) with respect to Y (obtaining the numerator) and then with respect to i (obtaining the denominator). When the marginal propensity to save is positive and when the interest elasticity of investment is negative, the IS curve exhibits a negative slope. Given an investment trap $(dI/di = 0)$, we may not differentiate implicitly because the denominator in (128) vanishes. A vertical IS curve does not satisfy the mathematical definition of a function. Considering the limit, however, we recognize that the IS curve is steeper the smaller the interest elasticity of investment demand. This is because the fraction (128) increases when dI/di decreases.

Slope of the LM curve. The procedure is quite analogous:

$$L(Y, i) - \frac{M}{P} = 0 \tag{129}$$

$$\frac{di}{dY}\bigg|_{LM} = -\frac{\partial L/\partial Y}{\partial L/\partial i} > 0. \tag{130}$$

We see that the slope of the LM curve becomes smaller the higher is the interest elasticity of liquidity demand. For the liquidity trap we obtain:

$$\frac{di}{dY}\bigg|_{LM} = \lim_{\partial L/\partial i \to -\infty} -\frac{\partial L/\partial Y}{\partial L/\partial i} = 0. \tag{131}$$

Hence, the LM curve becomes horizontal when interest elasticity of liquidity demand increases without bound.

Slope of the Y^d curve. Here, matters are a bit more tricky. In the Keynesian model, we derived the Y^d curve from the IS/LM schema, which constituted the demand sector of the economy. (Recall Figure 38 on p. 99) Mathematically, this means that the relationship between P and Y, the variables of the Y^d/Y^s diagram, is not described by one but by two equations:

$$F^1: \quad S(Y) - I(i) - G = 0 \tag{132}$$

$$F^2: \quad L(Y, i) - \frac{M}{P} = 0. \tag{133}$$

Thus, we are concerned with a *vector-valued* function **F** and must apply the implicit function theorem. But which variables adopt which role in the story?

First, Y is the variable on the abscissa of the Y^d/Y^s diagram and we look for dP/dY, the slope of the aggregate demand curve. Therefore, Y is the parameter t of the implicit function theorem.

Second, equations (132) and (133) determine P and i when Y is given. Hence, P and i correspond to the variables **x**.

After these preliminary considerations, the result is immediately obtained from the rule (124):

$$\frac{dP}{dY} = - \frac{\begin{vmatrix} F_Y^1 & F_i^1 \\ F_Y^2 & F_i^2 \end{vmatrix}}{\begin{vmatrix} F_P^1 & F_i^1 \\ F_P^2 & F_i^2 \end{vmatrix}} = - \frac{\begin{vmatrix} \dfrac{dS}{dY} & -\dfrac{dI}{di} \\ \dfrac{\partial L}{\partial Y} & \dfrac{\partial L}{\partial i} \end{vmatrix}}{\begin{vmatrix} 0 & -\dfrac{dI}{di} \\ \dfrac{M}{P^2} & \dfrac{\partial L}{\partial i} \end{vmatrix}} \tag{134}$$

In the denominator, we encounter the determinant of the Jacobian, which consists of the partial derivatives of (132) and (133) with respect to P and i. Because we are looking for dP/dY (the derivative of the *first* endogenous variable), the *first* column of the Jacobian has been replaced by the partial derivative of **F** with respect to Y. The resulting matrix forms the numerator. Computing the determinants yields:

$$\frac{dP}{dY} = - \frac{dS/dY \cdot \partial L/\partial i + \partial L/\partial Y \cdot dI/di}{M/P^2 \cdot dI/di} < 0. \tag{135}$$

The slope of the aggregate demand curve has thus been inferred from the assumptions concerning the functions S, L, and I. By taking the limits $\partial L/\partial i \to \infty$ and $dI/di \to 0$ it is easily seen from (135) that Y^d becomes vertical when there is a liquidity or an investment trap.

Slope of the notional equilibrium loci. In Chapter XI we discussed the separation of w/P-space into several regions, taking account of both the Classical and the Neokeynesian view. These regions differed from one another in the combination of excess demands that appeared in them. They were separated by the equilibrium loci for the commodity and the labor market, respectively, which were defined as those lines where there is no excess demand. The intersection of the two equilibrium loci was the general equilibrium.

We want to prove first that the notional equilibrium loci, associated with the Classical view, do have the slopes we assigned to them in the text. To that end, we take the equilibrium condition for the commodity and labor market, and differentiate it implicitly with respect to w and P:

$$C = Y: \quad C(\alpha) - Y(\alpha) = 0 \tag{136}$$

$$\left.\frac{dw}{dP}\right|_{C=Y} = -\frac{\overset{(-)}{\partial C/\partial P} - \overset{(+)}{\partial Y/\partial P}}{\underset{(+)}{\partial C/\partial w} - \underset{(-)}{\partial Y/\partial w}} > 0 \tag{137}$$

$$N^d = N^s: \quad N^d(\alpha) - N^s(\alpha) = 0 \tag{138}$$

$$\left.\frac{dw}{dP}\right|_{N^d=N^s} = -\frac{\overset{(+)}{\partial N^d/\partial P} - \overset{(-)}{\partial N^s/\partial P}}{\underset{(-)}{\partial N^d/\partial w} - \underset{(+)}{\partial N^s/\partial w}} > 0. \tag{139}$$

Recall that α comprised P and w, among others. The signs of the partial derivatives were assumed or inferred in the text. We arrive at the result that both equilibrium loci exhibit a positive slope. Why the slope of the equilibrium locus for the commodity market should be greater, however, cannot be established till the next section.

Slope of the effective equilibrium loci. In the Neokeynesian mode, the notional equilibrium loci were replaced by the effective ones. As already indicated, two of the latter have a slope which can be determined uniquely, whereas the slope of the boundary between regions I and K is ambiguous. The effective equilibrium locus of the commodity market, forming the boundary of regions C and K, is defined by the equation

$$CK: \quad \tilde{C}(\alpha, \bar{N}) - Y(\alpha) = 0. \tag{140}$$

In region C, there is excess demand in the commodity market while, in K, there is excess supply. Hence, the effective plans must match at the boundary of these regions. Since the households are rationed in the labor market in both regions C and K, they are rationed on the boundary, too. Thus we must consider their effective commodity demand. Firms are not rationed in the labor market in both regions; therefore, we have to consider their notional commodity supply. Implicit differentiation of (140) yields:

$$\left.\frac{dw}{dP}\right|_{CK} = -\frac{\overset{(-)}{\partial \tilde{C}/\partial P} + \overset{(+)}{\partial \tilde{C}/\partial \bar{N} \cdot \partial N^d/\partial P} - \overset{(+)}{\partial Y/\partial P}}{\underset{(+)}{\partial \tilde{C}/\partial w} + \underset{(-)}{\partial \tilde{C}/\partial \bar{N} \cdot \partial N^d/\partial w} - \underset{(-)}{\partial Y/\partial w}}. \tag{141}$$

In order to calculate the derivative of C with respect to P, the chain rule has to be applied. The ambiguous sign of the numerator may be interpreted in the following way: Increases in P reduce houshold's consumption; this is the first term of the sum, the *direct effect*. But they also produce an increase in labor demand, augment household's income and thus induce households to consume more; this is the second term of the sum, the *indirect effect*. The direct and the indirect effect of prices on consumption work in opposite directions.

Yet, the sign of the numerator is *negative*, which can be shown by some simple transformations:

$$\partial\tilde{C}/\partial P + \partial\tilde{C}/\partial\bar{N} \cdot \partial N^d/\partial P - \partial Y/\partial P$$

$$= \frac{\partial\tilde{C}}{\partial P} + c' \frac{w}{P} \cdot \frac{P}{w} \cdot \frac{\partial Y}{\partial P} - \frac{\partial Y}{\partial P}$$

$$= \frac{\partial\tilde{C}}{\partial P} + (c' - 1)\frac{\partial Y}{\partial P} < 0. \tag{142}$$

In the first step, we made use of the nominal marginal propensity to consume $(\partial P\tilde{C}/\partial w\bar{N})$ and of the fact that $\partial Y/\partial P = w/P \cdot \partial N^d/\partial P$. The latter, in turn, follows from

$$Y = f(N) \tag{143}$$

$$\frac{\partial Y}{\partial P} = f'(N) \cdot \frac{\partial N^d}{\partial P} = \frac{w}{P} \cdot \frac{\partial N^d}{\partial P}. \tag{144}$$

The last equation is due to the fact that, in the firm's notional equilibrium, marginal productivity of labor and the real wage rate are the same. Hence we can infer from (142) that the numerator is negative if the marginal propensity to consume is less than one.

The examination of the denominator is carried out in the same manner and yields the result that the denominator is positive. Therefore, the slope of CK is *positive*.

The reader should try to prove that IC, the boundary of regions C and I, exhibits a positive slope, too. It is defined by the equation

$$\text{IC:} \quad \bar{N}^s(\alpha, \bar{C}) - N^d(\alpha) = 0. \tag{145}$$

Hint: Employ the definition of the nominal marginal propensity to work which was assumed positive and less than one in Chapter XI.

This proves the effective classification of w/P-space we used in Chapter XI.

*4.5 Properties of Demand Functions

This is a typical problem of economic theory: How can we derive demand and supply functions from given preferences or technologies of production? The answer is, generally, not at all, a possible exception being the case of functions which are specified numerically. But this case is less attractive to the theorist who is typically interested in general results.

The theory of implicit functions helps to escape this dilemma. By means of implicit differentiation, we can investigate the *properties* of demand or supply functions without knowing these functions themselves.

Let us demonstrate this using the firm we introduced in Subsection *3.9. For this one-commodity-two-factors firm, we obtained the following first order conditions for a profit maximum:

$$p f_1(x_1, x_2) - q_1 = 0 \tag{146}$$

$$p f_2(x_1, x_2) - q_2 = 0. \tag{147}$$

The subscripts refer to the partial derivatives or marginal productivities. We now ask whether we can derive some information about the firm's behaviour from these equilibrium conditions: "How does the firm respond to an increase in the price of one factor?" Our analysis would be rather fruitless if we were unable to answer such a simple question. Yet, the answer is not very obvious.

We proceed from the following basic consideration: Equations (146) and (147) must hold for *every* given vector $(p, \mathbf{q})$ if the firm maximizes profits instantaneously. In particular, the equilibrium conditions must hold *before* some change in prices and *after* it. Therefore, (146) and (147) are explicit constant functions of x_1 and x_2.

It is possible then that there exist implicit functions of the form $x_i = f^i(p, \mathbf{q})$, and it is these functions we are interested in. Being unable to solve for $\mathbf{x}$ explicitly, the implicit function theorem gives information about the existence and properties of such functions.

To conclude, we are concerned with two simultaneous equations, (146) and (147). They comprise two endogenous variables, x_1 and x_2, and exogenous parameters such as q_1. By applying the implicit function theorem, we immediately obtain the slope of the factor demand functions:

$$\frac{dx_1}{dq_1} = -\frac{\begin{vmatrix} -1 & pf_{12} \\ 0 & pf_{22} \end{vmatrix}}{\begin{vmatrix} pf_{11} & pf_{12} \\ pf_{21} & pf_{22} \end{vmatrix}} = \frac{pf_{22}}{\begin{vmatrix} pf_{11} & pf_{12} \\ pf_{21} & pf_{22} \end{vmatrix}} \tag{148}$$

$$\frac{dx_2}{dq_1} = -\frac{\begin{vmatrix} pf_{11} & -1 \\ pf_{21} & 0 \end{vmatrix}}{\begin{vmatrix} pf_{11} & pf_{12} \\ pf_{21} & pf_{22} \end{vmatrix}} = \frac{-pf_{21}}{\begin{vmatrix} pf_{11} & pf_{12} \\ pf_{21} & pf_{22} \end{vmatrix}}. \tag{149}$$

The denominators are the determinants of the Jacobian of equations (146) and (147). In the numerator corresponding to x_i, the i-th column of this Jacobian is replaced by the derivative of the simultaneous functions with respect to q_1. At first sight it seems impossible to determine the signs of dx_i/dq_1 since these determinants may assume any sign or even vanish. But: *The Jacobians are identical to the Hessian of equation (106)!* From the information that the Hessian is negative definite at a regular profit maximum, we can infer that the determinante of the Jacobian is positive.

This ensures the existence of factor demand functions in a neighborhood of the profit maximum because the determinant of the Jacobian does not vanish. Moreover, it is easy to determine the derivatives of the implicit functions. If the denominator in (148) is positive and the second derivative of the production function (f_{22}) is negative (which implies decreasing marginal productivity), the derivative dx_1/dq_2 is certainly negative. Hence, the firm will reduce its demand for factor x_1 when the price of this factor increases.

But how will the demand for the other factor respond to such a change? Two factors are called *substitutes* iff their cross price elasticity is positive; they are called *complements* iff their cross price elasticity is negative. From (149) we infer that the two factors are substitutes iff the cross derivative of the production function (f_{12}) is negative; and they are complements iff this cross derivative is positive.

Let us interpret the two factors as labor and capital. From (149) we learn that investment demand is independent of the real wage rate, and labor demand is independent of interest, iff the cross derivative of the production function vanishes, that is, $f_{12} = 0$. In § 19 we made just this assumption. It served to simplify the exposition because, if $f_{12} \neq 0$, we would not have been able to draw a labor demand curve independently of the prevailing interest rate. Note, however, that the cross derivatives are very likely to be positive in reality since an increase in capital equipment is likely to increase the marginal productivity of labor and vice versa. Therefore, in reality, factors of production are probably *complements*: An increase in interest will diminish labor demand, and an increase in the real wage rate will diminish investment demand. Note also that a Neoclassical production function whose cross derivatives vanish is *strictly concave*. In Chapter IV, we could thus confine our discussion to the first order conditions since every critical point is a unique maximum.

To summarize: The implicit function theorem yields the properties of demand or supply functions without knowing these functions themselves. We obtain information about these properties when employing the information implied by the conditions for an optimum. The equivalence of the Jacobian in (148) and the Hessian in (106) indicates the intimate logical relationship between comparative statics on the one hand and optimization on the other.

*4.6 Fiscal Policy in the Keynesian Model

Finally we want to show how the implicit function theorem may be used for analyzing economic policy. Fiscal policy in the Keynesian model is taken as an example.

Let us commence with the most simple case: that of fiscal measures when prices are given. The IS/LM model is:

$$S(Y) - I(i) - G = 0 \tag{150}$$

$$L(Y, i) - \frac{M}{P} = 0 . \tag{151}$$

Here we have a model with two simultaneous functions, two endogenous variables, Y and i, and one exogenous parameter, G. Real money supply is taken as constant. The implicit function theorem – equation (124) – yields the multipliers dY/dG and di/dG whose signs indicate the impact of government expenditures on real income and interest:

$$\frac{dY}{dG} = - \frac{\begin{vmatrix} -1 & -I_i \\ 0 & L_i \end{vmatrix}}{\begin{vmatrix} S_Y & -I_i \\ L_Y & L_i \end{vmatrix}} = \frac{L_i}{S_Y L_i + I_i L_Y} > 0 \tag{152}$$

$$\frac{di}{dG} = - \frac{\begin{vmatrix} S_Y & -1 \\ L_Y & 0 \end{vmatrix}}{\begin{vmatrix} S_Y & -I_i \\ L_Y & L_i \end{vmatrix}} = \frac{-L_Y}{S_Y L_i + I_i L_Y} > 0 . \tag{153}$$

The subscripts represent the partial derivatives. The denominators are the determinants of the Jacobian of the IS/LM model; and in the numerators we encounter matrices which emerge from eliminating the i-th column in the Jacobian and replacing it by the vector $(-1; 0)$. This vector comprises the partial derivatives of (150) and (151) with respect to the parameter G. The signs in (152) and (153) show that government expenditures will increase both real income and the rate of interest when prices are given and there is underemployment at the outset.

Beyond this well-known result we can infer: If money demand is perfectly interest inelastic ($\partial L/\partial i = 0$), as in the Classical model, real income will remain unchanged. With an investment trap ($dI/di = 0$) or liquidity trap ($\partial L/\partial i \to -\infty$), (152) will assume the form of the elementary multiplier, $1/S_Y$. In the latter case, the impact on interest is zero as shown by equation (153).

Now we move on to the more ambitious case of *flexible prices*. As we had to learn in Chapter VI, the graphical derivation of the impacts is awkward here since there are counterveiling effects; and the net result is not intuitively obvious. All the more rewarding is an analytical treatment of the problem which will yield unique results. First, we reproduce the Keynesian system with sticky wages from p. 110, simply rearranging terms and setting $w = \bar{w}$.

$$N^d\left(\frac{\bar{w}}{P}\right) - N = 0 \tag{154}$$

$$Y - f(N) = 0 \tag{155}$$

$$S(Y) - I(i) - G = 0 \tag{156}$$

$$L(Y, i) - \frac{M}{P} = 0. \tag{157}$$

These simultaneous functions comprise the four endogenous variables Y, N, i, and P. Labor supply is insignificant here since the workers are rationed and employment is solely determined by labor demand. Government demand, G, is the exogenous parameter. The responses of the four endogenous variables to changes in G are obtained by applying the implicit function theorem. First, we want to define

$$X := \frac{\partial N^d}{\partial(\bar{w}/P)} \cdot \left(-\frac{\bar{w}}{P^2}\right) > 0 \tag{158}$$

to have a short-hand for this expression. The first multiplier will be written in detail whereas the others should be computed by the reader:

$$\frac{dY}{dG} = -\frac{\begin{vmatrix} 0 & -1 & 0 & X \\ 0 & -f_N & 0 & 0 \\ -1 & 0 & -I_i & 0 \\ 0 & 0 & L_i & \dfrac{M}{P^2} \end{vmatrix}}{\begin{vmatrix} 0 & -1 & 0 & X \\ 1 & -f_N & 0 & 0 \\ S_Y & 0 & -I_i & 0 \\ L_Y & 0 & L_i & \dfrac{M}{P^2} \end{vmatrix}} = -\frac{L_i \cdot f_N \cdot X}{|Jac|} > 0 \tag{159}$$

$$\frac{dN}{dG} = -\frac{L_i \cdot X}{|Jac|} > 0 \tag{160}$$

$$\frac{di}{dG} = \frac{\dfrac{M}{P^2} + L_Y \cdot f_N \cdot X}{|Jac|} > 0 \tag{161}$$

$$\frac{dP}{dG} = -\frac{L_i}{|Jac|} > 0 \tag{162}$$

$$\frac{d\left(\dfrac{\bar{w}}{P}\right)}{dG} = \frac{d\left(\dfrac{\bar{w}}{P}\right)}{dP} \cdot \frac{dP}{dG} = \frac{(\bar{w}/P^2) \cdot L_i}{|Jac|} < 0 \tag{163}$$

where $|Jac| = -I_i \cdot \dfrac{M}{P^2} - X \cdot f_N \cdot (S_Y \cdot L_i + I_i \cdot L_Y) > 0.$ \tag{164}

In order to compute the i-th multiplier, one must eliminate the i-th column of the Jacobian (the matrix in the denominator of (159)) and replace it by the vector (0; 0; 1; 0) which consists of the partial derivatives of the simultaneous functions with respect to G.

The signs of all the multipliers are uniquely determined. Due to an expansionary fiscal policy, real income and employment will rise and prices will rise, too. The real wage rate, however, will decline. The signs of the multipliers prove that the initial expansionary effect on real income is not offset by the increase in prices and interest. Geometry and the verbal explanations did not tell us that.

5. Ordinary Differential Equations

While the previous section was devoted to comparative statics, this one is concerned with dynamics. We deal chiefly with stability problems and show the close relationship between comparative static and dynamic properties of economic systems.

5.1 Function Equations and Functional Equations

It is likely that many readers have been confronted in their mathematical courses with function equations only, and are not familiar with functional equations. To bring out the difference, we define a *function equation* as an equation of the following type:

$$F(x_1, \ldots, x_n) = 0. \tag{165}$$

A certain function F is given, and we look for those variables **x** which satisfy (165). These variables are called solutions of the function equation.

Example: $x^2 - 2 = 0$ is a function equation with the solutions

$$x_1 = \sqrt{2} \quad \text{and} \quad x_2 = -\sqrt{2}.$$

On the contrary, a *functional equation* is defined thus:

$$F(f^1(x), \ldots, f^n(x)) = 0. \tag{166}$$

Again, a certain function F is given; but here we do not look for numerical values, but for *functions* f which satisfy (166) for *all* admissible x. Such functions are the solutions of a functional equation.

Example: $f^1(x) - (f^2(x))^2 = 0$ is a functional equation with the unknown functions f^1 and f^2. One solution for $x \in \mathbb{R}$ is

$$f^1(x) = x^2 \quad \text{and} \quad f^2(x) = x$$

since these functions satisfy the equation for all real x.

Differential equations form an important subset of the set of functional equations. We define an *ordinary n-th order differential equation* as

$$F(x, f(x), f'(x), \ldots, f^{(n)}(x)) = 0. \tag{167}$$

Equation (167) is called a *differential* equation since it involves, besides x and the unknown function f, the derivatives of that function. The differential equation is termed *ordinary* because f is a function of a single variable. (Differential equations involving functions of several variables are referred to as partial differential equations.) Finally, we speak of an *n-th order* differential equation since the highest derivative of f is of order n. Consider an ordinary first order differential equation:

$$F(x, f(x), f'(x)) = 0. \qquad (168)$$

Example: $f(x) - f'(x) = 0$ is an ordinary first order differential equation. A solution for $x \in \mathbb{R}$ is

$$f(x) = e^x \quad (\text{thus } f'(x) = e^x).$$

Since the derivative of f is f itself, the exponential function satisfies $f(x) - f'(x) = 0$ for all real x.

There is no universal method for solving ordinary first order differential equations; only certain types of them are capable of being solved according to general rules.

5.2 Solution of a Linear Differential Equation

The type important to us is the *ordinary linear n-th order differential equation with constant coefficients*, which we will refer to as a "linear differential equation" for convenience:

$$y'(x) = k\,y(x) + c \quad \text{where} \quad c, k, x, y \in \mathbb{R}; \quad k \neq 0. \qquad (169)$$

We are interested in whether a function y(x) exists which satisfies (169) for all real x. The answer to this question is in the affirmative:

Theorem 12: Assume a linear differential equation (169). There is a set of solutions which is given completely by

$$y(x) = a \cdot e^{kx} - \frac{c}{k}; \quad a \in \mathbb{R} \qquad (170)$$

Let us take the completeness of this set of solutions for granted and test whether it is correct. Differentiating the solution (170) with respect to x yields:

$$y'(x) = a \cdot k \cdot e^{kx}. \qquad (171)$$

The exponential term was differentiated in accordance with the chain rule; and the constant $-c/k$ dropped out. To ensure the correctness of the theorem, we substitute the solution (170) and its derivative (171) into the differential equation (169):

$$a \cdot k \cdot e^{kx} = k \cdot \left[a \cdot e^{kx} - \frac{c}{k} \right] + c. \qquad (172)$$

Obviously, (172) is satisfied by any real x; hence, the theorem gives the correct solution. Yet, it yields no *unique* solution because the constant a may be chosen arbitrarily. By (170) we obtain a *family* of functions. The solution $a = 0$ is called *trivial*, all other solutions are *non-trivial*. Hence, the trivial solution is simply the function $y(x) = -c/k$.

It is quite clear that the solution becomes *uniquely* determined if we require it to cross a given point. By means of this point, called the *initial value*, one function of the family is selected. The task of solving a differential equation subject to an initial condition is called the *initial value problem*.

Theorem 13: Consider an initial value problem with the linear differential equation

$$y'(x) = k\,y(x) + c \quad \text{where} \quad c, k, x, y \in \mathbb{R}; \quad k \neq 0 \tag{173}$$

and the initial value

$$y_0 = y(x_0). \tag{174}$$

Then, there is just one solution:

$$y(x) = \left(y_0 + \frac{c}{k}\right)e^{k(x-x_0)} - \frac{c}{k}. \tag{175}$$

The reader may check by differentiation that the solution satisfies the differential equation. With $x = x_0$, the exponential term of the solution assumes the value one and $y(x_0) = y_0$. Thus (175) satisfies the initial condition.

Example: Let

$$y'(x) = 2\,y(x) + 4$$

be a differential equation and

$$y(0) = 1.$$

an initial condition. From Theorem (13), we obtain the unique solution:

$$y(x) = 3\,e^{2x} - 2.$$

Differentiating the solution and setting $x = 0$ proves that it satisfies both the differential equation and the initial condition.

*5.3 Stability of a Market

A market equilibrium is *stable* iff the prevailing price will approach the equilibrium price in course of time. The market equilibrium is *(asymptotically) locally stable* if this holds only for small deviations from the equilibrium price. Testing a market for stability presupposes the existence of a market equilibrium but not its uniqueness. Using the results of the previous subsection we can investigate market stability. To that end we define an *excess demand function* which gives the difference in demand and supply for every price:

$$E(p) := D(p) - S(p). \tag{176}$$

Excess demand is supposed to exhibit the normal reaction, that is, E' is negative. While comparative statics gives changes in the equilibrium position due to shifts of the demand and supply curves, dynamics help to investigate those adjustment processes that arise when the market is *not* in equilibrium. We assume the "law of the market":

$$p'(t) = H(E(p(t))) \quad \text{where} \quad H(0) = 0; \quad H' > 0. \tag{177}$$

The "law of the market" requires that prices rise due to positive excess demand, and decline due to negative excess demand. If supply and demand match, i.e. if excess demand is zero, there is no price change. Since p' (t) is the rate of price change, the above function H gives the "price adjustment velocity". An *equilibrium price* is defined by

$$H(E(p^*)) = 0. \tag{178}$$

because prices were assumed not to change in equilibrium. Equation (177) is basically an ordinary first order differential equation: The functions H and E are given, and we look for some function p(t) which satisfies (177) for all t. But since nothing specific is known about the functions H and E, we cannot solve (177) directly because, as remarked in the previous subsection, there is no universal method for solving ordinary differential equations.

The following trick proves helpful. If (177) were a *linear* differential equation with constant coefficients, we could solve it according to Theorem 12 without difficulty. Therefore, we *linearize* the right-hand side of (177) by a Taylor-expansion with the rest term of the second order. Expanding at the equilibrium point p* and neglecting the rest term yields:

$$H(E(p)) \doteq H(E(p^*)) + H' \cdot E' \cdot (p - p^*). \tag{179}$$

We differentiated in accordance with the chain rule: first H with respect to E, and then E with respect to p. The derivatives H' and E' are evaluated at points E(p*) and p*, respectively. Owing to the neglect of the rest term, (179) is only an approximation and its application is confined to testing for local stability.

According to definition (178), the first term of the sum in (179) is zero, and (179) simplifies to

$$H(E(p)) \doteq H' \cdot E' \cdot (p - p^*). \tag{180}$$

In the following, we neglect the symbol for approximation ($\doteq$). The economic meaning of (180) is clear. Price will change faster the more it deviates from its equilibrium value. Given a positive deviation it declines, and vice versa. In order to simplify notation we define

$$k := H' \cdot E'. \tag{181}$$

Thus the differential equation may be rewritten as

$$p'(t) = k \cdot (p(t) - p^*). \tag{182}$$

This is a linear differential equation like (173). p(t) is the unknown function y(x), and $- k \cdot p^*$ corresponds to the constant c. Assuming an arbitrary price to prevail at time zero

$$p_0 = p(0) \tag{183}$$

we obtain an initial value problem which is easily solved by means of Theorem 13:

$$p(t) = (p_0 - p^*) \cdot e^{kt} + p^*. \tag{184}$$

The reader should ascertain that the solution (184) satisfies both the differential equation (182) and the initial condition (183). The solution describes the dynamic market behaviour in a neighborhood of the equilibrium. The market equilibrium is stable if

$$\lim_{t \to \infty} p(t) = p^*, \tag{185}$$

that is, if price p (t) converges towards the equilibrium value p*. Consider equation (184) to discover which condition is sufficient for stability. Obviously, the convergence of function (184) depends on the *sign of k*: If k is negative, the exponential term approaches zero for $t \to \infty$, and p (t) will thus approach p*. If k is positive, the exponential term grows without bound, and the equilibrium is unstable. The following figure depicts price adjustment in the stable case:

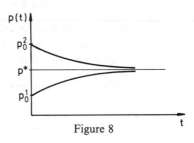

Figure 8

k being negative, p (t) will converge towards p*. Three cases should be distinguished:

- With $p_0 > p^*$, the coefficient $(p_0 - p^*)$ of the exponential term of (184) is positive. For $t \to \infty$, this term declines because of $k < 0$, and so does p (t). p* is reached in the end.
- With $p_0 < p^*$ the reverse is true. The negative exponential term will increase in course of time until in the end p* is reached.
- With $p_0 = p^*$, finally, the coefficient of the exponential term is zero. Hence, according to (184), $p (t) = p^*$. This meets the economic postulate that prices will not change in equilibrium.

Given a tatônnement, a market equilibrium is locally stable iff excess demand declines when the price rises. This is true iff, in equilibrium, the slope of the demand curve is smaller in value than that of the supply curve.

5.4 Solution of Simultaneous Linear Differential Equations

The result of the foregoing section was quite plausible and hardly astonishing since it was intuitively reasonable. In the case of many interdependent markets, however, intuition fails so that marginal returns to mathematical analysis are much greater. But first we have to become familiar with the solution of simultaneous linear differential equations. We begin with the following observation.

Lemma 2: The stability of the initial value problem (173), (174) is independent of the constant c.

The mathematical proof follows immediately from solution (175) of the initial value problem. The convergence of solutions for $t \to \infty$ depends solely on the sign of the exponent and not on c. Consequently, local stability in the previous example is independent of the initial value. The magnitudes p_0 and p* influence the "sooner or later" of the adjustment process; but they are of no importance to the question of whether the equilibrium is attained at all.

Supposing that Lemma 2 also holds for simultaneous equations, we can confine the subsequent analysis to the case of *homogeneous* equations where the constant c vanishes.

The vector-valued function

$$\mathbf{y}'(x) = \mathbf{K} \cdot \mathbf{y}(x) \quad \text{where} \quad \mathbf{y}: \mathbb{R} \to \mathbb{C}^n, \ \mathbf{K} \in \mathbb{R}^n \times \mathbb{R}^n; \quad \mathbf{K} \neq \mathbf{0} \qquad (186)$$

represents simultaneous homogeneous linear first order differential equations with constant coefficients. For short, we will speak of simultaneous linear differential equations. Multiplying out in (186) yields the equivalent representation

$$y^{1\prime}(x) = k_{11} y^1(x) + \ldots + k_{1n} y^n(x)$$
$$\ldots\ldots\ldots\ldots\ldots\ldots\ldots\ldots\ldots\ldots\ldots\ldots \qquad (187)$$
$$y^{n\prime}(x) = k_{n1} y^1(x) + \ldots + k_{nn} y^n(x).$$

Thus we have n simultaneous equations with n unknown functions and must look for a solution $\mathbf{y}(x)$ which satisfies (186) for all admissable x. This is clearly a complicated problem: all unknown functions have to be determined simultaneously since the derivative of each must assume a certain relationship to the other functions. Analogously to Theorem 12 (where c = 0) we try a solution

$$\mathbf{y}(x) = \mathbf{a} \cdot e^{\lambda x} \quad \text{where} \quad \mathbf{a} \in \mathbb{C}^n, \ \lambda \in \mathbb{C}, \qquad (188)$$

where $\mathbb{C}$ is the set of complex numbers discussed in Subsection 2.4. The derivatives of these alleged solutions are computed according to the chain rule as

$$\mathbf{y}'(x) = \lambda \cdot \mathbf{a} \cdot e^{\lambda x}. \qquad (189)$$

If our conjecture is valid, (188) and (189) must satisfy the differential equation (186), that is

$$\lambda \cdot \mathbf{a} \cdot e^{\lambda x} = \mathbf{K} \cdot \mathbf{a} \cdot e^{\lambda x}. \qquad (190)$$

Therefore, the solutions are found if numbers λ and vectors $\mathbf{a}$ can be determined which satisfy (190). Eliminating the exponential terms and multiplying by the identity matrix yields:

$$\mathbf{E} \cdot \lambda \cdot \mathbf{a} = \mathbf{K} \cdot \mathbf{a} \qquad (191)$$

$$\Leftrightarrow \quad (\mathbf{K} - \mathbf{E}\lambda)\mathbf{a} = \mathbf{0}. \qquad (192)$$

Equation (192) is the well-known *characteristic value problem* we became familiar with in Subsection 2.4 and equation (72). The characteristic value problem certainly has the trivial solution $\mathbf{a} = \mathbf{0}$ whereas non-trivial solutions emerge, as we know, from equalizing the determinant of $(\mathbf{K} - \mathbf{E}\lambda)$ to zero:

$$|\mathbf{K} - \mathbf{E}\lambda| = 0. \qquad (193)$$

(193) is the characteristic equation of matrix $\mathbf{K}$. It is a polynomial of degree n of λ:

$$b_0 \lambda^n + b_1 \lambda^{n-1} + \ldots + b_{n-1} \lambda + b_n = 0. \qquad (194)$$

This polynomial is obtained by computing the determinant in (193). Its coefficients consist of combinations of the elements of $\mathbf{K}$. By solving (194), we obtain the required characteristic values and can then find the sets of associated characteristic vectors. If these are called λ_i and $\mathbf{a}_i$, the *solution* of our differential equations (187) is given as:

$$\mathbf{y}(x) = \mathbf{a_1} e^{\lambda_1 x} + \ldots + \mathbf{a_n} e^{\lambda_n x}. \tag{195}$$

It is represented by a linear combination of the $n\,\lambda_i$ and $\mathbf{a}_i$. Some remarks are called for. First, there are of course very many solutions: We know that an infinite set of linearly dependent vectors is associated with every characteristic value. Therefore, the $\mathbf{a}_i$ in (195) are determined up to an arbitrary factor. This is simply analogous to the unknown constant in Theorem 12, which could be determined only if an initial condition was added. Here, the same applies: Provision of the n initial conditions makes the solutions unique.

Second, we have to emphasize that, while an n-degree equation such as (194) has n solutions, these are bound neither to be different, nor real. But it can be shown that complex characteristic values always occur pairwise, and these couples can be combined to real solutions.

Theorem 14: Assume simultaneous homogeneous linear differential equations with constant coefficients

$$\mathbf{y}'(x) = \mathbf{K} \cdot \mathbf{y}(x) \tag{196}$$

where $\mathbf{y}: \mathbb{R} \to \mathbb{C}^n$, $\mathbf{K} \in \mathbb{R}^n \times \mathbb{R}^n$ and $\mathbf{K} \neq \mathbf{0}$.

Then, there are solutions

$$\mathbf{y}(x) = \mathbf{a_1} e^{\lambda_1 x} + \ldots + \mathbf{a_n} e^{\lambda_n x} \tag{197}$$

The λ_i and $\mathbf{a}_i$ are the charateristic values and characteric vectors of the matrix $\mathbf{K}$. They are either real or complex; but the solution (197) is always capable of being represented in real form.

Example: Consider the simultanous differential equations

$$y^{1\prime}(x) = -3\,y^1(x) + 2\,y^2(x)$$
$$y^{2\prime}(x) = -4\,y^1(x) + y^2(x).$$

According to Theorem 14, we compute the characteristic values from the characteristic equation

$$\begin{vmatrix} -3-\lambda & 2 \\ -4 & 1-\lambda \end{vmatrix} = 0 \Leftrightarrow \lambda^2 + 2\lambda + 5 = 0.$$

This yields the two complex solutions

$$\lambda_1 = -1 + 2i \quad \text{and} \quad \lambda_2 = -1 - 2i.$$

Substituting these into the equation $(\mathbf{K} - \mathbf{E}\lambda)\,\mathbf{a} = \mathbf{0}$ we find the associated sets of characteristic values

$$\mathbf{a_1} = (1;1+i) \quad \text{and} \quad \mathbf{a_2} = (1;1-i).$$

According to (197), the solutions are thus:

$$y^1(x) = e^{(-1+2i)x} + e^{(-1-2i)x}$$
$$y^2(x) = (1+i)\,e^{(-1+2i)x} + (1-i)\,e^{(-1-2i)x}.$$

It is easy to prove that these two functions satisfy the above differential equations.

In considering this example the reader may wonder how complex solutions can be interpreted economically. Therefore, we supply a lemma without further discussion according to which complex solutions can be transformed to real solutions.

Lemma 3: Let $a_i\, e^{\lambda_i x}$ be a complex term of the sum (197). Then, there is another (conjugate-complex) term of the sum, and these couple can be transformed into the real terms

$$e^{ax}\,(\mathbf{r} \cdot \cos{(bx)} - \mathbf{s} \cdot \sin{(bx)}) \qquad (198)$$

$$\text{and} \quad e^{ax}\,(\mathbf{r} \cdot \sin{(bx)} + \mathbf{s} \cdot \cos{(bx)}). \qquad (199)$$

Here, a and b are the real and the imaginary part of the characteristic value $\lambda_i = a + b \cdot i$; and $\mathbf{r}$ and $\mathbf{s}$ represent the real and the imaginary part of the associated characteristic vector $\mathbf{a}_i = \mathbf{r} + \mathbf{s} \cdot i$.

Applying this lemma, we may transform the above complex solutions into:

$$y^1\,(x) = e^{-x} \cdot (\sin{(2x)} + \cos{(2x)}) \qquad (200)$$

$$y^2\,(x) = e^{-x}2 \cdot \cos{(2x)}. \qquad (201)$$

These real solutions represent *damped harmonic oscillations* The trigonometric terms cause oscillations with an amplitude not greater than one whereas the exponents exhibit negative signs and force a decline of the whole expression. For $x \to \infty$, the solutions converge towards zero:

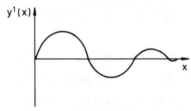

Figure 9

From this, we can already infer a conclusion important to economic theory. The characteristic values may be real or complex: in all cases, the convergence is determined by the *real* parts of the solutions. With real characteristic values, this is quite obvious from (197). Negative characteristic values guarantee the convergence towards zero. Complex characteristic values, however, may be transformed to real ones by means of Lemma 3. It is also clear that the convergence of solutions (198) and (199) is solely determined by the a, the real part of the characteristic values. The imaginary parts, however, determine whether the solution will converge *monotonically* (Fig. 8) or *harmonically* (Fig.9). If the imaginary parts vanish, the convergence will be monotonic, otherwise it will be harmonic.

The solution of homogeneous simultaneous differential equations is called *stable* iff it converges towards the null vector for $x \to \infty$. Thus, the above considerations may be summarized by the

Stability theorem: The solutions of the homogeneous simultaneous differential equations are stable iff the real parts of the characteristic values of $\mathbf{K}$ are all strictly negative.

In order to test the real parts of the characteristic vectors, however, these vectors must first be found. This is often a very difficult task because n zeros of the polynomial (194) have to be computed, and the coefficients of this polynomial are not given, but must be computed from the coefficients of the matrix $\mathbf{K}$. Therefore, some criteria have been developed which serve to determine the signs of the real parts without having to calculate the characteristic values. Two of these criteria are given below.

Lemma 4: Let the assumptions of Theorem 14 be satisfied, and let $\mathbf{K}$ be a 2×2 matrix. The real parts of the characteristic values of $\mathbf{K}$ are all strictly negative iff

$$\mathrm{Tr}\,(\mathbf{K}) < 0 \quad \text{and} \quad |\mathbf{K}| > 0. \tag{202}$$

Lemma 5 (ROUTH-HURWITZ): Assume the characteristic equation of the $n \times n$ matrix $\mathbf{K}$:

$$b_0 \lambda^n + b_1 \lambda^{n-1} + \ldots + b_{n-1} \lambda + b_n = 0.$$

From the coefficients b_i, form a matrix $\mathbf{B}$ with the following properties: Its first row contains all b_i with an odd index; every subsequent row emerges from diminishing the indices by one; and zeros are put instead of b_i's with a negative index:

$$\mathbf{B} = \begin{pmatrix} b_1 & b_3 & b_5 & b_7 & b_9 & \ldots \\ b_0 & b_2 & b_4 & b_6 & b_8 & \ldots \\ 0 & b_1 & b_3 & b_5 & b_7 & \ldots \\ 0 & b_0 & b_2 & b_4 & b_6 & \ldots \\ 0 & 0 & b_1 & b_3 & b_5 & \ldots \\ & & & \ldots & & \end{pmatrix}$$

$\mathbf{B}$ is square. The real parts of all characteristic values of $\mathbf{K}$ are strictly negative iff all leading principal minors of $\mathbf{B}$ up to order n and all b_i $(i = 1 \ldots n)$ are strictly positive.

Up to here, we have confined our considerations to stability of *linear* differential equations. This seems to limit the power of our theorems but, in fact, their realm is easily extended to non-linear systems:

Theorem 15: Let $\mathbf{y}'(x) = \mathbf{F}(\mathbf{y}(x))$ where $\mathbf{y}: \mathbb{R} \to \mathbb{C}^n$; $\mathbf{F}: \mathbb{C}^n \to \mathbb{C}^n$; $\mathbf{F} \in C^1$; $x \in \mathbb{R}$ represent simultaneous ordinary first order differential equations. $\mathbf{y_0}$ may be an equilibrium, that is $\mathbf{F}(\mathbf{y_0}) = \mathbf{0}$. This equilibrium is locally asymptotically stable if the real parts of the characteristic values of the Jacobian $\mathrm{Jac}\,(\mathbf{F}(\mathbf{y_0}))$ are all strictly negative.

This theorem may be made plausible in the following manner. We can linearize the above vector-valued function $\mathbf{F}$ by means of a Taylor-expansion with the rest term of the second order. Neglecting the rest term, we obtain a linear differential equation like (186), its matrix $\mathbf{K}$ being the Jacobian $\mathrm{Jac}\,(\mathbf{F}(\mathbf{y_0}))$. The neglect of the rest term is legitimate when investigating *local* stability because, in a small neighborhood of the equilibrium, the deviations $(\mathbf{x} - \mathbf{a})^2$ of the second order are small compared to the deviations $(\mathbf{x} - \mathbf{a})$ of the first order. Thus, the term of the first order governs the stability properties in a sufficiently small neighborhood of the equilibrium.

Observe, however, that the stability of the linearized system is only *sufficient* for the stability of the original system but not necessary: If the linearized terms vanish (and the system thus seems to be neither stable nor unstable), the terms of higher orders determine the stability properties.

*5.5 Stability of the IS/LM Model

We pass to some economic applications of stability analysis, starting with the stability of the IS/LM model with given prices:

$$I(i) - S(Y) = 0 \tag{203}$$

$$L(Y, i) - \frac{M}{P} = 0. \tag{204}$$

Government demand has been omitted since it do not alter the dynamic behavior of the model. The model may have a solution (Y^*, i^*) of the simultaneous equations which is depicted graphically as the point of intersection of the two curves. The essence of the "Keynesian logic" consists of the following two adjustment processes:

$$Y'(t) = H_1[I(i) - S(Y)] \quad \text{where} \quad H_1(0) = 0; \quad H_1' > 0 \tag{205}$$

$$i'(t) = H_2\left[L(Y, i) - \frac{M}{P}\right] \quad \text{where} \quad H_2(0) = 0; \quad H_2' > 0. \tag{206}$$

Real income will rise when investment demand exceeds savings and vice versa. With $I = S$, real income remains unchanged. Interest will rise due to an excess demand in the money market (accompanied by an excess supply in the bonds market) and vice versa. When supply matches demand in these two markets, interest will remain unchanged.

Now, will the simultaneous adjustment of real income and interest bring about the equilibrium when we start at an arbitrary point in the neighborhood? In order to answer this question, we apply Theorem 15 on non-linear simultaneous differential equations and compute the Jacobian of equations (205) and (206), evaluated at (Y^*, i^*):

$$\text{Jac} = \begin{pmatrix} -H_1' \cdot \dfrac{dS}{dY} & H_1' \cdot \dfrac{dI}{di} \\ H_2' \cdot \dfrac{dL}{dY} & H_2' \cdot \dfrac{dL}{di} \end{pmatrix}. \tag{207}$$

From Theorem 15 we know that the equilibrium is locally stable if the real parts of all characteristic values of the Jacobian are strictly negative. This is true, according to Lemma 4, iff the Jacobian exhibits a strictly negative trace and a strictly positive determinant:

$$\text{Tr}(\text{Jac}) = -H_1' \cdot \frac{dS}{dY} + H_2' \cdot \frac{dL}{di} < 0 \tag{208}$$

$$|\text{Jac}| = - H'_1 \cdot H'_2 \cdot \frac{dS}{dY} \cdot \frac{dL}{di} - H'_1 \cdot H'_2 \cdot \frac{dI}{di} \cdot \frac{dL}{dY} > 0 \,. \tag{209}$$

Thus we can conclude: The equilibrium of the IS/LM-model is locally asymptotically stable. Given a small deviation, Y and i will finally re-attain their equilibrium values.

Note that the complete Keynesian model with flexible prices is not generally stable. The reader should prove this as an exercise. It is stable, however, if we employ the assumption that Y and i move infinitely quicker than P. This very assumption is of course implied by the construction of the Y^d-curve. In this light, the reversal of the adjustment velocities in Neokeynesian theory does not appear as a genuine novelty.

*5.6 Stability of the Neokeynesian Model

We now want to examine the stability of the Neokeynesian model assuming a pure price tatônnement. In the commodity and the labor market a price tatônnement takes place according to the following rules:

$$P'(t) = H_1 [C(P,w) - Y(P,w)] \quad \text{where} \quad H_1(0) = 0; \quad H'_1 > 0 \tag{210}$$

$$w'(t) = H_2 [N^d(P,w) - N^s(P,w)] \quad \text{where} \quad H_2(0) = 0; \quad H'_2 > 0 \,. \tag{211}$$

Due to an excess demand in the commodity market, the price level increases, and vice versa. Due to excess demand in the labor market, nominal wages increase, and vice versa. In general equilibrium (P^*, w^*), prices and wages remain unchanged.

During the price tatônnement, both processes take place simultaneously. They are closely interconnected since the excess demand of every market depends on both prices and wages. The process is thus very involved: If prices increase in one market because of excess demand, supply and demand in the other market will change; this produces a price change in the other market; and that, finally, will influence demand and supply in the first market. Will the market equilibrium be locally stable?

First, we calculate the Jacobian of the model which is evaluated at (P^*, w^*):

$$\text{Jac} = \begin{pmatrix} H'_1 (C_P - Y_P) & H'_1 (C_w - Y_w) \\ H'_2 (N^d_P - N^s_P) & H'_2 (N^d_w - N^s_w) \end{pmatrix} . \tag{212}$$

C_P means the derivative of consumption with respect to P, etc. If the trace of the Jacobian is strictly negative and its determinant is strictly positive, then the real parts of all characteristic values will be strictly negative (Lemma 4) and the equilibrium will thus be locally stable (Theorem 15). The condition involving the Jacobian's trace is met according to the assumptions made in Chapter XI:

$$H'_1 (C_P - Y_P) + H'_2 (N^d_w - N^s_w) < 0 \,. \tag{213}$$

The condition involving the determinant, however, seems to be ambiguous since eliminating the H' yields:

$$(C_P - Y_P)(N^d_w - N^s_w) - (C_w - Y_w)(N^d_P - N^s_P) > 0 \,. \tag{214}$$

This expression can be interpreted in the following manner. If, "on the average", the excess demands respond more strongly to changes in the price of the own market than to changes in the price of the other market, then the left term of the difference exceeds the right one; and since it is positive, the stability condition is met.

In order to show that this is indeed true, we take Walras' law, neglecting all variables referring to government behaviour since this does not alter the dynamic behavior of the model. Walras' law reads:

$$P(C - Y) + w(N^d - N^s) + \Delta M = 0. \tag{215}$$

The short-cut "ΔM" denotes private money demand. Walras' law follows (as shown in the text) from a mere addition of all budget constraints. In the Neoclassical case, it holds both in equilibrium and out of equilibrium. Let us differentiate (215) with respect to P:

$$P(C_P - Y_P) + (C - Y) + w(N^d_P - N^s_P) + \Delta M_P = 0. \tag{216}$$

In equilibrium, excess demand in the commodity market $(C - Y)$ vanishes, and the rest of equation (216) can be rewritten as

$$|C_P - Y_P| > \frac{w}{P}(N^d_P - N^s_P), \tag{217}$$

because ΔM_P is positive according to the assumptions made in Chapter XI. Similarly, we obtain the following inequality from differentiating (216) with respect to w and taking account of $\Delta M_w > 0$:

$$|N^d_w - N^s_w| > \frac{P}{w}(C_w - Y_w). \tag{218}$$

Multiplying (217) and (218) yields:

$$(C_P - Y_P) \cdot (N^d_w - N^s_w) > (C_w - Y_w) \cdot (N^d_P - N^s_P). \tag{219}$$

This equation is identical to (214). Hence the model is locally stable.

We want to turn to the *correspondence principle* finally. The correspondence principle, as put forward by SAMUELSON, states a relationship between the dynamic and the comparative static properties of an economic model. Knowing something about the dynamic properties, it is often possible to determine some comparative static results without making further assumptions. The same holds in converse. Let us apply the correspondence principle to our Neokeynesian model.

By means of equations (137) and (139) of Subsection *4.4, we substantiated the positive slope of the notional market clearing loci of the Neokeynesian model. Confined to pure comparative statics, we were unable then to determine whether one of those loci is steeper than the other. In particular, we obtained the results:

$$\left. \frac{dw}{dP} \right|_{C=Y} = -\frac{C_P - Y_P}{C_w - Y_w} > 0 \tag{220}$$

$$\left. \frac{dw}{dP} \right|_{N^d=N^s} = -\frac{N^d_P - N^s_P}{N^d_w - N^s_w} > 0. \tag{221}$$

But in Chapter XI it was alleged that the equilibrium locus of the commodity market exhibits a *greater* slope than the equilibrium locus of the labor market. This amounts to saying

$$\left.\frac{dw}{dP}\right|_{C=Y} > \left.\frac{dw}{dP}\right|_{N^d=N^s} \qquad (222)$$

$$\Leftrightarrow \frac{C_P - Y_P}{C_w - Y_w} < \frac{N_P^d - N_P^s}{N_w^d - N_w^s}. \qquad (223)$$

Multiplying in (223), it is necessary to reverse the sign of inequality since one of the terms is negative:

$$(C_P - Y_P) \cdot (N_w^d - N_w^s) > (C_w - Y_w) (N_P^d - N_P^s). \qquad (224)$$

If inequality (224) is satisfied, the equilibrium locus of the commodity market will exhibit a greater slope than the other one. But – (224) is identical to the stability condition (214)! Therefore, we obtain the comparative static property (222) from the dynamic property that the model is locally stable.

Put differently, inequality (224) implies comparative static as well as dynamic properties. These two topics, appearing so remote at first sight, are thus closely related to one another.

To be precise, however, it must be remarked that inequality (224) holds only *in equilibrium* and in a certain neighborhood of it. This is obvious from the argument above. Therefore, strictly speaking, up to here we have only proved that the equilibrium locus of the commodity market is steeper *at the equilibrium point*. Yet, because in Chapter XI we assumed the *uniqueness* of the equilibrium, the equilibrium locus of the commodity market must be above the locus of the labor market if $P > P^*$, and below if $P < P^*$. This substantiates Figure 84.

Further Reading

GANDOLFO, G. (1980) Economic Dynamics: Methods and Models. Amsterdam etc.: North-Holland

INTRILIGATOR, M.D. (1971) Mathematical Optimization and Economic Theory. Englewood Cliffs: Prentice-Hall

SAMUELSON, P.A. (1947) Foundations of Economic Analysis. Cambridge: Harvard University Press. Second enlarged edition 1983 ibid.

Bibliography

ABRAMOVITZ, M. et al. Ed. (1959) The Allocation of Economic Ressources. Stanford: Stanford University Press

ACKLEY, G. (1978) Macroeconomics: Theory and Policy. New York etc.: Macmillan

ANDO, A. and F. MODIGLIANI (1965) The Relative Stability of Monetary Velocity and the Investment Multiplier. American Economic Review 55, pp. 693–728

ARCHIBALD, G.C. and R.G. LIPSEY (1958) Monetary and Value Theory: A Critique of Lange and Patinkin. Review of Economic Studies 26, pp. 1–22

ARROW, K.J. (1959) Toward a Theory of Price Adjustment. In: ABRAMOVITZ, M. et al. Ed. The Allocation of Economic Ressources. Op.cit.

ARROW, K.J. (1964) The Role of Securities in the Optimal Allocation of Risk–Bearing. Review of Economic Studies 31, pp. 91–96

ARROW, K.J and F.H. HAHN (1971) General Competitive Analysis. San Francisco: Holden-Day

AZARIADIS, C. (1975) Implicit Contracts and Underemployment Equilibria. Journal of Political Economy 83, pp. 1183–1202

BARRO, R.J. (1974) Are Government Bonds Net Wealth? Journal of Political Economy 82, pp. 1095–1117

BARRO, R.J. (1979) Second Thoughts on Keynesian Economics. American Economic Review (PP) 69, pp. 54–59

BARRO, R.J. and H.I. GROSSMAN (1976) Money, Employment and Inflation. Cambridge etc.: Cambridge University Press

BAUMOL, W.J. (1952) The Transactions Demand for Cash: An Inventory Theoretic Approach. Quarterly Journal of Economics 66, pp. 545–556

BENASSY, J.–P. (1973) Disequilibrium Theory. Unpubl. Diss. CRMS Working Paper No. 185. Berkeley: University of California

BENASSY, J.–P. (1975) Neo-Keynesian Disequilibrium Theory in a Monetary Economy. Review of Economic Studies 42, pp. 502–523

BENASSY, J.–P. (1977) On Quantity Signals and the Foundations of Effective Demand Theory. Scandinavian Journal of Economics 79, pp. 147–168

BENASSY, J.–P. (1978) A Neokeynesian Model of Price and Quantity Determination in Disequilibrium. In: SCHWÖDIAUER, G. Ed. Equilibrium and Disequilibrium in Economic Theory. Op.cit.

BENASSY, J.–P. (1982) The Theory of Market Disequilibrium. New York etc.: Academic Press

BLAUG, M. (1968^2) Economic Theory in Retrospect. London: Heinemann

BLINDER, A.M. and R.M. SOLOW (1973) Does Fiscal Policy Matter? Journal of Public Economics 2, pp. 319–337

BÖHM, V. (1978) Disequilibrium Dynamics in a Simple Macroeconomic Model. Journal of Economic Theory 17, pp. 179–199

BOULDING, K.E. (1955) In Defence of Statics. Quarterly Journal of Economics 69, pp. 485–502

BRUNNER, K. and A.H. MELTZER (1972) A Monetarist Framework for Aggregate Analysis. In: Supplement 1 to Kredit und Kapital

BRUNNER, K. and A.H. MELTZER (1976) An Aggregate Theory for a Closed Economy. In: STEIN, J. Ed. Monetarism. Op.cit.

BUCHANAN, J. (1969) An Outside Economist in Defense of Pesek and Saving. Journal of Economic Literature 7, pp. 812–814

BUITER, W. (1980) Walras' Law and All That: Budget Constraints in Period Models and Continuous Time Models. International Economic Review 21, pp. 1–16

CAGAN, Ph. (1956) The Monetary Dynamics of Hyperinflation. In: FRIEDMAN, M. Ed. Studies in the Quantity Theory of Money. Op.cit.

CHANG, W.H., D. HAMBERG and J. HIRATA (1983) Liquidity Preference as Behaviour Towards Risk is a Demand for Short-Term Securities – Not Money. American Economic Review 73, pp. 420–427

CHICK, V. (1973) Financial Counterparts of Saving and Investment and Inconsistencies in Some Simple Macro Models. Weltwirtschaftliches Archiv 109, pp. 621–643

CLOWER, R.W. (1965) The Keynesian Counter-Revolution: A Theoretical Appraisal. In: HAHN, F.H. and F.P.R. BRECHLING Ed. The Theory of Interest Rates. Op.cit.

The Commision on Money, Credit and Commerce Ed. (1963) Stabilization Policies. Englewood Cliffs: Prentice-Hall

Croome, D. and H.G. JOHNSON Ed. (1970) Money in Britain, 1959–1969. London: Oxford University Press

DAVIDSON, P. (1978²) Money and the Real World. Basingstoke etc.: Macmillan

DEBREU, G. (1959) Theory of Value. New York: Wiley

DRAZEN, A. (1980) Recent Developments in Macroeconomic Disequilibrium Theory. Econometrica 48, pp. 283–304

DRÈZE, J. (1975) Existence of an Exchange Equilibrium under Price Rigidities. International Economic Review 16, pp. 301–320

EATWELL, J. and M.MILGATE Ed. (1983) Keynes' Economics and the Theory of Value and Distribution. London: Gerald Duckworth

ESHAG, E. (1963) From Marshall to Keynes. Oxford. Basil Blackwell

FISCHER, St. Ed. (1980) Rational Expectations and Economic Policy. Chicago: Chicago Press

FITOUSSI, J.-P. Ed. (1983) Modern Macroeconomic Theory. Oxford: Basil Blackwell

FITOUSSI, J.-P. (1983) Modern Macroeconomic Theory: An Overview. In: FITOUSSI, J.P. Ed. Modern Macroeconomic Theory. Op.cit.

FOLEY, D.K. (1975) On Two Specifications of Asset Equilibrium in Macroeconomic Models. Journal of Political Economy 83, pp. 303–324

FRIEDMAN, B. (1979) Optimal Expectations and the Extreme Information Assumptions of "Rational Expectations" Macromodels. Journal of Monetary Economics 5, pp. 32–41

FRIEDMAN, M. (1948) A Monetary and Fiscal Framework for Economic Stability. American Economic Review 38, pp. 245–264. Reprinted in LINDAUER, J. Ed. (1968) Macroeconomic Readings. Op.cit.

FRIEDMAN, M. (1956) The Quantity Theory of Money: A Restatement. In: FRIEDMAN, M. Ed. Studies in the Quantity Theory of Money, Op.cit.

FRIEDMAN, M. Ed. (1956) Studies in the Quantity Theory of Money. Chicago: Chicago Press

FRIEDMAN, M. (1957) A Theory of the Consumption Function. Princeton: Princeton Univerity Press

FRIEDMAN, M. (1968) The Role of Monetary Policy. American Economic Review 58, pp. 1–17. Reprinted in: FRIEDMAN, M. Ed. (1969) The Optimum Quantity of Money and Other Essays. Op.cit.

FRIEDMAN, M. (1969) The Optimum Quantity of Money and Other Essays. Chicago: Aldine

FRIEDMAN, (1970) The Counterrevolution in Monetary Theory. London: Institute of Economic Affairs for the Wincott Foundation, Occasional Paper 33

FRIEDMAN, M. and D. MEISELMAN (1963) The Relative Stability of Monetary Velocity and the Investment Multiplier in the United States, 1897–1958. In: The Commission on Money, Credit and Commerce Ed. Stabilization Policies. Op.cit.

FRIEDMAN, M. and A.J. SCHWARZ (1963) A Monetary History of the United States, 1867–1960. Princeton: Princeton University Press

GALE, D. and H. NIKAIDÔ (1965) The Jacobian Matrix and Global Univalence of Mappings. Mathematische Annalen 159, pp. 81–93

GANDOLFO, G. (1980) Economic Dynamics: Methods and Models. Amsterdam etc.: North-Holland

GARVY (1975) Keynes and the Economic Activities of Pre-Hitler Germany. Journal of Political Economy 83, pp. 391–405

GORDON, D.F. and A. HYNES (1976) On the Theory of Price Dynamics. In: PHELPS, E.S. Ed. Microeconomic Foundations of Employment and Inflation. Op.cit.

GRANDMONT, J.-M. (1983) Money and Value – A Reconsideration of Classical and Neoclassical Monetary Theories. Cambridge etc.: Cambridge University Press

GRANDMONT, J.-M and G. LAROQUE (1976) On Temporary Keynesian Equilibria. Review of Economic Studies 43, pp. 5367

GURLEY, J.G. and E.S. SHAW (1960) Money in a Theory of Finance. Washington D.C.: The Brookings Inst.

HAHN, F.H. (1980) Unemployment from a Theoretical Viewpoint. Economica 47, pp. 285–298

HAHN, F.H. and F.P.R. BRECHLING Ed. (1965) The Theory of Interest Rates. London: Macmillan

HANSEN, A.H. (1941) Fiscal Policy and Business Cycles. New York: W.W. Norton

HARCOURT, G.C. Ed. (1977) The Microfoundations of Macroeconomics. London: Macmillan

HAYEK, F.A.v. (1933) Monetary Theory and the Trade Cycle. London: Jonathan Cape

HICKS, J.R. (1937) Mr. Keynes and the 'Classics': A Suggested Interpretation. Econometrica 5, pp. 147–159. Reprinted in: HICKS, J.R. (1967) Critical Essays in Monetary Theory. Op.cit.

HICKS, J.R. (1939) Value and Capital. Oxford: Oxford University Press. Second Edition 1946 ibid.

HICKS, J.R. (1965) Capital and Growth. Oxford: Clarendon Press

HICKS, J.R. (1967) Critical Essays in Monetary Theory. Oxford: Clarendon Press

HICKS, J.R. (1974) The Crisis in Keynesian Economics. Oxford: Basil Blackwell

HICKS, J.R. (1976) Some Questions of Time in Economics. In: TANG, A.M. et al. Ed. Evolution, Welfare and Time in Economics. Op.cit.

HILDENBRAND, K. and W. HILDENBRAND (1978) On Keynesian Equilibria with Unemployment and Quantity Rationing. Journal of Economic Theory 18, pp. 255–277

HONKAPOHJA, S. and T. ITO (1983) Stability with Regime Switching. Journal of Economic Theory 29, pp. 22–48

INTRILIGATOR, M.D. (1971) Mathematical Optimization and Economic Theory. Englewood Cliffs: Prentice–Hall

JOHNSON, H.G. (1970) Recent Developments in Monetary Theory – A Comment. In: Croome, D. and H.G. JOHNSON Ed. Money in Britain, 1959–1969. Op.cit.

JOHNSON, H.G. (1971) The Keynesian Revolution and the Monetarist Counterrevolution. American Economic Review (PP) 61, pp. 1–14

KAHN, R.F. (1931) The Relation of Home Investment to Unemployment. Economic Journal 41, pp. 173–198

KAHN, R.F. (1977) Malinvaud on Keynes. Cambridge Journal of Economics 1, pp. 375–388. Reprinted in: EATWELL, J. and M. MILGATE Ed. (1983) Keynes' Economics and the Theory of Value and Distribution. Op.cit.

KEYNES, J.M. (1936) The General Theory of Employment, Interest and Money. London. Reprinted 1964 New York etc.: Harcourt and Brace

KLEIN, L. (1966) The Keynesian Revolution. New York: Macmillan

KREGEL, J.A. (1975) The Reconstruction of Political Economy: An Introduction to Post-Keynesian Economics. London: Macmillan

KUHN, Th.S. (1970) The Structure of Scientific Revolutions. Chicago: Chicago University Press

LANGE, O. (1942) Say's Law: A Restatement and Criticism. In: LANGE, O. et al. Ed. Studies in Mathematical Economics. Op.cit.

LANGE, O. et al. Ed. (1942) Studies in Mathematical Economics. Chicago: Chicago University Press. Reprint 1968 ibid.

LEIJONHUFVUD, A. (1967) Keynes and the Keynesians: A Suggested Interpretation. American Economic Review (PP) 57, pp. 401–410

LEIJONHUFVUD, A. (1968) On Keynesian Economics and the Economics of Keynes. Oxford: Oxford University Press

LERNER, A.P. (1944) The Economics of Control. New York: Macmillan

LINDAUER, J. Ed. (1967) Macroeconomic Readings. New York etc.: The Free Press

LIPSEY, R.G. (1960) The Relation between Unemployment and the Rate of Change of Money Wages in the United Kingdom, 1886–1957 – A Further Analysis. Economica 27, pp. 1–37

LUCAS, R.E.Jr. (1973) Some International Evidence on Output-Inflation Tradeoffs. American Economic Review **63**, pp. 326–334

LUCAS, R.E.Jr. (1975) An Equilibrium Model of the Business Cycle. Journal of Political Economy **83**, pp. 1113–1144

LUCAS, R.E.Jr. (1976) Econometric Policy Evaluation: A Critique. In: Supplement **1** to the Journal of Monetary Economics

LUCAS, R.E.Jr. (1977) Understanding Business Cycles. Supplement **5** to the Journal of Monetary Economics

LUCAS, R.E.Jr. (1980) Methods and Problems in Business Cycle Theory. Journal of Money, Credit and Banking **12**, pp. 696–715

LUCAS, R.E.Jr. (1980) Rules, Discretion and the Role of the Economic Adviser. In: FISCHER, St. Ed. Rational Expectations and Economic Policy. Op.cit.

MACHLUP, F. (1983) The Rationality of 'Rational Expectations'. Kredit und Kapital **16**, pp. 172–183

MALINVAUD, E. (1977) The Theory of Unemployment Reconsidered. Oxford: Basil Blackwell

MARKOWITZ, H.M. (1959) Portfolio Selection. New York etc.: Wiley. Second edition New York 1970: Yale University Press

MARSHALL, A. (1890) Principles of Economics. Reprint of the 8th edition London 1952: Macmillan

MARSHALL, A. (1926) Official Papers by Alfred Marshall. London: Macmillan

MAYER, Th. (1975) The Structure of Monetarism. Kredit und Kapital **8**, pp. 191–218 and 293–316

METZLER, L.A. (1951) Wealth, Saving and the Rate of Interest. Journal of Political Economy **59**, pp. 93–116

MILL, J.St. (1848) Principles of Political Economy. London: Parker. Reprint Toronto 1965: University Press

MINSKY, H.P. (1975) John Maynard Keynes. London: Macmillan

MODIGLIANI, F. (1977) The Monetarist Controversy or, Should We Forsake Stabilization Policy. American Economic Review **67**, pp. 1–19

MUELLBAUER, J. and R. PORTES (1978) Macroeconomic Models with Quantity Rationing. Economic Journal **88**, pp. 788–821

MUELLER, M.G. Ed. (1967) Readings in Macroeconomics. New York etc.: Holt, Rinehart and Winston

MUSGRAVE, R. (1959) The Theory of Public Finance. New York etc. McGraw-Hill

MUTH, J. (1961) Rational Expectations and the Theory of Price Movements. Econometrica **29**, pp. 315–335

PARKIN, M. (1983) Modern Macroeconomics. Scarborough: Prentice-Hall

PATINKIN, D. (1948) Price Flexibility and Full Employment. American Economic Review **38**, pp. 543–564. Reprinted in: MUELLER, M.G. Ed. (1967) Readings in Macroeconomics. Op.cit.

PATINKIN, D. (1956) Money, Interest and Prices. New York: Harper and Row. Second edition 1965 ibid.

PESEK, B.P. and Th.S. SAVING (1967) Money, Wealth and Economic Theory. New York: Macmillan

PHELPS, E.S. (1967) Phillips Curves, Expectations of Inflation and Optimal Unemployment over Time. Economica **34**, pp. 254–281

PHELPS, E.S. Ed. (1970) Microeconomic Foundations of Employment and Inflation. New York: W.W. Norton

PHELPS, E.S. and J.B. TAYLOR (1977) Stabilizing Powers of Monetary Policy under Rational Expectations. Journal of Political Economy **85**, pp. 163–190

PHILLIPS, A.W. (1958) The Relation between Unemployment and the Rate of Change of Money Wages in the United Kingdom, 1886–1957. Economica **25**, pp. 283–299. Reprinted in: MUELLER, M.G Ed. (1967) Readings in Macroeconomics. Op.cit

PIGOU, A.C. (1943) The Classical Stationary State. Economic Journal **53**, pp. 343–351

POPPER, K.R. (1936) The Logic of Scientific Enquiry. Reprint Ney York 1961: Basic Books

QUIRK, J. and R. SAPOSNIK (1968) Introduction to General Equilibrium Theory and Welfare Economics. New York: McGrawHill

RABIN, A. and D. BIRCH (1982) A Clarification of the IS Curve and the Aggregate Demand Curve. Journal of Macroeconomics 4, pp. 233–238

RICARDO, D. (1817) Principles of Political Economy and Taxation. Reprint of the 3rd edition London 1924: Bell and Sons

ROBINSON, J. (1956) The Accumulation of Capital. London: Macmillan

ROBINSON, J. (1962) Economic Philosophy. London: Watts

ROBINSON, J. and J. EATWELL (1974) An Introduction to Modern Economics. London: McGraw–Hill

SAMUELSON, P.A. (1946) Lord Keynes and the General Theory. Econometrica 14, pp. 187–200

SAMUELSON, P.A. (1947) Foundations of Economic Analysis. Cambridge: Harvard University Press. Second enlarged edition 1983 ibid.

SAMUELSON, P.A. and R.M. SOLOW (1960) Analytical Aspects of Anti-Inflation Policy. American Economic Review (PP) 50, pp. 177–194. Reprinted in: MUELLER, M.G. Ed. (1967) Readings in Macroeconomics. Op.cit

SANTOMERO, A.M. and J.J. SEATER (1978) The Inflation Unemployment Trade-Off: A Critique of the Literature. Journal of Economic Literature 16, pp. 499–544

SARGENT, Th.S. (1976) The Observational Equivalence of Natural and Unnatural Rate Theories in Macroeconomics. Journal of Political Economy 84, pp. 631–640

SARGENT, Th.S. (1976) A Classical Macroeconomic Model of the United States. Journal of Political Economy 84, pp. 207–237

SARGENT, Th.S. (1979) Macroeconomic Theory. New York: Academic Press

SARGENT, Th.S. and N. WALLACE (1976) Rational Expectations and the Theory of Economic Policy. Journal of Monetary Economics 2, pp. 169–183

SCHNEIDER, E. (1953) Der Streit um Keynes. Jahrbücher für Nationalökonomie und Statistik 165, pp. 89–122

SCHUMPETER, J.A. (1954) History of Economic Analysis. London: Allen and Unwin

SCHWÖDIAUER, G. Ed. (1978) Equilibrium and Disequilibrium in Economic Theory. Dordrecht: Reidel

SHACKLE, G.L.S. (1955) Uncertainty in Economics. Cambridge: Cambridge University Press

SHILLER, R.J. (1978) Rational Expectations and the Dynamic Structure of Macroeconomic Models – A Critical Review. Journal of Monetary Economics 4, pp. 1–44

SMITH, A. (1776) An Inquiry into the Nature and Causes of the Wealth of Nations. Reprint Oxford 1976: Clarendon

STEIN, J.L. Ed. (1976) Monetarism. Amsterdam etc.: North-Holland

STEIN, J.L. (1982) Monetarist, Keynesian and New Classical Economics. Oxford: Basil Blackwell

SVENSSON, L.E.O. (1977) Effective Demand and Stochastic Rationing. Review of Economic Studies 47, pp. 339–355

SVENSSON, L.E.O. (1981) Effective Demand in a Sequence of Markets. Scandinavian Journal of Economics 83, pp. 1–21

TANG, A.M. et al. Ed. (1976) Evolution, Welfare and Time in Economics. Lexington: Lexington Books

TAYLOR, J.B. (1979) Staggered Wage Setting in a Macro Model. American Economic Review (PP) 69, pp. 108–113

TOBIN, J. (1958) Liquidity Preference as Behaviour Towards Risk. Review of Economic Studies 25, pp. 65–86

TOBIN, J. (1961) Money, Capital and Other Stores of Value. American Economic Review (PP) 51, pp. 25–37

TOBIN, J. (1965) The Theory of Portfolio Selection. In: HAHN, F. and F.P.R. BRECHLING Ed. The Theory of Interest Rates. Op.cit.

TOBIN, J. (1969) A General Equilibrium Approach to Monetary Theory. Journal of Money, Credit and Banking 1, pp. 15–29

TOBIN, J. (1970) Money and Income: Post Hoc ergo Propter Hoc? Quarterly Journal of Economics 84, pp. 301–317

TOBIN, J. (1980) Are New Classical Models Plausible Enough to Guide Policy? Journal of Money, Credit and Banking 12, pp. 788–799

TOBIN, J. (1980) Asset Accumulation and Economic Acitivy. Oxford: Basil Blackwell

TOBIN, J. and W. BUITER (1976) Long–Run Effects of Fiscal and Monetary Policy on Aggregate Demand. In: STEIN, J.L. Ed. Monetarism. Op.cit.

VARIAN, H. (1975) On Persistent Disequilibrium. Journal of Economic Theory 10, pp. 218–228

WALD, A. (1936) Über einige Gleichungssysteme der mathematischen Ökonomie. Zeitschrift für Nationalökonomie 7, pp. 637–670

WALRAS, L. (1884) Eléments d'économie politique pure ou théorie de la richesse sociale. Lausanne. Reprint New York 1970: Franklin

WALRAS, L. (1954) Elements of Pure Economics. London: Allen and Unwin

WALSH, V.Ch. and H.GRAM (1980) Classical and New Classical Theories of General Equilibrium. New York etc.: Oxford University Press

WEINTRAUB, E.R. (1979) Microfoundations. The Compatibility of Microeconomics and Macroeconomics. Cambridge etc.: Cambridge University Press

WEINTRAUB, E.R. (1983) On the Existence of a Competitive Equilibrium: 1930–1954. Journal of Economic Literature 21, pp. 1–39

WICKSELL, K. (1965) Interest and Prices. New York: Kelly

Author Index

Abramovitz, Moses 239
Ackley, Gardner 67
Ando, Albert 182
Archibald, George C. 147
Aristotle 13
Arrow, Kenneth J. 66, 197, 210, 239
Azariadis, Costas 207

Barbon, Nicholas 50, 51
Barro, Robert J. 187, 203, 204, 209, 210, 244, 248, 249
Baumol, William 154
Benassy, Jean-Pascal 209, 211, 215, 237, 249
Birch, Dan 92
Blaug, Mark 18
Blinder, Alan M. 166, 184
Böhm, Volker 237
Boulding, Kenneth E. 10, 251
Brechling, F.P.R. 170, 210, 249
Brunner, Karl 171, 179, 184, 185
Buchanan, James 150
Buiter, Willem 90, 166

Cagan, Phillip 170, 189
Cantillon, Richard 14
Chang, Winston W. 170
Chick, Victoria 96
Clower, Robert W. 72, 210, 212, 213, 245, 248

Davidson, Paul 71, 172
Debreu, Gérard 197, 210
Drazen, Alan 249
Drèze, Jacques 211

Eatwell, John 72, 249
Eshag, Epraim 58

Fischer, Stanley 189, 204, 207, 208
Fisher, Irving 17, 56, 189
Fitoussi, Jean-Paul 142, 211
Foley, Duncan K. 90
Friedman, Benjamin 205
Friedman, Milton 171, 173–185, 194, 195, 202

Galbraith, John Kenneth 70
Gale, David 294
Gandolfo, Giancarlo 315
Garvy, George 69
Gordon, Donald F. 240
Gordon, Robert J. 142, 193
Gram, Harvey 67
Grandmont, Jean-Michel 152, 211
Grossman, Herschel I. 209, 210, 244, 249
Gurley, John G. 149, 152

Haavelmo, Trygve 128
Hahn, Frank H. 66, 170, 207, 210, 249
Hamberg, Daniel 170
Hansen, Alvin H. 172
Harcourt, Geoffrey C. 211
Harrod, Roy F. 71
Hayek, Friedrich August von 205
Hicks, John Richard 71, 86, 96, 108, 153, 170, 210, 218
Hildenbrand, Kurt 236
Hildenbrand, Werner 236
Hirata, Junichi 170
Honkapohja, Seppo 240
Hynes, Alan 240

Intriligator, Michael D. 315
Ito, Takatoshi 240

Jevons, William Stanley 16
Johnson, Harry Gordon 29, 70, 172

Kahn, Richard F. 71, 83
Kaldor, Nicholas 71
Kalecki, Michal 71
Kant, Immanuel 253
Keynes, John Maynard 17, 18, 69–74, 78, 80, 82, 83, 86, 89, 102, 108, 112, 141, 143, 152, 160, 210, 212, 228, 236, 244, 245, 247
Klein, Lawrence R. 71
Kregel, Jan A. 71
Kuhn, Thomas S. 6

Laidler, David 171
Lange, Oskar 143, 145

Laroque, Guy 211
Lassalle, Ferdinand 15
Leijonhufvud, Axel 72
Lerner, Abba Petachya 172
Lindauer, John 113, 138
Lipsey, Richard G. 147, 192
Lucas, Robert E. Jr. 187, 196, 197, 200, 204, 206–208

Machlup, Fritz 206, 208
Malinvaud, Edmond 210–212, 235, 236, 249
Malthus, Thomas 15
Markowitz, Harry M. 153
Marshall, Alfred 1, 16, 38, 55, 58, 67, 210
Marx, Karl 15, 18, 21, 66
Mayer, Thomas 183, 185
McKenzie, Lionel 210
Meiselman, David 181
Meltzer, Allan H. 170, 179, 184, 185
Menger, Carl 16
Metzler, Lloyd A. 151
Milgate, Murray 72, 249
Mill, John Stuart 15, 54–59, 67
Minsky, Hyman P. 71, 78
Modigliani, Franco 71, 182, 185
Montesquieu, Charles 54
Muellbauer, John 225, 236
Mueller, M.G. 113, 138
Musgrave, Richard 115
Muth, John 190, 191

Negishi, Takashi 209
Nikaidô, Hukukane 294

Pareto, Vilfredo 17, 196
Parkin, Michael 208
Patinkin, Don 71, 108, 141, 143, 145–147, 152, 172, 209
Pesek, Boris P. 150, 152
Petty, William 13
Phelps, Edmund S. 187, 194, 195, 207, 240
Phillips, Arthur W. 192
Pigou, Arthur Cecil 17, 53, 55, 148
Plato 13
Popper, Karl Raimund 6
Portes, Richard 225, 236

Quesnay, François 14, 20, 21
Quirk, James 66

Rabin, Alan 92
Ricardo, David 15, 59, 67
Robinson, Joan 18, 71, 72

Samuelson, Paul Anthony 7–9, 70, 71, 193, 210, 314, 315
Santomero, Anthony M. 192
Saposnik, Rubin 66
Sargent, Thomas S. 187, 196, 206, 208
Saving, Thomas 150
Say, Jean-Baptiste 15, 58, 59
Schneider, Erich 212, 213
Schumpeter, Joseph Alois 13, 14, 18, 62
Schwarz, Anna Jacobson 180, 181
Schwödiauer, Gerhard 237
Seater, John J. 192
Senior, Nassau William 46
Shackle, George L.S. 71
Shaw, Edward S. 149, 152
Shiller, Robert J. 208
Smith, Adam 13–15, 66, 67, 80, 82
Solow, Robert Morton 71, 166, 184, 193, 200
Stein, Jerome L. 142, 166, 171, 185
Svensson, Lars E.O. 211, 216, 225

Tang, A.M. 96
Taylor, John B. 187, 207
Tobin, James 62, 71, 141, 142, 153, 154, 159, 160, 164, 166–170, 182, 208
Turgot, Anne Robert Jacques 14, 38

Varian, Hal 238

Wald, Abraham 66, 210
Wallace, Neil 187, 208
Walras, Marie Esprit Léon 16, 62, 65, 66
Walsh, Vivian Charles 67
Weintraub, E. Roy 66, 210
Whitehead, Alfred North 139
Wicksell, Knut 17, 57, 58, 151

Subject Index

Abstinence theory 46
Acceleration, theorem of 195
–, and New Classical theory 201
Activism 117
Aggregate 11
Allocation 12
Allocation, optimal 16
Allocation problem 16
Analysis, comparative static 9
–, dynamic 9
–, ex ante 10
–, ex post 10
–, partial 10
–, static 9
–, total 10
Approach, asset 161
Assets, financial 165
–, real 165
Auctioneer, Walrasian 62, 65, 208, 218, 224
Axiom of a closed flow 20

Balances, precautionary 86, 89
–, speculative 89
–, transactions 89, 154
Banking school 181
Bonds 39, 87, 161, 162, 173, 174
Budget constraint 48, 212, 248
Budget deficit 117, 118, 131

Cambridge-effect 57, 101, 151
Cambridge equation 56, 144, 145
Cameralism 13
Capacity effect 43
Capital as factor of production 35
Capital demand function 50
Capital supply function 50
Cash balance coefficient 55
Causation, reversed 181
Ceteris paribus clause 10, 11
Chain rule 257, 279
Characteristic value 273, 308
Characteristic vector 273, 309
Circular velocity of money 56, 180
Classical and Neoclassical theory 33
Classical model 59

Classical theory 14, 33
Classical unemployment 235
Cobb-Douglas production function 38
Commodity demand curve 98
–, slope of 295
Commodity market 51, 92, 98, 198
Commodity supply curve 98, 110
Complementarity of assets 165
–, of factors of production 299
Concavity 261, 283
Concentration of a portfolio 157
Consols 87
Constraint cf. rationing
Consumption demand 47, 73
–, effective 215
–, notional 213
Consumption function, Classical 47
–, Keynesian 73
–, Neokeynesian 225
Convexity 261, 283
Correspondence principle 9, 314
Cramer's rule 272
Cross derivative 37, 299
Crowding in 126
Crowding out 114
–, partial 129
–, total 119
Currency school 181

Deduction 6
Definiteness of a quadratic form 275
Definition 7
Deflation 103, 134, 177
Demand gap 59, 81
Demand signal 216
Demand, effective
–, effective in Clower's sense 215, 216
–, effective in Drèze's sense 215, 216
Depreciation 22
Derivative 255
–, n-th 257
–, partial 277
–, total 279
Determinant 269
Determinateness of general equilibrium 65

Dichotomy, macroeconomic 34
Difference quotient 256
Differentiability 256, 278
Differential 260
–, partial 282
–, total 282
Differential equation 303
Differential quotient 256
Diversification of a portfolio 157
Domestic products 25
Dual decision hypothesis

Earning capacity value of a firm 163
Eigenvalue 273
Employment, problem of 17
Equation, characteristic 273
Equilibrium 7
–, in the methodical sense 7
–, in the normative sense 8
–, in the theoretical sense 8
–, stable 8
–, unstable 8
–, with unemployment cf. under-employment
  equilibrium
Equilibrium analysis 7
Equilibrium income, in IS/LM model 94
–, in income-expenditure model 81
Equilibrium loci, effective 235
–, notional 234
–, slope of 294
Equities 173
Equivalence theorem, Ricardian 203
Existence of general equilibrium 66, 210
Expectations 188
–, adaptive 189
–, endogenous 188
–, exogenous 188
–, Rational 190
–, static 160, 189
–, subjective 155
Expected value 155, 190

Face value of a security 87
Factor income 22
Factor variation, partial 36
–, total 36
Factors of production 35
Firm, representative 38
Fiscal illusion 203
Fiscal policy 117
–, counter-cyclical 130
–, criticism of 132
–, mixed 241
–, pure 243
Fiscalism 136, 180
Fisher-effect 150
Fix price method 218

–, criticism of 248
Flow diagram 19
Form, quadratic 274
Formula flexibility 202
Full employment 49, 108
Function equation 302
Functional equation 302
Functions 255
–, continuous 255
–, differentiable 257
–, effective 216
–, explicit 291
–, implicit 291
–, notional 213
–, of a single variable 255
–, of several variables 277
–, real valued 255
–, vector valued 278
Fundamental theorem on partial derivatives
  278
Fundamentalists 196

General equilibrium theory 66, 197, 205,
  210
Government demand 24, 117
Government, in income accounting 24
–, and economic policy 115
Gradient 278
Great Depression 17, 69
Gross domestic product 25
Gross investment 22
Gross national product 25

Haavelmo-theorem 128, 132, 204
Hand, invisible 14
Helicopter effect 133
Hessian 281
Hoarding of money 54, 59
Homogeneity of degree zero 65
Household, representative 44
Human capital 173

IS curve 92
–, as depicting a commodity market
  equilibrium 92
–, slope of the 295
IS/LM model 94
–, stability of the 312
Identity matrix 269
Impact, monetary 167
–, fiscal 167
Imperfectionists 196
Implication 7
Implicit function theorem 292
Income, permanent 173
–, disposable 118
Income effect 46, 219, 230

Income hypothesis, absolute 173
–, permanent 173
Income-expenditure model 80
Indifference curve 45, 159, 213, 215, 226, 227
Induction 6
Inflation 172
–, repressed 235
Initial value problem 305
Inside money 149
Inside wealth 161
Interest rate, actual 50
–, natural 50
Inverse of a matrix 270
Investment demand 39, 78
Investment trap 101, 131
Investment, interest inelastic 80

Jacobian 280

Keynes' theory 70
Keynes-effect 101, 103, 106, 151
Keynesian model 97
Keynesian theory 69
Keynesian under-employment 235
Keynesianism and fiscalism 136

LM curve 85
–, slope of the 295
Labor as factor of production 35
Labor demand function 42
Labor market 49
Labor supply function 46
Labor value theory 16
Lagrange function 219, 220, 286
Land as factor of production 35
Law, empirical 6
–, fundamental psychological 74
–, of diminishing returns
Liberalism, economic 117
Liquidity preference, absolute 105
Liquidity preference theory 86, 160
–, and Monetarism 176
–, criticism of 160
Liquidity trap 105
Lucas' aggregate supply function 198
Lump sum tax 118

Macroeconomics 11
–, microfoundation of 211
–, new 141
Main diagonal of a matrix 268
Marginal efficiency of capital 78, 163
Marginal product 36
Marginal productivity 37
Marginal revenue 40
Marginal utility 16, 45
Marginal value productivity 40

Marginalism 16
Market clearance 197
Market equilibrium 10
Market rate of real capital 163
Market value of a security 87
Marxian theory 18, 112
Matrix 268
–, definite 275
–, square 268
–, symmetric 268
Maxima cf. optima
Mean value theorem 260
Mercantilism 13
Microeconomics 11
Minima cf. optima
Minimum rule 217
Model of the reduced form 197
Models 6
–, deterministic 188
–, stochastic 188
Monetarism 171
–, mark II 141, 187, 204
Monetarist theory 172
Monetary growth rule cf. rule of constant
   monetary growth
Monetary policy 133
–, by rule 184, 202
–, discretionary 184
Monetary theory 141, 143, 172
Money 53
–, and wealth 33
–, as part of a portfolio 162, 173
Money demand 56
–, stability of 175
Money illusion 144
Money market 55
Money prices 144
Money supply 56, 133
Multiplier

National income 25
National income accounting 19
Neoclassic 15
Neoclassical synthesis 71, 152, 248
Neokeynesian model 229
–, stability of 313
Neokeynesian theory 209
Net asset value of a firm 162
Net national product 25
Neutrality of money 54, 147
New Classical model 197
New Classical theory 187
Nominal products 25
Nominal wage rate 34
Null vector 267
Number, complex 273
Numéraire 144

Optima
–, local   263
–, regular   264
–, under constraints   286
–, unique   264
Output   35
Outside money   149
Outside wealth   162

Phillips-curve   191
–, criticism of the long run   194
–, modified   193
Physiocracy   14
Pig cycle   188
Pigou-effect   148, 151
Policy   115
–, by rule   184
–, discretionary   184
Policy rules, active   202
–, passive   202
Portfolio   153
Portfolio selection, theory of   153
Postkeynesian theory   71
Precautionary motive   86
Premise   7
Price dynamics in Neokeynesian model   237
Price taker   40
Prices, abstract   62
–, money   144
–, relative   62, 144
Principal minor   275
–, leading   275
Production function   35
–, Classical   38
–, limitational   38
–, Neoclassical   35
–, short-run   43
–, substitutional   38
Profit   39
Propensity to consume, marginal
   nominal   231
–, real marginal   74
Propensity to save, marginal   75
Propensity to work, marginal nominal   231

Quantity equation   56
Quantity equilibrium   223
Quantity rationing cf. rationing
Quantity tatônnement   236
Quantity theory   53
–, restatement of the   173

Rate of inflation   174
Rational expectations theory   187
Rationalism, critical   6
Rationing   213
–, 0/1-rationing   218

–, binding   215
–, efficient   218
–, manipulable   216
–, priority   218
–, proportional   217
–, stochastic   216
Rationing scheme   217
Real-balance effect   143
Real capital as part of a portfolio   162, 173
Real income   34
Real products   25
Real wage rate   35
Real wealth   162
Reinvestment   22
Rest term in Taylor's expansion   259, 281, 282
Ricardian equivalence theorem   203
Risk curve   158
Risk of a portfolio   154
Root, characteristic   273
Rule of constant monetary growth   184

Savings   46
Savings function, Classical   47
–, Keynesian   75, 77
Say's equation   58
Say's identity   147
Say's law   147
Scalar product   267
Securities, as part of a portfolio   162, 173
Simultaneous equations, homogeneous   271
–, inhomogeneous   271
–, linear   271
Solution, non-trivial   273
Speculative motive   87
Spill-over   235
Stability analysis   8, 305, 313
Stability theorem   311
Stability, of general equilibrium   66
–, of a single market   305
–, of the private sector   173
Stabilizing policy cf. policy
Stagflation   187
Stagnation   187
Stationary state   148
Steady state   148
Stock equilibrium   166
Substitution effect   46, 219, 230
Supply price of capital   163
Surplus   13

Tableau économique   20
Tatônnement   66
Taylor's theorem   258, 281
Theorem   7

Theory
–, normative   3
–, positive   3
Tobin's q   162, 163
Transactions balances, interest elasticity of
   154
Transactions motive   54
Transpose of a matrix   268

Under-consumption   236
Under-employment   108
–, Classical   235
–, Keynesian   235
–, equilibrium with   108
–, natural rate of   178, 195
–, with a flexible wage rate   108
–, with a sticky wage rate   109
Unemployment (cf. underemployment)
Uniqueness of general equilibrium   66

Utility function   45
–, with an absorbed budget constraint   225
Utility theory, cardinal   45
Utility, intertemporal   225

Value theory   16
Variables, endogenous   7
–, exogenous   7
–, stochastic   188
Vector   267

Wage and price policy   116, 117, 244
Wage stickiness   109
Walras' law   52, 65, 145, 245
Walras' model   62
Wealth effect   167
Wedge-diagram   229

Yield, non-pecuniary   174

Lecture Notes in Economics and Mathematical Systems

Managing Editors: **M. Beckmann, W. Krelle**

This series reports new developments in (mathematical) economics, econometrics, operation research, and mathematical systems, research and teaching – quickly, informally and at a high level.

A selection

Editors: **J.-P. Aubin,** Paris, France; **D. Saari,** Evanston, IL, USA; **K. Sigmund,** Vienna, Austria

Volume 257
Dynamics of Macrosystems
Proceedings of a Workshop on the Dynamics of Macrosystems
Held at the International Institute for Applied Systems Analysis (IIASA), Laxenburg, Austria, September 3–7, 1984
1985. VI, 280 pages. ISBN 3-540-15987-8
Contents: Neural Network Dynamics. – Ecological Models. – Genetic Systems. – Economic and Social Macrosystems. – Viability Theory and Multivalued Dynamics. – Stochastic Models for Dynamical Systems. – General Systems Theory. – General Aspects of Evolution.

C. Withagen, University of Eindhoven, The Netherlands

Volume 253
Economic Theory and International Trade in Natural Exhaustible Resources
1985. VI, 172 pages. ISBN 3-540-15970-3
This monograph deals with the economic theory of natural exhaustible resources with special reference to the international trade aspect.

M. Roubens, State University of Mons, **P. Vincke,** Free University of Brussels, Belgium

Volume 250
Preference Modelling
1985. VIII, 94 pages. Soft cover DM 27,-. ISBN 3-540-15685-2
Contents: Binary Relations: Definitions, Representations, Basic Properties. – The Concept of Reference Structure. – Usual Preference Structures. – Two New Preference Structures. – Complete Valued Preference Structures. – Complete Two-Valued Preference Structures.

Editor: **P. T. Harker,** University of Pennsylvania, Philadelphia, PA, USA

Volume 249
Spatial Price Equilibrium: Advances in Theory, Computation and Application
Papers Presented at the Thirty-First North American Regional Science Association Meeting
Held at Denver, Colorado, USA. November 1984
1985. VII, 277 pages. ISBN 3-540-15681-X
This book presents the results of recent research on the concept of spatial price equilibrium. It offers a useful state-of-the-art survey of the spatial economic literature dealing with computable and large-scale models.

Editors: **B. G. Hutchinson,** University of Waterloo, Ontario, Canada; **P. Nijkamp,** University of Amsterdam, The Netherlands; **M. Batty,** University of Wales, Great Britain

Volume 247
Optimization and Discrete Choice in Urban Systems
Proceedings of the International Symposium on New Directions in Urban Systems Modelling
Held at the University of Waterloo, Canada, July 1983
1985. VI, 371 pages. ISBN 3-540-15660-7
Contents: Categorical Data and Choice Analysis in a Spatial Context. – Optimization Models. – Spatial Interaction. – Discrete Choice. – Discrete Analysis.

Springer-Verlag
Berlin Heidelberg New York
London Paris Tokyo

Economics from ...

NEW BOOKS · NEW BOOKS · NEW BOOKS · NEW

... Springer